THIS LIFE

"POITIER TELLS THE RICH, PAINFUL, EXHILA-RATING STORY OF HIS LIFE, AN EPIC PERSONAL STRUGGLE."

Washington Post

"POITIER VERY DELIBERATELY WRITES IN A CLEAR PERSONAL VOICE, AS IF SPEAKING DI-RECTLY TO THE READER, ALTERNATELY POETIC, PROFANE AND COLLOQUIAL . . . A biographer, de-scribing Sidney Poitier's story could have called it *This Amazing Life, This Surprising Life, This Extraordinary Life*. Poitier simply claims it as his own."

Chicago Sun-Times

"I LOVED THIS BOOK—THIS LIFE. It will probably be to this year what Lauren Bacall's *By Myself* was to last year. Both tell lives of struggle and pain. Both are glamor-ous, funny, intelligent, triumphant . . . Poitier is lucky and smart as well as talented and has written a grand book."

Boston Globe

"NO BLAND, GHOST-WRITTEN SMOOTHIE BUT A FRANK AND FORCEFUL SELF-PORTRAIT BY AN ACTOR WITH DEFINITE OPINIONS HE NEVER HESITATED TO EXPRESS . . . This is an honest book which tells it as it was. Best of all, it bears the unmistak-able stamp of Sidney Poitier."

John Barkham Reviews

(please turn the page)

"A REVEALING JOURNEY THROUGH THE FIFTY-THREE YEARS OF SIDNEY POITIER, spotlighting a man who has a strong cause, to help the plight of black people creatively and politically . . . one is enriched learning about the life of Poitier and his heritage."

The Hollywood Reporter

"HIS CANDOR ABOUT HIMSELF AND OTHERS WILL LEAD READERS TO KNOW AND RESPECT HIM AS A MAN OF STRENGTH AND PASSION AND DEPTH, and to be moved by what he has achieved, what he has lost, what he values."

Publishers Weekly

"AN INTENSELY ABSORBING STORY OF A MAN'S SEARCH FOR HIMSELF."

Ebony

"A NOTABLY FRANK AND AFFECTING MEMOIR . . . A POWERFUL WORK."

People Magazine

THIS LIFE

Sidney Poitier

BALLANTINE BOOKS • NEW YORK

PHOTOGRAPH CREDITS

Home in New York City: C. G. Marshall Wilson, *Ebony Magazine;* with Mrs. Roosevelt, with civil rights protesters, with Joanna, *Cry, the Beloved Country,* stage production of *A Raisin in the Sun,* and Academy Award: Wide World Photos; "Harlem Homecoming," *Porgy and Bess, The Lost Man:* United Press International.

All pictures not otherwise credited are from Sidney Poitier's private collection.

Library of Congress Catalog Card Number: 79-3488

ISBN 0-345-29407-6

This edition published by arrangement with Alfred A. Knopf, Inc.

Manufactured in the United States of America

First Ballantine Books Edition: April 1981

Contents

My most heartfelt thanks to Alex Haley, whose firm insistence turned me toward the light and whose brotherly encouragement was a strong wind at my back. Tons of appreciation and thanks to my long-time friend, Louis Robinson, who knew where all the painful things were stored and, moreover, where I buried some of the keys. Thank you, Louis, for being there in a meaningful way all the time I was looking into myself. Words cannot express my appreciation to the best editor in the world, Robert Gottlieb. And most of all to my wife, for wonders too numerous to mention.

1 Cat Island

I WAS BORN in Miami, Florida, on the evening of February 20, 1927. My parents, Evelyn and Reginald Poitier, were two uneducated farmers from Cat Island in the Bahamas. They had arrived in Miami some weeks before with about a hundred boxes of tomatoes they had grown, picked, packed, crated, and accompanied, on the long journey across the Gulf Stream, with the expectation of selling them to the highest bidder at the Produce Exchange.

While Reginald Poitier haggled with middlemen over what he considered a fair price for the fruits of his labor, his wife, Evelyn, seven months pregnant, was happy to be away from home. She was looking forward to a long rest and having her husband all to herself away from the demands of their six children back on Cat Island.

Her rest was to be short-lived. At first she ignored the premature labor pains as false alarms, but they persisted. She began to pray that they *were* false alarms: Evelyn and Reginald wanted to have the baby on Cat Island. Birth in Miami would complicate their plans and keep them away from the other children much longer than they would like. And the dangers of a premature arrival frightened Evelyn. Yet while she hoped and prayed that this was only a false alarm, she discreetly made inquiry in the neighborhood about a good midwife. That afternoon she was introduced to such a person, with whom she made an agreement on the spot. Not a moment too soon, as it turned out, for at nine o'clock that evening, with her midwife in attendance, my mother gave birth to a very, very premature baby.

Mine was a highly uncertain entrance into this world. I weighed in at less than three pounds—a very peculiar kind of birth. To begin with, less than three pounds isn't much of a start, giving rise to the question: Is there enough there to take hold? Being less than three pounds

1

put me on the downside of the odds, so it was touch and go for quite a while. The consensus indicated that I should not be expected to survive: my father, having sired many children—and in fact I would turn out to be the last of them—had already lost several of his offspring to death by disease or stillbirth. At this point he still had four boys and two girls (quite a few to make it through), so the threat of another loss wasn't as devastating as it might have been under other circumstances. Not expecting that I would pull through, given my highly premature arrival and medicine being what it was in those days, he went to a local undertaker and got a miniature shoe box of a casket for my burial. But my mother was distressed by the prevailing opinion and stood alone against it.

Mother was an inarticulate, shy, and terribly sensitive woman, and because of her inarticulateness, she endured enormous frustrations that another person would avoid by simply being able to explain her feelings. But my mother could not express herself easily with most people other than my father. With him, she was able to find her tongue; with others, she couldn't quite—she would struggle through conversations with people, of course, but things that touch the heart, things that had to do with emotions, she wasn't able to put into words. Apparently she had an unusually strong resistance to any talk of my not surviving, insisting that the doubters were miscalculating—that they didn't really know. She felt in her heart that I could be saved, and she intended to do everything in her power to that end. She told my father that she loved him very much, as well as the children waiting for them back on Cat Island, but that she was determined for this child to make it—to come through—to get over.

My mother's concern grew far more intense than it might have if she hadn't continued to stand alone in her prayers and her actions, and eventually carrying so many unexpressed feelings inside became too much for her. She left the house one afternoon. For the only time in her entire life she paid a visit to a reader of palms and tea leaves—the local soothsayer. Sitting there in her quiet frenzy, Evelyn Poitier looked into the eyes of the neighborhood clairvoyant, pleading for a sign, a word, a glimpse into things as yet unseen, an arrangement of soggy tea leaves at the bottom of a cup to indicate there was life ahead for her baby. The steady, intense eyes of the clairvoyant seemed to be looking beyond the subject of her gaze. She silently took Evelyn's hand, closed her eyes, and sat quietly. Although Evelyn grew uncomfortable in the long silence, she continued to stare intently at the face of the reader. She didn't intend to miss anything —not a movement, not a sound, not a sigh. Suddenly there was activity in the clairvoyant's face. Eyes were darting about under closed lids, cheek muscles twitched, nostrils began to flare rhythmically. There was a burst of deep breathing, and a few unintelligible, throaty sounds gurgled up. As the reader tightened her grip on Evelyn's hand, Evelyn was transfixed by the violent turmoil reflected on the reader's face: some inner turbulence was loose in this woman, and she was struggling to harness those forces—bring them to order—regain control.

The reader's grip on Evelyn's hand began to loosen. When her eyes flew open, they seemed glazed and unfocused. As Evelyn continued to stare at that face, her fascination turned to embarrassment at being a close witness to such a private, unvarnished ritual. It put her in mind of the fits and trances of the Holy Rollers back in the Bahamas (many of whom she thought were fakes, taking advantage of an opportunity to let off emotional steam), but she shut that thought off quickly. Her need was too great to entertain the suggestion that what she was watching might be just a performance. She concentrated on the woman sitting across from her, examining the spotty gray hair done in braids all over her head to the loosely fitting gingham dress and the strand of imitation pearls she wore.

Evelyn allowed herself to speculate on how someone arrives at such a calling. Opportunists aside, the real ones must be "chosen." They must be. Because gifts are involved that just cannot be acquired; they must come directly from God, she thought. Suddenly without warning, the soothsayer spoke: "Don't worry about your son, he will survive and he will not be a sickly child. He will grow up to be"—and she paused for a moment, then shifted gears—"he will travel to most of the corners of the earth. He will walk with kings. He will be rich and famous. Your name will be carried all over the world. You must not worry about that child."

My mother was transfixed. Finally, at last, she had found support. Only later, after the euphoria, doubt was to creep aboard her consciousness for a short ride. She was to wonder whether the clairvoyant was indeed chosen by God or was she in fact just another Holy Roller type of opportunist, making a fast fifty cents off her troubles, selling her a cheap fifty cents' worth of feeling good about a premature child who probably had no chance at all of overcoming the odds. But that thought— that doubt—was also snuffed out quickly and thoroughly. She chose instead to believe, if only because it made her feel better; it was surcease from pain. Yet, somewhere deep down inside, Evelyn Poitier knew that she couldn't totally obliterate the idea that she was backing a long shot. After all, premature arrivals of this kind, among the women on Cat Island, were a fact of life, and there was no disputing the dismal survival percentages. No, being on speaking acquaintance with several women who had been victimized by those percentages, she couldn't dispute them. But she intended, by a sheer act of will, to *ignore* them. To that end, after paying the soothsayer, she hurried back to the house and demanded that my father remove the shoe box of a casket from the premises—there would be no need for it.

And so it was that Evelyn Poitier took her stand. And so it followed, for reasons that Evelyn and I believed were better left unquestioned, that I pulled through. When I was three months old and clearly on the way to surviving, Evelyn and Reginald Poitier took me back to Cat Island in the Bahamas, where we joined the other members of our family.

THE NAME "POITIER" comes from Haiti. Slaves bearing that name, having made successful escapes from the Haitian plantation system, ventured into the Bahama Island area, settling in on the first islands they encountered on their escape routes. Upon learning that the Bahama Islands consisted of seven hundred islands and cays, they set up a pattern of interisland migration that eventually brought our branch of the family to Cat Island. A generation later, my mother's branch (bearing the name "Outten") arrived from one of the numerous plantations scattered about these British-owned islands that begin 50 miles off the southeastern coast of Florida and run 400 miles in a jagged line due east, with Cuba, Jamaica, and Haiti lying between them and the Caribbean Islands farther to the south.

Cat Island stands out as one of the most beautiful

among the thirty-five inhabited islands in the chain. It has fantastically beautiful beaches on the north side, and a 400-foot-high ridge runs almost the entire 45 miles in length, like a miniature rocky mountain, from the top of which one has an <u>uninterrupted view of the ocean on both sides.</u> The beaches on the north side were lined and shaded by hundreds of coconut palm trees that simply grew at random along the waterfront. Flowers, edible fruit, and berries could be found growing wild almost everywhere, thanks to ample rainfall, abundant sunshine, and rich, but precious little topsoil. When Reginald and Evelyn Poitier returned to Cat Island from Miami, carrying me—the new baby they now called "Sidney"—they were greeted by their six children, who for more than three months had been eagerly awaiting their return: my older brother Cyril, fifteen; Ruby, thirteen; Verdon (Teddy), eleven; Reginald, eight; Carl, five; and Cedric, three. Also on hand were Mama Gina and Pa Tim, our grandparents on our mother's side, and Evelyn's two sisters, Yaga and Agusta, and her brother Tim. Within a few days of their arrival Reginald and Evelyn returned to the routine that had occupied most of their adult life, tomato farming.

Reginald Poitier was a perfectionist as far as his tomatoes were concerned. He planted by the moon and reaped his harvest at a moment dictated by a combination of rain, sunshine, and the unpredictable sailing schedule of interisland cargo freighters. He would plunder a cave in which millions of bats had lived for millions of years and had deposited tons of excrement. Hundreds of pounds of this bat waste would be transported on the back of the family's one horse and one donkey to the farm site, where it would be mixed with the natural topsoil. Reginald considered the contents of that bat cave the best fertilizer available in the world, and the uniformly fantastic tomatoes he raised with it stand in testimony to that belief. Adjacent to the tomato farm was an acre or two where the family did its subsistence farming. There they grew string beans, sweet potatoes, navy beans, yams, okra, onions, peppers, and corn. Corn was the foundation of our diet—the center of almost every meal. It was roasted, toasted, baked, broiled, stewed, and ground into grits by a small hand-operated grinder, but first it had to be plucked, shucked, and dried in the sun until the kernels, hard as pebbles, could be easily rubbed from the cobs. Grits and fish, roast corn and fish, grits and eggs, chicken and grits —cornmeal cereal and condensed milk. Whatever the time of day, whatever the meal, corn made its appearance.

Except, possibly, on the occasional Sunday when rice would dethrone King Corn and star for the day. Rice was quite a luxury, and to have it every Sunday was a sure sign that your family was one step above the crowd. Rice was imported all the way from England. On weekdays, Evelyn Poitier, working side by side with her husband and those of their children over six years old, would look at the sun to determine how close it was to noontime and start preparing the family's midday meal. From a carryall basket she would remove a cast-iron pot, some dried fish, some grits, and seasonings. She would build a fire around three stones, set the cast-iron pot on it, then drop in an ounce or two of hog lard, some onions, tomatoes, green beans, and okra, letting it all stew and simmer down, finally adding dried fish, grits, water, and seasoning. When the sun sat dead center in the sky she would call the family to lunch. Taking a large grape leaf from a sea-grape tree, she very quickly and artistically bent it into a plate, dished the food onto it, and passed it to her husband. Then repeating the action until all of the family had been served, she finally looked to herself. We ate with our hands mostly, but sometimes we would fashion a spoon from a sea-grape leaf. After lunch my mother would wash out her cast-iron pot, return it to her basket, collect the grape leaves we had eaten from and bury them at the root of a tomato plant where they would decompose and nurture that plant, and return to work beside her husband and children.

Evelyn hadn't always managed things so smoothly— the responsibility of being a wife and mother overwhelmed her from time to time. But she had no comparisons to make with how those responsibilities were met in other cultures, having never been away from Cat Island except for the occasional trip to Florida. She married Reginald James Poitier when she was thirteen and he was twenty-eight, and began to give him children while she was still fighting with the difficulties of being a child herself. A child one year—the next, a wife and mother with adult responsibilities for which she had very little preparation and no education. Fortunately, the relationship she found herself in was such a compatible one that she was able to

6

endure those difficulties and ride through. Not, however, without some subtle damage to her psyche. Now at twenty-eight with seven surviving children, one of them a three-month-old baby, she functioned in the field and at home out of a routine born of necessity. She was lean and fit in mind and body, having been exercised severely by struggle and adversity.

When the sun stood at the four o'clock position in the sky, Evelyn would leave the fields a full hour ahead of Reginald. The older children, gathering the firewood necessary for cooking the evening meal, would follow her the 5 miles home. Each mouth to be fed had to lend a pair of hands to that end, provided they were more than six years old. If she planned to bake bread that evening, one or more of her children would jam wood into the oven to make a band of red-hot coals, on which she would lay her freshly mixed dough. As efficient as she was, she couldn't put the wood in the oven plus do the cooking, plus fetch the water, plus shuck the corn, plus shell the beans, feed the chickens, wash and iron the clothes, grind the grits, slop the hogs, without the constant helping hands of her children. She taught them early and quickly the lessons that had been hammered into her and her mother before her by a hard life in a semiprimitive society: Survival requires everybody to carry a load. Her intention was simple: Discipline imposed on the children now not only will help the family but will also benefit the children in later years.

Evelyn Poitier was a dark woman, of my complexion; she was a thin woman all of her life. And she walked with a limp. I suspect the limp was congenital, because I don't remember hearing about her being in an accident or anything. But one leg *was* somewhat shorter than the other. She moved about with a noticeable hop to her walk. She had skinny legs, big jawbones, and smooth skin. She had the *smoothest* skin. When she was sixty-eight, her skin was the same as when she was a young woman—not a line in her face, not a line. And although her hair went gray, one would think she was a woman still in her late thirties. She was quick to anger—quick to anger. No, she wasn't. She was volatile, not angry. But when you *did* get her angry, O Lord!

I WAS DRAWN to dangerous things. Ever since I can remember I have enjoyed being scared a little bit, an attitude I believe began in the tenth month of my life, when my mother threw me into the ocean like a sack of garbage and stood by expressionless in a dinghy boat watching me go under, sputtering, splashing, and screaming. My pitiful struggle for life seemed not to affect her: she looked calmly on while I clawed at the water, stricken with panic. Even as I gasped desperately on the way down for the last time, she made no move to help. Suddenly, mercifully, my father's hands scooped me up, held me above the water for a moment, then passed me up to my mother —who promptly threw me back into the ocean again. That went on for hours over a two- or three-day period. At the end of which time I had learned to swim. Before I could walk they had taught me to swim. On an island that is barely 3 miles wide, it doesn't matter where a kid lives— as soon as he learns to walk, he will find his way to the water. My parents knew I would be no exception. Therefore, when I began wandering away from home, since I had already learned to swim, nobody worried about me until it was time to eat. At age four I was free to roam around the island with absolutely no restrictions. I knew where home was and I knew that food was there, so I would go back at various times during the day for pit stops, and then off again until the sun began to set. Save for these occasional returns for refueling and finally getting home before dark to bed down, I was completely free to make my own rules and captain my own ship. Naturally, by now the ocean held a particular fascination for me, and whenever I got word that a shark or a barracuda had been seen in the water, I would have a very strong urge to jump in. And often did. But I also had sense enough to scurry right back out again. So while it appears that I loved dancing close to the flames of danger, I was also prone, it seems, to proceed with caution. On balance then, the likelihood is that I was only a little crazy at that age, however much to the contrary the following recollection might suggest.

When I was five years old, there was a 100-foot-long, 6-foot-deep man-made ditch in the village of Arthur's Town on Cat Island. It was dug from the sea to an inland salt pond. When a hand-hewn wooden trap was lifted, ocean water would rush through this ditch into the inland lake and there evaporate into salt for the use of the island's inhabitants. The ditch, though 6 feet deep, was only 2 feet wide. A perfect death trap. It was covered over

8

by wood, since it was actually dug across the roadway that ran parallel with the waterfront. The awesome, dark, claustrophobic appearance of this ditch was enough to scare away most of the children on the island—and in addition, we were all regaled with stories about its properties as a death trap.

I found this ditch just up my alley, so to speak, and I planned to conquer it. It was my Mount Everest. One afternoon I entered the ditch at the salt pond end, and was soon swallowed up by darkness as I moved toward the trap door that kept the ocean out. About 25 feet in, as I was beginning to get deliciously scared, I discovered that the walls of the ditch were terribly narrow and growing more so, inch by inch. I realized that I couldn't turn around, that the water was getting deeper as I proceeded, and if I had to retreat, I would have to back out—how fast could I move backward if the trap door gave way and sent the ocean rushing at me at 50 miles an hour?

With images of moray eels, sea urchins, and other spiny creatures flooding my mind, I edge on toward the trap door. At 60 feet in, the water is too deep for me to continue crawling. I stand up and begin to wade the rest of the way. At 90 feet in, the darkness is complete and the water is up to my neck, and I'm scared shitless! I'm too scared to back up and petrified of pressing on. Then I hear someone walking overhead across the wooden cover of the ditch. I start to call for help, but change my mind when I realize the whipping in store for me when my father learns about this adventure. Then a moment later, whoever it is up there is gone, out of hearing range. While I stand there petrified, passionately regretting having undertaken this incredibly dumb thing, I become aware of the sound of the water hissing through cracks in the trap door, and I realize I'm fairly close. Another 10 feet and I'm home. Or, on the other hand, another 10 feet and I'm finished, depending on whether the tide is high enough to do me in or low enough to allow my swimming through to the rocks beyond. One way or another I'll know as soon as I reach that trap door and spring it open. Deciding to press on, I inch along on my tippy toes as the water grows deeper, and finally I arrive at the trap door and the moment of truth. I reach up with both hands and yank on the wooden trip-latch of the trap door. Nothing happens —and an "oh shit" feeling grabs hold of me. I yank again and again—nothing. I don't have the strength—am simply too small—to put enough pressure on the lever to trip the latch and open the door.

This is as scared as I've ever been in my life up to that time. I start to cry and call for Mama. Dear Mama, she certainly would save me. I holler for Mama—and I holler and I holler and I holler. But to no avail. Finally I take the only choice left open to me. I begin to slowly work my way out of the ditch. Too afraid even to try turning around, I begin to inch my way backward the entire 100 feet out of this hellhole.

The journey back was nightmarish, terrifying, but I made it and quickly scurried away from the ditch up across the main road and down to the water's edge to see if the tide was high or low. To my great shock and ever-lasting joy, the tide was high, which meant that if I had been able to open that trap door, my little ass would have been done for, swept at 50 miles an hour into the salt pond and buried there. Drawn as if by a magnet, I had gone down into that ditch to flirt with danger, and had come close to being wiped out. I was scared so badly from that experience, it was a week before I tried it again. But this time I checked on the tide, to make sure it wouldn't be running against me.

THERE WAS no welfare on Cat Island. Everybody worked except those who were too old or sick, and in such instances, of course, younger, healthier members of the family supported them with their labor. Older people were an integral part of the family structure, with tasks appropriate to their advanced ages, until things got too difficult for them, at which time they would sit down and do nothing, assured of their continued—and revered—place in the family unit. Consequently, grandparents like mine, on my mother's side, didn't have to worry about survival when their productive years were over, since everything was shared with them. Respect for the old ones was everywhere in evidence in this patriarchal society. Young people were required to be honest, live up to their responsibilities, and respect their elders. My father always harped on that. There was no juvenile deliquency, no marijuana, no gang membership, no drinking, and no prostitution. However, there were some chicks who were pretty promiscuous from time to time, and thank God for those.

It's amazing what happens to a young mind when it

begins to fantasize about things sexual. Always it starts with what you have "heard" about sex—or, more usually, overheard picking it up in snatches from older people's conversations, or getting it third-hand from another boy who was lucky enough to be within earshot of such grownup male ego-flexing. But however it comes, it's always titillating, inviting, mysterious, and wonderful—right? Through the ages, little boys everywhere have tuned in on men talking about some amorous experience with a woman, and that experience was always terrific. She was fabulous—and he really pounded her into the ground! And on the other side of the coin, if it's a woman talking and you overhear that, it's pretty much the same: how terrific this guy was, or how terrific he thought he might have been, whereas it was she who really did most of the work.

But the unmistakable conclusion is that "pleasure" is derived from this kind of involvement, and such deliciousness falling on tender ears creates anticipation. You say, "Gee, I'd like some of that." And you begin thinking of how you're going to *get* "some of that." Then, with the whole experience lying ahead of you, and your fantasies running wild, you say, "All right, boy, I'm going to get it on with somebody. I'm ready." So you devise an approach to the girls—you feel them out, trying within your little nine-year-old set of experiences to figure which one is going to be the most propitious, the most ready, the one who is going to receive your forays most graciously. The ones who aren't going to loud-talk you too quickly. The ones who, if they turn you down, are going to turn you down with as much consideration for your feelings as possible. And once those prerequisites have been taken into account, you lock in on one particular chick and start making your moves. You become so drunk with the fantasy image of yourself exploring the naked body of a young girl that your heart begins to pound in your head and your blood races as you think what it must be like to look at an exposed vagina. You ain't really ever seen one of them exposed—right there staring back at you.

My dearest friend on Cat Island was Fritz Campbell, a boy all the girls in the village found striking. At nine years old, with curiosity at fever pitch, he and I decided that the time had come for us to have a face-to-face with a nine- or ten-year-old vagina. Having heard that the girls were more likely to show their little "thingies" to a boy they loved, we set out to explore a list of ways to make them all fall in love with us forever and ever. Naturally, on the top of that list were the voodoo rituals—magical recipes and potions, rumored to be the best ways to cast spells on the little ladies. First we would capture two frogs, kill them, put their bodies in two matchboxes, and put the matchboxes in an ant's nest. We would go back a week later and find only the bones of the frogs—and if among the bones of the frogs we found a couple of bones looking like the letter V, each of us would take one such bone and write the name of the intended girl and our own name on a piece of paper, then obtain a strand of hair from the head of that girl and a strand of hair from our own head. We would wrap these individual strands of hair around the opposite branches of the V and, with the names written on the piece of paper, deposit them in the matchbox and bury it at least a foot underground. I never knew what forces were supposed to conspire in this little buried mixture, but the girl was expected to be smitten with feelings of love and affection for the person whose hair is there mingled with hers in the earth.

Right? It never worked for me—it just caused the death of a lot of frogs. We also recited magical incantations and various other utterances that were supposed to make the girls just go crazy for us, but—nothing happened. Fritz may have gotten a peek or two, but for me? Blank.

Then when I was nine and a half, I got lucky and struck gold. Or one could say that it took six months for the magic and voodoo to really do their stuff for me. Anyway, my first experience with a girl was somewhat more than a face-to-face. At nine and a half years old I had never had an erection, but according to my information, one good peek at a vagina would correct that situation. She was eleven, her name was Lurlene, and she was as curious as I was, which made her an ideal candidate for experimentation. Moreover, of all the girls in the village, she sent out the clearest signals. Plus she was one of the few girls I was really at ease with. And she, in turn, with me. But the most important advantage was that she was a member of the Thurston family. Her brother was married to my sister, and to my mind it seemed that everything would be more appropriate if we kept it all in the family. So with all the signs indicating go, I planned her seduction.

There was an old house built of limestone that had

gone into complete disrepair, and it was so situated in the woods that the likelihood of discovery was minimal. Having enticed her into the most remote corner of this old, broken-down, abandoned house, I nervously began to test, in real life, some of the fantasy images I had conjured up about seduction and discovery. I sent a cautious hand up under her dress, moving slowly, slowly, slowly, and then I stopped at midthigh and shot her a glance to check her reaction. She smiled her permission and I continued on, delighted and flushed with expectancy. I remember feeling a strong curiosity—a little nervous and plenty scared—since I waited to be overwhelmed by that most important of all feelings, sexual desire. According to my information, it should be grabbing hold of me just about now. My hand finally reached its destination, and I was a bit surprised to find that there wasn't any hair in the region, as my information had led me to believe there would be—I was told to be ready for hair and some dampness in the area. My fingers checked around for moisture and found none, which could only mean that she wasn't quite ready—yet. So there I was up under this child's dress, having to improvise for a few moments until Desire grabbed us both and made her damp and moist under there and me swell up into a powerful erection. And then, according to my information, I was supposed to make penetration into whatever I found up there.

But I wasn't in a condition to penetrate anything. I continued to improvise and ad lib. According to my information, the breasts were a sensitive area, and I immediately went to work up there with the other hand. They were just beginning to peak out like little buds, and I did what I imagined to be the proper things. A little stroking, some gentle rubbing—then the blowing of a couple of hot breaths . . . I knew what genital contact was, because I had seen chickens doing it and animals doing it, and I understood that people did the very same thing. We were now standing up trying to make contact, and obviously nothing was ever going to happen, because without an erection I just couldn't stuff my little dingaling into this child, whose receiver wasn't really ready to receive anything either. We were, it seemed, doomed from the start. But I liked the experience, and I think what I liked about it was the closeness of the two people and the trust in the exchange between us. We became closer than ever because we had shared that thing.

I wrote her a letter. I was going to school at the time, but I had barely learned to read or write. However, I was able to manage to write "I love you," which I did on a brown paper sack, in pencil of course, because I don't think there were two pens on the whole island. Would you know the note gets into the hands of her folks who put it in the hands of my folks? I came home one day—my mother, my father, my brothers and sisters, the whole family is on the front porch. Everybody—with this mysterious kind of smile on their faces—looking at me. I felt terribly uncomfortable and I thought: I must have done something, but what is it? And how bad could it be if everybody was smiling? Lo and behold, they laid it on me and as they began to talk, I puffed up in indignation and was about to deny the whole thing when they came up with the evidence in my own handwriting, such as it was. I can't tell you how embarrassed I was—I can't tell you how *embarrassed I was!* It was an exposure of a kind that was utterly, utterly devastating—that everybody there knew I had these feelings in me for this girl. And beyond that was what they *didn't* know about—my attempt to seduce her, and the closeness of the moments we had spent in that house. I hadn't written any of that in my note to her, so they couldn't know, but I assumed the guilt of their knowledge. It was awful. (As a matter of fact, I never— ever, ever—allowed myself to get caught like that again; I found it very difficult to write "I love you" later in life. I did it—but with great difficulty, I must tell you.) I got ribbed a lot by my family about that letter, but I'm not a quitter. I'm not easily discouraged. And when I am, I find on the other side of that discouragement a challenge to reenergize and to overcome the forces that created my discouragement in the first place. And as many times as I'm discouraged, I will reenergize and go back and tackle it again.

Well, that leads to me and the chicken. I hadn't achieved an erection and it worried me—how in the hell was I going to get my penis into a girl if it remained so tiny and refused to swell up as it was supposed to (according to my information)? So I looked around and picked out a good-looking chicken: A hen, naturally. Under the house, there was a very small crawl space between the floor and the ground, and it was somewhat enclosed. And I sneaked up under there with this hen. Having witnessed many times the behavior of those horny roosters

14

around our yard, I immediately began my experiment by placing her in the mounting position. Then I unsheathed my little dingaling, found the entrance to her damp area, and tried to "stick it to her." But again I didn't have enough stiffness to get in. I really tried—and of course the chicken wasn't too cooperative. She fluttered about hollering, squawking, and yelling "rape." I wanted her to shut up, dammit, and hold still, but she wouldn't. Instead, she stepped up her protest. I was very frustrated and more than a little concerned that the chicken would create such a fuss that somebody would come along to find out what was wrong. That was all I needed on top of the other exposure—for the family to find out I was trying to hump a chicken under the house! Needless to say, that chicken remained a virgin—at least *I* never got into her. After that experience, I tried to reestablish the whole thing with Lurlene, but I couldn't find conditions favorable enough. I never did negotiate another go at that lady. And then, when I was ten, my mother and I left Cat Island for Nassau.

2 Nassau

WHEN IN THE MID-1930s the United States government placed an embargo on the importation of tomatoes from the Bahamas, Reginald Poitier and his fellow tomato farmers on Cat Island searched frantically for another market for their goods, but found none. One by one they succumbed to the economic disaster that had ravaged America and was now spilling over beyond her borders. Reluctantly, Reginald made the hard decision to leave Cat Island and try to find work in Nassau, the capital of the islands. My mother and I made up the advance party he sent on ahead to find a house for the family. We left Cat Island by sailboat on a sunny afternoon, pushed by a firm breeze flowing out of the northeast. As we sailed away, I kept looking back at Cat Island until she disappeared on the horizon, as if the sky and the ocean were slowly coming together and squeezing her out of existence. For a long time I went on staring at the spot where I had seen her, but she was gone, not to reappear except in my mind, when I was seeking comfort in daydreams. I turned around to look in the direction we were going and couldn't make out anything but yet another horizon, with no sight of land.

We sailed all that evening and into the next day, until someone called out, "There's Nassau." In the distance off the bow of the ship was the hazy, undefined outline of an island. As we got closer and closer to it, the outline became sharper and sharper. Suddenly I could make out objects in motion, scurrying about at great speed. I asked my mother what they were and she said they were cars. I had never seen a car before, and as we drew nearer to the island these beetlelike fellows absorbed my complete attention. With eyes wide and mouth dropped open, I stepped ashore into this fascinating new place, this big city with people—cars—electricity—and other strange things I had never seen before. There were stores with all kinds of goodies—shoes and clothes and food. My mother bought me an ice cream cone. I had never tasted ice cream before in my life and it looked like mashed potatoes to me. I bit into it and the shock was overwhelming. I almost fainted, it was so cold. The truth is, I had never been exposed to anything so cold in my life.

We stayed with friends for a few days, while my mother scoured the island in search of a house that would fit our needs while falling comfortably within our economic means. She came upon such a place consisting of three rooms on "Ross corner" near East Street. My sister Teddy and her husband would take one room because she had two children by then. The middle room would be for my father and mother, and the farthest room would house my brothers Cedric, Reginald, Carl, and myself, the four boys. My sister Ruby would marry shortly and be off in her own house. My brother Cyril, having slipped away to America, was living in Miami.

My father arrived with the rest of the family and immediately began looking for work, but the job market was tight and for several months he had no luck. During this time my mother took to "beating rock." That was what we called it. She took large rocks and broke them into very small stones. In the backyard, under a tree, with a hammer in her hand, she would beat—smash—pulverize—

16

those big rocks into gravel. We would roam around, my brothers and I, looking for big rocks to bring home. Some were enormous, weighing twenty or thirty pounds. She would hammer away eight or ten hours a day, breaking them all down into little pebblelike stones in the hopes of selling them to builders to be used in cement mixture. It sometimes took her three months or more to crack a ton of stones into pebbles. She earned an average of twenty cents a day.

Then after many frustrating months, my father finally found a job as manager in a bicycle shop owned by a wealthy black Bahamian. He learned about bicycle repairs, rental, sales, and kept that job for three years, until for reasons unknown to me, he lost it. Unable to find another job, this fifty-nine-year-old displaced farmer tried unsuccessfully to return to the soil. He claimed "squatter's rights" to some small acreage of government-owned land in the middle of the island. With no bat excrement at his disposal to enrich the poor soil, he was never able to coax from it a crop worthy of his labor. In fact, that land with only his blood and sweat to fertilize it never yielded enough to meet the family's minimal food requirements. Consequently, with ends never quite meeting even in the face of his best efforts, subtle signs of despair began to surface in his actions. But however subtle, they could not go unnoticed in the sensitive presence of my mother. She could only rage helplessly against the punishing body blows poverty was inflicting on her displaced farmer. Her only comfort was in the knowledge that she knew her husband well. This new, ruthless, sophisticated system of tourism and colonialism, however relentless, would never succeed in dismantling her husband's pride. She knew that he would die before he would live one day without his pride, and she loved him for it, because that quality in him strengthened her and kept her going. Indeed, at times she knew better than he how rough things were. Because she had no fertile, producing farm to go to for our food, circumstances directed her to the grocer, and going to the grocer meant taking money with her. In order to take money with her, Reginald Poitier had to have a job. If he didn't have a job, the grocer wouldn't deal with her, and if he didn't deal with her the family wouldn't eat. Unlike Cat Island, Nassau required the selling of one's labor for a price, and using the returns from the sale of that labor for the food buying and the rent paying and the clothes buying and the doctor bills. Her new neighbors did not exchange corn for beans, yams for peas, or papayas for sugar apples. Nor did they use the free age-old root medicines; instead, when sickness came, they bought from a pharmacy the medicine that probably originated from the very root that used to be free but was now packaged and refined and cost money.

In an attempt to cushion and protect her husband as best she could, Evelyn Poitier kept the relationship between the family and the grocer outside the range of his immediate attention. The skillful juggling of our woefully inadequate resources, plus a little cash slipped to her by my sister Teddy and her husband, or my sister Ruby and her husband, enabled her to somehow keep the lines of communication open between the family and the grocery store. Sometimes in a quiet moment when she was alone, Evelyn Poitier would allow her mind to wander back to Cat Island. Free living. Happier times, in a place where a family could live from year to year without exchanging a dime. Where her husband built their first house with his own hands. She recalled vividly how day after day he mixed lime and sand to a firm consistency, then worked by torchlight into the night, pouring the foundation for their new home. With machetes they worked side by side cutting down the trees used to erect the frame. Then stone by stone, nail by nail, from the ground up, this hardworking man fashioned, almost exclusively from material generously supplied by nature, a home for his family. Evelyn would linger on such recollections, reliving some of the moments of great happiness she had spent with her family on Cat Island. But she refused to acknowledge that she missed that life. That would weaken her for the tasks ahead. A backward glance from time to time, to brighten a few moments in her day while she completed her adjustment to a city existence, was all that Cat Island could mean to her now.

My parents' financial difficulties and adjustment problems did not filter down to the eleven-year-old level where I was finding life in this new environment, in this new rented house, a remarkable experience cramjammed with excitement. For the first time in my life, I was in a neighborhood so dense that I could make friends with boys my own age who were living just next door or across the street or around the corner. I was checked out —looked over—questioned—and finally accepted into the

18

various "buddy-buddy" groups, street-corner factions, and neighborhood clubs. At eleven, I was still terribly shy of girls and stayed away from them for the most part, but I was able to manage with the fellows and fitted in rather easily after finding my place in the pecking order. In no time I became one of the boys. The new house was ideally located for my social life. It was situated only 60 yards from the busy thoroughfare where Ross and East streets intersect, the spot where all the teen and preteen boys of the neighborhood gathered to plan or improvise the secnarios of mischief that would send them off to gleefully tie tin cans to dog tails, "accidentally" break windows with slingshots, and otherwise reduce to a shambles the established order of the community. However exasperating it may be to the adult world, it cannot be denied that some of the happiest boyhood moments in history can be traced to street-corner gatherings such as ours, where a contingent of little bastards can be stylishly creative at being "up to no good."

Be assured, we were not free of dissension in our ranks. Bickerings would occasionally lead to fisticuffs, and leadership struggles were rampant in the hierarchy. My first fight took place on "our corner." It was a one-punch affair that immediately made me a feared and grudgingly respected figure in the group. A peculiar set of reactions, since I was the one who was punched out cold. No, slapped out cold would be more like it, since he hit me with an open hand. I was on the corner one day shooting the breeze and skylarking with six or seven of the other guys, when along comes a bully named William . . . *something*. Within thirty seconds I sensed that this William *something* was looking for somebody to beat up. His testing and probing through the guise of conversation confirmed that he was searching for a victim. I tried desperately to shift his attention elsewhere when his eyes fell on me—no good. I tried introducing new topics of conversation. But he was fixed on *me*—it was settled, as far as he was concerned; he had chosen me to express his authority, and that was that. We sparred with words a few seconds and then he challenged me. Quickly reviewing my options and finding that I had none, I reluctantly rose to the challenge. The first shot in the exchange was a slap. He hit me across the face—but with such power that I went out like a light! Do you hear me when I tell you? But this guy was much bigger than I was. Not to say I wouldn't have gone out if he was smaller than I was—anyone who could hit that hard was certainly going to rattle your marbles, and he *hit* me. I guess I was elevenish, and he was about fifteen or sixteen. Some of the other guys ran to my house and got my sister Teddy, who rushed out, surveyed the situation, picked me up, and took me back to the house. She put cold water on my face and brought me around. As soon as she saw that I was okay she got up, walked back to the corner, and said, "Where's William?" One of the guys said, "He's across the street and he'll be right back."

Teddy waits there for a couple of minutes, and sure as hell, here comes old William *something* from across the street. My sister walks over to him and smacks him so hard his knees buckle, and she proceeds to beat the daylight out of him. She beats his tail to a frazzle. She slaps, punches, and kicks William's behind and warns him that if she ever has to come after him again she will destroy him. "Keep your hands off my brother or I'll mess you up some more," she warns before turning away from the decked and dazed William and walking back to the house.

My reputation took a giant leap as news of my powerful ace-in-the-hole quickly spread around town, and for a full week the fat lip and bruised eye of William *something* confirmed like prime-time advertising the retaliatory power behind little Sidney "P." In fact, even William *something* would smile respectfully when he passed me on the street, and it filled me with pride when I overheard one boy saying to another, "Don't fuck with him or he'll call his sister—and she's *mean*."

Yorick Rolle, Godfrey Rodriguez, and Samuel White, Jr., were my closest friends during that period. We all lived on the same street, and I attended Western Senior School with Yorick and Godfrey. Yorick Rolle was slight, frail, with an undernourished appearance in a face that exploded into sunshine when he smiled. This little, skinny, high-strung kid was an absolute delight to be with, and he became my number-one "tight buddy."

MY FIRST LOVE AFFAIR—which wasn't quite a love affair—was with Margaret Ferguson. She lived down the street about midway between Yorick's house and mine—right next door to my friend Godfrey Rodriguez. She had a sister and a mother, but I don't think the father was there. The two sisters and the mother were in the straw business—they plaited palm leaves to make straw hats and pocketbooks and other stuff to sell to the tourists. I saw her, and just like that, I was in love. But I was too shy to ever approach her. I was in love with the child and never said "hello" to her. Never! The closest I came to expressing my feelings for her was to walk past her house on the pretense of visiting Godfrey. I watched Margaret and her sister sitting on the porch, plaiting those things while their mother made hats and bags from them.

By now, I was going to the movies, and the most important thing for me was Westerns, to watch how the cowboys swaggered down the street. I developed a cowboy swagger. I figured that would impress them. I must have looked like an idiot swaggering along in that swivel-hipped motion of Bob Steele or Wild Bill Elliott. Through good peripheral vision I could tell they were looking at me as I strolled by and I would swagger away—not even once looking over at them, as if they didn't exist. I guess Margaret wondered: What the hell is he doing walking up and back this way five and six times a day? I don't remember *ever* talking to Margaret.

After two years of living in the house on Ross Street, my mother found a cheaper rental about ten blocks farther south on East Street. Again we had three rooms, but this time we were on the main drag, where the family's privacy was considerably reduced. By my evaluation, the new surroundings were definitely not a move up. But bundles of interesting memories will be retained from my life in this new house, among them the second time I did any exploring with a girl—in this case my niece, daughter of my sister Teddy. We played a little "doctor," but before we could get into anything incestuous, my mother unexpectedly walked into the room. She stopped. She looked at us a moment. Then, as the picture sank in, her brow wrinkled and her eyes narrowed to a cold stare before she asked, in a tone laden with disapproval, "What are you all doing there?" We said, "Ooh, nothing, just talking." There is my niece with her dress up and me with my pants down and we're saying, "We're just talking." At which point this volatile, inarticulate mother of mine—grandmother of my niece Lois—began her familiar deep and uneven breathing: a sure sign that fire and brimstone were about to rain down on us. Then with arms akimbo, she started circling us silently, melting us down with an angry stare.

As we trembled inside the circle waiting for the world to end, I flashed back on the time on Cat Island when her anger flared to its awesome fullest. It was that terrible day when my father and his brother, my Uncle David, had a fight. I never knew for sure, but I think it was about land left to them by their father—they argued over it constantly. My Uncle David had a small grocery shop to which my mother sent me on occasion to purchase sugar, salt pork, or hog lard. On that fateful morning she gave me money for a bit of all three, and off I scurried to the shop about half a mile away. As I walked in, I noticed that my Uncle David was furious about something. When I went over to him and placed my order, he asked, "Where's your father, boy?" I said, "He's at home." He said, "Tell him I want to see him." He filled my mother's order and I left. A little ways along, I saw my father coming up the street heading in the direction of the store. Just as he reached me, Uncle David came running from his shop, picked up some great big rocks, and began to stone my father viciously. One stone caught him on the upper arm and tore deep into his flesh, and several others found their mark before my father responded in self-defense. The two brothers fought like two gladiators. I watched in complete shock for a while before running off to the nearest house for help, spreading the news as quickly as I could and bringing to the scene enough neighbors to separate the two men. They had to be dragged away from each other and forcibly returned to their homes, which were located about a quarter of a mile apart from each other, across a pond on the far side of which was a bridge leading to Uncle David's house.

When my mother heard about Uncle David's unprovoked attack on her husband, off she went. She started screaming at the bridge where Uncle David's house was, and immediately Uncle David's wife, Lena, came out onto the bridge and answered in kind. My mother took off after her. I had never seen her that angry before, and I have never seen her that angry since. She was frothing at the mouth. I saw veins pile up in her face—she was trembling and absolutely incapable of controlling herself—charging for the pathway that led to the bridge on which Uncle David's wife stood with every intention of destroying her and then moving on to demolish Uncle David, the house, and everything else on their side of the pond. My older brothers had to do a nine-second 100 to overtake her, and they found that every ounce of their strength was necessary to contain her.

That day I saw with my own eyes the other side of Evelyn Poitier, that part of my mother that hardly ever came up from the deep-down place where it lived. When she was back in control of herself, she washed and dressed my father's wound and gave loving care to all his other bruises, stopping from time to time to look daggers across the bridge at Uncle David's house.

My father and his brother never spoke again. Our family moved from Cat Island soon after. In our absence, while we were in Nassau, Uncle David died. The news of his death was brought by a seaman who asked me to pass it along to my father. There was a profound sadness in Reginald Poitier about that incident with his brother. It was a terrible wrenching that never healed. And only now, looking back, can I see how heavy it must have been on him and also on my Uncle David. My father didn't say much when I told him his brother was gone. He just nodded his head. But despite this minimal reaction, it was my judgment that he took the news of his brother's death very deeply to heart.

I REMEMBER the day after their fight, I wondered about that other side of Evelyn Poitier and hoped that I would never, ever, have to face it—and now, years later, here I was in this circle of doom, in our rented house on East Street in Nassau, with my pants down, guilt written all over my face, about to be shredded by Evelyn's fury.

At last she stopped circling and stood in front of us. My niece Lois couldn't wait for the roof to fall in: she started to cry. Watching her weep, Evelyn slowly began to soften, and I glimpsed the hope that maybe, just maybe, if Lois kept up her crying we might miraculously wind up with a reprieve.

Lois came through like a champion. In fact, I think she overdid it, once she realized it was working in our favor, but she was effective nonetheless, and I shall forever be grateful to her. Evelyn administered a stern lecture peppered with warnings suggesting that nieces and uncles who play doctor are likely to wind up with the most severe whippings ever administered in the history of the world. It was not the custom of parents in those days to have open and frank discussions of sex with their children, so when Evelyn left the room, Lois and I were not one whit

23

more enlightened than when she came in. No, we were not enlightened, but we were definitely relieved.

A LITTLE enlightenment might have made a difference a few weeks later when I lost my virginity. From the new friends I had made in this new location, I learned there was an old lady—I guess about twenty-five or thirty years old—from whom, it was rumored, "You could get your stuff," and the price was reasonable. I said to myself: I think I'll go and have myself a shot of that. It's about time I got myself fixed up. So I put together the necessary finances—fifty cents, as I recall—and set out for her place to make my deal.

By now I'm at the age when I no longer worry about having erections; in fact not only am I having erections, but I'm also enthusiastically tinkering with masturbation. Anyway, I go to this lady, pay her fee, and ready myself for my first trip to the moon. She is pleasant and business-like, and I try to appear casual and experienced.

As I now recall, it was really very nice. Absolutely neat. But the old broad gave me the biggest dose of clap I have ever seen, and because I wasn't one whit "enlightened," I didn't even know what it was. I thought I was having a prolonged ejaculation. There I was five days later saying to the fellows—just to show how dumb you are as a kid—I would say to them, "Hey, man, I can come." They'd say, "Yeah?" I'd say, "Yeah, I've got some in my pants right now." They would say, "Let's see." I'd say, "Never you mind. I can do it whenever I want to do it." Little did I know. Well, it starts to burn after a while. I say, "Hell, there must be something wrong here." So like the little idiot I am, instead of going straight to my old man, who is the right fellow to go to, I figure the best way to treat it is like a sore. I begin bathing my penis in hot water, and after two days it catches cold and swells up. It swells up pretty big, and now I'm scared. I don't know what to do. I finally go to my father. He says, "You're going to have to go to the hospital." He takes me there to the outpatient clinic, where they look at it and tell me I have gonorrhea. To cure it, I have to come in regularly for sulfur treatments (they had no penicillin then). At the clinic they would put a tube up the head of my penis and the sulfur stuff would drip in. I went there for weeks and ultimately licked it, but I was gun-shy after that.

24

For some time thereafter, masturbation was quite satisfactory.

IN ADDITION to losing my virginity in the thirteenth year of my life, I also quit school, working for a time as a waterboy to several hundred pick-and-shovel laborers digging a 40-foot-wide, 25-foot-deep, 2-mile-long ditch from the ocean through what is now known as Paradise Island, up to and underneath the stately mansion of the European industrialist Axel Winergren. Upon completion, this gigantic ditch was to be flooded to its capacity, as rumor had it after the fact of his deportation from the Bahamas, allowing a miniature Nazi submarine from a mother ship to pay discreet visits to the pro-Nazi Mr. Winergren. All of which had to be terribly clandestine and grossly illegal, seeing that the Bahamas were a British possession and dear old Britain was locked in World War II with Nazi Germany. Subsequent to Mr. Winergren's involuntarily "'splitting" for Mexico, I went to work in a wholesale warehouse where I stacked hundreds of bags of flour, sugar, and rice, each weighing up to 125 pounds. There I developed a classic pattern on my buttocks and shoulders of the stretch marks that are usually associated with pregnant women. Also, a ribbon of a varicose vein curled itself around my lower leg between the knee and the ankle. I hung in there for several months, although I was obviously not yet man enough for that kind of job.

Before my thirteenth year slipped away, I went to work for the United States government, which had been given permission by the British to build a military airbase in Nassau, using mostly Bahamian labor. I fell in love with a wonderful, beautiful girl named Dorothy. And I lost my best friend, Yorick Rolle, to the colonial prison system of the Bahamas.

Poor Yorick had been sent to reform school for stealing a bicycle on a day I was supposed to be with him and just by chance wasn't. On that rare day our inseparable twosome was separated for no more than a few hours—time enough, however, for fate's grand design to alter our directions and set new courses for us that would lead to Yorick's being dead before thirty, and me . . . well, we shall see. My father, on hearing of Yorick's difficulty, said, "There but for the grace of God goes my son, whom I can't seem to handle anymore—I must get him off this island." Since I was an American citizen, due to my

Miami birth, he thought his little hard-headed, restless, pain-in-the ass son might have at least a chance not to wind up in reform school. Fate, no doubt, remained at work guiding my father's hand when he wrote to my brother Cyril in Miami, saying, "Your mother says it's time for him to leave. I agree. He has no life here, so we would appreciate it if you could see your way clear to help us get him off the island." My brother responded positively and it was set in motion, although more than a year would pass before I was actually to leave.

In the interim—no more than a month after Yorick's downfall—I was arrested for stealing corn. With seven co-conspirators, I raided a cornfield. We carted off sacks of succulent tender ears of corn deep into the woods, where we built a bonfire, roasted them, and feasted for hours. Of course the glare of the bonfire guided the police and the angry farmer directly to us. Rounded up and locked away in a cell at the police station, we waited for our respective parents to arrive with the ten shillings necessary to get us out. My father couldn't raise the money that night and had to wait until the next day to borrow it from somebody, so I spent the night in jail. That was scary, especially after all the other guys had been bailed out by their parents and I was alone in the slammer. I began to imagine what it must be like for Yorick in reform school, and I got really, really scared. The next day I was taken to the chambers of the judge, where my father had to pay for the corn, again with borrowed money. On the way home, he said to me, "You know, boy, I can't run after you anymore. I'm getting on in years and you seem determined to get into trouble . . . you were born in the United States and we want you to go back there. You will have a chance to go to school and try to make something of yourself. In the meantime you have got to—you hear me, boy?—you have got to toe the line or you'll never make it back to America. You hear me, son? You hear me?"

There I was still dancing close to the flames, with the stakes getting higher and higher. Playful mischief by now had escalated to petty larceny. From Cat Island, where theft was practically unknown, to this place where it came close to being a survival tool. Yes, sir, Nassau was different from Cat Island, and the nature of the daring chances I had grown used to taking was a reflection of that difference. I had a devil-may-care attitude, while at the

26

same time I was scared of what the devil might decide to lay on me. I knew if I got caught at some of my devil-may-care stunts, I was gone—four years gone.

Yet, with those scary four years looking me right in the face, I continued my wicked ways. For instance, I would walk into a hardware store, saunter upstairs as if I knew exactly where I was going, stroll around, pick up a pair of skates, walk back downstairs and out the store. It's not as if there's nobody in the store, mind you. I mean there are salespeople and customers all over the place. I obviously was seen by them but not *noticed*. Looking back, I shudder at the nerve—or was it ignorance, stupidity, insanity or a cocktail blend of all four—which made me completely oblivious to the objective reality which stated that I couldn't get away with what I was getting away with! How, O Lord, at the age of fourteen, did I arrive at the kind of reasoning that enabled me to say, "I'm going to dazzle them with simplicity." And it was not only roller skates, but comic books, milk bottles returned to grocery stores to "retrieve" never-paid deposits, and any number of other items that could be stolen and converted into funds for food and tickets to the movies. With no rational explanation offering itself as to how an afflicted little boy, reeling from the culture shock of the transplant from Cat Island to Nassau, survived those dangerous, treacherous early years, one is forced to lean on phrases like "chance," "guardian angel," "dumb luck." Or, again, was it "fate's grand design" that separated my friend Yorick and me, sending us off in different directions to suffer, to love, to give, to take, to be lonely, to be creative, to be forgiving, and never, ever, telling us why?

One day I took a long, lonely walk to the far eastern end of the island to see my friend Yorick in reform school. They had shaved his head and put him in a little dark ocean-blue uniform, and he could never come home for four years. He had to eat there, sleep there, work in the garden there, daydream about "running with the fellows" there, and hope that on Sunday an old friend or a member of his family would come to see him. That place was scary as hell, yet it was only the junior jail, not the forbidding grownup slammer where my brother Cedric was sent to similarly live out a gargantuan sentence for a flea-size crime. My friend Yorick looked skinnier than usual, dressed as he was in a uniform that looked two sizes larger than necessary, issued, no doubt, in the expectation that he would grow into it. He said he was glad to see me and I believed him, but his rhythm was off as he tried to impress me with his casual, cucumber-cool, who-gives-a-damn attitude. He was bluffing—I could tell from the hurt in his eyes. He was frightened at having abruptly lost control over his life. He tried desperately to keep me from seeing how vulnerable this experience had left him, but my instincts side-stepped the subterfuge and went directly to the corner where the real, insecure, little boy Yorick was crying. An insight that made me uncomfortable because it brought to mind my father's words, "There, but for the grace of God, goes little Sidney P." In trying to keep my own uneasiness and fears out of sight, I smiled a lot and made nonsensical small talk about the other guys and the neighborhood, but all to no avail, because the expression on Yorick's face quickly told me that his instincts too had hurdled those obstacles; he was looking at the real me in my own frightened little-boy corner, being glad that it was him and not me in this awful reform school. There we were, my friend and I, two little boys naked to each other, already so deeply trapped in the macho myth that we couldn't say to one another, "Hey man, I'm scared." Or better still, have a good cry together and, if the need arose, holler for our mamas.

My brother Cedric at sixteen was two years older than me and had been working for a man in a little grocery store before he lost his job because of some impropriety. In other words, I think he was going home with more than the man was paying him. The man blew the whistle and my brother did some time in the poky. After his release, with jobs very difficult to come by, he entered into a conspiracy of mischief with a friend of his, a guy named "Billy-O." They were about the same age, Rooster and my brother Cedric, and seemingly of the same mind. Do you know what those little mothers did? There was a man in the food business named Mr. Royale. He had two successful shops and was also in the real estate rental business. In fact, the second house we lived in on Nassau was owned by Mr. Royale. My brother Cedric and Rooster wrote a letter to Mr. Royale saying that they were going to burn down his houses and blow up his stores if he didn't bring x number of dollars to such-and-such a place, at such-and-such a time, on such-and-such a day. Just to show you that the little bastards were seeing too many movies, they added a P.S. that said, "Do not be in touch with the police or you will regret it." The letter was delivered to Mr. Royale, who promptly disregarded the P.S. and called in the police, who in turn made up a phony package. On the evening designated, my brother and Rooster are underneath some brush in the woods, looking out on the road and waiting for Mr. Royale to drop this stuff. A car goes by and the package comes out of the car. It's lying there on the side of the road. My brother and Rooster, lying deathly still in the underbrush, look up and down the street for the double cross, but the street remains empty. No cars or people anywhere in sight; Mr. Royale's car seems to have gotten back on the main road and driven away. With success just a few feet away, my brother and Rooster beam congratulatory smiles at each other, then out they come, pick up the package, and head back for the safety of the underbrush. Only to have dozens of cops pounce all over them. Well, needless to say off they go to court, and from court to jail for six months.

After his release, Cedric figured that Nassau was too small for him. He's got to go. Must split. Move. And the ideal place to go is the United States. But not being a citizen poses a huge problem that requires his having, once again, to put on his mischief cap and think up a sure-fire way to enter the U.S. My sister Teddy by now was separated from her husband and going around with a guy named "Blood." This guy Blood decided that he too had to get out of Nassau, forging another union to hatch another conspiracy. Blood used to work for the slaughterhouse—was a killer of animals—hence his nickname. Anyway, Cedric and Blood hatched an intricate plan to stow away to Miami on a cargo freighter. It was a beautiful plan that worked like a charm—until they got to Miami, where they were caught and sent back to Nassau and off to jail, the third and last time for my dear brother Cedric. I left the island before he came out of jail, but years later—I'm doing very well—I go back. He is there. He is married. He has a family. I said to him, "Now you can go to America. I can get you there." He said, "No, I don't want to go." I said, "Why don't you want to go? I can fix it." He said, "Because our mother and father are getting old and there is no one here to take care of them." He said, "I'd rather stay. You're gone, Cyril is gone, Teddy is gone [by now Teddy was dead], Ruby is married, and she's in Florida. Reginald has his own family to worry about. Which leaves just me and Carl, who as you know is a little touched in the head and is not quite right. No, I don't want to leave them or my children or the Bahamas. I'd rather stay here." At that point he'd gone straight and had a job as a maître d' in a hotel, where he'd been working many years and doing quite well. In the process of being a maître d', however, alcoholism slipped up on him. Eventually, after ten or twelve years, he lost his job and went to work for a big construction firm, servicing their heavy equipment at night. One night it starts to rain and it's a little cold and he's been drinking. He goes into one of the trucks to sit there, rolls up the windows, turns on the motor to keep warm—and asphyxiates himself by carbon monoxide. He's dead at the age of thirty-six. By the time he was seventeen, barely three years removed from a life of innocence on Cat Island and before he could get a fix on the rules of the game as it's played in this new, fast, corrupt place, he was had. Enticed, seduced, fucked, and infected—never to recover.

That place Nassau was not good for raising tomatoes or children. There were not then, and there are not now, many imaginative attempts to discourage the impact of negative cultural images on the minds of Bahamian children. There was at that time available to all Bahamian children, albeit in segregated theaters, a continual display of flagrant, unvarnished brutality. One-on-one, group-on-group violence, with guns, clubs, fists, knives—how to shoot, how to steal, how to kill Indians. And these same things make up much of what is available to today's kids —only in a more intense, compact, and streamlined manner, on top of which they are being double-dosed: once or twice a week at the movies, and nightly on television. My brother Cedric learned a lot about life from movies. For instance, the classic extortion formula applied by him and Rooster to Mr. Royale could only have come from books, which he didn't read, or movies, which he saw a lot of. Let me hasten to add that all Bahamian children did not turn out like my brother—not by a long shot: many of the children who saw the same pictures my brother did went on to be doctors and lawyers, prime ministers, and in a few cases, movie stars. But on careful scrutiny one would have to admit that all too many failed.

To shift to a lighter side of the same subject, Tom Mix, Bob Steele, Gene Autry, Wild Bill Elliott, Roy Rogers, Ken Maynard, and Charles Starrett with his white horse and big white hat were my first exposures to film. I was transfixed by their every move—I accepted them as real. In fact, as I sat in the theater, I used to think that they were all actually there behind the screen—backstage. For the longest time I was firmly convinced of this, to the point of dashing out of the theater the moment "The End" appeared on the screen and rushing around to the rear, fully expecting to see them strut out through the stage door, followed by their horses and their cows and the bad guys and the good girls—the whole ensemble. After waiting and waiting I would grow heavy with disappointment and try to puzzle out how could they have got out so quickly—or could it be that they were really still back there, taking a break? Maybe. . . . But the most resilient of bubbles will burst in time, and when I discovered that Bob Steele and Wild Bill Elliott did not actually come in person to our Saturday matinées I was crestfallen; I even changed my swagger to resemble a couple of other guys.

Hearsay had it that all these guys worked in a place called "Hollywood" where they rode around on horses, branded cows, and had gunfights every Saturday afternoon on Main Street in a town whose name kept changing from week to week. One day, while I was still locked into my fixation on cowboy heroes, I told my sister Teddy that I was going to Hollywood and be a cowboy. But I meant a real "cowboy"—I had no idea what being a movie star was. What I meant to say was that I was going to be a cowboy because I liked working with cows. I just thought you worked with cows in Hollywood, rather than Texas or Oklahoma or somewhere like that. Her familiarity with my fanciful imagination permitted a straight face that dissolved into a sympathetic smile before she responded with, "You are, huh? Well, when are you going to do this?" I said, "When I go back to America."

Teddy was a lovely lady, the freest spirit and the most courageous of all the Poitiers. Let me tell you about her. Her true name was Verdon. She had mischievousness, she had presence, an eye for the ridiculous and the ability to laugh with anyone. Indeed, to laugh at life. She was hugely affectionate and very sensual. She was married on Cat Island to a very nice, conservative, strait-laced kind of guy named Vincent Williams, with whom she had two children—Lois and Christine. The Williams family moved down to Nassau with the rest of us, but the marriage didn't work and they separated. After a while she took

31

up with that guy named Blood, the killer of animals, who was a very neurotic and dangerous fellow. Naturally, she kind of liked him because he was "so alive." Anyway, they started to live together, but they were incompatible and their life together became increasingly tumultuous over a four-month period. Deciding to separate from him for a while, she came home and said to my father, "I don't want to live with him anymore. I want to come home for a while." He said to her, "Okay, you can come home for a while. But while you're here, you don't belong to him—you become a part of our family once again. We're going to put the protection of this family around you. Therefore, you have a responsibility to this family. You can see him but not until you ask my permission. You're not to go back to his house. You're not to see him unless you say 'I am going to see him' so that I know where we stand as a family. If you want to come home under those conditions, you are welcome. If not you'll have to go someplace else to work out your problems." She said, "No, I want to come home. Those conditions are fine with me." She came home and stayed a while, living very comfortably, until she started seeing him again without telling my father. I'm sure it was a difficult, ambivalent thing for her to see Blood again and not tell the old man. I think probably what she had going on inside of her was the need to feel out the situation, to ascertain whether she really wanted to have another shot at a relationship with this guy or not. Maybe she only saw him once or twice briefly, and figured: I don't have to tell Daddy about this because it isn't a serious attempt to get back together.

I was at home the afternoon my father heard about it, and as soon as my sister came walking in the house I knew she was in for it. He said to her, "Is it true what I've heard?" She hesitated, trapped between an honest "yes" that would certainly doom her, and a fraudulent "no" that might stay his hand, at least temporarily. Her hesitation was a beat too long, leaving him to interpret her silence as a reluctant admission of guilt. At which point he filled the void with, "You know what I'm going to do? I want you to go out there to that tamarind tree and bring me a switch." The tamarind switch is the worst thing to get a whipping with, because it has so many thornlike knots and jagged edges. He said, "I want you to bring me a switch. Don't bring me anything small or you'll get it twice as hard." Now my sister by this time was well into

32

her twenties—a grown woman with two children of her own. But she was aware that this fact would make no difference to Reginald Poitier. She knew he lived by a code, and the code was fair, and she had broken it, and since he was and always would be her father, she went out as she was told and brought him a big, fat switch. He took it and pulled the branch right through his hand to shed all the leaves from it. He took her by the hand, led her outside, and he whipped on her with that tamarind switch. He said, "When I tell you that this house is my home and if I tell you under this roof you have to do what I tell you —you have to respect this house and respect me—you listen and you do it. Under my roof you never get so old or so big that you're outside the jurisdiction of my parentship." And he beat the daylight out of her—and she hollered and screamed and cried and stormed and fussed—and he whipped her behind for about twenty minutes, I mean really beat her up. At the end he said, "If you want to go—go. If you want to stay, you may stay. If you stay you're going to stay under my terms. You will see that man when you say to me, 'Daddy, I am going to see him.'" My sister didn't respond, she just jumped and hopped around the yard, twitching from pain as if he were still applying the switch to her. And myself, having spent loads of time on my sister's end of the tamarind—I knew exactly what kind of pain was making her do that peculiar dance. Evelyn Poitier sat looking on impassively. Much, I imagine, the way she did when I was being thrown in the ocean to sink or swim at the age of ten months. But indifference would be a mistaken reading of what she was expressing, because the truth is that Evelyn was a touch wiser than both of us. She knew that certain things had to be done to preserve life and certain other things were necessary to preserve dignity.

A few days later, my sister went to my father and said, "I'm going to go back to Blood." My father said, "Okay, if that is what you want, but remember when you are in his house I can't protect you and your brothers can't do anything for you. You're his woman then." She said, "I understand." My mother helped her to collect her belongings and back she went to live with Blood. Things worked out pretty well and she was happy—for a while. About two months later he got drunk. For some reason he thought she had done something to bruise his ego, and since he was a killer of animals, he knew all about the cow's cock. If you've never heard about a cow's cock, it's precisely what the name implies. The cock of the cow. When the animal is killed, they take his cock, including the extension that runs along his back up through his spine. They cure it. They smoke it. They salt it down until it dries into a hard, jagged-edged weapon. It is light-weight, and its contours twist and turn in such unexpected ways that to be hit with it can cut you all to pieces. He found her on the street that day, in his drunken stupor, and he began to beat on her with his cow cock. He beat her up pretty good. None of the boys—my father, his sons—none of the boys were at home. My father heard about it that evening, and being the kind of man he was, he said, "Well, there's not much we can do about that," since she was not under his jurisdiction. He quickly let it be known among his sons that a certain rule of behavior must be respected. No one was to move against Blood— no one. The killer of animals never knew that his hide— possibly his life—was saved by an unexpected ally with a very stiff code of behavior.

Teddy left him after that and began her evolution into an independent woman. In a matter of weeks, with Blood finally behind her, she was bubbling with laughter again. Soon she would be relying on herself to look after herself, and the more she outgrew Blood, the more full of life she became. She was a roustabout, a joyous life-lover who would sip her rum on a Saturday, dance barefooted in my mother's kitchen, and sing the old songs of Cat Island until my mother and my father joined in with hand-clapping and foot-stomping. She stirred their memories of happier times and brought smiles and laughter to us all. She was a very sturdy, big-boned woman, tall like me—weighing about 160 pounds. One day she took sick and she fell away to nothing. The doctors couldn't figure out what it was. Finally they put her in the hospital and when she was down to 100 pounds, they discovered that there was some failure of a vital organ. They tried to work on her, but there wasn't much they could do. My father and mother went to the hospital every day and were finally told there was nothing that could be done for her; the de-terioration of the vital organ was such that it was just not possible for her to survive it. So they sent her home.

My father, who was always a believer in bush medicine with a dash of voodoo, made inquiry as to the where-abouts of a certain bush medicine man. They told him that this medicine man lived on another island, and my father decided to send for him. The man came to Nassau, was met at the boat, and brought to our house. He was a tall man, slender and dark. He wore an old frayed and worn gray jacket, dark gray wrinkled pants, a bluish shirt, and an old black hat. He was wearing his Sunday best, which clearly revealed how poor he was. He saw my sister alone for about half an hour, sitting silently by her bed the whole time. When he came out he asked my father what the doctors said it was, and my father told him all that he had been told. He asked my father where the woods were—because we were living in the city. My father told him. He went away and he didn't come back for two days. When he reappeared he had a bag full of roots and leaves and told my mother to bake them slowly for several twelve-hour periods. They had to remain constantly under heat in order that the roots be completely parched—not burned, but parched—so that they could be ground to powder. The leaves had to undergo the same process, but for a shorter period. Then, combining the roots and leaves in certain amounts, she was to make tea for my sister to drink, and a designated amount of this powder had to be sprinkled on her food morning and night. My father paid him with money he'd scratched together for this purpose, and that strange medicine man went away. My sister Teddy was on her feet within a month. She was back to 160 pounds within the year. She got a job and came to the United States to work for a family in Syracuse, New York, as a domestic. She stayed there for ten years, and then there was a recurrence of the illness. I was by that time at Universal Studios, making a film called *Red Ball Express*. I got a call informing me that they'd put Teddy in the hospital and that she'd died there. But that old man had fixed her up and she'd lived ten years— that was something. Ten years. And she had a terrific life. I remember our last meeting, in a hotel room in Miami. I was passing through on my way to Nassau and she was on her way back to Syracuse. She was full of life—big, robust, and laughing. She was happy that I finally got to "work with cows in Hollywood." I told her that I had met a girl and that she was a very nice girl and that I was thinking of getting married. She said, "What for?" I said, "Well—" She said, "Don't you talk to me about getting married." Without losing the sparkle in her eye or the warmth in her smile, she was dressing me down. She

said, "Live, Sidney, live, live, live. Life is too beautiful.
Get married when you're twenty-eight—when you're
thirty—when you're older is time enough. Marriage at
your age? Ridiculous! Enjoy yourself, travel a lot, see
things and learn and eat and taste and sleep and do whatever you want to do with your life. It's yours, Sidney, enjoy it. Don't get married now." I remember her saying
those things. And you know, in fact, I didn't get married
to that girl.

3 Miami

THERE AS A BELIEF among the poor people of
Nassau that America was the land of opportunity where
the streets were paved with gold; all you had to do was to
get there. On a January morning in 1943 I was fifteen
and I was on my way. Before I left the house that morning, my mother stood me before her. She looked deep into
my eyes, focusing, it seemed, on a place beyond my understanding. After a long silence she smiled, engaged the
top button of my shirt, touched my face, and finally, as
tears began to well up in both of us, turned me away from
her and gently shoved me out the door. She did not go to
the boat. My father took me by way of the main thoroughfare, as if he sensed I had goodbys to say. Once we
arrived at the dock, he introduced me to a couple of the
boat's crew members and said they were going to look out
for me on the crossing. I stepped on board the old passenger steamer called *Ena K*, and immediately I felt
cut off from all that my life had been before. As if I
had stepped away from my first fifteen years, leaving
them behind. As I turned and looked at my father, there
was uncertainty in his eyes and a contemplative curl to his
lips, as if he were weighing the merits of his decision to
send me away from Nassau. He looked the way an eagle
must at the moment of turning its young out of the nest.
Painful though it is—it has to be done; nature requires it.
As I stood there on the boat, filled with anxiety, ambiva-

lence, anticipation, curiosity, and flush with the excitement that surrounds new adventure, I kept searching his face for signs of regret. I found none. He had solicited the aid of my brother Cyril, the illegal alien in the United States, who had since married an American girl and gained legal citizenship. Cyril, upon agreeing to receive me, sent my father ten dollars to cover travel documents and incidentals. Since we had no money beyond my passage, ten dollars was a blessing indeed. Part of it was used to obtain my passport from the American Embassy in Nassau and to buy me a pair of pants, a shirt, a pair of shoes, and a sweater. The remaining three dollars would be squeezed into my hand just before I sailed and Reginald Poitier, my father, without a smile and with no tears that I could see, sent me out into the world with these few simple words—"Take care of yourself, son."

For many days before my departure I had been anxious about leaving, mostly because of the girl I had gotten involved with. Her name was Dorothy. A part of me didn't want to leave her, yet much of me was straining to go and see this Miami—this America—this *other* part of the world. As a matter of fact, "this Miami, this America" was all there was to the world outside the Bahamas; beyond them there was nothing. I had no more than a marginal awareness that two major wars were being fought in remote and hazy places called "Europe" and "Asia." Even the mother country, colonial Great Britain, which had sent its own royal son, the Duke of Windsor, to be our governor, was no more than a faint, distant blur.

My father waved to me, and the boat pulled out of the harbor and on into the open sea toward Miami. I was alone now. For the first time in my fifteen years, I was on my own—with a small battered suitcase and three dollars against the world. I had third-class accommodations, which meant down in the hole where the smell of motor oil from the engines quickly made me seasick. I stayed up on the deck as long as I could, but ultimately the cold night air forced me down into the hole where I retched myself to sleep. The next morning I scrambled up for fresh air and off in the distance saw the outline of Miami coming up on the horizon. The closer we got, the larger it became. The tall buildings—the whole sight of it was really magnificent. The harbor was the largest I had ever seen, of course, with its hundreds of boats of every shape, size, and description. As we were easing into the dock, I

37

tried to pick out my brother Cyril from among the crowd on the wharf. I hadn't seen him since I was a baby and didn't know what he looked like, but I thought that if he looked like us, he wouldn't be too difficult to recognize. And he wasn't. Cyril wasn't as tall as I was, but slight, dark, and sort of handsome, and he seemed glad to see me as he took me and my bag through customs. We got into a car and drove to his house, my eyes feasting on everything along the way. He lived in Liberty City with his wife and six children in a three-bedroom house that had one bath.

Instantly upon meeting my sister-in-law and my nieces and nephews, I realized I was in an entirely new set of social and cultural circumstances. I didn't understand these people—and they didn't understand me. I had come from a place seemingly as far away as Mars; they had heard about the Bahamas, but most of them had never been there. It was a strange time for me. I spoke with a different kind of an accent from theirs. I knew nothing of the kind of life they lived, and because their values were quite foreign to me, naturally communication was difficult. It was just bizarre for the first couple of months. In fact, it was so traumatic, that whole experience, that I was never able to adjust to Miami.

I soon realized that my sister-in-law was not too thrilled having me around. She made it known rather quickly that I would have to go out and get a job pronto. Mind you, I was just about fifteen and under the mistaken impression that I would be able to return to school. Instead, she informed me, "You have to pull your own weight in this family structure." Quickly then, before I might have wanted to, I was out looking for a job, and jobs were not too difficult to find because the war was on. However, the unskilled hands of an immature day laborer who was totally, totally, inexperienced in the ways of this Miami—this America—could not be in great demand. In looking for that job, I began walking the streets of Miami and acquainting myself with the physical nature of the city—so many streets that I became confused, lost, even overwhelmed. But day after day I would go back, looking the city over, checking it out, and suddenly I would remember that I'd gone down this street day before yesterday and this street empties into another street, and that one connects with yet another one, and slowly I began to learn my way around.

After a week of looking for a job in this fantasyland where everything was newness to me, my sister-in-law's impatience pressed my brother into taking me to see someone he knew at Burdine's Department Store who gave me a job delivering packages from the drug and pharmacy section of the store. I joined a cadre of little black kids who made deliveries on bicycles. I didn't know the city all that well, but I could ride, so they assigned me a bike and I hit the road. As a delivery boy I had to deliver packages all the way over to Miami Beach from downtown Miami, and I didn't know Miami Beach either. I found my way by asking questions and getting directions from the other kids. Also, I could read well enough to be able to identify the street if not pronounce it, and in a pinch could get someone else to pronounce it, and of course I would know what the street numbers meant. So it seemed I might manage to get the rhythm of it—eventually.

Except that on one of my first deliveries, I was sent to Miami Beach to a very wealthy area. I walked up to the front door of a beautiful house and rang the bell. A lady came to the door and said, "What do you want?" I said, "I've brought the package from the drugstore." She said, "Get around to the back door." Not knowing what the protocol was in such circumstances, I said, "Why?" She said, "Would you just go around to the back door with the package?" I said, "But I'm here. Here is the package." It was easy enough, from my point of view, for her to just take the package. She slammed the door in my face and I put the package down on the doorstep and I left. I wasn't accustomed to such behavior on the part of ladies, white or black, and having been reared in an area where I never ran into that kind of thing, I was definitely not about to accommodate myself to it in this strange new place. Furthermore, while admittedly I was not completely naïve about racial matters, I was certainly not afraid of white people. I went back to the store and continued with my deliveries.

Two evenings later, returning from the movies with one of my cousins, I noticed that my brother's house was completely dark—at a very early hour—which seemed a bit peculiar. As we approached the porch, voices from within the house whispered, "Get on in the house. Come on in the house." We stepped inside and found the whole family moving about in an atmosphere of heavy tension as if they were under siege. In hushed tones, my sister-in-law asked accusingly, "Where have you been?" We said we had gone to the movies. "Did you see those white men?" she inquired. I said, "No," and she said, "They had on robes and hoods. They said they were looking for you. We've got your clothes packed. We've got to get you out of here." It still didn't scare me. I'd heard about the Klan and the nightriders, and white folks who were always trying to intimidate black folks, but I wasn't frightened by them. Possibly because I didn't know any better at that time, which was due in part to my spending the first fifteen years of my life free of the crushing negative self-image hammered into black children by this system, in this Miami, in this America. Under cloak of darkness I was hurried out of my brother's house and ten miles across town, to Uncle Joe's place on Third Street, where my brother had made arrangements for me to retreat. I settled in there and immediately started looking for another job, having been told by my brother never to go back to Burdine's.

I decided that I wanted to park cars because everywhere I went I saw parking lots with signs saying "Attendants wanted." Moreover, it seemed like quite a glamorous job in those days to be an attendant zipping around in all those different cars. My only difficulty was that I hadn't the faintest idea how to drive. I went downtown to a car park place and stood at the little hut where customers drove up and turned their cars over to the attendant. I stood there looking directly into the cars and saw exactly what the customers did when they left their cars. Then I looked into the window at the attendant who was parking the car, to see exactly what he did with his hands and his feet. I concentrated on the hands first and memorized the sequence of movement that triggered the car into motion. Next I made mental note of every movement made with his feet, however slight. After a while I thought: I can do that—it's just a matter of coordinating the hands and feet. Yes indeedy, I'm ready to give it a shot. So I went to another place that had a sign hanging out. I walked in and said, "I've come to see about the job." They said, "Can you drive?" "Yes, I can drive." "Do you have a license?" "Yes, I have a license." They said, "Fine. Take that car and put it in the slot over there." I said, "Certainly." I walked over, got into the car, put it in reverse, and right away began stripping the gears. The guy ran over and grabbed me out of the car and almost beat me, he was so angry, but finally he just shooed me away. I went another five or six blocks away, not wanting to try places too close together, walked into another place with a sign, and announced I was looking for a job. They said, "Where have you worked before?" I said, "Downtown at such-and-such a place." They said, "Okay, put away that car, over there." Now, I've learned you don't get into a car and put it in gear the way I did with the last one. So I put my foot on the clutch and sure enough it's in first gear and it starts off—not jerky, kinda smooth, and I'm rolling along—but I panic because I don't know what to do after that. I kept it in first gear and suddenly I hit the brakes. The car jerks a little. I look around and there's the guy watching me kinda funny. So I turn the car toward an empty slot and as I do I run right into something—bang! I got thrown out of that place, too. But now I know two things you do—you ease up and press down on the accelerator ever so softly, and when you hit the brakes you don't have to crash down on them. I figure finesse is the name of this game, so here I go one more time.

By the time I go to the next place I know the whole protocol required to apply for a job at a place like this. I walk up with a lot more confidence—having got the other wrecks behind me—and there is a guy and his wife and I say, "I'd like to apply for a job." They both are busy parking cars and obviously need help. She says, "Do you have references?" I say, "I've worked in Coral Gables and Fort Lauderdale and I've been parking cars for a couple of years." He says, "Okay," and takes down my "particulars" (all made up on the spot). "You'll start over there and fill up that southwest area, and you must always park them with the front end to the wall. And back the next car against that one so that people can get out easily, and make sure that the keys are left in the car." In those days people weren't as afraid of their cars being stolen as they are today. Anyway, I get into a car and lo and behold, it's one of those foreign makes and I don't know what the hell to do with that car. I figure I'll have to take a chance, so I cross my fingers, press down on the clutch, turn the key, and the car jumps into life. By now, I know about finesse, so I push into a gear, ease up on the clutch, and noticing that the car has started off backward, I say, "Ah-ha! That's reverse." Then I get it into—maybe not first, but second. I take off and I'm driving, but before I can get the car where I'm supposed to park it, I crash into something, and again I get tossed away.

By now I've realized that my biggest fault is in depth perception. You're going to have to make your turns wider, I said to myself. You're going to have to realize that you're dealing with five feet behind where you're sitting, and you've got three or four feet ahead of you, therefore, you have to gauge how you're going to get that much hulk—rather than your own dimensions—into a particular space. Armed with this new insight, I moved on in search of the next job. At the end of a single day, I had gone through six or seven places and I had wrecked six or seven cars. The next day I had to try a whole new area because I had wiped out an awful lot of cars and I think my reputation had preceded me in downtown Miami. So I went to a new place and worked there for a whole day before I got fired, which meant that I successfully parked a lot of cars before getting kicked out of there for not being smooth enough. The very next job I got I was driving, and driving very well—considering. Again, without much finesse, without much style, without much evidence of experience in the way I handled the cars; and again I was fired. But by this time I was a driver. I had learned how to drive on those parking lots with no lasting damage done except to the string of wrecks I left behind me. Then, now that I knew how to drive, the realization hit me that I was going to need a driver's license if I was to hold a job in a parking lot or even work as a truck driver; either way, I needed a license. I rushed over to the License Bureau and discovered that at fifteen I wasn't old enough to get a license. That ended my driving career, and I started doing other things.

I WAS HAPPIER living with my Uncle Joe and his wife, who were elderly people from the Bahamas. They had this little house in which they gave me a room. I liked them very much and they seemed to like me too, but being on in years, they didn't have the energy to spend much time with me or otherwise be of much help in my development. In between unsuccessful tries at jobs—as cleanup boy in a motor hotel, a car washer, and a warehouse laborer—I spent a lot of time in the streets just roaming around and learning the survival game, American style. I decided that Miami wasn't so good for me when I began to run into its not so subtle pattern of racism. I didn't understand it—I really didn't understand it. I couldn't even, at the time, define it as racism. Instead, I characterized it as white people being unnecessarily unfair. The thought of joining the Navy came to mind, but remembering quite clearly that my mother had cautioned me against *ever* joining the Navy—a reaction to her having been one of the few surviving passengers on a Nassau–to–Cat Island sailboat that sank in rough seas, resulting in a heavy loss of life—caused me to hesitate. But the thought persisted, and in time I came to see the Navy as a possible attractive escape route from Miami. So I figured, What the hell— Mama will understand. The Navy will be easier than the Army to get into, since I'm only fifteen. I decided to give it a shot. But before I could do that, I would have to get my birth certificate, and before you could get your birth certificate, you had to go to the main police station in downtown Miami—get permission in the form of a pass— then walk across the street to the building that housed the city jail and the Bureau of Vital Statistics where all birth records are kept. I walked into the police station, and the desk sergeant—a big, burly, rough-looking guy—says, "Take off that cap, nigger." I turned around to see who was behind me and then I suddenly realized that he was talking to me. So I said, "Are you talking to me?" He said, "Yes, I'm talking to you." I said, "Are you crazy?" He said, "What?" I said, "Are you crazy?" He said, "What did you say, boy?" I said, "Boy? My name is Sidney Poitier, you calling me names? Do you know who you're talking to?" The room is full of lots and lots of cops, and at this point they're falling down on the floor with laughter. Never in their lives have they seen such a nutty little black boy—he's got to be insane, or somebody's paid him fifty cents to come in and play this little charade. The guy behind the desk is looking at me—his mouth is wide open —and he says, "What did you say your name is, boy?" I say, "My name is Sidney Poitier—it's not 'boy.' " He says, "Okay, Mr. Poitier, would you mind telling us what it is you want?" I said, "I've come here because I want you to give me a pass to go across to the Bureau of Vital Statistics to see about my birth certificate." He said, "All right, sir," having decided he would go along with the joke, whatever it was. And then he said to me, "Where are you from?" I said, "I'm from the Bahamas." And he said, "Oh, I see." At which point they realized that I just

43

didn't know what was going on; that I just wasn't familiar with the established behavior pattern, the reflex conditioning, that would activate automatically if I stayed on in Miami much longer. He gave me the pass and I got my birth certificate and made inquiries at a recruiting station about joining the Navy and was told I couldn't, because I was too young even for the Navy. And that being the case, I decided it was about time for me to move on to another part of the country. It seemed obvious to me that there was a basic incompatibility between Miami and me; this place was simply not ready for Sidney Poitier.

I was getting a little money now from my Uncle Joe (my brother Cyril was contributing a few bucks a week toward my expenses), and I decided to run away. In fact, the only way I could leave town was to run away, since I had only about three dollars in liquid assets. Before my sudden decision to run away, I had left some clothes at the cleaners, and in order to get them immediately, I had to go to the factory itself instead of the local outlet.

The factory is located about thirty blocks across town in a white area, and I take a bus to that place because I'm really anxious to shake the dust of Miami from my tail. Mind you, I don't know how I'm going to get out of town. I have no particular plans beyond a vague vision of freight trains, but don't even know where the railroad yard is. Still, first things first—I get my jacket and two pairs of pants from this cleaning establishment and return to the bus stop and find that the buses are no longer running. It's a little after seven in the evening, and faced with no acceptable alternative to a very long walk home, I take off reluctantly in the direction of "colored town." About five blocks into my journey, I start hitchhiking. I'm smart enough now to know better than to expect to be picked up by white people in their cars, so I wait until I see black people going in my direction and I give them the thumb. Soon, a dark sedan comes rumbling along with what looks like a lot of black people inside. I give it the thumb and discover too late that it's an unmarked police car with five white cops inside, two in the front and three in the back, all in uniform. It pulls up right alongside me and the guy in the driver's seat with stripes on his sleeves says, "What are you doing?" and I say, "I'm trying to hitch a ride back to colored town." He says, "You are, are you?" He looks at me in silence for a moment and then says, "Do you see that alley over there?" and I say, "Yes." He says, "Go up in that alley." Now I ain't gonna question that, so I walk up into that alley and he backs their car in behind me in a way that puts me face to face with the officer on the passenger side of the front seat. Now here I am boxed in an alley with five cops in their unmarked car. I stand waiting. Then slowly, deliberately, the guy in the passenger seat beckons me to him, and as I lean in toward him, he takes out his gun and places the nozzle of the revolver right between my eyes—on my forehead. He starts moving the nozzle of the gun around ever so slightly in a circle on my forehead, and he's talking to me at the same time, but not so much to me as to the sergeant behind the wheel. Looking dead at me he says, "What should we do with this boy?" The sergeant says, "I don't know—find out where he's from." The guy with the gun says, "Where're you from?" I say, "I live on Third Street." He says, "Well, what're you doing over here? You're not supposed to be over here at this time of night." I say, "No, sir, I wasn't aware that I wasn't supposed to be over here at this time of night. I've been to the cleaners to get my clothes." He says, "Why did you have to come over here to go to the cleaners—all the way over here?" I say, "Well, the cleaner that I go to said my clothes wouldn't be ready for a couple of days, and I was going away, and in order to get them out I had to come all the way over here and the buses had stopped running." Well, my story obviously is the truth and it begins to register with them, but also at the same time I'm getting madder than a son of a bitch. Instead of being scared I'm getting mad at this attempt to intimidate me. The guy with the gun says to the sergeant, "What do you say, Sarge?" The sergeant, taking his time, ponders my fate a full ten seconds, then he says, "Boy, we're gonna let you walk home. If you turn around we'll shoot you. If you look back just once we'll shoot you. Do you think you can walk home without looking back?" I say, "Yes, sir." I head out of that alley with my little package of clothing and turn toward home when I hit the main street. I'm on the right side of the street, walking by stores with plate-glass windows, and I can see the reflection of the cops' car. It's pulled out of the alley and is right behind me. Now I don't move my head a fraction of an inch, either to the right or to the left. I keep my head dead center, but I can turn my eyes toward the windows I'm passing—and as I'm passing those windows, out of the corner of my eye I can see that police car. For thirty-five fucking

45

blocks they *stay* behind me, until I'm back in the black community. I walk all the way to Third Street, where I turn right and head toward Uncle Joe's house. Then, and only then, do they accelerate and continue on. Now I *am* scared—I realize that they were dead serious. It must have taken me an hour to finish that walk, and they must have been laughing all the way and deciding who was going to take the first crack at me. Now I'm scared and absolutely must get out of this town, because I cannot make it here; this place is too strange.

All right—quite soon after that I figured out the freight train situation and found out where the railroad yards were. If I was going to leave town, this would have to be the way, since I had no money and sure in hell wasn't able to earn any seeing that the few jobs I did get I wasn't experienced enough to hang on to. Besides, hadn't I seen it done many times in the movies? Next day, I packed my belongings in my little battered suitcase, went down to the railyards, and hopped into a boxcar. The first car I got into was an open-topped one hauling some kind of earth-like material that was to be processed into something else. It looked like a lot of rocks and gravel. Anyway, I jumped into that car and lay down and the long train of boxcars left Miami. It ran and ran and ran—night fell. About 9:00 p.m., the train stopped on a siding outside of a town. I looked up over the side and there were no lights in sight, and I thought: What the fuck is this? but consoled myself with the thought that this was a temporary stopover and we would be moving again in a little while. Hours passed and I fell asleep, only to wake up the next morning and find that some of the freight cars had been detached during the night while I slept, and the rest of the train had gone on without us. I started walking and wound up in Tampa, Florida.

I remembered my family saying we had relatives in Tampa, so I asked around and sure as hell, there were some Poitiers in town. I found them living in a little shack on the outskirts, and they seemed genuinely pleased to see me. When I told them I was on my way north, they fed me, gave me bread and other things to carry away with me, and wished me well. I went back to the railroad, but I couldn't negotiate another boxcar. I spent hours and hours waiting for something to come through—and nothing. So I wound up back in Miami with Uncle Joe.

My brother had heard that I'd run away and was quite

upset. I told him I just couldn't take it there anymore and that I was going to leave if I could, but I promised that the next time I tried to leave it would be with a job or something. He told me where to go for a job that would take me out of town—a place that hired help for resorts. The resorts needed all kinds of help—gardening help and kitchen help. They'd give you a room and you'd stay for six weeks or something and make a few bucks. The season wasn't quite ready, but I registered. And in the meantime I decided to take another crack at the freight trains. I'm gone this time for sure, I thought, as the train clickety-clacked into the night, but I still didn't get out of the state of Florida. When I woke up the next morning, I was on the outskirts of this little town beyond Tampa, and again they'd left some boxcars stranded on a side grading while the rest of the train went on to other places. I had just imagined that if you got in a boxcar, it would go all the way north. Frustrated and hungry, I walked away from that abandoned freight car in the direction of the little town nearby. I remember that it was a terribly clean, manicured, little town, and I kept looking for the "colored" part of it, and I couldn't find it.

Now I'm really getting hungry. I decide that I'm going to have to get something to eat, because it's going on twenty-four hours since my last meal. I walk down a residential street and there are lovely little tract homes—all clean and neat. I walk up to a house and a white woman comes to the door and says, "Yes?" I say, "Excuse me, I do hope I'm not interrupting you, but you see I'm hungry and I wondered if there's something you would like to have done around the house—some job. I can mow lawns, I can clean out a garage, I can wash things. I can do almost anything that you would want me to do. If there's something you need to have done—I'd be more than glad to do it in exchange for something to eat." The lady is so impressed—she is overwhelmed. She says, "Well, my goodness, where are you from?" I say, "From Miami." She says, "Miami—you're a long way from home." I say, "Yes, I am, and I've run out of funds and I haven't any money and I'm hungry and I always want to earn my keep." I don't know where I got all that nerve from, nor all the know-how for dealing and negotiating with people, but I got it, and I'm cooking. That lady says to me, "Come in." She takes me in the house—into her kitchen—and feeds me at her dining room table, the biggest meal. And as I leave, she gives me a bag full of fruit and sandwiches. She doesn't ask me to do one thing and she says, "Good luck, and take care of yourself." I thank her and go.

That episode buoyed me. It also developed an ambivalence in me, because on the one hand Miami was awful—the white people were awful—and here is this lady. It was then I began to learn that there are middle grounds, and an awful lot of grays in between white and black.

I kept heading for what I thought was the North—I had some food now to last a couple of days. I slept in some woods near the train depot, waiting for another train to come. I waited—and waited—and waited—and nothing. So I roamed around the town again and wherever I went—whenever I was hungry again—I would ring a doorbell and say, "I'm looking for work in order to get food," and I would always get a lawn to mow or a garage to clean out or a car to wash, and every time I would do the best job I possibly could. I had a terrible, fierce pride. I guess it came from my folks and that whole early time in the Caribbean, but I wanted people to think well of me. And in order for someone to think well of me after I was gone, I had to leave them with a good impression. And in order to leave them with a good impression, I had to do whatever job I did for them so well that when they thought of me, they thought favorably. (There were exceptions to that rule, of course—the Miami parking lots, for example.)

Well, I'm hanging around this town and it's time for some conclusions. I can't sleep out in the woods any longer—it's frigid out there at night. So on this my third day in that town, whose name I don't remember, I am nose to nose with the following dilemma: I can't sleep out in the woods any longer, and I certainly can't sleep in town because the moment I'm caught, that's vagrancy, and I'm well aware of what vagrancy could get me. The ideal solution would enable me to sleep in a warm place in town and at the same time beat the vagrancy rap, but what could it be?

Bang! like a flash the ideal solution lights up my mind. When night falls, I walk into the local police station. Inside there is one guy on duty who looks up and says, "Yeah?" I say, "Good evening, sir, I have no place to sleep tonight and I'm not interested in being arrested for vagrancy and I thought that if I came here and told you that, you'd allow me to sleep in jail and tomorrow I'll be on my way." The guy looks at me as if he doesn't understand a word of what I'm saying. He says, "Come again?" I say, "I would like to sleep here tonight because I have no place to sleep and tomorrow I'll be on my way. I don't wish to break the laws of the town by being found sleeping in hallways or some place that would make me a vagrant." And he says, "Aha, I see. What's your name?" I tell him. He says, "Where are you from?" I say, "Miami, Florida." He says, "Where are you going?" Now I lie a little bit. I say, "I'm going to Liberty City, Florida —I'm going home." He says, "That's a new one on me. All right. You'll have to give me some information." I give him my brother's name and all that and he says, "I tell you what I'm going to do. You can stay here, but I'd like to call your brother. Is there a phone there?" Now I'm stuck. I say, "Yes," and give him the number and he calls and my brother Cyril answers the phone and the man says, "Do you have a brother named Sidney?" Cyril says, "Yes." The man tells him I want to spend the night there since I don't have any funds, and Cyril thanks him and says he'll come up in the morning and get me.

The deputy was satisfied. He gave me a cell to sleep in, and the next morning Cyril came up on the bus and took me back. Boy, was he steaming mad. He said, "Let me tell you something. I have got a family of my own—I love you and I love all my family—my father, my mother and my brothers and my sisters. You're my baby brother, but I've got a family of my own—I have children of my own and I have to be concerned about them. I cannot, I *cannot* assume responsibility for you—I just simply can't. You are going to have to stop this shit, because I can't be negotiating your extrication from these involvements anymore. Now you just straighten up and fly right or I'm going to have to send your ass back to Nassau." He was not the kind of guy to come on that strong, so I knew it was close to straighten-up time. And back to Uncle Joe I went.

But within a week, my restlessness and frustrations were bubbling over. I spent practically every day hounding those people who hired for the resorts, and as luck would have it they offered me a job working in the mountains in Georgia. I was to be kitchen helper—which means everything: you wash dishes, you scrub floors, you peel potatoes, you do everything. I said I'd take it, and they gave me a one-way ticket and told me what bus to take. I got on that bus with my little suitcase—well, Georgia is a fucking long way from Florida. I just had no idea of the length and breadth of this country. I figured when I was running away on the freight train that I'd be in New York in no time—like the next morning I'd wake up in New York. Instead, every time I woke up I was still in the state of Florida, which was an education in realizing that America isn't the same size as Nassau.

So now I went to Georgia. The bus stopped in Atlanta at the main terminal, where I transfer to another bus in a few hours, and during the layover I roamed around Atlanta. It was fantastic. The buildings were taller than in Miami. The black community was a big one—busy, active, and inviting. But it wasn't a place I wanted to stop, and soon it became time to catch the other bus and head for the mountain. That evening, before the sun went down, we pulled into a one-street town where I was scheduled to be met by someone at a particular time; those were my instructions. With about forty-five minutes to kill before being picked up, I went exploring. One post office and three stores—that's all there was to the town. But it had a black community consisting of one bar, one church, ten dwellings "behind the tracks," with no paved roads or street lights—in reality, just a cluster of shacks with a gin mill and a place of worship. I roamed around and did strange things there. It was the first time I had been exposed to rural American blacks—they were mostly workers on the farms. I was welcome because I was black, and so I was able to walk up to people's homes unchallenged. At one house I saw some kids around my age and I just moved in and stood up next to them and mingled in with the crowd with nobody knowing that I was an outsider. Later, I walked into the local bar and sat down. Listening and studying—watching these new faces and trying to figure what kind of people exist behind them. In time, I was challenged by the owner, who wanted to know why I was sitting and staring and not drinking, and finally he asked, "Who are you anyway?" I said I was waiting for someone. He looked at me intently, screwed up his brow trying to place me in some familiar frame, but couldn't, and finally turned and walked away. I continued to sit in the midst of these new people, watching their every move. There was nobody in that town that I'd ever seen before. The girls were new, the men were new, the

50

women, the mothers, the children, the white people were new. Every place was new. In forty-five minutes I got a real education in the lifestyles playing themselves out "behind the tracks" in this little nondescript town.

I got back to the bus stop with no time to spare and, sure as hell, a car pulled up with a white guy and some black people inside. He introduced himself as one of the owners and we headed up the mountain. The resort consisted of a fifty-room, two-story motel-type structure, with a main dining room, a snack bar, a gift shop and other tourist trappings, and it was nestled on a plateau at the very top of the mountain. Scattered in among the pine trees around this main complex were fifteen two-bedroom bungalows. The view was absolutely spectacular—a vista of green sloping sharply down and running unevenly toward a fusion with the horizon a hundred miles away. I spent a month and a half in that fantastic setting, working seven days a week, twelve hours a day—and let me tell you they got their money's worth, which is to say my ass was dragging at the end of the day. The boss wouldn't pay us our salary at the end of each week but would give us a "draw" of a buck or two against it. Occasionally, at his discretion, he would let us have an afternoon off to do as we pleased, and of course we would go down the mountain and behind the tracks, where some of the other black guys would seek out the ladies who offered favors for a fee. But I wasn't into that so much because in my head I was still into the romantic imagery of love affairs—you know, my girl Dorothy back in Nassau. I saw romance, rather than sexual release, as my main need. I preferred drifting about observing, listening, watching people, and weaving scenarios about them from the impressions they gave off.

One day the beautiful mountain began to lose its magic. My work was good and I got along well in the kitchen, but respite from the prolonged isolation was too infrequent, causing the restlessness in my nature to heat up to the moving-on point. I went to the owner, thanked him for the job and told him that I had to leave. He paid me thirty-nine dollars, which is what I had accumulated after deductions, plus the cost of a one-way ticket back to Florida. Someone dropped me down the mountain, and before catching the bus back to Atlanta, I took a farewell stroll behind the tracks in that little mountain town, but there was no one to say goodby to me because no one ever knew that I was there.

Obviously, I never had any intention of going back to Florida, but now that I was able to go somewhere else, I didn't know where. I get off the bus in Atlanta and before I leave the station, just to make sure I don't get trapped in Georgia, I go to the ticket window and ask the man, "Where is the next bus going to?" He says, "Where do you want to go?" I say, "I don't know—I want to know where the next bus is going to." He says, "Well, the next bus is going to Chattanooga and it leaves in five minutes." I say, "How far is Chattanooga?" He says so many miles. I say, "How much is that?" and he says, "Two dollars and five cents." I say, "No, it's not far enough." He says, "What is it that you want?" I say, "Well, where is the next bus going after that?" He says, "The next bus after that is going to Birmingham." I say, "How much is that?" He says, "Two forty-five." I say, "No, that's not far enough." He says, "Well, if you tell me what you want . . ." I say, "I don't know. Where is the next bus going after that?" He says, "The next bus is going to New York." I say, "How much is that?" He says, "That's eleven dollars and thirty-five cents." I say, "Okay, that's far enough."

Well, a part of it is the distance away from Florida, but there's also everything I've ever heard about New York—Harlem and stuff like that. It's a combination of the two. The clerk at the window says, "Round trip?" I say, "No, one way." After paying for my ticket, I've got twenty-seven dollars left from my wages plus the amount of my one-way bus ticket back to Miami. I wander around Atlanta double-checking first impressions and looking longingly at colored girls in plaid skirts and silk blouses, because I'm still missing my girl back in Nassau. Then at departure time I step onto a bus and take off from Atlanta, Georgia, for New York City. I know no one in New York. Have no relatives, no friends, no address of anybody who is known by anybody. I'm a sixteen-year-old total stranger on the way.

4 New York

DURING MY twenty-eight hours charging north-ward on a Greyhound, I saw much of America streaking by on the other side of a splattered window. The schedule, mercifully, required periodic stops to disgorge and receive passengers, but more importantly it allowed "through" passengers to make necessary relief runs on the toilets and snack bars.

We arrived in New York around three in the afternoon —an uneventful entrance, considering my anticipation, along an obscure route, up 8th Avenue to 50th Street, which in no way let one see the full extent of the city. But what do I know? And who cares? What's the difference? The Greyhound has done its job, I said to myself. I'm here. Tingling with an excitement fueled by expectations, I disembarked, taking precise note of the moment my feet made contact with the legendary island of Manhattan. My eyes and ears immediately began drinking in the sights and sounds swirling around me as I waited for my little battered suitcase. As the porter yanked it out of the luggage compartment on the underbelly of the bus, I noticed it had been busted into. Possibly by one of the people who were loading and unloading luggage at the various stops we made. Whoever it was had lifted a couple of items of clothing, one of which contained the money left over from my wages and the one-way bus ticket back to Miami. But again I said to myself, what the hell, I've still got what's left in the suitcase, plus three dollars and change in my pocket.

As I walk out of the bus station onto 50th Street, a well-dressed colored guy walks up to me and says, "Hey, would you like a girl?" I'm caught off guard—I hesitate: "What do you mean?" He says, "I can get you a girl." I ask, "What kind of girl?" He answers, "A white girl." I say, "Noo-oo." He tries, "Colored girl?" I say, "I don't think so. Not now, but maybe I'll see you later." He asks,

"Where're you going?" I tell him, "I'm going to Harlem."
He asks, "You know anybody over there?" I assure him,
"Oh, yes, I know a lot of people out there." He says,
"Well, how long are you going to be around?" I say, "I'll
be here—I'll see you." He says, "Okay, I'm usually
around here and that'll be fine," and he takes off.

But I don't know where to go. I see another colored
guy and I walk up to him and say, "Could you tell me
how to get to Harlem?" He says, "Yes, you take the subway there." I say, "The what?" He says, "The subway."
I say, "What's that?" He says, "Well, you have to go down
under the ground there." "I've got to go down under the
ground?" I ask suspiciously. He says, "Yes, there is a
train there and you can take that train." I say, "How
much is that?" He says, "Five cents." I say, "Oh." He
says, "You don't know anything about—are you from
the South?" I say, "Yeah." He says, "Well, what are you
going to do up there?" I say, "I'm going to find a place to
stay. You could tell me the name of a hotel." He says,
"Yeah, there's a hotel called the Dewey Square Hotel at
116th." I say, "Thank you very much." He says, "Don't
mention it and good luck."

I go down some steps and into the ground. There is a
booth and a tiny revolving gate. Now I don't know how to
get into this revolving thing, so I say to the man in the
booth, "How do I get the train to get me to Harlem?" He
says, "You put a nickel in that thing and you walk in
and when the trains come, look for a train with the letters
AA." I say, "Fine." I take a nickel, put it in the turnstile,
go in, and stand on the platform. These fucking trains
start coming with all kinds of names and letters. There's
the A train and the C train and the D train, and some of
them don't stop because this is 50th Street and the express
stop is 59th Street. So I wonder, how do people get on that
train that doesn't stop? It whizzes right by and swoosh it's
gone in nothing flat! I've never been down under the
ground, and I say to myself: How can trains run under
the ground? How far can they go? And do they go deeper
as they go along? And if they get so deep into the ground,
maybe you can't ever get out. I'm standing there fascinated by the whole thing and here comes a train with the
letters AA lit up on its forehead. It pulls up and it goes
"ha-chet shish!" The doors open up and some people
rush out and other people rush in. I step in behind them
and the door closes . . . SHASSSS! Un-chun . . . un-chun

54

. . . un-chun . . . the train goes. I look around and I'm on a TRAIN UNDER THE GROUND . . . it's FANTASTIC!!! I glance about at everyone else and notice that nobody is scared that they're under the ground. I say, "Hey, this must be okay." We get to 59th Street, which is the next stop. But wow! Now I'm really awe-struck, because 59th Street is an express stop and they've got all kinds of platforms, not just one, and trains coming in—and going out—and coming in and going out. . . . I say, "Jesus, all of this underground!" I have no idea how far this underground thing runs, but I figure there are cities underground. People have got to be living under here too. And through it all, I'm thinking that I have to remember where to get off: 116th Street, the guy told me, so I'm looking for it. From 59th Street the next stop is 72nd Street—and I am watching. The next is 86th Street—then 96th Street, 110th Street, and finally 116th Street. So I get off. But I don't know what to do next, and I just follow people. I see them heading in a certain direction and I flow right behind them. They pass through a revolving gate and proceed up a flight of steps and I, bringing up the rear, follow the leaders up those steps—and wham!—I'm out on top of the ground again. I'm on 116th Street and 8th Avenue and I see nothing but colored people. I see a few whites in the stores functioning, I guess, as clerks, owners, and managers. But I see colored people everywhere, colored people in profusion, and I feel completely at ease as I start walking around in search of the Dewey Square Hotel, and as I walk, I'm marveling at the tall buildings. Colored people live in these buildings? Yes, colored people are all over this place, and they live in these tall buildings—that's great. I find the Dewey Square Hotel, which is a kind of nondescript little hotel, and walk up to the front desk and the guy says, "Can I help you?" And I say, "Yes, I would like a room." He says, "Very good. For how long?" I say, "How much are they?" He says, "Three dollars." Now I figure the man is talking about three dollars a month or if push comes to shove, three dollars a week, which would be absolutely too extravagant for me, but the man is talking about three dollars a night! I say, "Three dollars a night?" He says, "Yes, that's about the best you're going to do." I say, "Three dollars a *night!*" He says, "Yes, sir." I say, "Thank you very much," and get out of there fast. Now I say to myself: What the hell am I going to do? If a hotel room is three dollars a night, I can't have any place to stay. I figure I'll go back to square one and start figuring from there. I find my way back to the subway—I go on the other side—I take the train and go back down to 50th Street. I get out and I go into the bus station, where I invest a dime by putting my little suitcase into one of those lockers good for twelve or twenty-four hours. With three dollars and change in my pockets, unburdened by my suitcase, I come out of that terminal thinking: To hell with it. I'm going to worry about my sleeping quarters later on. Now I'm going to see me some New York. I walk one block. I don't know what pointed my nose toward Broadway—I could easily have gone the other way, but I head toward Broadway, I guess maybe because the buildings are tallest in that direction. I walk one block from 8th Avenue and 50th Street to Broadway and 50th Street, and I turn and look around, and never in my life— now it's beginning to be twilight time and the lights are on—have I ever seen such tall buildings or such bright lights. I mean lights everywhere—flickering on and off— making designs and turning into all kinds of funny-looking things like people walking, dancing, doing flips. Then the lights all go out and suddenly you see a train move on a great big signboard of flickering lights. I am absolutely entranced. It's as good as watching a movie.

Well, here I am, man. I start walking down toward 42nd Street. Mind you, I don't know there is a place called 42nd Street, but I'm walking down Broadway mesmerized by, among other things, a huge sign of a Camel smoker puffing smoke out all over Broadway. Well, I'm walking and marveling and the people are jammed together and the traffic is fantastic. It's like a marvelous circus. I get down to 42nd Street and I go crazy—because on 42nd Street in one block between Broadway and 8th Avenue they've got at least fifteen movie houses. And pinball parlors, gift shops, dirty bookstores, haberdasheries, restaurants. The place that sucks me in and almost destroys me is a malted milk stand, right at the corner of 42nd Street and Broadway. It leads down into the subway. A malted milk stand with hot dogs—oh, my Lord! I have me a chocolate malted—you hear me when I tell you. Never have I tasted anything so good in my life. And I eat a big, fat, juicy, hot dog that's just unbelievable. So I say to myself, "Shucks, this New York is really neat— this New York is absolutely fabulous." Now I don't want to get out of here. I don't want to go anywhere but Broadway and 42nd Street. So I start walking up Broadway, back down to 42nd Street, back up Broadway. Each trip I sneak in for a malted milk and a hot dog. Well, my stomach is bursting. And my three dollars are gone. And it's now about 9:00 p.m. But there is a practical side to Sidney Poitier too. Well, I say to myself, my three dollars are gone because I spent it all on hot dogs and malted milk. I've got to have money to eat with tomorrow and I've got to have some place to stay. I know I can't find a place to stay tonight, because I have no money, but tomorrow has to be addressed. How am I going to manage? That's the problem I'm dealing with as I'm walking up and down Broadway for the tenth time.

At 49th Street I'm passing a place called the Turf Restaurant when I notice a sign in a window that says "Relief dishwasher wanted." I say to myself: Hey, I'm going to see about that job. Whereupon I walk in, search out the night manager and tell him, "I'm here for the dishwasher job." His eyes run me over quickly before he says, "Okay." He gets on the phone and talks to someone and apparently they say, "Send him down," because he points me toward a door at the rear and says, "Go downstairs." The kitchen is located in the basement of the restaurant, and all the food comes up to the dining room on dumbwaiters. The guy who meets me asks, "Can you start right away?" and I say, "Yes." He says the pay is $4.11 per night and I can have two meals. Four dollars, that's a lot of money, I think, and I say, "I'll take it." The job is hard, since I've never worked with big machines like these—or in such an enormous place. The regular dishwashers ran the machines while the relief guys sorted, stacked, and shelved the tons of dishes and silverware spewed out by the monster machines. It took me all night to catch on to the ritual, but I learned it.

As I climbed up out of that kitchen basement at four o'clock in the morning I was tired to the bone, and at the same time delighted to have been asked back. Out on the street I was amazed to find that *my* lights and *my* Broadway were still going strong, with hundreds of people moving around at this late (or early) hour. It was wartime. Back at the bus station with a change of clothing taken from my little suitcase stashed in the locker, I went down into the nickel pay toilet to take a birdbath and hopefully find somewhere to catch a fast forty winks. After my "bath" I took up occupancy in a pay toilet booth at the extreme end of the men's room. With the seat down and my feet up against the door, I settled into a sleeping position and tried to doze off. I'm sure there are more uncomfortable ways to take a nap, but none come readily to mind. Still, what was I to do? Spend three dollars a night for a hotel room and be left with one dollar? I couldn't do that. So I slept in the pay toilet, miserably, for an hour or so—enough to refresh me sufficiently to get me back out into the swing of things. And back I go exploring New York, loading up on malted milk and hot dogs, penetrating a little deeper into the unknown regions of this infinite city, until the last precious minute in the evenings before reporting back to work in the basement of the Turf Restaurant.

The pay toilet didn't work out for sleeping purposes, and I had to find a more suitable place. It was the rooftop of the Brill Building at 51st Street just off Broadway, a building that housed the offices of music publishing firms, composers, songwriters, agents, and managers for musical groups and recording companies. I found it by chance. In my wanderings through the Broadway area, I entered many buildings just to ride the elevators, since riding elevators above three or four stories was a newness to me. Just being so completely anonymous in a vast wonderland like New York was amazing. I would walk into a building and get into an elevator with a panel of buttons from one to thirty, punch any button, and that elevator would take me anywhere I wanted to go. What power! In the Brill Building, on such an excursion, I decided to go up and look at the roof. I think my reason was simply to get an overall view, because the streets of New York are canyonlike—you're always looking up—and I figured if I got up high enough, I could look down and around from one section to another, from one street to another. The panorama of the entire city that greeted me as I stepped out on that rooftop was breath-taking, especially those buildings reaching toward the sky that were taller yet than the one I was on. Nighttime must be brilliant up here, I thought. That's when the idea flashed on me to sleep in this setting under the stars. Later I asked the elevator operators what time the building closed and was told it never closed. Never. I mean it closed, but they had maintenance guys around at night cleaning the lobby and hallways while a crew of women cleaners attacked the offices. These ideal conditions for entering and exiting, coupled with my fluctuating hours at the dishwashing machine, allowed me to use the roof of the Brill Building as my penthouse dwelling for the next few weeks. On spread-out copies of the *New York Times* and/or the *Journal-American,* I was finally able to stretch out and sleep. A vast improvement over my former habitat, and it served my needs quite well, except that occasionally it got as cold as hell up there, and the *New York Times,* however many uses it may be put to, was clearly never intended to see service as a blanket.

So, in time, I saved some money, went up to Harlem, rented a five-dollar-a-week room, and moved in. I didn't have a bathroom, but I could use the one in the hall. It was great: now I could take real baths in a tub instead of birdbaths in a public toilet. The room was plain and terribly small and furnished with only the minimum essentials—a little cot bed, a small chiffonier with a few drawers in it serving in the absence of a closet, and a naked 40-watt bulb, placed noticeably off center in the ceiling. But never mind, I was making an attempt to set down roots in this new place.

By now I had found out where to go to get dishwashing jobs when the Turf didn't need me. At 88 Warren Street —way, way down in the southern end of Manhattan—I found a bank of employment agencies that dealt in restaurant help of all sorts, with relief dishwashing being in very big demand. For months to come I would be sent by one or another of those agencies into each of the five boroughs, into scores of restaurant kitchens, dozens and dozens of times.

I'm now getting to know New York more than a little bit, and the romance is really thick and heavy between us, with my leisure time happily divided between 42nd Street and Harlem.

Being unaware of the winter's insidious preparations, I found no warning in the occasional brisk morning or chilly evening. In innocence and ignorance I went about my life, making the simple choices that carried me across a day, with no hint to alert me to the assault that soon would drive me to the wall and do me real damage. In the meantime, with weeks to spare, I went about getting my bearings and committing to memory the rules by which the game of life was played in the "Big Apple"—a very different kind of town from Nassau or even Miami. In this fastest of cities, survival might very well have depended on how quick a study I was. By leaving nothing to chance and paying strict attention to the daily lessons that necessity was laying on me, I was somehow managing to survive from week to week, growing just a little wiser along the way.

It was during this time that I was in a race riot. Or was it two? (I remember one of them being characterized as a "disturbance.") Anyway, riot or disturbance, I was in them both. In one of them I got shot in the leg. I was living on 127th Street in my little rented room—in those days, as I suspect is still true, many colored people had to rent out one or more rooms of their apartments to help make ends meet. In a restaurant downtown where I was working I heard that there was trouble in Harlem. After work I took a train uptown, came up out of the subway, and there was chaos everywhere—cops, guns, and people running and looting, with shots going off everywhere and debris and broken glass all over the street. Many stores had been set on fire, and the commercial district on 125th Street looked as if it had been bombed. Lenox Avenue was also ripped up, but I lived near Lenox, so I tried making my way home.

I'm not essentially a looter—I don't think—but how can one tell? I'm making my way home and I see all these people piling out of this grocery store with stuff in their arms. The front of the store has been busted down, and where the plate-glass window was, people are just vaulting over it into the store and grabbing things. They're coming out with cases and bags of stuff, and for some reason I join in. I run into this store, but I don't know what the fuck I'm going to come up with because I'm not going for anything in particular, I'm just rushing around in there among dozens of other people who are moving fast—grabbing, scooping up, putting down boxes, picking up unopened cases and running out—and finally I hear bang! bang! bang! The people start flying out of the store in every direction. Deducing from the sound of the gunshots that the cops are very close, possibly right outside the store, I run into a little storeroom looking for an exit, but there isn't any. No windows, no doors, nothing; it's simply a storeroom containing large bags of flour, sugar, and various grains. I'm in there and there's no way out—right? I close the door behind me. Now I hear the cops coming into the store. In the distance people are screaming and hollering and shots are going off. Well, I've got no fucking alternative now—they're not shooting in the air, they're shooting at people. I have no alternative now but to employ my survival instinct. You know what I do? I flop down on the floor across some bags, and I just lie there stretched out over those bags in a way meant to give the impression that I'm dead—right? I'm lying there and my head is kinda leaning over and I stop breathing. They're approaching the storeroom and I listen—they're coming nearer and nearer—and as I hear the door about to open, I take one last breath and stop breathing again. Bang—the door opens and there isn't a twitch moving. Not a hair in motion. I am not breathing. Whomp! I'm just gone. Suddenly a light shines into my face—then I hear the words "Oh, shit" and the door closes—bang! Slowly I start breathing again. I wait for what seems an eternity, but it can't be more than about five or six minutes, and I'm saying, "Oh, Lord, how did I get into this?" Then I decide that they've looked at me and figured I was dead and didn't want to get involved—so they just closed the door and split. When I finally open the door and peek out, there's nobody in the store, but they're still rioting outside everywhere. I can see people running frantically about the streets, screaming, shouting, cursing. Some loaded down with foodstuffs or furniture, heading home with their loot. I say to myself: Now is the time for me to get the hell out of here. With that I leap out through that broken plate-glass window and take off —wham! Everybody is running in one direction or another, and some of them are being shot at. I run along Lenox Avenue heading for 127th Street, get to the corner, make my turn, and head for home. When I hear bang, bang, bang, and I feel something cool on my foot. Needless to say I don't stop to investigate it. But when I get to my room, the blood is soaking in my shoes. I've been shot. The slug has torn through the fleshy part of my lower calf and gone on out, leaving me with a bloody shoe and a nasty painful gash, but not seriously wounded. Even through my pain, I have the presence of mind to be grateful that the slug didn't hit anything solid. I was, I thought, very lucky under the circumstances. It hurt like hell after I calmed down, but I wrapped it up and stayed home the rest of the evening and most of the next day. Then I went out and got some Vaseline—I didn't know anything about medicine, so I got Vaseline—put it on the wound, and wrapped it up. I limped around for a couple of days and went back to work; I could barely walk on it, but I had to work. It healed eventually and everything was cool. Another riot (or disturbance) followed in Harlem later on, and again I was a bit player in its cast. Terrible, terrible times they were. But I wasn't sophisticated enough then to understand the underlying causes that brought them about.

THE BEAST OF WINTER came, and she was a bitch! I had never in my life been in a winter. I had never been near snow—I didn't know what it looked like. I knew it was supposed to be white—I'd seen it in the movies—but I had no experience with it. I had no experience with temperatures of 30 degrees and freezing. And I had no wardrobe. As a result, I was hit by the winter with such fierce impact that by the end of November I was fractured, disoriented, almost immobilized. My feeble defense was to wear all of my clothes at once—but they were summer clothes—are you listening? The little fad styles of summer, shirts of summer, trousers of summer. I had never been so cold in my life. I had a light jacket, but that was it. No topcoat—no nothing—and I was freezing. Every day I went out it was freezing. As a matter of fact, the only warmth I ever experienced was when I was dishwashing in some kitchen, or in the little five-dollar room I was renting. I remember standing one day on the platform of the elevated train at 125th Street in very cold weather, waiting for a downtown train. Chilled to the bone, I said to myself: Lord, one of these days— one of these days—I'm going to be able to stay in bed as long as I want to. I'm not going to have to get out of bed because I don't care what I've got to do, I'm going to make out in this world. While waiting for the train, I stood on that platform dressed in my insufficient clothing, freezing my ass off—not to mention my toes, my ears, my lips, my nose, and my fingers. *Everything* was frozen. And by the time I got on that train and defrosted a little, it was time to get off and out into the cold again.

Striking as she did without warning, Lady Winter threw me off balance and kept me staggering long enough to get me dispossessed from my room for nonpayment of rent and leave me penniless, sleeping on a bench in Pennsylvania Station, where I was arrested and booked for vagrancy. Someone tapped me on the shoulder and said, "Get up." Jarred from sleep, it took me a moment to focus on the cop hovering over me. I scrambled to a sitting position. He asked my name and said, "What are you doing here?" I said, "I'm going to take a train." He said, "Where's your ticket?" I had no ticket. He said, "Do you have any identification?"—and I had no identification. He said, "Well, you come with me." He took me to a precinct on 32nd Street, where they booked me for vagrancy, put me in a cell with one light on over my head, then slammed and locked the iron door to that awful cell, leaving me shaken and alone, wishing they would turn out the lights because I couldn't hold back the tears that had already begun to blur my vision. They kept me there all night, never once turning out that light. The next day they let me out, saying they had run a check on me with the information I had given them—plus, my fingerprints had turned up nothing of consequence. As a result, I was free to go, but not without a warning: "Another arrest for vagrancy will surely get you some time in the poky." I said, "No, sir, I'm not going to get arrested for vagrancy anymore. I am going to join the Army." (Another on-the-spot invention.) They said, "That's a good idea." One of the officers gave me a quarter to have something to eat and I left.

Now hear this. I got the address of a Catholic orphanage in Brooklyn. I don't know if I just stumbled onto it in my wanderings, or if I was directed to it, but I went out to that orphanage, walked in, and told a nun that I had no room and had just been arrested for vagrancy and needed some place to spend a few days while I got myself together. Her sympathetic eyes studied me briefly before she went off to consult with the Lady Superior of the orphanage. Soon she returned smiling and said, "Yes, you can stay here." They put me in a dormitory with other kids—mostly white—they gave me a bed, food, and a toothbrush. I stayed out there and went back to work as a dishwasher. But I still found it very hard to deal with that fucking winter, mostly because it was so new to me and I hadn't worked through it yet. Also, I still didn't know how to deal with it in terms of clothing. Gloves, for instance, I didn't have.

Well, one day while at this orphanage I decided the best thing to do was really go into the Army, because that would get me off the streets, get me three squares a day, and get me some warm clothes. And I hoped they'd send me some place warm. I went to a recruiting station in Brooklyn and said, "I've come to join the Army." They said, "How old are you?" I said, "Eighteen." They said, "When were you eighteen?" I said, "Last birthday." Which wasn't true—I was just sixteen. They said, "Okay. Have you ever been arrested?" I said, "No." They said, "All right." And handed me an application. "After you've filled that out, you go and take a physical." A couple of days later I took my physical and passed. Ten days after that—I was in the Army. I had successfully hiked my age and had been accepted in the U.S. Army.

Before leaving the orphanage, I went in to say goodby to the nuns and thank them for their generous hospitality. I offered them my little battered suitcase and its contents as partial payment for their many kindnesses, and because they accepted it as if it were a very important gift, from someone they cared about, I was moved. Taking particular notice of the nun with the sympathetic eyes who first received me, I think I witnessed a tear falling, but then again I wasn't sure. She did, however, definitely smile and wave her farewell as I walked away from the orphanage on my way to the Army.

5 The Army

THEY SENT ME on a train with a lot of other inductees to Camp Upton on Long Island. They gave me clothing and ran me through a little basic training for a few weeks, and from there they sent me to Northport, Long Island, to work in a Veterans Hospital which housed returning GI's who were shell-shocked. There were about 150 of us, including a captain, a lieutenant, and a master sergeant. We were a real company—or was it a detachment?—anyway, we were supposed to augment the civilian employees at this particular hospital. We learned to do physiotherapy, to tend wards, to administer cold packs, shock treatments, and other supposedly rehabilitative therapies that were destined to come to naught, because despite our training, we would become, in time, no more than jailers. Due, you see, to the fact that the Army was not heavily into the mental health business.

On weekends those of us who were off duty would pile into two trucks and head for a place called Oyster Bay or another called Huntington, each of which had a small colored community with a couple of bars—lots of girls and unlimited music to boogie by. Military police accompanied us on such outings to make sure we didn't fuck up and do something wrong. One of their responsibilities was to cover the whole town—both sides of the tracks, so to speak—making certain that wherever we may have wandered, they were there to keep the peace. On one particular night, while patrolling the town of Oyster Bay, one of our MP's said to another, "Hey, let's get a beer and a sandwich." The MP behind the wheel nodded in agreement, and they maneuvered their truck into the parking lot of a roadhouse restaurant located in the white section of town. The place was jammed as they walked in, and of course they noticed there were no blacks anywhere in sight, but they walked up to the bar and asked a lady bartender if it was possible for them to have a couple of sandwiches and two beers to take out. The MP's were certainly not looking for trouble, having made it clear that they intended to take their purchases outside to eat. The lady bartender gave them a level look and said, "We don't serve niggers in here." Neither MP registered an outward reaction—their smiles weren't even dimmed—but internally they sensed a holocaust in the making, and in an attempt to abort it one of them said, broadening his smile, "Well, Miss, all we want are two sandwiches and a beer and we're going to take them out, we're going to eat in the truck." She repeated with pronounced emphasis, "We don't serve niggers in here." The MP's said, "Well, may we speak with the manager." She went and came back with the manager, who was behind the bar at the other end. Our MP's said, "Good evening, sir, we just asked for a beer and a sandwich and the lady said that she's not going to serve us." The manager said, "That's right—we don't serve niggers here." Our MP's said, "Okay, thank you," and left followed by a trail of derogatory remarks, catcalls, and laughter from the patrons of that roadhouse restaurant. The two MP's got into their truck and drove over to where the rest of us were, dancing and romancing, and they called us outside for a meeting. None of us knew what was going on, but we sensed it was important and hustled out-side. After the MP's told us what happened, they asked us what we as a group thought we should do about it. One of our guys said, "Well, I think we should all go over there and order fifty sandwiches and fifty beers." That sugges-tion met with unanimous agreement. We piled into our two trucks, drove across town to the roadhouse restaurant, and backed the trucks up to the entrance. Every one of our guys, numbering about sixty in all, walked up to the bar with our two MP's at the head of the group. The manager and the bartender lady came up and said, "What do you want?" The MP's said, "All of us would like to have sandwiches and beers." The manager said, "I thought I told you we don't serve niggers in here." And that was all he got out, because one of the MP's shot his right fist smash into his nose. With that all hell broke loose. The bartender lady screamed and started to run to the back of the room. She climbed up to the window to jump out and somebody caught her right in the rear with an army boot —and out the window she went. We tore that place to ab-solute shreds—do you hear me? I mean to shreds! We broke damn near every bottle in the place, the white people were flying out of there—out through windows, through doors, wherever there was the slightest chance of escape they dashed for it. We only stayed in there about three minutes, but we went through that place and de-stroyed it. Completely destroyed it. Then we got back into our trucks, returned to our base, and went to sleep.

The next morning there was a wake-up bugle call and the captain was out on the parade ground madder than a hatter. He said, "Everybody out—everybody." We all got up and out on the parade ground—all 150 of us, the guys who were in the brawl and the guys who weren't. The captain said, "There was a disturbance at Oyster Bay last night and there are a lot of people in the hospital, and there's been extensive damage done to the place. It is my understanding that at least half of you were there. Now in order not to punish people who weren't involved, I would like it if all those who were in Oyster Bay last night would take one step forward out of formation." At which point 150 guys took one step forward *in* formation. The captain fumed. "It's going to be like that, eh? All right," he said, "for that reason everyone is restricted to base. There will be no leaves whatsoever for six months." One of our guys was a lawyer, and he said, "That's not legal. You can't do that." The captain said, "I know that I can only put you on for one month, but I'm going to put you on for one month and take you off, and put you on and take you off, and put you on and take you off, and you won't get off this base for six months, until somebody tells me what went on last night. And we're going to have Army investigators coming from Staten Island to get to the bottom of this, and those of you who are involved are going to be court-martialed." Nobody talked. The investigators came from wherever, and nobody talked. They never got to the bottom of it. They never knew who started it. They never knew anything about it—nobody talked. We were put on restrictions, but they remained in force only three months. And on the first weekend following the lifting of the restrictions, one of our guys said, "You know, we never did get our sandwiches and beer," and another guy said, "We'd better go and see if they're ready." So sixty guys got into two trucks and went back to Oyster Bay, and the first stop we made was at the roadhouse restaurant. It had been refurbished, and it was packed. We backed our trucks up to the entrance—sixty of us stepped out and walked into the place. The same two MP's walked up to the same manager who was behind the bar. The woman wasn't there. The MP's said, "Good evening, sir. We would like to have sixty sandwiches and sixty beers." The manager said, "It will take a little while because it's busy back there, but we'll see what we can do." We waited twenty-five minutes and we got sixty sandwiches and sixty beers—you listening to me? We didn't press the issue because the place was already crowded. We didn't ask to be seated or anything. We just took our beers and said that it was okay to wrap the sandwiches to go. They put the beer and the sandwiches in a box. Everything was neatly packed and courteously delivered. We thanked the manager for his troubles, we paid him, and we left. Interesting story, huh?

I HAD JOINED the Army hoping to be sent to a warmer climate, but it never happened. I spent my entire service on Long Island, although I visited New York often on weekend passes, spending most of my time dancing at the Savoy Ballroom. The best dancer I've ever known in my life was James Culmer, my roommate in the Army. I would make sure to be in his company when we visited the Savoy, because that way I was in line for all of his rejects, and there were plenty of those. He was a very handsome, smooth guy who conked his hair and danced the lindy hop as if he'd invented it. On the way into the city, on the Long Island Railroad, this tall, graceful, virile roommate of mine would give me lessons in how to make out with the girls, and when we reached the Savoy, I would follow his instructions to the letter and from time to time would hit the jackpot. The only place I would see him in the city would be the Savoy, because he would always get locked into some young lady and then he'd be gone until it was time to get back to the base. I was very fond of him, but strangely enough, the way I got out of the Army killed my ties with most of the guys I knew then. I got out before most of them, and by the time the war was over and they were being mustered out I had been out of the service for a full two years and had gone on to other things. I was in the Army for one year and eleven days and was out before I was eighteen.

Now, let me tell you how I got out. After nine or ten months in the Army, I realized it wasn't for me, and that physiotherapy was not a profession I was comfortable with. I didn't like the way the civilian help and the military help abused the patients in the hospital. Most of the civilian help was white, and all of the military help was black, but black or white, it seemed as if they were unaware of the meaning of mental illness. They did awful things to the patients—certainly not all of them, but enough so that it hurt just the same. After about nine months there, I decided I wasn't going to stay. But I wasn't about to say, "I'm too young to be in the Army and I want out." I preferred getting out of the Army in the most dramatic way I could think up. The question was how? I had heard a great deal of talk about guys who buck their way out on a Section 8, which means being discharged at the convenience of the government. The only way you could get that kind of Section 8 was by being declared crazy, and in order for you to be declared crazy, you had to *do* something "crazy." Then you had to go before a review board of psychiatrists and they had to say that you were not able to function well within the confines of the military establishment.

I had heard of three or four guys who had made it out this way, and on investigation, it turned out to be the *only* way. Remember, the war was on. I also heard about dozens and dozens of other guys who had tried it, and when it didn't work for them they wound up being court-martialed and going to jail. I said to myself, "Well, I have to do it, and I have to do it right." So I devised an approach, and once it was settled in my mind that it was the correct approach, I rehearsed it thoroughly in my head before setting it in motion.

I woke up on the day I had decided on for this drama, got dressed, and walked around the hospital grounds, knowing it would be my last trek over some very familiar terrain. I didn't say goodby to anyone—I just kind of talked to people I liked because I knew that this was it. At about eleven o'clock, which I had chosen as kick-off time, I walked over to the administration building where the civilian head of the hospital had his office. There was a secretary in the reception area who looked up and said, "What can I do for you?" I said, "I've come to see the head of the hospital." She said, "What is your name?" I said, "My name is Private Sidney Poitier." Then she went into the main office, closed the door, stayed about half a minute, came out again, and said, "All right, you may go in." I got up from my seat, walked through the door, closed it, turned around—and there he was. A middle-aged, sturdy-looking man, sitting behind a great big desk. Behind him was an enormous bay window looking out over the lawns of the hospital grounds. I looked at him. He looked at me. He said, "Yes, what can I do for you?" In front of the desk were two wooden chairs—two huge, bulky, heavy, wooden chairs that looked as if they had been hewn out of redwood. I picked up one of those chairs and threw it at the man. He ducked just in time, as I had hoped he would. The chair went right through the bay window, shattering it to pieces and falling two stories to the ground, to be followed by a shower of broken glass. The man was now under his desk. I turned, walked out of the office, and closed the door. I walked past the secretary and down the steps. I walked back over to the Recreation Center. Casually I picked up a pool cue and I began to play pool—by myself. About fifteen minutes into my pool game, three MP's came in with drawn guns and said, "Ah-hh, Poitier, you fucked up now, boy—your ass is in a sling. You've got to come with us." They took me to the captain, who said, "What did you do?" I said, "I threw a chair at the man." He said, "Wha-aat!" I said, "Yes, I did." He said, *"What?* Why?" I said, "I don't know." He said, "You don't know!" He said, "You walked in there

69

and tried to hurt this man—threw a chair—broke the window—what are you trying to do?" I said, "I don't know." He said, "Do you know I've got to send you to Mason General Hospital for observation? That's the dumbest thing I've ever heard. You go and pack your stuff because you're going to Mason General Hospital. You have to be locked away." I packed my stuff. They put me in a jeep with two MP's and they took me for an hour-and-fifteen-minute ride to a place called the Mason General Hospital in Amityville, Long Island, where they checked me into a psychiatric ward with about fifty other guys. I noticed that all these other guys had their shoelaces, had their belts, they were eating with knives and forks—plastic ones, maybe, but they were still knives and forks. I knew from tales I'd heard, therefore, that I was not in the right place. Because if you're considered really dangerous, they don't let you have your shoelaces, they don't let you eat with knives and forks, and belts—certainly not. So I said to myself: Oh, Lord, I'm really in trouble because I ain't where I'm supposed to be. Then I thought: I'd better do something to get me to where I *am* supposed to be.

I was sitting in this ward on a regular wooden chair leaning back against the wall with my feet up on the bottom rung of the chair when someone announced that the dinner cart had arrived. Into the ward came an enormous steam cart pushed by two or three guys. This steam table had everything on it—hot, hot, hot water on the bottom of it, and sitting on top were trays—enormous trays, with all kinds of food: meat, potatoes, carrots, and whatever else was on the menu that day. There was another section that had ice, and on the ice great big pans of desserts and fruits. This thing was so huge it looked like a big automobile. These guys were pushing it around the room, and dishing out food on plastic trays and passing them on to the patients. This monstrous steam table on wheels could feed fifty men in twenty minutes. As they moved around the room coming closer to me, my heart began to pound, and when finally we were lined up opposite each other, I planted both my feet against the side of the steam table and I pushed. Over went the steam table in the middle of the ward with baked beans and chicken and hot water and string beans and Jell-o and ice cream and pudding *everywhere*.

Shock electrified the room for a moment. The guys

kept staring in disbelief at the mess on the floor, then over to me, saying to each other, "What the fuck is going on?" "Who is that?" Well, I didn't move from my chair. I tried to keep a kind of calm, collected exterior by just sitting and looking around very quietly at everybody. In no time, the guards arrived. They said, "Stand up." And I stood up. They said, "Turn around." I turned around. "Put your hands behind you." I put my hands behind me. And they tied my hands behind me. And they took me upstairs to the eleventh floor, and there was the ward I was looking for. I thought: Ah, now I'm in it—everything is cool now. On the eleventh floor they put me in a room that had no bed in it, only a mattress on the floor. They took my belt, my shoelaces, *and* my shoes. They gave me some slippers and a great big gownlike robe to put on. When they fed me it was on a simple kind of tray with no utensils. I had to eat with my hands. They gave me water in a paper cup. I said to myself: Everything's cooking now.

The next day the head psychiatrist for that ward came by. He said, "How are you doing?" I said, "Fine." He said, "Wow, that was some display you were involved in yesterday." I said, "Yeah, it wasn't too bad, was it?" He said, "No, it was quite spectacular—quite spectacular." He said, "You want to talk about it?" I said, "No." He said, "Well, it seems to me that if you do a thing like that, you would want to talk about it somewhat." I said, "No, I don't want to talk about it." He said, "Well, I tell you what we're going to have to do—and I hope you don't mind. We're going to have to give you some shock treatments. How do you feel about that?" I said, "Okay." Expecting that he wouldn't expect that response, I looked at him to try and determine if I'd made a score or not. But he was as noncommittal as I was. So he said, "Okay. We'll arrange for you to start having your shock treatments this afternoon." And I said, "Fine." We played cat and mouse with each other for a while and then he got on to other questions. He started asking about where I came from and whether I was an inductee or a volunteer, and went on probing deeper and deeper into my background, obviously searching for motives. Judging from the many questions he asked and the way he was behaving, I began to sense that he was very serious about those shock treatments. Now, listen, I know what shock treatments are and I ain't about to let them put no fucking wires to my head. So I said, "Listen, how often are those shock treatments going to be required?" He said, "Oh, I don't know, sometimes you'll get three a week or—depending on the severity of your situation we may give you more." He paused to let that sink in and held my gaze looking for a crack. I didn't oblige and he continued. "Or less. And it could go on for a month, or two, or three." Again this clever shrink paused. My mind raced quickly around this dilemma, seeking an appropriate response to avoid the big fucking trap the doc was setting for me—and *Bingo!* I came up with a stunner. "I'll tell you what I want to do," I said finally, "I want to tell you why I did what I did." One of his eyebrows flexed—clearly he wasn't expecting that. "Because," I continued, "I don't want any shock treatments." He said, "You don't?" I said, "No." He said, "Well, I can't promise you that you won't get them, but if you want to talk about what you did . . ." I said, "Yeah, I want to talk about it." He said, "Well, first question, why did you do what you did, why did you turn over the food cart?" I said, "Well, it was calculated." He said, "Was it?" I said, "Yeah." He said, "To what end?" I said, "To get out of the Army." He said, "You kicked it over to get out of the Army?" I said, "Yes, I did. Not only did I do that to get out of the Army, but I also threw the chair at the head of the hospital. That too was calculated to get me in here. But when they brought me here, they put me on that other ward which is not really a dangerous, violent ward. And my understanding is, if you are in here you ought to buck for the dangerous, violent ward, because being in that ward is an admission on the part of the hospital and the Army that you are dangerous enough or incompatible enough or crazy enough to require being taken care of in this extreme manner—and such an admission means that half the battle is won. So my intent was to get here on this ward." He said, "So you did it all because you're bucking out of the Army?" I said, "That is absolutely correct." He said, "Then why are you telling me this at this time, knowing that it will surely bring about a court-martial for you? And if in fact you are telling the truth, and it's proven that this is your motivation, you could go to jail for twenty years." I said, "Yeah, I know that." He said, "Are you still willing to take the chance?" I said, "Yes, I am." He said, "Okay, what else?"

And I ran the whole thing down for him. I told him

how I conceived of the idea, how I got bored with the Army after nine months, what was going on at the hospital that I didn't like and couldn't cope with. How incompatible I was to that kind of discipline. I gave him my background as a kid. I gave him everything. He said, "Well, I'll tell you what. You have been honest with me so I'll be honest with you. If you would like it, I would like you to come and see me for fifty minutes a day—every day, at least five days a week—for a few weeks, maybe a month. At the end of that time we'll be able to decide whether you are going to have a discharge, or whether you are going to jail for twenty years." I said, "That's a deal." He said, "Okay—under those circumstances you won't have to take any shock treatments. But you have to promise me no more violent displays, because you've already gotten what you want. You are on the violent ward and you can't go any farther." I said, "Okay, that's a deal." He said, "Suppose I put you on another ward where you'll be less restricted —you're going to have to be cool." I said, "I'll be cool." So they put me on a less restricted ward, and every day I went to see him for about fifty minutes. We talked— just talked and talked. We talked about how I felt, where I was from, what life was like where I came from. He was psychoanalyzing me. That went on for about five weeks, and then one day he said to me, "You won't have to come anymore. This is your last visit."

Apparently, in the discussions we'd been having, I kept repeating that I was as *good* as anybody. That no man was better than I was—no man. No man in the world. I was not ever going to conceive of myself being less than any other man. He said to me on that last day, "Of all the things we discussed, there is one thing that I want to talk to you about. There are differences in men. There are men who are smarter than you. Stronger than you, tougher than you, smarter than you." Then he said, "They are not better than you, tougher than you, smarter than you because they are white or black. Because that's no way to judge men. But there are men in the world with different strengths from yours. There always will be. For every man that you find better than you in areas one, two, and ten, you will find men that are better than *him* in areas one, two, and ten. Don't judge people on color, because there are as many black men better than you as there are white

73

men better than you. There are as many black men better than white men, so don't judge people on color." He said, "You and I have been here now for five weeks. What do you think of me?" I said, "I like you." He said, "Why do you like me?" I said, "Because I think you're fair." He said, "Okay—" And we left it at that.

A lot of lessons I learned from him. The principal one was on this question of some men being better than other men. He helped me to understand that because I was surrounded by a society that seemed to be perpetually hostile to blacks, I assumed a position, a pose, designed to say: I am *not* going to let you dismiss me, hostile world. He led me inside myself, where I discovered that my psychological guard was constantly up, sometimes unnecessarily. And I'll be grateful to him forever for telling me that there are men I won't be as good as in certain areas, and that it won't be because of their color; it's just the way life is. There are guys who'll be able to run faster than you, guys who'll be able to calculate faster than you, guys who'll be able to lift heavier weights than you. There are guys who'll be able to fly planes better than you . . . I don't know where that doctor is today, I don't know if he's still alive or not, and I never heard from him or saw him again. I don't remember his name. I only remember he was an Army psychiatrist. A white man.

A few days after that I was told I would be going to Camp Upton to wait for the decision on my case. I returned to my company at the Veterans Hospital in Northport, collected my belongings, and was sent on to Camp Upton. The decision stated that I would not be court-martialed, but would be sent to Fort Dix, New Jersey, from where, after three weeks of processing, I would be mustered out of the United States Army.

Now with it all decades behind me, and sober, quiet moments permitting me to reflect, a large puzzling question arises. Why? Why, one will surely wonder, did I take such chances considering the fact that all I had to do was say, "Look, I'm not old enough to be here, fellas," and they would have sent me home. Well, I did not want to do it that way. That was a cop-out, an admission a child would make, and I wasn't a child—I didn't think of myself as a child. I'd rather do it the manly way. But obviously the manly way was full of shit too. Then why did I have to do it the so-called

74

macho way? For years to come I was to ponder that and other related questions. For instance, was I in fact an emotional defective, even though the Army released me on other grounds? My subjective appraisal told me I wasn't crazy. But who is to know? Who is to say that I wasn't, in fact, living through some temporary insanity through the whole period of my early exposure to America? From the moment I got off that fucking boat, I began to experience this new, different, strange, complex, crazy society. And once I became attuned to the strangeness of the racial situation in Miami, that did weird things to my head. Who knows what it did to me emotionally? I must have been terribly disoriented, I mean to throw a chair at that man—that has to suggest a certain kind of violence in me. Granting that I didn't intend to hurt him, still it took a lot of something to pick up a chair and throw it through that window. And if that "something" is violence, then there has to have been a lot of it in me. To be perfectly honest, I feel that there has always been in me this potential for violence. Because there has to be on the other side—this is my own reading—there has to be on the other side of my enormous effort at being likable and friendly and fair and honest and dependable, there has to be on the bottom of that an awful fucking violent fear that if somebody makes me angry and I let go completely I might not be able to control it. Crucial personality questions of this nature were to remain unanswered for years to come, except by the rationalizing I felt it necessary to do in order to feel comfortable about myself. After all, *I* had to like me too, wouldn't you agree?

The real importance of those questions would not be fully understood for years to come, even after certain clues became evident in my personality; for instance, in my work as an actor I would discover that it's easier for me to go on to the set prepared. Even now I don't like a director to say to me, "Jesus Christ, you don't know your work. You aren't prepared. You're not quite right in that scene." That does something to me, and rather than ever put myself in that position, I will be overprepared. But on the other hand, what is it that I don't want to happen? What is it that happens if I'm *not* prepared and he *does* say something to me? I believe what I don't want to happen (shades of my mother) is to lose control. Because if I lose control, I go absolutely crazy. I get *so* angry sometimes—and I remember these times —that I can't speak, and then I could tear a house apart. Now on the other side of that coin, I have on innumerable occasions in my life bent over backward to give the other guy the benefit of the doubt. Because I don't want to justify myself in letting out whatever is festering down there. So I make all kinds of adjustments and compromises—within reason. I'm saying, I suppose, that there is a part of me I haven't been in touch with yet, and from all indications I have every reason to fear an introduction.

On December 11, 1944, after my year and eleven days in the service, I became a civilian again, returning to the streets of New York two months before my eighteenth birthday. I received the customary mustering-out pay, and I had taken out an allotment for my mother that was never sent to her. So I was back in New York City with quite a few hundred dollars in my kick. I bought some clothes, marking the first time in my life I was able to buy a suit. In fact, I bought *two* suits. I rented a room again in somebody's apartment and went back to dishwashing.

I had planned to go home to Nassau, but the money wasn't enough. By now my mother was sure I was dead. Because they never sent her the allotment, she didn't know where I was, and she hadn't known where I was most of the preceding year. When I found out they were returning the allotment to me, it meant that they had never let my family know about my being in the Army, and that created an anxiety in me to rush home with my few hundred dollars. But on second thought, I discovered I'd be needing every penny of that money for my immediate survival. And an unwritten rule in Caribbean life says that if you ever go to America, don't write home unless you put something in the envelope. After renting a room, buying warm winter clothing, and generally reestablishing myself in the city again, I didn't have any money to send home, so I didn't write. I was totally out of touch. Later, my mother was to tell me how she prayed that God would give her some sign as to whether I was alive or dead during that period.

Well, I *was* alive, and I had determined that things were going to be different now between New York and me. Being less vulnerable to the winter and considerably more streetwise, I brought to the relationship hints of the tough, self-reliant maturity I so strongly admired in men who seemed to be in control of their lives. This time around, I vowed, New York City would not be fucking with a little boy. It was going to be dealing with Mister Sidney Poitier, man to man.

6 Learning to Act

As I SAY, after being separated out from the Army, I returned to New York City in the winter of 1944-45, fully confident that this time I would be able to manage, armed as I was with an additional year of experience, several hundred dollars, and a frighteningly fresh memory of what the city and the winter had done to a bewildered sixteen-year-old boy. This time they would be faced off against an eighteen-year-old man who knew the score—or so he thought. Alas, it would only be a matter of time before they had me begging for mercy again. My confidence eroded, my new-found manhood turned out to be not nearly so resilient as I had imagined, and my enemies seemed to have awesome powers in reserve just for the purpose of teaching a lesson to cocky little know-it-all bastards like me. They worked me over with a swiftness I'm ashamed to acknowledge, leaving me broke and deflated at the hand-to-mouth existence level, heavily dependent on my accumulated skills as a dishwasher. From my seven-dollar-a-week room on 118th Street I would go to wherever my job happened to be, work my customary eight hours, then back to Harlem, where most of my free time was spent wandering around in the hope of finding someone willing to become my steady girl. I daydreamed a lot about that kind of relationship, hungry for a boy-girl relationship that fitted my fantasies. Dorothy, the girl I'd left behind in Nassau, had by this time married someone else, and of all the girls I met during my Army sojourn, none of them expressed much interest in me beyond a dance, a shared bottle of beer, or the occasional roll in the hay.

One evening, walking along 116th Street, I notice a girl standing alone on the steps of an apartment building, and as I approach, we make and hold eye contact for a few seconds. I read volumes of potential into those few seconds, and as I stroll past her I detect a faint but unmistakable smile, and then she adds a slight movement of her head that seems to be halfway between a friendly nod and an invitation. My heart speeds up, my walk slows down, and I shoot her a smile broader than her own and cap it off with a movement of my head, hoping to leave absolutely no doubt that I'm interested. Oh, God, was I interested! She says, "Hi." I say "Hi" and move toward her. We exchange names and bits of information—I learn, for instance, that she lives in that building on the fifth floor with her father, mother, a sister, and a brother, and that she's in her last year of high school and looking forward to entering the job market. Then I become tongue-tied and can't sustain even a casual conversation without embarrassingly long pauses during which I'm frantically trying to think of something to say. Small talk, cute sayings, funny stories, where the hell are they now that I need them? Afraid that I'm going to scuttle all of this potential on one tongue-tied evening, I lie and say I have an appointment to meet someone and have to go, but would it be possible for me to see her again? She says, "Yes," she'll be at the same place the next evening at about the same time. All of which I take to mean that my tongue-tied stupidity hasn't seriously damaged my chances.

Furious with myself as I walked briskly along 116th Street to keep my bogus appointment I began to think of all the wonderfully witty and impressive things I should have said, instead of standing there like a dummy. What would any girl in the world want with a dodo like you? You can't even talk to them, I thought as I kicked myself all the way home. The next evening I turned up with dozens of well-rehearsed mental notes around which I could build a conversation, if and when it looked as if I was about to fall into one of those long, deep pauses that had almost finished me off the evening before. Her smile was very big this time and I sensed that she'd been looking forward to our meeting again. She was a plump girl, her skin was dark brown, her eyes were misty and soft, and her face was round and pretty with lips I yearned to make contact with. From appearances, this very sweet eighteen-year-old girl fit snugly in the fantasy images I had of what a girlfriend of mine had to be, but our second meeting wasn't much better than the first. Neither was our third or fourth. She obviously liked me in spite of myself, because on our fifth date I took her to a movie and bought her an ice cream cone and she took me home to meet her folks, all of whom drifted off after the introduction into other rooms in the apartment, leaving the two of us to sit and make small talk. I wasn't accustomed to that kind of one-to-one with a girl, and with there being no television at that time to salvage the evening we would just sit there teetering painfully on the brink of those long, deep, embarrassing pauses that left us both feeling insecure and uncomfortable. The relationship fell apart, for obvious reasons.

Through what seemed like an endless winter, psychologically at my lowest point, I moved from 118th Street to 146th Street into the home of a Spanish family from either Puerto Rico or Mexico. They rented me a very nice room for six dollars a week which included fairly liberal kitchen privileges. But the winter and the city had me on the ropes again, off balance and dazed, to the point where I said to myself: I've got to get out of this place and go back home. But I can't go back home. First of all, I can't write to my folks—they don't have the money. In fact, they don't even know where I am— whether I'm alive or dead. Second, it would take at least a hundred dollars to take a bus back to Florida and a boat to Nassau. I have neither the hundred dollars nor any practical way of getting a hundred dollars. Yet I make up my mind to go, because the winter is just too fierce for me. I concede. Hell, I can manage in Nassau— I can go fishing, I can work in the warehouse, something like that. I would rather do something like that than struggle on through a winter that's killing me.

Then one cold evening an idea strikes with lightning force, bringing me to my feet. Standing there in my six-dollar room I look at all sides of this potentially brilliant solution, rerunning it over and over in my mind, weighing its merits against its flaws and coming out each time convinced that it could indeed be a brilliant solution. Convinced by the soundness of the idea, I immediately put it to the test by writing a letter to the President of the United States: "Dear President Roosevelt, my name is Sidney Poitier and I am here in the United States in New York City. I am from the Bahamas. I would like to go back to the Bahamas but I don't have the money. I would like to borrow from you $100. I will send it back to you when I get to the Bahamas. I miss my mother and father and I miss my brothers and sisters and I miss my home in the Caribbean. I cannot seem to get myself organized properly here in America, especially in the cold weather, and I am therefore asking you as an American citizen if you will loan me $100 to get back home. I will send it back to you and I would certainly appreciate it very much. Your fellow American, Sidney Poitier." I sent that letter off and never heard from the cat. Never heard from the cat. And I'm very glad I didn't, because if I had received a hundred-dollar check in a letter, I would have been long gone. I would have spent the next thirty years on a rock with a line in the water, trying to catch me a fish or two. Mantan Moreland would likely have made *Blackboard Jungle*. Eddie "Rochester" Anderson would probably have played in *Guess Who's Coming to Dinner*.

In all sincerity, ignorance, and possibly insanity, my letter was an honest appeal, but there was no response at all from the White House—not a word. I was very displeased about that for a while too. Boy, I would get up every morning and rush down to the mailbox looking for that hundred-dollar check. I even had visions of him sending an Army truck to take me to the train station or the bus station. Finally I gave up—listen, how long can you wait for a hundred dollars? By the time spring arrived, I said, "Well, I'm obviously not going to hear from old President Roosevelt, so I'm back to washing dishes," and that's when I found my way into the American Negro Theatre.

How I stumbled into the theater is something that's been written about a lot, but now I'm going to tell you exactly what it was like. I used to read the *Amsterdam News,* a black paper in New York that carried, among other things, one hell of a good want-ad section from which I could almost always obtain a dishwashing job. One day while browsing through the listings for chauffeurs, maids, dishwashers, porters, janitors, etc., my attention was drawn to the opposite page, the theatrical page, which carried a gossip column, advertisements for movies, night clubs, cocktail lounges, and an article under the heading "Actors Wanted by Little Theatre Group." I said to myself: Hey, here they say actors wanted and on the other page they say dishwashers wanted, janitors wanted, and porters wanted. Well, I've done all those other things, but I've never done acting. Maybe I should go in there and see what that's all about and . . . like I'm carrying on a conversation with myself. And then I said: Yes, I'll drop in there, see how much they're paying, check out the working conditions. They certainly can't be any worse than what I'm into now. So I go down to a place on 135th Street near Lenox Avenue. It was the address of a library that housed the Shomberg Collection on the first floor and the American Negro Theatre downstairs in its basement. I knock on the door of the theater and am admitted by a man who introduces himself as Frederick O'Neal. He says, "Come on in," and I say, "I've come to look after this job that was advertised in the paper." He says, "Are you an actor?" I say, "Yes." He says, "Well, we didn't advertise, exactly. You see, that was an article about us doing a play and we were seeing certain actors. But you *are* an actor?" I say, "Yes, sir." He says, "Okay, where have you acted?" I say, "Oh, a lot of places." He says, "Where?" And I say, "Oh, a lot of places down in Florida and Nassau." He says, "You did?" I say, "Oh, yeah." He says, "Okay, why don't you take this script and go up on the stage and read the part of 'John' on page twenty-seven, and I'll read the other part, but I'll stay down here in the orchestra." I say, "Okay," and go up on the stage.

It is the first time I have ever been on a stage—I didn't even know what a stage looked like—but I'm up there now and I open this "script" but I don't know what it is. It's a book, I think, with a soft cover but it's called a "script." I turn to page twenty-seven and find an awful lot of writing and I see names right above each little patch of writing, so I figure that's what he wants me to read because he told me to read the part of "John." Everywhere I see "John" I'll read everything under that, so I turn to him and he says, "Any time you're ready." The first person to speak on page twenty-seven is John, so I read his line, and O'Neal reads back his responding line. I read back—but no responding line comes from Frederick O'Neal. I see him sitting in the orchestra staring at me with the most peculiar look. He says, "Boy, get off that stage." I'm always ready to do my number, so I say, "What do you mean?" He says, "Just come on down off that stage and stop wasting my time." I say, "I don't understand." He says, "You're no actor." I say, "Yes, I am." He says, "No, you're not. You don't even know how to read." I say, "I can too read." He says, "You cannot read. Get out of here." He meets me halfway as I'm getting off the stage and he grabs hold of me and leads me to the door and as he pushes me out, he says, "Just go on and get out of here and get yourself a job as a dishwasher or something." How the hell does he know I'm a dishwasher? What the hell is this? Can he read me—is there a sign on me somewhere?

I walk off down the street—O'Neal of course goes back inside the theater, quite justifiably peeved at being messed about like that. I walk off down 135th Street saying to myself: Why would he say that to me? He also said to me, "You can hardly talk. You've got an accent, and that accent—you can't be an actor with an accent like that. And you can hardly read. You can't be an actor and not be able to read." I begin to contemplate what he'd said to me. Now I knew I couldn't read too well, I knew that. And I knew I had an accent— a bad, crippling accent—I knew that because on more than one occasion people would find it funny and would laugh at it. I knew those things, but what I hadn't come to grips with until then was that if I didn't do something about myself, I would be trapped forever as a dishwasher. If he can read that in me through my inexpertness in reading and speech and my general deportment, if he can read that much lack of potential in me, then my life is not going to be worth shit. I'm going to be a dishwasher when I'm forty—and when I'm fifty— and when I'm sixty. Here I am, I'm eighteen years of age, and if I live to be eighty, for the next sixty-two years I'm going to be a dishwasher. I'm not going to be able to impress people. I'm not going to be able to get a hearing from people. No, I'm not going to be able to command attention from anyone unless I'm able to create some idea or present some point of view or successfully put forth some real image of some kind—positive or negative. I am going to be of no consequence for the next sixty-two years. People will walk by me and I won't register. I will always feel inadequate. I will always be a dishwashing nobody, to be dismissed out of hand. Always overlooked. Never considered. That will be my destiny if I do not, by myself, take my life into my own hands and work it into something worthwhile.

But how do you do that? I wonder to myself. And I know right then as I'm walking toward 7th Avenue and 135th Street that I have to find a way to prove that man wrong. To prove—just to him, and by reflection to myself—that I can be more than a dishwasher.

But now the question arises, what more than a dishwasher? What should I start with? Well, the first thing to start with is, I *will* become an actor, because it's around that issue that the challenge originated. First and foremost I have got to prove to him that I can become an actor. Then I'll walk away from it and go on to other things, because once I can prove to him and to myself that I can be more than a dishwasher, the sky's the limit and I can be anything I want to be. But until I get over that first hurdle, he'll be correct in his estimation of me. I saw clearly that this was a crossroad and that I had to make a dramatic choice. And I did. I decided that I was going to be an actor.

Look who's deciding who's going to be an actor—a kid who didn't even know there was such a thing as a book of plays, a kid who had never been in a theater in his life except the once he walked onto a stage and got thrown off. I knew nothing about theater, nothing about acting, knew no actors or actresses except those I had seen in movies and that was different: first of all they were white; second, they were in California; and third, they were mostly working with cows and there were no cows in New York that I knew about. Still, I had to be an actor. But I couldn't start out being an actor until I overcame the handicaps that had caused me to be thrown out of the theater I had just left. He had itemized them for me—he said I could barely read and that I had this horrible accent. Well, I had to rid myself of the accent and I had to learn to read well. How do you rid yourself of an accent? I asked myself. I decided the best way was to listen to the way Americans speak, and to copy it. And what's the best way to listen to Americans speaking? Because I just can't go following people around. A radio, I thought to myself. The best thing for me to do is get me a radio. That very same day I went back to the want-ad section of the

Amsterdam News and picked out a dishwashing job. Out of the first week's salary, I bought a thirteen-dollar radio. For the next six months, except when I was working or asleep, I listened to that radio morning, noon, and night. Everything I heard, I would repeat, it didn't matter what it was. If the radio said, "This is WOR bringing you the news," then I would say, "This is WOR bringing you the news." WOR, WEAF, WQXR, Lux Radio Theatre of the Air, commercials, soap operas, panel discussions—everything I heard from whoever was speaking, I would repeat. Six months of that and I noticed that my *a*'s were lightening; that my rhythm was changing considerably and I was no longer singsong in my speech pattern as Bahamians generally were. I noticed too that I was developing the pronunciation rhythms most New Yorkers had. Certainly there were still traces of the old accent remaining, but all in all there were some definite signs of improvement.

During the same six months I was working with the radio, I spent as much time as possible reading. One of the restaurants I worked in during that period was in Astoria, Long Island—a big place requiring three dishwashers with machine experience. The work was hard and heavy, but we would almost always have most of the dishes cleared away by 11:00 or 11:15 p.m., and the only dishes after that were a straggly few from the waiters having their own meal after the restaurant was closed. While waiting for the waiters to finish their supper, it was my custom to sit out near the kitchen door and read the *Journal-American*, a fairly conservative newspaper of those days. I didn't have a political view, however, and didn't care if it was conservative, liberal, or what—it just happened to be a big, fat paper. I bought it and read it because it helped me improve my reading. At the waiters' table there was an old Jewish man who used to watch me trying to read that paper. I asked him one night, what does this word mean, and he told me. I thanked him and went back to my paper. He went on watching me for a few seconds and then said, "Do you run across a lot of words that you don't understand?" I said, "A lot—because I'm just beginning to learn to read well," and he said, "Why don't you—I'll sit with you here and I'll work with you for a while." So at about 11:00 p.m. every night when he sat down for his evening meal, I would come out of the kitchen and sit down next to him and read articles from the front page of the *Journal-American*. When I ran into a word I didn't know (and I didn't know half of the article, because anything past a couple of syllables and I was in trouble) he explained the meaning of the word and gave me the pronunciation and then sent me back to the head of the sentence so I could grasp the word in context. In half an hour he would teach me the meaning and pronunciation of twenty-five or thirty words. Then I would take the paper away with me, armed now with the meaning of those words, and reread and reread the article so that the meaning of those words would get locked into my memory. Every evening we did that. He paid no attention to the content of the articles, just dealt with the words, and it was beautiful the way he did it. When I would place the stress on the wrong syllable, he would explain the difference to me, and he didn't have an accent—sometimes I would overemphasize a word and he would say, "You should go softer," or "You should hit this part." From this gentle man I learned about silent letters, abbreviations, words that are pronounced the same but spelled differently, and tricky singulars and plurals like "phenomenon" and "phenomena." This soft-spoken, natural teacher, with thick bifocals, bushy eyebrows, and silver-white hair, sat with me night after night in the twilight of his years and gave me a little piece of himself. I stayed there at that job for about five or six weeks and I learned a pattern from him, then I was off to other things. I have never been able to thank him properly because I never knew then what an enormous contribution he was making to my life. I don't know if he's alive or dead, probably dead by now, but he was wonderful, and a little bit of him is in everything I do.

After my relationship with my teacher, the waiter, I always looked for the meaning of words, and when I ran into words I couldn't pronounce and didn't understand, I would work on them until some sense began to come. I would keep going over and over the sentence they were in, and after a while I would begin to get an idea of what the word meant just by repeating the sentence. That became a habit, as did all the other things he left me with.

Now it's time to go back to the American Negro Theatre—six months later. You ask why would I go back to the American Negro Theatre? I could go anywhere else and try to be an actor. I could find out where there are other theater groups or I could go to a professional agent or something. But I don't even know that there are such things. Besides, I have to go back there to show one man that I can do this. So back I go. But that man isn't there. I'm told he's away for a few days, but that they're soon going to be having auditions for a new class of actors and he'll be one of the men in charge of the auditions. I say, "Terrific, I'd like to audition." They say, "Fine," and tell me when to come.

The American Negro Theatre had by now moved to larger quarters on 127th Street between Lenox and Fifth Avenue, in an Elks' Hall building where they had a larger theater, larger stage, and more classroom space. In other words, the American Negro Theatre was moving up in the world. I arrived at the theater on the afternoon of the auditions to find about seventy-five other people gathered for the same purpose. I sat down in the audience and waited, ready with my material. The clatter in the auditorium came from clusters of auditioners having a last-minute run-through of *their* material. Some like me will be auditioning alone. Some will play scenes with other people. All—unlike me—will be reading from plays. I wonder where the hell they got those plays, because what I've got is a *True Confessions* magazine that I've bought and memorized two paragraphs from, and I'm growing fearful that I may be disqualified for not having a scene from a play for my audition. At that point the lights start down and someone in authority calls the applicants to order and makes a brief welcoming speech in which he explains the aims and aspirations of the American Negro Theatre and officially opens the auditions by calling the first applicant up onto the stage to show his stuff. I think to myself: Hell, it's too late for me to worry about my material now. It's sink or swim with *True Confessions* magazine. I sit there watching intently as other applicants go up on the stage and play out dramatic scenes, comedy scenes, monologues, pantomime . . . and then my turn comes. I hear them say, "Sidney Poitier"—panic! I think: Oh, Lord—here I go now. Do I know how to speak without my accent? I run a few lines in my mind to see if I'm accent-free, and in my mind I say: That's not too bad. Then I go.

The theater holds two hundred or so people. Besides

those taking auditions, there are also friends, parents, and others who've come along to lend encouragement and support. Then there are members of the American Negro Theatre's staff, including the president and the drama coaches. The president's name is Abram Hill and, yes, Frederick O'Neal is there, one of the leaders and founders. A lady named Osceola Archer is the drama teacher and head of the drama department, and also present are those heading the body movement and speech classes. So the faculty is well represented.

The bare stage is high, with good depth and width. They're in the middle of doing a play, but the scenery has been moved aside so the applicants can audition on an empty stage lit by two naked lights. I walk up on the stage from the little steps on the side, and immediately I feel self-conscious standing under those two bright lights that seem to accentuate everything and will no doubt accentuate the fact that I'm carrying a *True Confessions* magazine instead of a play. And I'm further disquieted by the fact that, though I'm under the spotlight where everybody can see me, I can't see anybody out in the auditorium. A voice coming from the direction of the faculty table asks, "Sidney Poitier?" "Yes," I reply. "Mr. Poitier, what are you going to do for us?" I say, "I am going to read something from *True Confessions* magazine." I hear a snicker in the audience and I say to myself: Oh, shit! I must have made a mistake, because why would they be laughing? The teacher says, *"True Confessions* magazine?" I say, "Yes, ma'am." She says, "All right. You can begin whenever you're ready." Out of the breast pocket of my suit I pull my magazine. The best suit I've owned to that point in my life is a brown suit, and needless to say, I'm dressed in my brown suit with my brown tie and my brown socks and my brown shoes and my brown shirt. I am dap! Most of the other kids are not as sartorially stunning as I am because, apparently, they are intelligent enough to know that you don't dress up to come to an audition. So I begin to read this *True Confessions* magazine that I've whipped out of my breast pocket. I turn to a page of some innocuous story about "Frank and Melinda." All of these stories are told from a woman's point of view, and in this one Melinda is telling how she first met Frank, and I'm reading this shit. I'm saying, "I met Frank as I walked down the street going towards so-and-so and there coming towards me is this handsome man and I said to my-self 'just look at—' " Well, I can feel the people in the audience—I can feel their jaws drop. I can feel them thinking: What the fuck is he doing up there? Such thoughts are reverberating everywhere. Mercifully, Osceola Archer, the drama coach, interrupts. "All right, that's enough," she says. I stop. After a few seconds she says, "Mr. Poitier." I say, "Yes, ma'am." She says, "I would like you to do an improvisation for us. Would you do that?" I say, "Yes, ma'am." Now I don't know what the hell an improvisation is. I just hope that they'll ex-plain it to me so that I won't have to expose my ig-norance. She says, "All right, let us presuppose that you are in the jungle . . ." I'm thinking, what the fuck has the jungle got to do with that big word "improvisation." She says, ". . . and you are in the Army and you are in the middle of combat." I'm hearing what she's say-ing, but I'm trying to put it together to see how the word "improvisation" fits, because I still don't know what the word means. Well, finally, it dawns on me what it means. It means that I'm supposed to act out the part of a guy in the Army who's caught in the jungle behind enemy lines and there's no way to escape and the enemy is shooting at me from everywhere and I have to make my last-ditch stand—how do I do it? I say, "All right." She says, "Take a few minutes and think it over and let us know when you're ready." So I turn my back to the audi-ence, because I've seen other people do that to prepare themselves, but I'm not preparing anything. I'm think-ing: Oh, shit, now, what am I going to do here? This place ain't no jungle. I don't see no jungle, but now I've got to create all that stuff in my imagination. Well, I think, I'm going to give it a shot because I've seen some movies like this. I turn back around and I say, "I'm ready." She says, "All right, begin." I hold my arms out in the shape of a machine gun and I start looking around —I spin around suddenly as if I'm being surrounded by enemies and I'm saying like James Cagney—that's the only thing that comes into my mind—I'm saying, "Oh, you dirty rats, you can come and get me. I'll kill you." And I go brrr—rrrr—rrrr, bang, bang, bang. I'm carrying on like this and suddenly I get shot in the belly by one of the enemy's bullets and start sinking slowly and agoniz-ingly to the floor—when I suddenly realize that this is a dirty floor and I'm wearing my best suit! My very best suit in all my life! What's going to happen if I fall down on this floor and dirty up my suit! So on the way down to the floor, in the most dramatic moment of my improvisation, I reach out my arm and hold myself half on the floor and half off the floor, and I go on holding that position in the hope that all concerned will realize that I'm supposed to be *on* the floor but am just not going to fuck up my suit doing this improvisation. At which point the drama coach says, "All right, thank you —thank you." I get up and walk off. Now, I don't know whether I've done good or bad. I have a feeling I've done terribly, but I figure I'll brave it out, so I go back and sit in the audience and watch some of the other kids audition, and some of them are really brilliant, but mostly the girls. I finally leave with the understanding that they'll be sending me a card within a week to let me know if I'm accepted or rejected.

A week goes by, and a card arrives that says, "Would you come down and visit with us. We would like to have a talk with you." I dash down there and talk with someone representing the school who says, "We're going to take you on a trial basis for three months. We don't feel that you'll make it, but we want to give you every opportunity. If we feel, at the end of three months, that there hasn't been sufficient improvement we ask you not to continue. Is that understandable, and if so, is it agreeable to you?" I said, "That's understandable and it's agreeable." Little did I realize what the real bottomline reason for my being accepted on a trial basis was. As it turned out, they had forty students who got passing marks and all forty of them were girls. No men. As rotten as the men were, they had to take ten or twelve of us to fill up the new class, and I was the least likely to succeed among the twelve.

Well, I sure as hell was delighted I was accepted. I set about really determined to learn how to become this actor I needed to be in order to show this guy O'Neal, whom I'm seeing now from time to time around the school, and who, by the way, never acknowledges me. He just passes me by, which makes me feel he's ignoring me because I'm of very little worth. Not realizing that the man has other, more important things to think about than running a judgment on me. Anyway, now I'm in a class, I'm beginning to learn about acting. And right away, because of my accent, I'm being laughed at when

I'm playing scenes, so I withdraw a little and I'm reluctant to come out.

There was a brilliant student who was a carryover from another period—he wasn't one of the auditioners —named Richard Jones. He was fabulous—a college graduate, very handsome, a beautiful actor—and he took a liking to me. We became friends, and in time he helped me out of my introverted stance and fear of being ridiculed by playing scenes with me. Also he would very gently explain to people that it wasn't nice to laugh at my accent because "he's trying." After a while he got everybody to kind of cool it, for which I was very grateful because that kind of fun-poking could have developed into something very unpleasant. Richard was instrumental in getting the others off my back. He was brilliant, subtle, and quick of mind. He was also an epileptic. One evening while he and I were playing a scene, whack! he got hit by a seizure—stretched out on the floor, got completely rigid, then started to quiver. Someone who knew about epilepsy said, "Push his pipe into his mouth." I jammed his pipe into his mouth, but he quickly broke it in biting down. After jamming something more substantial in his mouth, we all stood around apprehensively waiting for him to ride through it. In fifteen or twenty minutes he was in control and up on his feet, but he never came back to class. I've never seen him again.

After three months, the faculty of the Theatre School said my first twelve weeks suggested I really wasn't improving and they would rather I didn't come back. I said, "Please! I'm just beginning to get a feel for what it's all about. I realize that there's a hell of a lot more to it than I had thought, but that only strengthens my determination. So please, please reconsider." They said, "No." Devastated at being cut from the class roster, I drifted about in confusion for a week or so before I struck on an idea. I said to myself: Maybe I can barter. I went back to the school, searched out Abram Hill, the president, and said, "Mr. Hill, I want to continue to be a student here. What I would like to do is this: You don't have a regular janitor to clean the theater, to sweep down the hallway and take care of the steps and the stage. You leave that haphazardly to students and they don't do a very good job. I will take over the cleaning of the auditorium and I will take over the cleaning of the stage if you will let me continue on for another semester." He said, "Well, I'll think about it. It's unusual, but I'll think about it. You really want to study that badly?" I said, "Yes, sir." He said, "I'll think about it." I came back a few days later and asked if he *had* thought about it and he said, "Yes. We've discussed it and you've got a deal." So back into the class I go, delighted to be back on track again, happily closing out each evening with a little floor scrubbing, stairway mopping, and whatever other janitorial tidbit I laid on the institution under our agreement.

By then I had switched from dishwashing to working in the garment district as a "packer" in a blouse factory. The pay was not as good, and there were no free meals, but the hours were stable, and they dovetailed conveniently with my schedule at the American Negro Theatre. The Alberta blouse company was owned by a certain Mr. Abzug (he had a son named Martin, who was married to a lively young girl named Bella—who in the years to come was to add refreshingly to New York's political scene).

My job was split between packing blouses for shipment to various parts of the country and pushing a hand truck around the garment district to pick up or deliver large bolts of material. Mr. Abzug and his son Martin treated their employees like family; you couldn't ask for nicer bosses. This would have been an ideal job if a restaurant job's two free meals could have been applied to the garment district and especially to the packers of blouses.

One day, on my lunch break, a girl sat down next to me at a busy lunch counter and smiled before she started munching on a sandwich. I smiled back and much to my surprise found that it was easy to make conversation with her. Her name was Laura Brown and she was beautiful. Her dark chocolate complexion accentuated a perfect set of pearls in her mouth and also served as an ideal background for a pair of eyes that sparkled like diamonds. She too was a "packer," working in a dress factory nearby. The ease with which small talk flowed between us excited me to such a point that I asked if she would like to go out to a movie that coming weekend. She delighted me by saying, "Maybe—I'll let you know tomorrow." The next day I floated over to the luncheonette and there she was with a smile beckoning me to come sit next to her. At the end of another wonderful lunch hour, I asked what her decision was about the weekend movie. She glanced up at the ceiling as if she was playing "Should I or shouldn't I" in her mind. Then without a word she wrote her address on a paper napkin, folded it, and gently tucked it in the pocket of my shirt. I like your style, Laura Brown, I thought to myself. Before the weekend arrived, I developed such a thing for that girl, I actually prayed that she wouldn't turn out to be too sophisticated and refined for the likes of me. The first date ended gloriously with a kiss at the door which pushed me over the edge. I was in love.

On our second date I mentioned that I was going to the American Negro Theatre. She wanted to know, "What's that?" And I said, "Well, it's a little-theater group. I'm studying to be an actor." She said, "An actor?" I said, "Yeah. I'm studying to be an actor." She said, "You mean like people on the stage and on the screen? Are you serious?" I said, "Yes, I am." She said, "What do you want to be that for? You'll never be able to get any work." "Well," I said, "I hope to." That was as far as we explored my work in the theater. Lord knows, I was really crazy about her and wanted to spend all my free time with her, but my schedule at the theater school couldn't accommodate more than a couple of evenings a week and daytime hours on weekends. Also I was constantly short of money. After rent, food, and ordinary expenses I had practically nothing left for entertainment. The most I could do was take her to the movies once in a while and buy her an ice cream soda, after which we'd walk back to her house and sit around. Her sisters were lovely and her mother was really nice too. We would sit up in her house and Laura and I would neck on the couch while everyone stayed clear of the living room. It was like my fantasies coming true. She was tall and skinny with an angelic face. Laura's smile was pure sunshine—warm, friendly, ingratiating. It absolutely floored me. I used to walk around New York City just thinking about her smile. Her name would reverberate in my consciousness, and I would feel all kinds of marvelous things in my body. I was crazy about that child. And I think she really liked me a lot too. But—she wanted to go to the movies more often, out to night clubs, parties, dinners at expensive restaurants. Even when I could find the time, I simply didn't have the money. It was very frustrating, I'm sure, for a girl who wanted to have a "jumping time."

Comes Christmas. I had no indications. From time to time, I had noticed a slight irritability at my not being able to afford certain things or not being free to take her somewhere, but otherwise I had no inkling that a bomb was about to be dropped on my head. With Christmas arrives the time for giving, and I gave to Laura Brown all that I could afford, topping it all off with a giant Christmas card in the shape of a heart, covered by smooth pink satin over an undercushion of cotton. Apart from being pleasing to the eye and sensitive to the touch, this oversized card was intended to convey the huge treasure of feelings I had for her even though I couldn't come down the chimney with a bagful of material goodies. On the big envelope, in my very best penmanship, I wrote "Merry Christmas to Laura," slipped the card inside, and set out for her house. The door flew open and there she was, looking lovely and wearing a broad smile that, unless I was mistaken, seemed to dim considerably as she stepped aside to let me in.

The first door inside her apartment opens into the kitchen and there are four or five people in there. She takes me into the living room and I give her my present. She thanks me for it, says, "Excuse me," and goes back to the kitchen, where she stays—and stays—and stays. I begin to get the picture after about forty-five minutes, because all I can hear from the kitchen is a party, and I'm sitting in the fucking living room! They're laughing and talking and telling jokes and falling on the floor and clicking glasses and stuff. Forty-five minutes goes into an hour, and after about an hour and a half it has sunk in deep, but I'm too paralyzed with shame and humiliation to leave, because I'd have to go by the open kitchen door. Two hours go by—I know because there's a clock. Now I have to go, because the longer I stay, the bigger the humiliation. I simply have to go, I think. No matter how difficult it is to get past that kitchen door, I have to go. Grace under pressure, it's called. I get up, walk down the long hallway toward the front door and stop at the kitchen. I look in and them cats are having a party. She's in the middle, laughing, clicking glasses, and carrying on. As soon as they become aware of my presence, they all look up and a sudden silence descends. She looks at me and I can see in her face a satisfaction—

93

like: How do you like them apples? I say to her, "Excuse me. I'm going to have to leave now, good night." She looks me dead in the eye and says, "Good night." I will never know why I smiled at her before stepping into the hallway and allowing her to close the door firmly in my face.

Clomping down those six flights of stairs was like descending into an abyss of shitty feelings. My showcase smile had disappeared long before I hit that cold street. Anger, hostility, fear, and confusion were whirling around in my head, punching out the question: Why did this child I was so crazy about choose emotional mutilation as a means of ending the relationship? Could I have unknowingly wronged her in some monstrous way, to trigger such overkill, or could it have been an instinctive reflex action from a killer bitch expressing her annoyance at some minor irritation in our somewhat flawed relationship? *And how could I not have seen it coming?* A heavy-handed *coup de grâce* of this nature should have been spotted a mile off; to have missed spotting it suggests a big flaw in me. If I didn't really miss it but just chose to ignore it, then I'd been an idiot and henceforth must guard against my head giving way to my heart in emotional involvements.

For six broken-hearted weeks, I was a wreck. Given to lovesick, irrational behavior like standing in the darkened hallway of the building across the street from where she lived, hoping to get a glimpse of her returning from work. Between 6:00 and 6:15 p.m. she would appear like clockwork from around the corner, walk the thirty or forty yards to her door, mount the steps leading into the front entrance, and check the mailbox before disappearing into the building. Three or four nights a week for six weeks I watched her come around that corner and walk to her door. Then, because everything has its season, the time came for me to stop that sophomoric crap. On the last night of the sixth week, I strolled out of the darkened hallway into the light of a Harlem evening, sufficiently recovered to have a kind thought for Laura Brown as I walked along 7th Avenue. I pondered: Yes, she messed over me—but am I not a touch wiser for it? A bit more enlightened because of it? I sure in hell hope so! Pain, heartache, joys, disappointments, all were behind me now. She was obviously not the lady I was looking for. But she does exist, I'm sure, this lady of my dreams, and she's waiting somewhere up ahead. Maybe next week or next month, or maybe around the next corner.

I never saw Laura again, from that last night I watched her coming around the corner and going into her building, until this day. That has to be thirty-two or thirty-three years. I often wonder where she is and what she's doing now. Whether she's still alive. Did she get married? Did she have children? Did she move back South? Or is she still having that same old party every Christmas Eve in the same old kitchen, exploding into laughter at the same old raucous jokes, having forgotten that I was ever there, a long time ago.

7 On the Road

THE WILDLY SUCCESSFUL Broadway production *Anna Lucasta* starring Hilda Simms originated at the American Negro Theatre, or more accurately evolved in the theater's laboratory from a drama about a Polish-American family into a comedy-drama about a black American family. Almost all of the supporting cast, naturally, were American Negro Theatre members, including that titan of an actor, who gave the most stunning performance of Frank, the brother-in-law, ever seen in the five-year history of that fabulous production—Mr. Frederick O'Neal. Various other productions were mounted at eight- or ten-week intervals. A popular favorite at the time, *On Strivers Row,* was written by Abram Hill, the president of the theater. Such productions offered the new, as well as the seasoned, black actors the opportunity to test their mettle in front of an audience.

Once or twice a year a student production was presented, solely to showcase the talents of the new students. In my second semester such a production was announced by Osceola Archer, our drama coach, who was to direct it. I don't remember who wrote it, but it was quite an interesting play about college life, and like *Anna Lucasta*, and most of our other productions, it was not specifically written for blacks. In this play, called *Days of Our Youth*, there was a character named Liebman whom I desperately wanted to play, but Mrs. Archer brought in another actor who was not a student, and had never been part of our theater—a complete outsider by the name of Harry Belafonte. Looking at this guy who suddenly appeared at the theater on the first day of casting, I wondered who he was, and so did everyone else in the class, because this was supposed to be a production for "us" students of the freshman class. Mrs. Archer explained that she'd gone outside the school to get someone because there simply wasn't anyone *in* the class to do justice to that particular part—implying that it was her prerogative to make such a judgment. I think Osceola Archer had a certain prejudiced view of me. No, I don't think she thought I had much to offer. And to be fair to her, Harry's credentials were somewhat more impressive than mine. He was a very handsome man who made a striking appearance on stage. Moreover, many black Americans were heavily into a color bag in those days, and there was a considerable color differentiation between Mr. Belafonte and myself, leading me to think that Mrs. Archer leaned toward Harry because of it—thus underscoring the value system of the black bourgeoisie at that time.

In case you have never heard of the black bourgeoisie, it was a group of mostly middle-class, fair-complexioned or brown-skinned black people who on the basis of color husbanded themselves into a "higher society," apart and distinct from the darker majority. Second-hand elitist values and codes handed down from white "high society" were rigidly and sometimes ruthlessly adhered to, with characteristically little regard for the human suffering incurred. The darker you were, the less likely you were to obtain admission into that particular community. It was my understanding that Washington, D.C., stood as a mecca for the black bourgeoisie in the twenties, thirties, and forties. Washington was said to have been as bourgie as you could get and still be colored, and I believe Osceola Archer was from Washington. I think some of the above was definitely in play during the casting of this student production—it was certainly voiced among the other students, who passed it on to me out of sympathy—

but I never raised the question with Mrs. Archer, nor did I ever discuss it with Belafonte. I was content to—no, I was not content, because I didn't get a shot at the part—but I was glad to be around the process of the play.

Mrs. Archer was approached by my fellow students and asked if it wouldn't be fair to offer me the understudy to Harry Belafonte, since there was nothing in the play itself for me to do. This request, made without my knowledge, met with her agreement, and she called me up and said, "You can be the understudy to Harry Belafonte. You learn the part as well as Harry, and if one night he can't go on, you will stand in for him." I was thrilled at that.

But in the process of rehearsing this play, Harry and I have an awesome clash. Beneath the stage is a storage area containing trunks full of old costumes amid a variety of props, bits of old scenery, half-used cans of paint, plus innumerable odds and ends, all untidily strewn about, gathering dust. Harry and I are assigned to look through the costumes, and almost immediately as we begin digging into the costumes we start sparring, feeling each other out through a cat-and-mouse game initiated by Harry, who knows by now that I'm a kind of threat because I've been made his understudy. I already know who he is: he's the man that came in and got the part I wanted. What interests me now is: What makes him so special? He opens up the exchange by saying, "You know, I've heard about you from somewhere. Were you ever in jail?" That is the first thing Harry says to me. I am on the defensive right away, which is where, I suspect, Harry wants to put me. I say, "Where did you hear that?" He says, "Oh, I heard that. Let me see, Jesus, yeah, I heard that. Did you really spend some time in jail?" I say, "No, I did not. Where did you hear that kind of stuff?" Well, I am very sensitive about this because I had been in jail that one night for vagrancy. Anyway, Harry senses that he's struck gold and he begins to mine. He starts a psychological demolition attack on me. I say to myself: Well, fuck that, and hastily try to size up the situation and get a fix on where he's coming from, but he jabs away, not allowing me time to think. Which brings me to the realization that this bright, tough cookie who knows where jugular veins are located is going to be very difficult to deal with. I say, "No, I've never been to jail, but I will probably go to jail because I'm very hot-tempered and I will cut, stab, or hit somebody in a minute. I can't control myself. That's the one thing that scares me—I'm very frightened of doing harm to people. But no, I've never really been in jail. I just hope that it never comes to that."

So the gauntlet is down on both sides. He says, "Oh, I see," and I say, "Yes, that's the way it is with me. Tell me about you. Where do you come from? How do you come right in and get that part and you've never been a member of the American Negro Theatre?" He says, "No" —then skips a beat, as if searching for the right words, and in that briefest of pauses, I think he wavers ever so faintly—a flash, a flicker, no more, but enough to tell me that I've edged him onto the defensive. Then he goes on, "No, I've been around theater work a long time. I used to belong to other theater groups—that's where I knew Osceola Archer from." I figure aha! At least now he feels it necessary to clarify his position to me, so I keep him on the defensive as long as I can. I say, "But most of the kids here—I don't want you to think this is my position necessarily—but most of the kids here think that you just walked in from nowhere. They're a little upset, because after all they've been here for three months, for six months —and you just stroll in off the street and get a part like that." He says, "Yeah, I know that. And that isn't the way it really is. But anyway I'm here and I'm going to do a good job and you shouldn't be concerned in any way because you've got the understudy and some nights I might not come in and you'll get a chance to play it." With that he neutralizes me, because I'm dying for a chance to play it—so much so that I'm forever hoping that he'll fall off the stage, break a leg, sprain an ankle, dislocate a shoulder, anything to give me a chance to go on for one or two performances; in fact, Harry Belafonte will be well advised not to walk down the steps in front of me, if he doesn't want to find himself in a heap at the bottom of them. And that was the extent of our first exchange.

Before the play opened, a miraculous thing occurred. Harry Belafonte's stepfather was a superintendent of a building that was heated by coal. On certain evenings Harry had to help his father transfer the ashes from the furnace into great big garbage cans, then carry them up from the basement to the street to await the arrival of the garbage trucks. Those sixteen huge cans, each more than

98

120 pounds of dead weight, required maximum effort on the part of the young Harry and his aging father. It was one of those evenings with Harry unable to be present for a six o'clock rehearsal that Osceola Archer invited a Broadway director named James Light up to Harlem to see what she was doing with the play and possibly give her some suggestions, since he was the original director of *Days of Our Youth*. Harry didn't show by twenty past six, and thinking that any further wait would be an abuse of her guest's generosity, Mrs. Archer signaled the start of the rehearsal by asking me, "Would you read Harry's part until he arrives?" Naturally, I didn't have to "read" it—I knew the part backwards by now, every word, every nuance, so I said, "Certainly." More than a few of my classmates were moved to applause by the unexpected turn of events that had offered me an opportunity to "get up in the part." Harry didn't show at all as we ran through the play under our coach's direction and the watchful eyes of James Light, who was scribbling notes on a yellow pad. At the end of the rehearsal, he turned his notes over to our director, complimented her on her work, and thanked her for having invited him to spend the evening with us. And as he was leaving, he came over to me and said, "Would you come to my office on Monday? I'd like to talk to you about something." I had no idea what he wanted, but you can bet I was impressed that a big director had asked me to come and see him.

I walked into his office the following Monday, still not knowing what to expect. What could he want to talk to me about? I was wondering to myself. I hope he's not going to tell me to forget about acting. Go out and get a job as a dishwasher. Maybe that's it—Jesus, Lord—could I have been so bad when he saw me in the play? He's probably seen that part played lots of times by brilliant actors before watching me butcher it like an untalented amateur—no, not like an amateur, like an untalented dishwasher. Well, the gentle Mr. Light offers me a chair and says, "Very shortly I will be doing a play called *Lysistrata* using an all-black cast." He runs down a list of people he's going to use, including Etta Moten, Babe Wallace, and Mildred Smith, and then he says, "*Lysistrata* is a Greek comedy, and in it we have a small part, the role of Polydorus, that I'd like you to play. Do you think you would be interested in playing Polydorus for me?" I'm sitting there in shock. Mr. Light obviously doesn't read it as shock, because he goes on to say, "It's really quite a good play, written by Gilbert Seldes." Now I don't know from Gilbert Seldes—I don't know from Greek comedies—I don't know the people he's mentioned. I don't know nothing. All I remember him saying is, "I'd like you to play Polydorus." I say, "Yes, sir—r!" He says, "So when we're ready to go, I'll let you know and we'll get together." Well, I'm flying now.

Back at the school my classmates pinned me down for every little detail. They wanted a word-for-word re-creation of the scene in Mr. Light's office and my reaction when he laid the magic question on me. I saw Belafonte and he said, "I hear that you went down and probably got a job." I said, "Yes." He said, "Hey, that's nice." It was a genuine response from him—and it stunned me. It was devoid of competitiveness; he genuinely felt: Hey, that's nice—either that or he was the best damn actor in the whole wide world, which is a definite possibility.

I kept on at the American Negro Theatre, and after the student production of *Days of Our Youth* closed, the renegade actor Harry Belafonte stayed and soon became a full-fledged member, evidencing a ferocious determination to make it on his own terms. This proud, arrogant, good-looking, intensely political West Indian bears watching, I said to myself, at least as closely as he's surely surveying me.

A group of six actors including Harry used to get together after class at the top of the stairwell to sing songs as a form of relaxation. They harmonized, vocalized, belted, soothed, cooed, hummed their way through lots of songs, and had a hell of a good time doing it. A marvelous, infectious camaraderie enveloped them as they launched into song after song with their arms thrown around each other, swaying from side to side to the rhythm tapped out by their feet on the marble steps. One evening, trying to become the seventh member of the group, I walked over and put my arms around the guys as they were singing, and I chimed in with a "toot-eee—tooot-ee—tootee-toot!" They just stopped and turned to me with hard looks as if to say: J-e-s-u-s! Will you please go away? I had no idea why—I thought I was simply being rejected out of hand—but I learned later that I was tone deaf. I couldn't carry a tune, and my toots immediately threw them off. I was confined to listening from a distance.

But Harry and I would see each other from time to time. I kind of liked him—didn't trust him one bit, but I kind of liked him because he seemed very complex. On the one hand, he could kill you; on the other hand, he could be very outgoing, very open, very giving, and very helpful. The trick was, you never knew which was which on what days. We were both content to get along on an arm's-length, "Hello, how are you?" basis. It was safer.

Finally, someone from James Light's office called me in to sign a contract, offering me $65 to $75 per week for the play. My Lord! Can you beat that? I thought to myself. Nervousness reduced my much-prized penmanship to chicken scratching as I signed my first contract as an actor. Money loaned to me by the company to join Actors' Equity, a prerequisite to my working on Broadway, would be deducted later from my salary. In one stupendous month of firsts, I signed my first contract for a Broadway play, promising me more money than I had ever earned in one week before, the first tangible indication that my still-embryonic self-improvement program, far from being a useless exercise, was in fact beginning to pay. The first time seeing my name in a newspaper, announcing additional cast members for the production of *Lysistrata*. The first time seeing a Broadway play, to get a "feel" of what the professional theater was like (it was wonderful). And last, but far from least, my first initiation into the fraternity of actors, making me a bona fide members of Actors' Equity. I beat Harry Belafonte to that!

From day one of rehearsal I was well prepared, on my toes, paying attention to everything. I was fascinated by the other people in the cast—watching them move around, listening to the way they read their lines. It was from watching these gifted black American artists that I began to understand the real magic of theater. The rehearsal month for *Lysistrata* was the best four weeks of my life.

Opening night of *Lysistrata*. After all the rehearsals and run-throughs, I am opening in New York on Broadway, and I'm feeling pretty good with myself. In fact, I've decided not only can I become an actor, I *am* an actor. I've proved that—I have an Equity card. Now is the time for me, according to my original plan, to simply thumb my nose at Frederick O'Neal and say, "Bye-bye. See—I *can* be more than a dishwasher," and go off and do other things. But now I'm stuck—because I love this new life and I don't want to go off and do anything else. "Half hour" comes and goes. I'm all dressed and ready. Somebody says, "Everybody get ready, curtain in five minutes." The actors take their places on the stage. I don't enter for a little while, but I'm ready.

Babe Wallace, on his way to the stage, stops and looks through a little hole about the size of a dime in the proscenium curtain. I wonder why he's peeking through that little hole. Soon he turns to another actor, whispers something, then peeks through the hole again before turning once more to the actor who is waiting for *his* peek. Smiling to himself, Babe wanders off to take his place on the stage. The other actor looks through the hole, shakes his head, and also drifts off to his first-act position.

So I say, "What in the world are they peeking at through there?" An overwhelming urge instantly develops in me: I walk up to the curtain, I look through the hole, and I discover that it looks directly out on the audience—about 1,200 people! As the lights begin to dim, I suddenly realize that I'm going out in front of those 1,200 people (most of whom are white). Lord have mercy—what have I gotten myself into? I quickly dash away from the curtain, but the damage is done. I am now petrified. I've got stage fright.

At that moment, the stage manager says, "Curtain going up." Sure as hell that curtain goes up, boy. I hear this thunderous applause and it sounds as though there are 12 million people out there. The play is supposed to be a Greek *comedy*, the audience is supposed to be laughing, but they ain't laughing. I don't know why. From the wings, I just hear the lines going and the audience quiet. My time grows nearer and nearer. Finally my cue is there and I have got to go out on the stage.

I can't move. The stage manager gives me a shove and I go stumbling out. The first thing I do, instead of looking at the actor I'm supposed to give my first line to, I look dead into the audience, where I see nothing but faces (most of them white). I say to myself: Mama, what am I doing here? It's time for my line. I don't remember it. The first line has gone completely out of my mind. I hear the silence, however, and I say to myself: Come on, Sidney, you've got to say something. You've got to start it. The first line that comes to my mind is line number three, so I give that line to the actor. His eyes open wide, indicating: That's not the right line. He tries to get me back to the head of the scene by giving me the line that was supposed to come after my *first* line. I'm stuck now, and can't pick it up, so I give him line number seven—at which point the juxtaposition of lines is coming out hilariously to the audience. We finally have to wait for them to calm down from laughing.

I know they are laughing at me. They can't be laughing at the humor in the play, because my scene isn't supposed to be funny. The other actor gives me line number three. I give him line number twelve. Now, the audience is not only laughing—they're beginning to applaud. Oh, shit, I realize, they want me to get off the stage. I'm finished. I've taken all the humiliation I can stand. The other actor, in desperation, throws yet another line at me. Instead of answering him, I gear myself up, turn around, and walk away. I walk off the stage and the audience is applauding. I'm saying, "Screw you. You're just applauding because I've left."

Backstage nobody says anything to me about having messed up the lines—they're ecstatic because, they say, the audience thinks I'm so terrific. But I don't believe they think I'm terrific, nor do I listen to anybody who tries to tell me so. I rush upstairs to my dressing room, whip out of my costume, put on my street clothes, and get the hell out of that theater. Everyone is supposed to wait for the curtain calls; I'm not there. They have a party after the show; I'm not there either.

Next morning, after what felt like the most agonizing night of my life, I reluctantly went out to buy some of the thirteen newspapers that were expected to carry reviews on the disaster of the previous evening. I just knew I was about to read about a certain young boy named Sidney Poitier who called himself an actor but was in fact a dishwasher and who messed up a good play. All thirteen reviewers panned the play—more correctly they "destroyed" the play. But according to a few reviews, the only saving grace of the evening was an unknown young actor who came out in the first act and absolutely devastated the audience with his acute comedic approach to the part of Polydorus. I said, "Uh-oh. Wait a minute now. Back up here a second."

I read and reread each paper. The words never changed. According to them, I was a hit. Overnight I was a hit! In a play that lasted only four days, of course, but I was a hit.

Next night I go to the theater feeling much better, but I can't repeat that first performance because I'm not fucking up all the lines now. And I proceed to give the three most disappointing performances of my life. Because now I'm not scared—now I'm a hit. I'm playing it straight, with each line coming in its proper sequence. Nobody laughs. The director and my fellow actors, being professionals, all understood and were sympathetic about my nervousness on opening night. Some of them said they even recognized a theatrical instinct in me, an instinct that said: Hey, I'm in the throes of some panic, some stage fright, and some other things, but I'm not going to be overwhelmed by those negative energies. Instead I'll theatricalize them, bend them to artistic use. Well, that instinct may have been there, but I was one person in that theater who wasn't aware of it!

In the audience on the opening night, watching me give my unexpected once-in-a-lifetime performance, was John Wildberg, the producer of *Anna Lucasta*. On the day of *Lysistrata*'s last performance, I received a call from Mr. Wildberg asking me to work for him as an understudy in a road company of his hit show. I had never been given to stuttering, but this swift, unexpected turn in my fortunes left me at a loss for words. I managed no more than something like: "I . . . I . . . bu . . . uh . . . uh . . . , Mr. Wildberg," and he interrupted with a smile in his voice, asking if I could come by his office the following day. All being mutually agreeable, I would there fix my signature to a contract guaranteeing me the record sum of eighty dollars per week, plus the excitement of work and travel in the company of professional actors. Within a week I was a member of *Anna Lucasta*'s family of traveling performers.

This experience brought me warm relationships of varying durations with Y. A. Janey, Duke Williams, Maxwell Glanville, Roy Glenn, Lance Taylor, Rosetta LeNoire, John Proctor, Doris Proctor, Albert Perkins, Laura Bowman, Lawrence Criner, Ruby Dee, Ossie Davis, Frederick O'Neal, John Tate, Wesline Foster, Hilda Haynes, Kenneth Manigault, Betty Haynes, Alice Childress, Alvin Childress, Claire Jay, Claire Lyba, and Earle Hyman. In one or another company, made up of most of the above, I traveled "the theatrical road" of

America, playing at various times Chicago, Philadelphia, St. Louis, Cleveland, Montreal, Cincinnati, Washington, Pittsburgh, Toronto, and many others.

Maxwell Glanville, a wonderfully boyish man and a very, very fine actor, was the first person I became friendly with in the company. He stood 6 feet tall, weighed about 190 pounds, and had a head shaped like an egg. He also had a marvelous sense of humor and by reputation was judged to be attractive to women. I never could understand it, but the girls indeed seemed to fly to him as if he were wearing a sugar mask. Due to an impressive percentage of successes (all of which cannot be verified), Maxie had to be classified as a "ladies' man," a label I was not qualified to quarrel with, since my credentials in that area were so meager. Besides, mine was not to reason *why* Maxie got so much poontang, mine was to learn from Maxie, so I too could come upon my fair share. Because of his boyish charm, the considerable difference in our ages was never noticeable to me. Maxwell Glanville was a trustworthy, dependable friend to whom I will always be grateful for the many things he tried to teach me—one of which was how to appear forceful and seductive when I spoke to women, thereby creating an aura of self-confidence and outgoingness. In keeping with his firm belief that women had a particular weakness for aggressive men, he set about giving me "aggression lessons" by going through pantomime routines on effective ways to approach women. He would act out, for example, how an aggressive man appears to a woman, then point out how a woman sees a man who has no aggression in his attitude. He then would lecture on the differences between the two, and how they manifest themselves in a man either being sought after by the ladies or completely ignored and left alone to hold up the wall. At first he was very patient, but he grew more and more infuriated as I turned out to be disappointingly slow on the uptake.

I was also tutored in lady killing by Roy Glenn and Duke Williams, two other guys in the company. Let me tell you who these guys were. Duke Williams was the most handsome man in the whole company, in the whole history of *Anna Lucasta*, and possibly in the whole history of black actors until Belafonte came on the scene. Duke was from one of the Carolinas, I don't remember which. He was a deep brown, 6 feet 2 inches tall, slender, twenty-two years old, built tough like a leopard. The set of teeth in his mouth could have guided ships through shoals, they were so pearly white and bright. Duke was a charmer, totally unaware that he had his *and* twenty-five other people's share of the masculine macho thing. I mean, he had it in abundance and it came naturally to him. When he walked on stage, the women in the audience tended to forget the play and just "watch that hypnotic sailor boy walk around the interior of that Brooklyn waterfront bar." That's the kind of magnetism Duke Williams had. To compound his situation, Duke had an enormous appetite for women. He was playing Lester, the youngest sailor in *Anna Lucasta*. Maxwell Glanville played Dannie, the older sailor.

Then there was Roy Glenn, a huge man with a great basso voice. Standing more than 6 feet tall and weighing about 225 pounds, he could sing beautifully, and he too loved the ladies. (Twenty years later he would play my father in *Guess Who's Coming to Dinner*.)

Glanville, Williams, and Glenn ran as a trio. When they walked into a party on a given evening, three ladies were destined to fall, and if they didn't—well, as yet no one has surfaced with testimony that such an event ever happened. They began taking me along on social outings, partly because they wanted me to study their approaches and try my own hand, and partly because it pleased them to have an appreciative novice along to witness and applaud their excellence. Maxwell Glanville coached me on approaches. Duke Williams taught me by example: "Just watch how I do it." They were all genuinely concerned about my shyness and inability to talk to girls. When we'd go to a party, I would sit down, wait for a girl to ask *me* to dance, and meanwhile I'd watch other people doing their number. I simply didn't have the esprit de corps to get out there and talk to the girls. I remember a party where Duke Williams picked out a girl, told me to watch him carefully, then, setting out to teach me by example, approached the young woman and said, "Have I seen you before?" The worst, the corniest line you ever heard—but it worked. The girl went all aflutter and said, "No, I haven't seen you before." He responded: "Oh, I thought I had. Well, anyway, that's my loss. Where're you from?" She told him, and he forged on with, "How many pretty girls are there in that town?" Following right up with, "If you're an example, that place must be Paradise. And I bet you're as sweet as you're pretty." Then, abruptly switching tactics, he turned off his smile, took a half step backward, narrowed down those haunting eyes, and asked, "You're not married, are you?" The tone of his voice together with the look on his face seemed to be pleading with her not to crush him with a "yes" answer. The poor girl, grateful that her single status would not damage this young Prince or otherwise abort such a gloriously promising start, said happily, "No, I'm not married," then waited the anxious moment or two before the smile gradually returned to Duke Williams's face. As she smiled up at him, he knew and I knew that he had her where he wanted her. But shoot, I knew that if I approached a girl with dumb, unimaginative, corny lines like that, she'd probably spin in her tracks and walk in the opposite direction—after laughing in my face.

Following several weeks of intensive tutoring in this crash course on how to "charm 'em into the sack," my trio of sponsors took me to a special party at which they proudly intended to unveil their handiwork. Alas, their protégé left much to be desired. The miraculous transformation into a smooth operator with all the finesse and skill necessary to becoming a "lady killer in full standing," so to speak, never materialized. My best efforts, falling woefully short of expectations, reduced me to a dependency on my Guardian Angels as ice-breakers—I would only try talking to girls they had already approached for themselves. Because I was a friend of theirs, I felt more comfortable walking up to a girl and laying my stuff on her if one of them was standing right there. For this rash, unforgivable act, I was practically drummed out of the corps. I eventually earned for myself the nickname "Sam Huff": like the real football player, I apparently broke up a lot of plays. It seemed I always came up at the wrong time, just when one of the trio was about to seal the fate of some unsuspecting young lady. Mind you, there were more than a few young ladies who were not so unsuspecting, but were rather looking forward to having their fate sealed.

My progress was dismally slow, essentially because lady killing wasn't my style, "quick as lightning" wasn't my pace, and excellence in the sexual wizardry known as "stud calisthenics" was certainly not my ambition—yet. Despite their sneaking off without me after a while, my trio of tutoring Guardian Angels refused to abandon me entirely as a hopeless experiment, attesting to my strong conviction that they liked me very much despite the massive failure of their very best combined efforts.

These larger-than-life characters, whose principal interests appeared to be work and sex, taught me a lot. It *seemed* that as long as they could find work in their chosen field and maintain an enviable rate of success in their ceaseless hunt for sexual conquest, that was all there was to life. But such would be the mistaken conclusion of an untrained eye, for such a narrow vision would ignore the many qualities that made these men, in some unexpected ways, American originals. They lived full (if unseen) relationships with relatives and friends; they had fears and hopes and desires, unspeakable self-doubt and secret visions. None of these emotions lent itself to easy articulation or ego-stroking as handily as work and sex do. To know my friends in the fullness that included their private selves, one had to be around when the masks were down, to witness their rage at their own helplessness when conflicts and failures that could no longer be denied forced them into confrontation. As characters in the real world they were richer and more complex than anything they possibly could have been involved with on the stage, since they were far from expert in their theater skills. Talented—yes. Well-trained—no. Had I known then what I know now, I could have learned more about acting from watching them as people than from imitating them as actors.

Having started as an understudy with the *Anna Lucasta* company, my job was to memorize several parts and to be ready to go on at a moment's notice for any actor who, for one reason or another, might be unable to appear. The first time I stepped on stage in Philadelphia, my feeling was: Fantastic! Exhilarating! Though I had no technique, or any real understanding of what acting was about, I was somehow finally on home ground. Yes, I was scared, but not to the point of panic, as I had been my very first time in front of a paying audience.

I now knew that I was a novice without any technique or the discipline of an artist, yet what I felt on that stage was akin to magic. Best of all, I was smart enough to realize how dumb I was about my new world, the world of professional theater acting. When the curtain fell that evening, I felt important—and worthwhile. And my friends took me out on the town to celebrate (even though to them I was still a dismal failure as a ladies' man).

Toward the end of our engagement in Philadelphia, through rote, osmosis, or brainwashing, I began to show small but encouraging signs of being able to make a play for a girl. For instance, I met a girl at a party who wore no makeup (I hated makeup wearers). She was a nurse from the South. She was country, and she was sensuous. I took a liking to this lovely woman who fitted into the image I had of the Ideal Girl. She was renting a room in a house in north Philadelphia, and when I saw her to her door, and kissed her sweet lips in the moonlight, I felt the earth move under my feet. Dynamite! (Or was it just the underground subway rumbling by?)

I didn't press it the first night—it was my habit not to —being too much of a gentleman, and too shy. Other guys would have ravished her that very evening, and she would have been discarded bones by the next morning. But me—I settled for a kiss, and was quite satisfied.

I saw her the next evening after the theater and we had a lovely time. After three or four similar evenings, I finally maneuvered myself into her bedroom. It was sensational! It was the first time I realized how wet some women can become, and that discovery served to make me hornier than ever, so much so that I found it very difficult to exercise restraint. But I had to manage it somehow, because I was taught by my tutors that it is essential to one's self-acceptance, indeed to the very nature of one's manhood, that one be able to really exercise control, stay cool—grace under pressure again. That child was a lot of pressure! The sex was mind-blowing. Absolutely mind-blowing! It was at that time that I seriously thought of taking the sex act two or three steps beyond the missionary position into forbidden regions where my tutors, by their own admissions, were legendary dwellers. That young country nurse from the South was a perfect partner with whom to take that giant step—or two. But I wasn't quite ready. I made a couple of feeble attempts, then postponed it. The following day, when asked by the trio for details, I lied and said nothing had happened, remembering when each of them would come back with stories of his evening out that sounded as if he were reading from a pornographic book. I chose to pass, leaving a tremendous evening with a wonderful woman where it should rightfully be, between the two of us. That delicious young black lady, in a very short time, gave me much love and lots of tender care. Then just before I left Philadelphia, she stepped into my mind and found a comfortable spot somewhere in the back of my head where she has remained through the years, providing memories that warm me even now.

From Philadelphia we moved on to Baltimore. The fact that Baltimore is renowned for its white marble steps is coincidental (I think) with its also being the city where I finally took a giant step—or two—of my own, partnered with a poker player. Whenever we arrived in a new town, one or another of the cast members, most of whom loved to play poker, would find out where games were being held and drop the word about us recently arrived devotees. Swiftly, the poker circle of Baltimore took us all to its breast and more than a few of us to the cleaners. Did you hear me? On the most memorable evening in that city, I sat down to poker in the comfortable apartment of our host, a local businessman, and found there was a most stunning woman in the game. She was a slender ebony lady, very sophisticated in appearance, very articulate, quick, good sense of humor and laid back. Laid back! Introductions around the table revealed her to be a schoolteacher in the local system whose hobby was poker, of which she was an excellent practitioner. Lady Luck was not in a sisterly mood that evening, however, flirting outrageously with a couple of men sitting directly across the table from the beautiful schoolteacher, who caught only second-best hands. Tapped out eventually by a full house against a straight, she was faced with relinquishing her seat to one of the many players anxiously awaiting a vacancy. She stood up, paused a moment to scan the faces of her adversaries, then asked, "Is there someone here who will lend me some money?" The silence that followed, after much shifting about and averting of eyes, gave her the answer. She smiled softly and turned when I said, "Maybe." Then she looked sheepishly at me for a moment and said, "I don't want to give up my seat. If you would be kind enongh to lend me some money, I promise to return it tonight. I live just down the street." I said, "Fine." From my modest winnings, I counted off the twenty-five-dollar table stakes required of each player, and pushed it across the table to her. Noticing that the soft movements at the corners of her mouth were followed

110

by a slight curtsy of her head as she slipped back into her seat, I knew instantly how much she genuinely appreciated my gesture. But Lady Luck's indifference continued to neutralize the skill of Baltimore's beautiful schoolteacher, who went on playing consistently admirable poker to rotten results. Later in the evening, after I had issued her an additional twenty-five-dollar loan, she tapped out completely, going all the way in support of a spectacular full house that was bested by four little deuces. She had had enough.

She told me a little about herself as we strolled the four blocks to her apartment, outside which she absent-mindedly fumbled for her key, preoccupied, I assumed, with deciding whether to invite me in or ask me to wait at the door while she dashed inside to fetch the fifty dollars necessary to square her debt. Between locating her keys and the releasing of the lock tumblers, she made a decision in my favor that became immediately apparent when she pushed the door open, stepped inside, and, with a gesture of reverse chivalry, asked me inside. "Have a seat," she said, disappearing into her bedroom and leaving me a few moments in which to look around the living room for telltale signs of a masculine roommate. But there were none among the objects making up her delicate, feminine room—put together more with taste than with dollars.

My review of the surroundings was interrupted when, emerging from the bedroom, she walked over to me with the fifty dollars in her outstretched hand. I hesitated. She folded the bills, stuffed them in my pocket, then asked, "Would you care for a drink or a cup of coffee?" "Tea," I answered. In the midst of light conversation, over tea and cookies, I decided to make a move at that lady. As you can notice I'm getting a little bolder in my approaches. I made my move, and she responded. After leading me to her bedroom, she disappeared into the john, leaving me alone long enough to have a brief conversation with myself about how best to create the impression that I was a seasoned player in this game. First and foremost, I told myself, "remain cool." Second, maintain a moderate amount of aggressiveness throughout. Third, be prepared for mutually acceptable diversity beyond the missionary position. Dressed in a nightgown that couldn't have been more perfect, she emerged from the bathroom with the scent of a delicate perfume swirl-

111

ing about her, forcing me to remind myself of the first and foremost ground rule. It took her only seconds to reduce the lighting in the room, arrange for some tender music to flood the semi-darkness, slide into bed, and, with inviting open arms, reach out for me. As I lowered myself into those lovely arms, knowing how important it was to start off with a kind of foreplay that would spell "experience," my mind riffled through the various possibilities gathered from my trio of mentors who, the day after every score, would relate in generous and vivid detail the approach that had sent the poor girls of the night before into a frenzy of orgasmic pleasures. In a moderately aggressive manner, with my "cool" in full operation, I started out by caressing her neck, ears, and mouth to immediately encouraging results. If I can build imaginatively on this promising start, I thought, I may very well join the ranks of the professionals by morning. There comes a time in the heat of moments such as these when a young, inexperienced man must resolve to go for broke, throw caution to the winds and press on, or risk the almost certain humiliation that seems to be reserved for young boys who fall short in their attempts at doing a man's job. The moment of truth was at hand. A seasoned player or a counterfeit lover—which will I be?

Surging up suddenly from these contrasting images came old memories of my first awkward, inept attempts at "ad-libbing" with older women, to remind me that I was, in those novice years, forever anticipating (or was it hoping?) that I would be stopped. "Ah, but not this night, no siree not this night," I silently proclaimed. However, if, on the off chance, she unexpectedly turned ambivalent and *did* move to stop me, I stood ready to negotiate smoothly around any such roadblocks with gentle attention to sensitive areas until her resistance weakened, because (according to my mentors) inventive ad-libbing in bed requires cooperation. Vowing then and there never again to view myself as a boy, I resolved to go all the way that night with that woman in the city of Baltimore. The chips were down. With objective fixed and perserverance as my game plan, I was, at last, heading for maturity along the route called "improvisation." And so it followed on that wonderful evening, with my temperature escalating and with little more than instinct as my guide, that I gingerly started on some serious improvising, inventing, ad-libbing.

I noticed right away that there was no resistance, but I was moving slowly, you know—I didn't want to break the speed limit. Moving slowly—I touched delicately on a sensitive area here, brushed across another there, pressed gently and steadily onward, kept moving—slowly, slowly. And instead of resistance, I found that each move was being matched by encouraging responses. I said to myself: Sidney P., you are about to come of age, young man, then pressed on to join the ranks of the Seasoned Player. Now I was not an artist, obviously, but what actually determines expertise? I loved that moment, because it was a consummation of wonderful things. I was very impressed by the lady. There was, I think, a giving of herself to me and my giving of myself to her, in a totally human way. Both enjoying not only what we were receiving, but what we were giving. And that was the best way for me to enlarge and diversify my sexual activities, the best possible way.

I left when we were done—I didn't want to stay, not knowing what her circumstances were. I didn't know whether she was married, or had a boyfriend, or had a family, or what, though from appearances she was a single girl living an unattached bachelor life. In any event, I chose not to ask, on the off-chance that questions might have been embarrassing to her. Besides, if she wanted me to stay she would have asked. And I didn't offer to give her the money back. I wanted to, as a gesture of friendship, but it would have been the wrong gesture. I'm sure she understood that and would have been disappointed by such a gesture, however well intended. We were only in Baltimore for a short time, and I saw her before we left, but it was at someone's house. We were never again in touch. She never came to New York, at least when I was there, but I stayed on the road a long time with *Anna Lucasta*—from 1946 to 1949, three years, on and off, and I never went through Baltimore again. So that was the end of that. But I remember Baltimore by remembering her.

Washington, New Haven, Boston followed before we swept into the Midwest. It became clear to me by the time we reached Boston that my being an understudy on this tour would teach me very little about acting or theater in general, but would undoubtedly off a rich education in life experiences which, over time, would turn out to be much more important than the primitive acting techniques that were the current vogue. An interlude in Boston with a wonderful woman I knew by the name of Ann Gurdine is typical of the "life experiences" that were at work shaping, molding, and honing away at that hunk of raw material recently transported from the Bahamas and known in very limited circles as Sidney Poitier, dishwasher-actor. The beautiful, sensitive Ann Gurdine was one of three children in a very middle-class black family headed by Colonel Ned Gurdine, one of the highest-ranked black officers in the United States Army. Pride in their strong family ties was visible to anyone who ever saw the closely knit Gurdines operate as a unit anywhere, but especially in their Roxbury, Massachusetts, home outside Boston. I met the gentle, sweet, warm Ann when she came to see the play in Boston. She too looked like my dream girl. She agreed to our first date on condition that I pick her up at her home, allowing, I'm sure, for her parents to take a look at me. They smiled pleasantly as we were introduced, and proceeded to behave in the civilized, courteous manner that is typical of intelligent middle-class parents who can't stand unknown young men coming into their homes sniffing around their daughters. Though Ann and I saw each other almost every day during my stay in Boston, there was no way for me to make a move at her sexually, due to subtle but effective maneuvering on the part of her clever parents, who invited me to the house a lot during the day while placing tight restrictions on her dating at night, refusing even to let her visit me backstage during performance. In the time allowed by these restrictions we became very close, very fast. It was a matter of a few weeks. Before the end of *Anna Lucasta*'s run in Boston, Ann and I found ourselves locked into a strong relationship and galloping toward emotional commitment. Then the old bugaboo of "How much future can an upper-middle-class colored girl find with someone dumb enough to want to be an actor in the American theater?" started coming from her parents. This bugaboo, alas, was all too valid, and was to haunt me for years to come. I moved on from Boston, but returned many times in the next three years to see the beautiful Ann Gurdine. In the meantime, we kept in touch with letters. At one point we even talked about getting married, but we knew that she would have trouble with her family. It was beyond our capacities to resolve all the questions that marriage would bring up, so we cooled off, letting our desires die at the hands of the bugaboo while we wandered off in different directions along the pathways of the Grand Design. (Years later I would return to Boston to promote a film and find that she had grown very, very militant in her politics, very pro-black in her outlook and social behavior. I only saw her briefly, but was able to grasp that she had matured a lot and aged very well, through what must have been very difficult years, changing from the sweet, warm Ann Gurdine into a politically tough and worldly wise woman, who was still as exciting as she had been a dozen years before—if not more so.)

From Boston we plunged into the Midwest, hopscotching from city to city over the following four months, before settling into St. Louis for a two-week tune-up engagement preceding an expected long run in Chicago. By the time we opened in St. Louis, I was seeing someone in the show on a regular basis—the young, vibrant, full-of-life actress Y. A. Janey, who was married to a New York musician I knew mostly as "Frank." I had met this quiet, cerebral man of music once, and had pegged him as a very pleasant person, strikingly economical in words and action, the kind of man who constantly keeps you wondering what he's thinking. The free spirit of Y. A. Janey infused the title role of *Anna Lucasta* with an infectious love of life, making the tragic moments in that character's troubled life unbearably close to reality. We were opposites, Janey and I. At the time we met, she had been for many years a liberated woman, while I, just recently off the adolescent dime, had miles to go to my manhood. The attraction of opposites took hold between us somewhere on the road, developing into a romantic flourish by Pittsburgh, blossoming across Indiana and Ohio, and ripening into a full-fledged affair that included being together almost every night before we rolled into St. Louis. We tried, with only limited success, to keep it cool because of her marriage.

In St. Louis all the female members of the cast checked into the Phyllis Wheatley Home for Women, a kind of resident hotel for colored women, while all the men checked into a local colored hotel. One night Dizzy Gillespie came to town for a weekend engagement at a local club and checked into the same hotel. Responding to an invitation from the club's owner, the entire cast attended Dizzy's opening after the curtain rang down on our own show, and we stayed on until one-thirty, stomping, whistling, and applauding. After Janey and her sister actors returned to their Home for Girls, our guys joined Dizzy and his musicians in his suite back at the hotel. We were in Dizzy's place for five minutes and out comes the pot, and everyone starts rolling and telling stories—unbelievably funny and risqué tales, from both musicians and actors. Finally the grass had mellowed everyone out to such a point that someone only had to mention the punchline of a previously told joke to send everyone else into another round of hysterics. Not being a grass smoker at that time, I was more of an observer than a participant. Logic insists that I must have experienced at least a low-grade buzz from the density of the marijuana fumes in the smoke-filled room, but I wasn't aware of having a contact high, unless rolling around helplessly from laughter with tears streaming down my cheeks was one of its characteristics. Possibly because Janey was sitting in her hotel lobby waiting for me, or possibly because I was supercautious about dope, I kept my wits about me until it came time to split. At which point I made a loud bogus announcement, saying, "Oh, well, I think I'm going to have to dash off and get me some sleep." My fellow actors, who were privy to my real reason for departure, quickly shared their knowledge with Dizzy Gillespie, saying, "He ain't going off to get him no sleep, he going off to pick up a lady and then *they* are going off and get some sleep." Gillespie said, "Well, we won't let him go until he admits where he's going." I said, "Fellows, I'm simply going to sleep." They said, "Well, if you're going to sleep, go to sleep in there. Go to sleep in Dizzy's bed." I said, "Look, I've got a room in this hotel. I'm going upstairs to my room and get in bed." They said, "Oh, no, you ain't, we know where you're going and it ain't upstairs." I said, "Please, fellows, let me out." They formed a human barricade between me and the door. They said, "Now, we know where you're going. We know what's happening. The longer you stay here, the longer she's going to be upset and figure that you're not coming and she's going to sleep and you're going to miss your little poontang for the night, so why don't you tell us where you're going and then we'll let you out the door." I said, "I'm going upstairs to my room. Come with me and see me get into my bed." They said, "Oh, no, you're going to stay here until you 'fess up." You know what I had to do? I had to jump out a window! I said, "Okay, I will go into Dizzy's bedroom and I will sleep in Dizzy's bed. How is that?" They said, "Cool." I go into the bedroom, open the window, and jump two stories down to the ground. Luckily it had snowed earlier, leaving two feet of powder to cushion my fall. They came to the window shouting down at me, "Aha, aha! We know where you're going—we know where you're going." I dashed to the corner, flagged down a cab, rushed over to the Phyllis Wheatley Home for Women, picked up Janey, and returned to the hotel. Stepping out of the taxi, I glanced up at the bank of windows in Dizzy Gillespie's suite. All seemed quiet—whacked out of their skulls, I thought, as we walked into the hotel and mounted the stairs leading to my third-floor room. As we hit the third-floor landing, turned into the hallway leading toward my room —wha—aam! There they were! Those dirty, rotten, no-good bastards were all lined up against the wall on both sides of the hallway smoking their grass, smiling mischievously, tipping their hats or bowing from the waist, uttering innocent pleasantries like, "Good evening." "My, my, my, I hope you had a wonderful evening." "I think it's so nice of her to see him to his door. Don't you?" "Maybe she's going to tuck him in." "Oh, I hope so." Shifting my eyes to Janey to see if she was ruffled by these little boys and their game, I caught a smile of bemusement moments before it bubbled into a cascade of laughter. She had great class, that Y. A. Janey. Instead of being ruffled, she didn't give a damn. She took my arm as we walked through this garland to my room and just before we entered she turned back to that stoned bunch of musicians and actors, gave them a suggestive wink, waved night-night, stepped in, and closed the door. In unspoken admiration, that band of gypsies stood in silent salute to a unique young woman who had just capped an outrageously great evening with a very classy finish.

Janey and I continued our backstage romance until months later when we were separated by her transfer to another of the national companies of *Anna Lucasta*. In her absence, I took a step backward by returning to the fold of my former mentors and running buddies, Duke Williams, Roy Glenn, and Maxwell Glanville, in

an attempt to replace her free spirit with their camaraderie, an exchange as impossible as swapping night
for day. Because, as I was shortly to discover, I had already shared all I could with them, they with me, and
one of us had to move on. It was only then that I understood that Janey too had to move on, leaving me where
I was. She was drawn like a magnet, not so much away
from me, but on to other experiences that were waiting
to fill out her life. More than once in a lifetime we ask
ourselves the big question: Do I settle here? Or do I go
on? If we elect to go on, it is almost never without a
pinch of regret for someone or something we leave behind. I hope that's the way it was with Janey in relation
to me. I know that's the way it was with me in relation
to my three mentors.

Among the people capturing my imagination at that
time was a young, brash, highly intelligent and determined man named Julian Mayfield, who came from
Washington, D.C., and who intended to make his mark
in theater and literature. He was quick, constantly reaching beyond some girl's skirt or a poker game, and while
he was a fun-seeker like the rest of us, it was also obvious that he had other things to do. I liked his mind.
Also about that time I met a tall, impressive-looking
black man, another accomplished girl chaser, by the
name of Omar Van Prince. Van was interested in acting,
but more than anything he was a wheeler-dealer. He
was always very well dressed, always had a little piece
of a car, and on a moment's notice he could turn a dollar
out of the most unlikely circumstances. A consummate
lover of games of chance—cards, poker, dice, any kind
of gambling. Rounding out this trio was William Marshall, the tallest man I had ever seen in those circles, a
young actor well versed in Shakespeare who was fittingly
blessed with a deep basso profundo voice, making him
the perfect candidate to play Othello. This highly educated student of the classics, together with Mayfield and
Prince, represented my next level of friends after the
Anna Lucasta crew, and we stayed together as a group
until I left for Hollywood. Mayfield's and Marshall's
willingness to make the heavy investment of time and
energy toward their self-improvement as artists and as
men impressed me so much that I was encouraged to
raise my sights several notches in an attempt to close
the gap between them and me. In time, this small circle

118

widened to include Bobby Slater, a good-humored sausage salesman who had no personal interest in the theater beyond a predilection for choosing theater-oriented people as his friends, and Leon Bibb, the golden-voiced actor/singer.

Along with these new friendships I developed a very special relationship with a woman named Alice Childress, an actress and a writer. I learned more from her than I did from any other person I knew during that period of my life—things about life that no one else ever took the time to explain. She opened me up to positive new ways of looking at myself and others, and she encouraged me to explore the history of black people (as opposed to "colored" people). She was also instrumental in my meeting and getting to know the remarkable Paul Robeson, and for that alone I shall always be grateful. Between Alice and me there was never the slightest trace of a romantic relationship—she was a friend in the purest sense—but alas, such a relationship with a female had its shortcomings, so whenever I felt the need to prowl (which was fairly often), I roamed the streets with Omar Van Prince, William Marshall, Bobby (the sausage salesman) Slater, and that determined young artist, Julian Mayfield, who was an integral part of the circumstances that took me to Hollywood.

8 Hollywood

IN 1949 word got around town that the Theatre Guild of America was about to produce a musical called *Lost in the Stars*. Most of the parts, except one, were for actors who could sing, that one exception being Absalom, the son of the central character. Turning up backstage where the auditions were being held, I discovered I couldn't get in because I didn't have an agent. Standing to one side watching other young actors being admitted under the auspices of various agents, I began to search my head for a solution, because one way or another I was determined to get in there.

At that moment a white man shepherding four or five young black actors came hurrying along the alley toward the stage door. Knowing he would have to wait a few minutes because of the backlog that had developed, I kept my eyes on him, and finally found a moment to approach him. "Excuse me, sir," I said, "you're an agent, aren't you?" "Yes, I am," he said, "and you're an actor, aren't you?" "Yes," I said. "And you want to get into the audition but you don't have an agent," he said. "Yes," I admitted. He looked at me silently, then tilted his head up and blew smoke toward the fire escape before asking, "What is your name?" "Sidney Poitier," I said. Again he fell silent, filled his lungs with smoke, and held it trapped for a second before expelling it once again in the direction of the fire escape. "You can come in with me. If anything materializes from it, you will of course let me handle it." I said, "Certainly." "My name is Bill Nichols," he said as we shook hands. "Tell me what you've done as an actor." I ran down my career activities for him, acutely aware that while my minimal credentials did allow me to call myself a professional actor, they were of such a piddling nature that Mr. Nichols would surely see that I didn't know very much and (God forbid) would reconsider the hastily made promise to take me in under his banner. Whipping out a notebook over which he poised an expensive-looking Waterman pen, this Mr. Nichols, with no discernible look of disappointment, said to me, "Would you repeat that for me? I'll keep a record of all the things you've done in my files—just in case. By the way, I knew I'd seen you somewhere before—up in Harlem in a one-act play called *Freight* and again on opening night of *Lysistrata*. You were pretty good." I beamed, and dove into a recapitulation of my fabulous credits. "I've been working in *Anna Lucasta* on the road. First as an understudy, then as Lester and Rudolph. I've also done some off-Broadway small plays here in New York, plus a couple of films, but they were for the Army—inconsequential films—training films for the Army." (One of them had been called *From Whom Cometh My Help*—a ten-minute religious film for which I was paid about a hundred bucks for a job that took three days to film.) In addition, I had a one-day job as an extra on a black film called *Sepia Cinderella*.

"William Nichols from the Jules Ziegler Agency, next," announced the assistant stage manager. Following behind Mr. Nichols and his other actors, I was challenged briefly at the door but was allowed to enter when Mr. Nichols said, "He is being represented at this audition by the Ziegler office." When my turn came to step on stage in the presence of the director of *Lost in the Stars*, my cool had melted into nervous perspiration on my forehead and a clammy wetness in the palms of my hands. Walking out on the naked stage, carrying a script I had been given just twenty minutes before, I found the drought condition in my mouth was worsening. The stage manager addressed the shadowy figures somewhere out there in the back of the theater: "This is Sidney Poitier, also represented by the Jules Ziegler Agency, here to read for the part of Absalom." No response from the shadows. With the stage manager reading the role of the father against my interpretation of the son Absalom, we began my audition. Instantly, as if some chemical change had come over my body, I detected an inexplicable control over the panic of nerves that had been engulfing me, a control that somehow was helping me to harness the energies springing from my stage fright, and even to make use of them in my reading. Without being commanded or conjured up by me in any way, this control simply appeared, out of nowhere, charging and infusing my audition with qualities not yet in my bank of skills. Where did it come from? How did it happen? Oh, dear Lord, I thought, if ever I can control that "control," *then* I will be an actor.

At the end of my audition, the voice of one of the shadowy figures somewhere out in the back of the theater said, "Thank you, Sidney, maybe we'll have you back to read for us again. We'll let you know." I said, "Thank you, sir," and left, thinking they were impressed at least a little bit, else why would they mention my coming back? They hadn't said that to any of the other actors in Bill Nichols's stable. Within three days I was called back for a second reading and I walked out on stage the second time with the same afflictions. When, out of nowhere, came old reliable "control" galloping to my rescue, making the second reading a definite improvement over the first and prompting one of the faceless figures out there somewhere in the darkened theater to say, "Thank you, Sidney. Now would you mind terribly if we asked you to come back a third time to read for us with a girl?" "No, sir, I wouldn't mind. I'd be happy to," I said. In fact, I read three times more with three different girls before the director said, "Mr. Poitier, we would like you to play this part. We'll be in touch with your agent." "Thank you, sir," I said.

Outside the theater, bursting with joy and excitement, I leaped into the air, landed on cloud 9 (or was it the crosstown bus?), floated over to the Jules Ziegler Agency, and rushed into the office of that Mr. Bill Nichols, and blurted out the good news. Triumphantly, Nichols marched me into the big office of the head honcho, Jules Ziegler himself. Who, after the proper introductions, said, "I will start negotiations immediately with the Theatre Guild for your salary. In the meantime, you go home and celebrate. We'll take care of it." The fatherly appearance of the short, stocky, partially bald Jules Ziegler was a fitting and reassuring contrast to the suave, Ivy League, laid-back, gray-flannel-suitism of the much younger Bill Nichols. I thanked them both and headed for home, stopping long enough to share the news with my friends Julian Mayfield and William Marshall, who themselves were hoping for parts in the same production. The odds on realizing those hopes were heavily in Mr. Marshall's favor, because of his musical talents, while Mr. Mayfield, a nonmusical actor, had been virtually knocked out of the box by the very news I had come to share with them. His hopes reduced to slim or none, Mayfield somehow managed to express enthusiasm over my good fortune through a sturdy handshake that followed a warm bear hug and a broad smile. "You son of a gun. That's great. Maybe I'll get to be your understudy," he said. "Hey, wouldn't that be something—the two of us in the same show—playing the same part." I said, "Yeah." "Let's hope it works out," said Mayfield, raising his right hand and crossing his fingers.

Walking from the subway to my rented room, I ran into another young black actor I knew named Thompson Brown, with whom I also shared the news. In addition to congratulations, I received the following information: "I hear Twentieth Century-Fox is looking for black actors for a movie they're going to do called *No Way Out*. I'm going to go down there and check on it. You want to go with me?" "Okay," I said. "When are you going?" "How about tomorrow?" I said, "You got it," and went on home, where I spent the rest of the day and most of the evening in sweet hypnotic daydreams about how fabulous I was going to be in the upcoming Broadway hit *Lost in the Stars*. Sweet and hypnotic enough, in fact, to produce hallucinations in which I even saw myself carrying a tune—singing a song in perfect pitch to the wild, riotous acclaim of a tuxedo-clad first-night audience. (Most of whom, of course, will be white—again.)

Walking into the reception room at Twentieth Century-Fox, Thompson Brown and I found it filled with young black actors and their agents hoping to get a screen test for the new picture. The scuttlebutt indicated that Fox was looking to fill six or seven parts with black people. Men and women, young and old. Until that moment I was not really interested in seeking a screen test because I already *had* a job, but the news of so many parts available initiated a conversation in my mind between me and myself. "You should try for this screen test too," was the way I opened the exchange, "not so much because you want to get a job, but look what an opportunity it would be for testing your ability to impress a potential employer with your reading." Said I convincingly to myself. Myself responded with: "Yeah—what the hell—why shouldn't I take a shot at that?" Thompson Brown and I both got appointments to come back and see the casting director, a Mr. Joe Pincus, who would be selecing the candidates for actual screen testing. Within a week we both would return to sit and answer questions under his searching eyes, and Mr. Pincus kept us both alive in the screen test race by placing us among those he had chosen to present to the film's director, Mr. Joseph L. Mankiewicz. A short preliminary screen test was made of each of the candidates and shipped to California for Mankiewicz's consideration before he came to New York for the definitive screen tests. And we, the competing hopefuls, waited day after anxious day through a torturous week that moved slower than refrigerated molasses for the arrival of the final arbiter—the maker or breaker of other men's dreams. But with the arrival of the soft-spoken Mankiewicz came a swift and merciless reduction in the number of candidates, leaving no more than six of us to square off in the

123

final free-for-all. My friend Thompson Brown, having not survived the cut, went off to sharpen his tools and await the coming of another chance in the daily battle against impossible odds.

A few days later, on a summer morning in 1949, the six remaining combatants assembled at the Fox studios, where one by one we faced the camera under the direction of Joe Mankiewicz. Seconds before my turn came I debated with myself the wisdom of telling him I already had a job, but decided not to until I saw what happened with the test. My moment came. I stepped in front of the camera. Someone called for quiet, then waited before saying, "Roll 'em."

The hum of the activated camera was all I could hear in the deathly silence, until Mr. Mankiewicz's directorial instructions drowned it out. He asked me to reach for character nuances that were not immediately evident in the scene as written, but were nevertheless essential to the realization of the character as a whole person. Damn, I thought, this guy sure is smart. After working through three takes under three different sets of directions, I heard Mr. Mankiewicz say, "Move in for a close-up while I have a word with the actor." Gesturing to the chair next to him, he invited me to be seated and said, "Tell me about yourself." I said, "Well, there's not much to tell. I'm from the Bahamas"—and I told him my history very quickly. He said, "Where have you worked before as an actor?" I said, "I've done *Lysistrata, Anna Lucasta*, and a few plays around town." He said, "Well, what would happen if I told you I want you to play this part?" I want to tell you that it was strange. Strange in that it was not unexpected. I was not flabbergasted—I just thought that my inexplicable luck was holding firm for reasons best known to God—toward ends only He could fully understand. I said, "I would love to play it if you're offering it to me, but—" He interrupted with, "Yes, I am offering it to you. I'd like you to play this part." I said, "I'd love to play the part, but I can't." He said, "Oooh!" "No, sir," I said, "I can't play the part—I have a part." He said, "Doing what?" I said, "I'm in *Lost in the Stars*. I've already been accepted to play the part of Absalom, it goes into rehearsal soon, and that's what I have to do. I came here because I wanted to try —I wanted to see—I want to work in films—but if you're going to go with your film very soon, I've al-

124

ready made a commitment." He said, "Well, can you get out of it?" I said, "I don't think so." He said, "Why don't you talk to your agent?"

Well, just as I'm not too surprised I got the part, he's not too surprised to hear I already have a part. Because little did I know it at the time, but now I'm dealing with Hollywood, and what Hollywood wants—Hollywood gets. He said, "Talk with your agent. Tell him I want you to play this part and let him talk to me about it." Dashing over to the agency, I said to Mr. Ziegler, "They want me to play the part at Twentieth Century-Fox in *No Way Out.*" He said, "What is that?" I said, "It's a new movie and Joe Mankiewicz is in town testing for it, and he tested six guys today and he wants me to play it." He says, "But you can't play it." I say, "I know I can't play it, but.he wants you to call him." He said, "All right, I'll call him."

He calls and says, "I'm sorry, Mr. Mankiewicz, but we already gave our word to the Theatre Guild." Mr. Mankiewicz says, "Well, did you work out the salary scale yet?" Jules says, "No, but I'm about to do that right now." Mr. Mankiewicz says, "Well, why don't you do that and see what their situation is and if you have any problems—if anything can be worked out, I certainly would appreciate it."

Now if Jules Ziegler is anything, he is sharp. He knows that I'm probably going to be offered a hell of a lot more money from Twentieth Century-Fox than I am at the Theatre Guild. He gets on the phone and calls Victor Samrock, who is the negotiator for the Theatre Guild. He says, "Victor, this is Jules Ziegler. I'm sitting in my office here with Sidney Poitier, the youngster you want to play Absalom in *Lost in the Stars,* and I want to tell you he just got an offer from Hollywood, and we want to work out the salary scale so that we will have no misunderstanding between us. You know what I mean? So that he doesn't lose out on one job and not have one in his hand." Victor says, "Bullshit, Jules—don't start that crap with me. If he's got a job in Hollywood, let him take it." Jules says, "I'm not kidding—the kid has got a job in Hollywood." Victor says, "Look, I've got no time for this, what kind of job in Hollywood, for Christ's sake? You're trying to push up the price on this kid. I'll tell you what we're going to pay him—we're going to pay him seventy-five dollars a week—take it or leave it." Jules says, "Now, Victor, you know me. I've been doing business with you for a long time." Victor says, "Yes, I know you, that's why I'm telling you take the seventy-five bucks or forget it." Jules says, "I want you to know that when this thing comes back at you—I want you to know that I've given you ample opportunity. The boy has a part in a Hollywood movie and if you are going to offer him seventy-five dollars a week in face of what he's being offered, I'm going to have to turn you down. Later, I want you to remember you had the opportunity to come up with meaningful negotiations." At which point Victor says, "Jules, go blow it out of your ass—don't give me this bullshit. The kid's got a picture? Let him go do the picture in Hollywood. He doesn't do the picture in Hollywood, you come back and we'll take him for the seventy-five bucks—is that clear?" They hang up their phones.

I didn't know anything about negotiating strategy and approaches and stuff, so it was years later before I realized that Ziegler had no intention of letting me do the play for Samrock, since I could get at least $750 a week for doing the movie. And he was clever enough to know that Samrock would never believe I had a movie to do, and probably wouldn't pick up the phone to check. Jules was taking a safe gamble when he said, "Please don't do this, Victor, we want to do the play." He knew that Samrock would suppose he was trying a too often used and essentially dishonest ploy to get him to go up to $100 or $110 a week. After Jules hung up the phone I must say I saw a look on his face that should have told me then that this was all a program, clearly designed to outwit a clever adversary. He picked up the phone again, dialed Joseph Mankiewicz, and said, "You've got us." And Jules Ziegler sold me to Hollywood for $750 a week— ten times what the play offered. About a week later Samrock called Ziegler and asked, "What about this boy—have you made up your mind yet?" Jules said, "Oh, he's gone to Hollywood." Samrock hit the ceiling. "You can't do that to me," he screamed. "We're depending on him to do the play . . ." and so on and so on, but of course it was too late. But guess who played Absalom in *Lost in the Stars*? My very dear friend Julian Mayfield.

I went off to Hollywood for the first time on a train called the Twentieth Century Limited. My posh accommodations on that luxury streamliner were, to say the least, impressively different from the cold, damp, dark freight trains I had once used as getaway vehicles in those repeated attempts to put Miami (that strange place) behind me. The long ride across America was made even more pleasant by the fact that this time I knew where I was going, and I was looking forward to getting there. Boy, this America is some big place, I remember thinking as countryside, mountains, and farmlands seemed to stretch out forever, day after day.

By the time we pulled into the station in downtown Los Angeles, I was beside myself with excitement. The anticipation was almost unbearable. I was met by a representative from Twentieth Century-Fox who took me to an apartment hotel in Westwood. The California sky was pure blue, the streets were clean, the humidity was low, and everybody seemed to be on vacation. All of which prompted me to think to myself: Hey, this place is all right, boy. After I checked in, it didn't take much exploring to discover that I was in an all-white hotel—in an all-white neighborhood—in an all-white part of town. And, as I expected, I soon found that living exclusively among white people with no other blacks around was like being a visitor in a foreign culture, on the alert and at the ready twenty-four hours a day. In pondering this matter, I tried to isolate the "whys" and found that they were legion—some valid, some not. But matters of more immediate concern forced my attention away from the white folks and their ways. I had to make the most of what was essentially a rare and important opportunity. Moreover, I had no doubt that in time my homing instincts would locate the places where the black folks were to be found.

On my first day at Twentieth Century-Fox, I was amazed by the number of in-person, real, live movie stars I saw almost everywhere I turned. When I first lunched in the commissary there, my head might as well have been on a swivel, the way I gaped and gawked and cased the dining room picking out familiar faces. That same day Darryl Zanuck was pointed out to me as he stood outside his office looking up at the sun through very dark glasses, wearing a horseman's habit with high boots and slapping himself on the side of his leg with a riding crop, while three assistants stood a few feet away, waiting in silent respect for the communion with nature to end. If the work force at Twentieth Century-Fox was not completely white, the exception was only an occasional kitchen worker or janitor, but the impact of this lockout was obscured by the fact that the studio had hired so many black actors and extras for the eight weeks we would be shooting the picture. Twentieth Century-Fox was not untypical of Hollywood studios in its almost complete exclusion of minority workers on all levels.

My part in the film was the biggest and most important acting job I had been offered to date. In spite of having no acting technique to speak of, I researched that part as thoroughly as I possibly could. I spent many evenings at the Los Angeles General Hospital observing young interns and making notes on their behavior in the emergency room. This was my first picture, mind you, and I was delighted to find that I was at ease in front of the camera. There was some nervousness, but nothing resembling the massive attacks I had been subject to when I stepped on a theater stage; in a movie set, on a sound stage, I seemed to be more at home.

My greatest anxiety came from the fact that I was only twenty-two years old, and I had told Joe Mankiewicz and the people in New York that I was twenty-seven. Because I knew they were looking for someone to play a young doctor interning in a county hospital, I figured he had to be at least twenty-seven, so I lied, and now I was afraid that if they found out, they'd fire me. That was my big worry. That is until Joe Mankiewicz allowed me to see some rushes one evening and I saw myself for the first time up on the big screen. "Oh, my Lord, look at that," was my first panic-stricken reaction. "What a long head he's got. Wow, that funny-looking, old, nappy-headed fellow doesn't look like an actor. Hell, he doesn't even look like the Sidney I know." I left the projection room with doubts chipping away at whatever fantasies I had about being motion picture material. Of course, there was the outside chance that others wouldn't see me as I saw myself.

The conscientious and very capable actor Richard Widmark, who was then at the summit of his popularity garnered from playing mostly rotten, vicious characters, was the most pleasant and refreshing surprise in my initial exposure to the Hollywood scene. The reality of Widmark was a thousand miles from the characters he played. That shy, gentle, very private person helped me to learn the ropes of film-making and was among the first in Hollywood, along with his lovely wife Jean, to open his home to me socially. Playing scenes day after day with professionals like Widmark, Ossie Davis, Linda Darnell, Ruby Dee, and many others taught me very quickly how to conduct myself like a professional. The thought of being worthy of their artistic company filled me with pride. Each and every one of them at some time in the production of that film urged, encouraged, or inspired me to stretch toward goals outside my previous reach, thereby ensuring my growth as a professional actor. I worked extra hard in between scenes to make sure that when Mr. Mankiewicz called me I was there with all my lines committed to memory, knowing exactly what I had to do, and doing it, because, most of all, I wanted to impress him with my professionalism. In the ninth week of filming, he came over to me and said, "What are you going to do when this is over?" I said, "Oh, I'll go back to New York and try to find another job." He said, "I tell you what I want you to do. I have a friend of mine who's going to be making a film in Africa. I want you to go and see him. Maybe he'll have something for you. His name is Zoltán Korda." He made me promise I would go and see this gentleman as soon as I returned to New York, but I had no idea that unbeknownst to me, he would then get on the phone to this man, recommending that he see me.

With my contractual obligations to Twentieth Century-Fox fulfilled, I boarded a plane for New York for my first cross-country flight. It turned out to be the roughest, scariest trip I have ever had in the air. Sitting next to John Garfield, a man I have always admired, I was frightened to death. That old prop plane was bouncing and tumbling around something fierce in what seemed to be an interminable stretch of bad weather. A very cool Garfield was lying back in his seat, undisturbed by the storm. He saw that I was scared out of my wits and leaned over with a reassuring comment: "Everything will be all right." I said, "You're John Garfield." He said, "Yes," and began talking to me, telling me a story about Joe Louis. He said, "You know I used to be nervous on planes myself, but I'm not nervous anymore because once I rode on a plane with Joe Louis. It was a very bad storm —worse than this. I struck up a conversation with Joe Louis because I was scared, helpless, and just had to talk with someone who wasn't petrified the way I was. Seeing how wrecked I was, Joe Louis said to me, 'Take out your handkerchief, put it over your face, lay back, and just don't think about anything. Think about absolutely nothing. Don't let one thought come into your mind, and everything is going to be all right.' I did it," John Garfield continued. "I spread my handkerchief over my face and lay back. Joe Louis spread *his* handkerchief out over *his* face and lay back. We didn't think about a thing, and in half an hour the storm was over and everything was fine. Later on, Joe Louis said, 'It doesn't matter what happens—you can't do anything about it anyway.' I was never afraid on a plane again. There are fears you can do something about, Sidney, and there are fears you can't do anything about, so with the latter, give yourself up to whatever is going to happen and you'll be okay." Well, I reached for my handkerchief—to find that I ain't got no handkerchief. I said to myself: That's all right for you and Joe Louis, but this is my first trip on an airplane and I'm gonna need a hell of a lot more than a handkerchief to spread over my face. So Garfield went under his handkerchief and switched off his mind while I spread the dinner napkin over my face and then sat fidgeting and sweating under it, too scared even to close my eyes, much less tamper with the shutoff switch in my mind, until we touched down safely in New York.

After dropping my luggage off at home, I rush to a local bank, where I open my first savings account with the three thousand dollars I've netted from my work on the picture. Then I proceed downtown to look up this Zoltán Korda fellow Mr. Mankiewicz has asked me to see. As I walk into the reception area of Korda's office, located in the upper reaches of the Empire State Building, a white man about fifty years old wearing a big fedora hat and a cape comes out of the inner office sniffing something into his nose from between his forefinger and thumb. He says to his secretary, "Well, I'm off now. Call me tomorrow about five o'clock London time. Meanwhile if anything important comes up you can leave word at my brother's house." As he starts to leave, I say, "I'm supposed to see Mr. Korda. Mr. Mankiewicz told me to come and see him." He stops halfway through the outer door, turns around, and says, "You're the boy Joe Mankiewicz told me about." I say, "Yes, sir." He says, "I see—well, I'm on my way to London and I don't have time to talk to you." He looks me up and down as if

130

measuring me for a suit, then adds, "Would you like to come to London?" I say, "Bu—uu—uuu—t." He says, "Yes, if you come to London I would like to do a screen test on you. Would you like to do a screen test for me?" I say, "Yes, sir!" He says, "All right—you'll come to London. When can you come? Next week?" I say, "Yes, sir." He says, "Okay. I'll see you next week," and he slams the door. Here I am with the secretary—she doesn't know me and I don't know her. I say, "What do I do?" She says, "You go to London next week—give me your name and address. You'll need a passport. Do you have a passport?" I say, "No, I don't have a passport." She says, "Do you know how to get a passport?" I say, "No, I don't." She says, "Well, I'll give you the address of the passport place and you go down there and make an application—you'll tell them that you need it right away because you'll be leaving for London within a week, and ask if they'll please put a rush on it. Once you've got it, let me know immediately so I can make the necessary arrangements for you to fly to London." I was in there two or three minutes, got no more than a passing glance at a strange man, and out of nowhere, I'm invited to London.

It was astonishing. I wondered who was that crazy-looking, cape-wearing, snuff-sniffing guy with the funny accent who looked as if he needed a shave. Zoltán Korda was his name—but what was a Zoltán Korda? If, I thought, he in fact turns out to be the genuine gift horse the situation suggests he might be, I could wind up being sorry if I tried looking into his mouth by asking too many questions, especially of his secretary. With my feet barely touching the ground, I made my way to the passport office and made my application. The passport came through within a few days, the necessary travel arrangements were completed a few days after that, and a week to the day after my meeting Zoltán Korda, I was on a Pan Am Clipper in the first-class section with a bed assigned, heading for London. Can you imagine me with a bed all to myself on a transatlantic airplane going to Europe—Lord, will wonders never cease? That evening somewhere over the Atlantic, after I had stuffed myself with food and drink, the steward came to me and said, "Your bed has been turned down, sir. You may retire at your leisure." I "retired" immediately, even though I was far too excited to sleep, because I wanted to see what the sleeping arrangements were behind that curtain, plus I was eager to have the experience of putting on my pajamas, and going to bed in a plane 25,000 feet up in the air. They were upper and lower berth beds, similar to those found in the sleeping cars of trains. I lay awake in my upper berth for hours wondering what London would be like. Dear old England! The Britannia that ruled the waves. The British who never, never, never will be slaves. At that point in my life, my political ignorance allowed no more than a vague awareness of colonialism and its impact on the lives of black people throughout the world, so I was not yet at the point of thinking that England was full of crap. I was still seeing her through the eyes of a naïve member of the Commonwealth.

9 Cry, the Beloved Country

SOMEONE FROM Zoltán Korda's office met me at the airport, checked me into a hotel, then took me to see that snuff-sniffing, cape-wearing stranger, who said, "Welcome to London, Mr. Poitier. Tomorrow morning we're going to test you." Giving me some pages from a script, he continued, "This scene is self-explanatory. I want you to study the part of the Reverend Msimangu, the twenty-five-year-old priest, and I'd be happy if you would come tomorrow ready to try it with an African accent. Do you think you can?" "I'll try, sir," I said. Mr. Korda's assistant dropped me back at the hotel, reminded me to be ready for an early start the next morning, then drove off, disappearing in the London traffic. The moment he was out of sight, I set out on foot through the streets of London, frantically searching for an African from whom I could pick up the rhythm of an authentic African accent. The only black people I encountered for the first hour were from the West Indies or the United States. Not one African showed his face. But I persevered. I trudged through the unfamiliar streets of this great big fantastic city with one eye out for this African person and the other gawking at the sights. It was weirdly fascinating to hear

English spoken by nearly everyone with such crisp pronunciation, such heavy emphasis on preciseness. Midway in my second hour I came upon an African chap with whom I shot the breeze for the better part of an afternoon, picking up in the process the rhythmic pattern of the English language as it flowed from the lips of a Kenyan whose principal languages were Kikuyu and Swahili. By the time we took leave of each other in Trafalgar Square, an authentic African accent was locked in the chambers of my memory.

With my mission accomplished, I returned to the hotel, ate dinner, studied my script, and went to sleep. The next morning at a London studio I made a screen test under the direction of Zoltán Korda for the movie to be called *Cry, the Beloved Country.* Halfway through the second take, he said, "That's enough—that's enough—you want this part?" I said, "Yes, sir." He said, "You got it. Okay, I won't need you for some months, so here's what I want you to do. Go back to New York, get on with your life, and we'll let you know when we want you to go to work." I said, "Thank you." I'm really kind of excited, because this means going to Africa and I'd like to go to Africa. Little did I know it would be South Africa (and in any case, I had no idea what South Africa was about). "Have you ever been to Paris?" Mr. Korda then asked. I said, "No," and he said, "Would you like to go to Paris?" I said, "Yes, sir." He said, "Good. I'll have them reroute you through Paris and you'll go from there to New York."

Paris was the city of cities. I loved it, even though I couldn't understand a word of French. The dozens of risqué tales I had heard flooded my mind with images of a kind that left me no alternative but to hit the boulevards in search of that naughtiness that lies at the heart of this city's worldwide reputation for night life. As soon as night officially fell, I made my way as fast as I could to the hunting grounds, where I purposefully roamed the terrain for the legendary Parisian experiences. And I found them in profusion when I wandered down a side street with an unusual number of transient hotels. This short, narrow street appeared to be the homing ground from where the "ladies of the evening" sallied forth to service the big tourist hotels and the busy thoroughfares in the Quarter. Upon entering the street I was immediately approached by a young woman who threw her arms around me and said, "Looking for a good time?" I said, "Yes." She said,

"You wanna come with me?" Well, I'm king of the walk now, boy, I said to myself. I've got a pocketful of money and I'm not going to grab up the first one I see. Besides, she was a little fat—a little tough to take, period. So I extricated myself from her grasp and moved on down the line, where there were more and more girls. After making a deal with a beautiful young lady who spoke some English, I followed her upstairs in one of the tiny hotels. In preliminary conversation she told me she had two children. It was my first time in that kind of situation. I like to talk to people, try to get to know them, so I encouraged her to talk about herself—her family, her country, and its customs. The residual hardships from the war had extracted from this young woman a brutally heavy price in exchange for an uncertain, elementary survival. She had no blame for her frail young husband, who had collapsed under the strain of being a husband and father in postwar France. He had split, leaving an apology on a slip of paper, yet she wished him well and hoped that life was better for him wherever he was.

This sociological excursion into her life turned me off as far as jumping on her was concerned, but it turned me on to finding out more about her because it seemed fascinating to me that a woman with two children would be out there hustling (to show how immature I was). While talking about her children and showing me pictures of them, she said, "I have to support them somehow since I don't have a husband to support me." There was no self-pity in the statement—that was the way things were and that was what she had to do. I found that refreshing. We chatted about the early days in both our lives. A dreamy haze filled her eyes as I told her about the Bahamas—the lovely beaches and fantastic weather. After laughing and talking for the better part of an hour, I gave her some money, she thanked me for it, and I left. In no time I'm back on the street, looking for somebody who ain't married—who ain't got no kids—and who ain't so nice. But what was still available was not to my taste, so I didn't connect that night.

The next morning I decided to spend the day trying to make some black contacts. The bilingual people at the hotel desk told me there was no specific area in Paris with large numbers of blacks. That impressed me. They said, "Blacks live pretty much all over the city because there is a diplomatic corps in Paris, there are students in

134

Paris, working people in Paris, musicians in Paris . . . there is no special place." With no particular area to go to, I just roamed around the city that day. I made my way to the Champs-Élysées and bounced in and out of a lot of movies. I was fascinated by them—the French language films with no English subtitles, or English movies dubbed into French, or American films dubbed into French. And when evening came, I hit the trail. This time I came up with somebody who spoke no English, and since I spoke no French we made a lot of gestures that turned out to be all the language necessary. We got along very, very well and that was the end of that.

Back in New York, where friends and old habits were waiting, I gradually picked up the rhythm of familiar routines. But wait a second. Something somewhere is out of tune. What is that undefinable pressure I sense, and why am I perceiving it more often than not as an urgent reminder of unfinished business? Anxiety? Certainly. But over what? Here I am with time on my hands and money in the bank—times have never been better—but still some question needs to be addressed, or why would it be ramming so consistently at the door of my consciousness? Whatever that pressuring question was, I realized it no longer could be ignored. But how do you give attention to something you cannot articulate? Something tearing itself upward from a region you aren't familiar with? On the other hand, I could be wrong. I thought, maybe I'm simply having difficulty adjusting to this sudden life of leisure. After all, I've never been idle before without the terrifying presence of hunger and defeat walking in my shadow. They say the psychology of poverty works in peculiar ways, so maybe my being a few dollars ahead in the game of life has unsettled me. Sure —that's more than likely what it is—but I'll adjust, give me a little time. After all, it ain't normal to feel guilty because you're a few dollars ahead of—guilty—guilty— guilty! Oh, my God! There she is. I'll be damned. For eight years my folks don't know where I am—they don't know whether I'm alive or dead. That powerful, tenaciously clung-to myth that all American streets are paved with gold can produce guilt of unmanageable proportions, in certain poor people who arrive on these shores to find that it isn't possible to scoop up boxes of that precious metal or its equivalent in dollars and send them back to those at home awaiting relief. Because I had very little to send during those years, the resulting guilt was so punishing I had elected to dissociate myself from the responsibility. I just simply cut it away. The image of my mother opening letters from me only to find there was nothing inside haunted me. Vividly I could see that dear woman's eyes filling with tears and disappointment and not wanting to face all that in myself, I just never kept in touch. In the beginning, for the first few months, I did, but later I just didn't.

Now I want to see my mother, if she is still alive. I want to see everybody, if they are still there. Now that I finally have enough money to buy a ticket, I must go home to Nassau and see my folks. That is what has been distressing me so.

I flew to Miami to change planes for the flight to Nassau, and between planes I thought of calling my brother Cyril and my Uncle Joe, but I resisted the urge, preferring my first contact to be with the family in Nassau, whoever is still there. It would also be true to say that I wasn't yet ready to contact the Miami of those earlier years. So after a quiet wait in the Miami airport, I boarded a flight for home.

I was a little baby of fifteen when I left on a boat, but now I am a man pushing twenty-three when I get off the plane at Nassau airport—and nobody knows me. I remember the airport as I walk into the terminal that evening because I had worked there with a pneumatic drill when I was fourteen years old. I look around and recall my childhood running through the swamps and bathing in the ponds that have since been filled in and pounded into runways. Inside, as I collect my luggage, I see faces I knew when I was a kid. I smile at them but they don't recognize me! I'm now a big man—6 feet 2 inches tall, weighing 179 pounds—and their last contact was with a little boy. I hire a taxi—the driver's face is familiar—and I tell him where to take me, but he too doesn't know who I am. Arriving in front of my father's house, I notice it hasn't changed a bit, except that the weather-beaten, two-room wooden structure looks considerably smaller than I've been remembering it. For a full minute, I remain motionless in the moonlight looking at my father's house and wondering how all the members of our family could have lived in such a tiny place. Then as I walk toward the house on that Saturday evening, I pass several people who either live in the other little houses in the yard or in the immediate vicinity. They don't know or much care who the tall stranger with a suitcase is; a casual, barely audible, mostly reflex "Good evening" comes my way as they pass me by.

Before I left, my parents lived in one room and the rest of us lived in the other, the toilet was an outhouse, and our source of light after the sun went down was the glow from a kerosene lamp. Nothing has changed, I think, as I'm drawn to the faint shimmering of the familiar light escaping from a window on my parents' side of the house, the window held open by a four-foot stick, one end jammed against the sill, the other end holding the window hoisted skyward. My heartbeat quickens at the sound of familiar voices reaching my ear after so many long years. A few inches from the window I hesitate and take several deep breaths in an attempt to arrest the pounding of my heart, but it doesn't help. The knowledge that I'm only seconds away from laying eyes on my parents after eight years is creating an unbearable mixture of tension and excitement in me. I step in front of the window and a bolt of adrenalin shoots through my system. There they are—my mother and father. I look at those two people talking to each other as they have always been able to talk to each other—my father can talk to anyone, but my mother can talk only to my father. They're talking in a very low, calm way, just exchanging ideas and energies back and forth. They don't see me. My father, who is sixty-seven, is wearing the same kind of work clothes he always wore. My mother is wearing an old print dress I'm sure I've seen before. I can't tell if they've aged beyond their years, because the kerosene lamp isn't that sharp, but I notice that they've partitioned their room into two sections—one for sleeping, one for eating! Now they are sitting at a table in the new dining area, just talking, the supper dishes already cleared away. The Poitier family has been reduced to these two people in their twilight years, alone with each other on a Saturday night, their children all gone—some into marriage, others off into worlds where Evelyn and Reginald cannot follow. And the youngest of them all—the baby of the bunch—has simply disappeared somewhere in America nearly eight years ago.

I walk around to the back door. It's open. I step inside, put down my suitcase, and just stand there looking at them. Seconds tick by before they become aware of my presence. My mother looks at me—blank. My father looks at me—blank. Then my mother looks at my father —blank—then he looks at her and my mother says to him, "Who's that, Reggie?" My father says with a smile on his face—but it's a smile of ignorance—"I don't know." However, his smile tells us he thinks it's someone he *should* know. As my mother continues to stare at me in the imperfect light of the kerosene lamp, I can see a thought come to her mind. She says, "Kermit?" I don't say anything. Now, Kermit is my older brother Cyril's son. He would be a couple of years younger than me and she hasn't seen him since he was small, and later it turns out that my brother has said to them in a letter that maybe he would be sending Kermit out to visit them soon. My mother smiles a quaint little smile while she's trying to figure out who this stranger is. My father, also smiling, his brow knotted with the question, looks to my mother for a clue and, never having taken her eyes off me, it suddenly strikes her like a bolt out of heaven—and that woman leaps out of her seat and starts to scream—such a scream I can't tell you what was in it. It's a scream so penetrating, so agonized, so anguished, so joyful, so filled with relief. She closes her eyes and her hands go to her head and she just screams, screams, screams. My father is looking on and he's beginning to get caught up in the excitement, but he still doesn't know. My mother leaps from where she stood—a good six feet across the room, one leap—and she's on top of me. Her arms fly around my neck and she starts to put some words to her screams —"Oh, my God—my Sidney, my Sidney, my Sidney." Then she breaks down. At that point my father jumps up and all he can do is laugh nervously and say, "Sidney? Sidney? Sidney? That you, Sidney?" My mother is sobbing convulsively and patting my shoulder, patting my shoulder. My father says, "Is that you, boy?—Sidney." I say, "Yes, it's me." Well, in no time they are all over me, exploring my face with their hands, hugging me, squeezing my hands as if their eyes and ears aren't to be trusted, until what they can see and hear is validated by the sense of touch. My father's joy is naturally tempered by his concern for my mother, who has never in her life been in this kind of emotional state. He grabs hold of her because he can see from her trembling and bubbling at the mouth that she's close to coming apart. Through her tears, my mother says something that I will carry to my grave. She says, "God, thank you for my boy. Oh, son, you don't know—I've prayed to God to give me a sign. Send me a sign to tell me if my boy is alive or dead. I asked God for that sign for seven years to tell me—just tell me if my boy is dead, then I won't worry about him anymore."

There I stood, a rotten, inconsiderate, ungrateful shit of a son who hadn't written to his mother in all those years. There I stood, fresh from cavorting in Parisian whorehouses—jumping on unfortunate women—while here was my poor mother waiting for a sign.

Well, we sat down and my father held my mother and tried to keep her from going to pieces. We talked. He tried to find out where I was living and what I had been doing—punctuating every third question with, "You should have written." They were just overwhelmed by the whole experience. After my mother began to pull herself together she did what mothers do. She went over to the leftovers, dished up a plateful, put it in front of me, and I ate it. As we talked and talked I tried to tell them everything that had happened to me. I started to tell them about the movie I had just finished, but there was no comprehension of that, they didn't know what actors did. I tried to tell them what an actor was, but my mother had never been to a movie. They simply couldn't see what kind of meaningful work one could do in front of a camera, or for that matter on a stage, where hundreds of people just sit and stare at you. But the polite bewilderment that greeted the information about my being an actor in theater and films gave way to enthusiasm when they learned that I had just come from London and Paris and would shortly be off to Africa. That bit of news brought a special shine to my mother's eyes, as if travel was much more in keeping with a mother's private expectations. After all, thought Evelyn, if there is still time for him to walk with kings, he must first travel to the places where kings are, even if he has to do silly things in front of the camera or on the stage with people staring at him to get there.

Yes, it was an extraordinary evening. I felt as if nerve ends, joints, muscles, practically every part of my body was experiencing a release, a relaxation, the likes of which I had never known in my life. I began to let go all of the tensions, the desperations, the fears, the anxieties, the insecurities leading all the way back to my letter to the President. Leading all the way back to the cold and terrifying days when I walked around New York with too little clothing to protect my body from the ten-degree weather. Back to all the loneliness and to the painful realization that I was, to all intents and purposes, in the world by myself, because I was so far away from the people who loved me, people who couldn't have helped me anyway—they didn't have the funds. My mind went back across eight years—across the time when I was arrested for vagrancy, across the time I was shot during the riot, across the time the policeman held a gun to my head in Florida. It ran across all the times in the Army when I did those terrible things and never knew why. The whole eight years replayed themselves, and at last I felt relief.

Evelyn Poitier, still unsteady, lay securely in my father's arms. The fragile, premature birth of her last boy, with all its attendant hopes and fears, flooded her mind, along with the collaborative fifteen years of effort among herself, her husband, and God Almighty, that somehow managed the survival of that child to the threshold of manhood. She remembered with absolute clarity the shirt he wore that morning—the one with the imitation pearl buttons that she helped him to fasten before she looked deeply into his eyes for such a long time without saying a word—before she touched his face, kissed him goodby, and sent him off to America. Out into a world she knew almost nothing about. Then came those painful years of silence that ravaged her confidence in a mother's intuition. Her once passionately held belief that I would be all right had been chipped away year after year by my persistent silence. Until that day when the strain of worry was beyond her endurance and she asked God to verify —to send a sign. Just one.

When her reflections had traveled full circle through her mind, enabling her to reconcile all those images from the past to the man who presently sat before her, very, very different from her little boy in his pearl button shirt, she arose from my father's arms plainly in control of her emotions once again and stood with arms akimbo looking down at me. Old habits die hard, I thought, and correctly predicted her next move. As she circled the tiny room marshaling her thoughts, a wave of apprehension swept over me and it was now my turn to reflect. A circling Evelyn Poitier, with hands on her hips, always spelled trouble when I was a boy. It was her way of revving up. Reaching way back across the years for a response, I said to myself: If she starts breathing deeply, I'm gonna have to get the hell out of here. We only played out those old roles for a few moments—but it was long enough for each of us to be in touch with a fundamental part of our mother-son relationship. And then I began to relax with the knowledge that we were both in a different place now, and I was put completely at ease when Evelyn's circling produced no more than some gentle questions about my odyssey.

Late in the evening, several hours past their bedtime, we called it a night. I went to a hotel because, you see, I can't go home again in certain ways. I prefer not to use the outhouse with its brown paper bag or green leaves instead of toilet paper. I don't want to walk to the corner and carry a bucket of water a quarter of a mile to have a washup. I don't want to have to build a fire to heat that water before I can use it to take a bath. I want to flip a switch or turn a faucet. So although I have been able to return to my father's house, in certain ways I have not been able to come back home.

At the hotel, I began getting calls, as word spread to the rest of the family. The next day my brothers and sisters converged on the hotel for a joyful reunion; we all filled in the missing years for one another. At first, they came down hard on me for not writing, but in time they understood. They forgave me, and I promised them I would never do that again. I gave my father most of the three thousand dollars, keeping just enough to see me through until it was time to go to Africa.

Back in New York, feeling good again, I met a girl in a fast-food restaurant on 155th Street and St. Nicholas Avenue. The luncheonette was owned by a man named Wilfred Weekes, and he had four daughters who worked alternate shifts as waitresses. They were the prettiest girls I had ever seen—especially two of them, Winifred and Dolores. My first time in the restaurant I took notice of Dolores while she was taking my order. She wore no makeup—her skin was newborn baby-smooth—and she was too pretty not to know it, and too smart to let you know she knew it. Clear, searching eyes and dark brown curling hair in combination with a sprinkling of walnut freckles gave her already distinguished face the appearance of being constantly alive, not to mention a sensual

141

innocence that came flashing your way every time she smiled. While her father, the short-order cook, prepared my breakfast of bacon, eggs, and orange juice, I struck up a conversation with this angel of the luncheonette, inquiring into her working hours with the full intention of regulating my eating habits to her shift. But because of school and family requirements, her shifts were frustratingly unreliable, resulting in my becoming acquainted with all four daughters within a week of eating three meals a day in their father's lunch room. Muriel, the oldest, was attractive. Dolores was beautiful. Winifred was a show-stopper. And Joy, the youngest, still in her early teens, was well on her way to upholding the family tradition. Although my eyes were on Dolores, my first date was with Winifred—I took her to see *Death of a Salesman*. While Dolores and I were about the same age, Winifred the show-stopper was about five years younger, and involved with a guy by the name of Norman Skinner, who played basketball for N.Y.U. She loved him to death, he loved her, and they looked as if they were bound for glory. She went out with me simply to raise her basketball player's temperature and at the same time see the most popular show on Broadway. I didn't mind being used by Winnie to "zing" her basketball player; my eyes were still on Dolores, and dating Winnie kept me within striking distance. Besides, the teenage Winifred, who wore her first pair of high-heeled shoes that night and who wasn't too steady on them, as I remember, was too young for an old roustabout like me.

Finally, after weeks of putting my best foot forward, I got the angelic Dolores to agree to a date. We spent an exhilarating evening out on the town during which I found her captivating beyond my expectations. She was a student at Hunter College, studying to be a psychiatric social worker. Her mother and father worked very hard in the luncheonette, putting in hours you would not believe in their efforts to educate six children (in addition to four daughters, they had two sons). Wilfred and Nettie Weekes were strict West Indian parents who believed wholeheartedly in education. Their life's aim was to send out into a complex world six well-equipped, self-sufficient people. I poured all the charm I could muster into that first date to enhance the possibility of a second. The second produced a third—and so on and so on, until we were constantly together and head over heels in love. I proposed—she accepted. I bought her an engagement ring and waited for the traditional meeting with her parents to ask officially for her hand. That meeting never took place.

Just before I left for Africa, there was a puzzling estrangement between us, the reason for which I could never quite put my finger on, but I suspected strongly it was engineered by her mother. Nettie Weekes was a delightful woman, but she didn't think there was any future for her daughter with an actor. With all the investment they were making in that girl they were certainly expecting a more secure life for her than would be afforded by someone messing around in the theater carrying a spear on the white folks' stage maybe twice a year. In lobbying against the relationship, her mother's hand was strengthened by the fact that I had no education to match Dolores's; and that raised indirectly the specter of her having to support me.

In any case, before I left for Africa, Dolores cooled and backed off. I went into a depression for weeks, suffered a severe loss of appetite, wandered aimlessly through the streets of New York by day, and in my rented room wallowed in a sea of self-pity every night. I had never been down that long from a blow to the heart and consequently didn't quite know how to handle it, until resentment against my own helplessness developed into rage, allowing me to fight back. Not against Dolores, but rather against the prevailing circumstances that had momentarily wrestled away control over my life. In a desperately furious effort to collect my shattered self, I jumped back into the dating game with a vengeance, and met, among others, a young lady named Vivian Cervantes. I started dating that devastatingly beautiful girl, but my heart was with Dolores. When I finally told her that, she said, "That's all right, I understand—I like you anyway." She became a tight close friend who eased my pain a little—for a time. But Dolores had penetrated deeper into my being than Vivian's efforts to erase her could reach. I missed her so much at times that I would relapse into moping about, particularly vulnerable in the late, lonely hours of the night. Despite the invaluable comfort Vivian lent to my recovery, I couldn't control the rot and continued to lose ground. I simply could not shake loose from Dolores's spell.

Then, as could have been expected, there came a time

when I couldn't bear to be without her another day and sought her out again. Lurking in the hallway of a tenement building along the route she customarily took to her father's luncheonette, I waited until the very last meticulously timed second before exiting to the street in the casual manner necessary to give my planned interception the appearance of an accidental encounter. Her eyes widened and instantly sparkled. She smiled and tried to speak, but surprise had left her at a loss for words. Instead, she slowly walked into my arms and nestled her head on my shoulder. In that joyful reunion I discovered that her misery had been just as intense as mine, she had missed me just as much as I had missed her, and she wanted us to be together more than anything. In a matter of a week we had resumed our relationship with full force and decided to go ahead with the marriage, despite an obvious, though unarticulated, ambivalence in her.

Happily back on track, I went off to Africa with a promise from Dolores that she would write to me every day until I was safely back home. I boarded a plane that took me from New York to London to Rome to Athens to the Sudan to Ethiopia to Kenya to Tanzania and eventually down to South Africa. Flying into Johannesburg, I could see that it was a huge, sprawling, urban center. I was barely through customs when I noticed signs saying "Bantu" and "White." Damn, I thought, nobody told me this. I got into a car with a representative from the film company for the ride into the city. I had visions of flopping down into a comfortable bed as soon as I hit my hotel and sleeping for days. Little did I know. We drove for a long time, but I saw no signs of the city. Finally, we came to a little farm with a little house way out in the woods. "What's with this?" I asked. He said, "This is where you're going to stay." I said, "I thought we were going to stay in a hotel." He said, "Oh, no, you're not going to stay in a hotel." I said, "Why? How come?" He gave me no response.

The renowned black actor from America, Canada Lee, was already inside the house, having arrived before I did. The representative from the film company introduced me to Mr. Lee and said, "This is where you will live." "How far is the city?" I asked. He said, "Twenty-six miles." I said, "Twenty-six miles! And we're going to be working in the city—how come we don't live in the city?" Dumb me—I didn't know anything. Canada Lee said,

144

protectively, "I'll tell you about that later." I said to the representative, "Well, can we have some beer and some booze? And maybe I would like to go into town and buy some foodstuff." He said, "You can buy some foodstuff, but you cannot have beer and you cannot have booze." I assured him: "I'm old enough to drink." And he said, "That's not the point. You see, black people are not allowed to drink in South Africa." I said, "No shit! Well, I'll tell you what. I want some whiskey and I want some beer and I want some food. I don't know who you have to tell that to, but I want you to tell them that now. Today. If it isn't here today, please tell them to send a car to take me back to the airport. I am going home." He said, "All right, I'll tell them," and left.

Canada Lee said to me, "Bravo—that's telling them, kid." He then gave me a tour of the little house and the yard surrounding it before sitting me down in my room and easing gently into the cold, stark facts of our situation. "Let me explain something to you. You know, we're officially here as indentured laborers. We are vouched for by Zoltán Korda." Then he began to explain all the ramifications of South African society as it relates to black people. He said the reason we were living out there was because we were not allowed to live within the city limits. It was against the law. "We can't live in the hotels because black people aren't allowed in the hotels. We're facing from twelve to sixteen weeks of work here, so let's do our work and get the hell out. I'm sure we're going to get some booze, beer, and food, but that's all and that's the way it is. I don't like it and I know you don't like it, but we're going to have to make the most of it. And in the meantime, we're not going to let anybody shit on us while we try to maintain our dignity within the confines of these restrictions—so let's relax and enjoy things as much as we can." He flashed me a big, warm smile, gave me a friendly pat on the shoulder, and said, "If you have any questions about all this, don't hesitate. I'll gladly try to answer them for you," then left the room, leaving me to unpack and digest all that he had said. Right away I liked that Canada Lee.

By evening they brought us several bottles of booze, lots of beer, and tons of food that we stacked in the refrigerator. They assigned an African man to cook and clean house, and hired an Indian driver to chauffeur us back and forth between the farm and the city. At first

145

we only went into Johannesburg during the day for costume fittings or for rehearsals; then at the end of the day we would get into our car with Dickie Niaka, our Indian driver, and drive back twenty-six miles to the farm to sleep. Canada Lee, my new, level-headed, practical, and mature friend, was also, as it turned out, one of the most courageous characters I have ever met, as complex as he was talented. In South Africa, where it was clearly a major crime—punishable by death—to cross the line racially, this man who was lecturing me on the strategy necessary to our survival in fascist South Africa, this practical sage who took me under his wise and protective wing, was a Duke Williams, a Maxwell Granville, and a Roy Glenn all rolled into one. A lady killer of the first degree. There was this particular woman —white, attractive, intelligent, very well educated—who today would be considered a liberated woman in Western terms. An active member of South Africa's upper class, with homes in Johannesburg and Durban—this high-placed lady met and was mesmerized by the fabulous Canada Lee. Wanting to know him better, she extended an invitation for dinner at her home. He accepted the invitation. She lived in the penthouse of a fashionable high-rise apartment building. Taking the service elevator up, he arrived at the apartment to find he was the only dinner guest expected. Over good food and an excellent wine in a candlelit surrounding, Canada Lee stayed for dinner—until six o'clock the next morning.

But wait—we started the movie and went to Durban to do some shooting. Remember, the lady has a house in Durban, so naturally she goes down there to be with Canada, who is living in a room next to me in the home of some Indian people. After work each night Canada would check into his room after dinner, slip out the back door, and disappear into South Africa. We wouldn't see him until the next day. By then I was fully aware of what South Africa was really like, and I said to him, "Please, remember the words of wisdom you gave me when I first arrived. Don't get us both killed in this country." He said, "Don't worry, I've got it under control. But hear me, good young friend. I will bend within reason to the madness that is required of us in this sick place, but *I* will decide what is 'within reason.' I will not twist my dignity out of shape to fit anybody's

146

custom. I don't live that way in America and I'm not going to live that way in South Africa."

Back in Johannesburg as we went on filming, we began to be invited into the homes of some of the white liberal element who wanted to express sympathy with us and help us collect a few good impressions of their country. They were almost all wealthy, living in the chic suburbs of Johannesburg. Many Jews, some English, and a few Afrikaaners. We were visitors, and though we weren't staying in the city, we were well within our rights as visitors to come inside the city limits on social trips as long as we got out by the end of the evening. We went frequently to dinner parties held in the homes of these very nice people who were brave enough (and wealthy enough) to challenge the system in this small way, and at those dinners Canada was always spellbinding in discussions of politics, America, the rest of Africa, and just about any subject you could name. Then at around eleven o'clock in the evening we would get back into our car and go back into the countryside where we were staying. (Dickie Niaka, the driver, would never go into a white home because, he said, "I don't want any white friends when the showdown comes.") We went to one dinner party where "that lady" was—as a matter of fact, she had engineered that particular dinner and spent the entire evening looking soulfully at Canada across the table. I have never spent a more uncomfortable evening in my life. I was expecting the secret police to pounce on Canada's ass at any minute! At the end of the evening as we're riding back to our bailiwick out in the country, Canada said to the driver, "Drop me off at such-and-such a place." I said, "Oh, no!" But sure as hell we did drop him off, and the next morning on the way in, we picked him up on such-and-such a corner. Nerve? Yes!

Cry, the Beloved Country's wrenching impact as a novel centered on the soul-crushing tragedy that engulfed two typical South African families, one black and one white. Zoltán Korda's movie script was as faithful to the novel as possible, resulting in well-rounded roles for all the principal actors. I played the Reverend Msimangu, a young African priest whose compassion and fighting spirit combined to make him the most artistically exciting character I had so far been asked to play. Insights into social characteristics and other subtleties of character were generously supplied by the author of the novel,

147

the remarkable Alan Paton himself, who was on hand during much of the filming. Alan Paton had drawn the young African priest in such completeness as a character that a mildly uncomfortable awareness began to dawn on me suggesting that my acting skills were as yet far short of what would be required to fully realize the character. There seemed to be more to acting than I had been led to believe—much, much more. But having no idea just how much more there was to know, I settled for the realization that what I did know was not nearly enough for a run at distinction.

We were also received in the homes of many black and Indian people, and we were feted by two political organizations, the South African Black Congress and the African-Indian Congress. In a real cloak-and-dagger manner, on successive Sunday afternoon picnic outings of their rank and file, we met and spoke in private with some of their leaders, who overwhelmed us with facts and figures relating to their constant struggle against a political system that considered both Indians and blacks less than human. So seldom did they have a sympathetic ear from the outside world that they leaped at the opportunity to outline in detail every aspect of their struggle— their aims and aspirations, and what they had so far cost in human life and suffering. With a casualness peculiar to men who live their lives dangerously, they apologized for the extensive briefing by saying, "You must excuse our long-windedness, but since we may never meet again, given the politics of our lives in South Africa, we would appreciate it if you could in the fullest sense tell our friends in America about our struggle." I remember thinking: Funny how men of great courage look just like other men. Shouldn't they be more serious? Solemn? Aren't they doomed to unnaturally short lives, as men of politics in a land that forbids it? Well, then, their readiness to laugh, and easiness with which they give themselves to eating, drinking, dancing, is a contradiction— unless a lust for life automatically intensifies in men who know that their days are numbered. (And indeed, it was only a matter of time before both organizations were outlawed, and many of their leaders jailed, some to die in confinement.)

During my first two weeks in South Africa, Dolores wrote to me every day as she had promised to. I answered instantly, sometimes getting off two letters a day.

148

But after those two weeks her letters stopped—cold. The first four or five days I supposed it had something to do with a malfunction in the postal system. After about a week and a half, I realized that probably wasn't the problem, since I was receiving other mail from the United States. I sent off wires to her. No response. Finally, I tried to phone person-to-person. The operator got through to her house, but Dolores was not available. After several more calls placed at strategic times produced the same polite "not available" reply, it became clear that she *was* available but not to me. Why? If, as seemed likely, her mother's influence had raised its head again, why didn't she write to say she was having trouble? At the very least, some frail opposition in defense of our relationship might have been mounted on the basis of my right to know what the hell was going on. There I was so far away from home, suddenly and mysteriously cut off—abruptly disconnected—from the girl I was going to marry.

Finally, after many days, I managed to get through to her by phone. She told me she had decided to call off the engagement in the face of the many practical difficulties that seemed inevitable to a union such as ours. Well, if you want to talk about a guy carrying a heavy load—that was a bitch! My angel of the luncheonette, to whom I was irreversibly committed, had left me stranded and defenseless on a hostile shore. But wait— such a one-sided assessment by a wounded partisan doesn't allow for the possibility that his love, Dolores, was deep in comparable anguish on the other side of the breach. Perhaps at the moment of impact, psychological devastation is always perceived as cruelty—to be on the receiving end of such a paralyzing jolt has to blur and distort one's vision. Right? Perhaps. But—the fact remains that she had socked it to me at a time and in a way that left me wide open to scars in the regions of my self-esteem. In years to come, standing in the clear objective light that is hindsight's major advantage, I will recognize the hard, uncompromising truth behind Dolores's behavior. Nettie and Wilfred Weekes needed desperately that one of their children emerge a "winner" in the remaining years of their difficult lives. Being the most likely, the bright and gifted Dolores was expected to break the cycle of poverty—indeed, she was earmarked from the earliest display of her intellectual gifts to carry other people's dreams. Her decision, made out of her compassionate understanding of her family's vulnerability and the shattering disappointment that would surely drown her parents if they were to lose her to a "loser," is from this perspective hard to quarrel with. But let me not get ahead of myself. At twenty-three years of age, in Africa, over the telephone, I got the shaft from Dolores Sheldon Weekes. With words so blunt they numbed, she accomplished a massive internal upheaval within me in just three minutes and then she hung up. I was left hurting in Africa; she was free in New York; and, as far as I knew, she was already in somebody else's arms. Whoever that dumb-ass, middle-class, college-graduated bastard was, I remember hoping his nose would fall off. I was to suffer for a long time.

Before I left I had asked Vivian Cervantes to occasionally send me the *Amsterdam News* to keep me abreast of what was happening in the black community back home. New York was my home now, and after my visit with my parents in Nassau, during which I was reconciled to that part of my life from which I had been cut off for so many years, I dreaded the thought of being cut off again for sixteen weeks in the remote reaches of Africa. The *Amsterdam News* once or twice a month would be a reminder, I thought, that someone cared. Vivian sent me the *Amsterdam News,* she sent me presents, she wrote to me every day, and she never knew until I returned to New York that the relationship with Dolores had self-destructed. Her consideration and generosity held me in one piece through a fearful four-month nightmare and propelled me deeply into an indebtedness to her from which I shall never completely emerge.

During our stay in South Africa we saw the real nature of the system operating against black people in the coarsest and most brutal ways. I remember a time we were driving from the house to the city and saw a young white man on a motorcycle playing "tag" in and out of traffic. Darting in and out—slowing down, speeding up—weaving intricate patterns through a steady flow of cars and trucks heading toward the city on a Sunday afternoon. Suddenly there was a collision between himself and a van filled with black people. He fell from his motorcycle but was unhurt beyond a few bruises. In the meantime, passing white motorists began to stop and before long they had formed a group of fifty or sixty around the van of blacks who were trying to explain what had happened. A police wagon arrived. At that point, Dickie Niaka, our driver, said it would be best for us to go on. In our car were myself, Canada Lee, and Lionel Ingakanye, a young South African black actor. Lionel said no and, pointing to a hill nearby, suggested that if we drove to the top of it, we would be able to see what was going on and at the same time be out of range of the tensions that seemed about to explode. We had barely arrived at the top of the hill when we saw fifty or sixty whites begin beating up the group of six or seven blacks from the van, one of whom was a pregnant woman. They beat them unmercifully before the police threw the black people into the wagon and drove off. We had seen the accident and knew that it wasn't their fault. Nothing they had said to the cops or the crowd could have warranted that kind of response. But by now we had begun to learn that in South Africa such an abuse of power was typical behavior on the part of the police and the white minority it represented. It was simply normal procedure.

We witnessed many, many such incidents, and naturally they had an emotional impact on us. I remember that one day at the studio in Johannesburg I went to the bathroom—they had one for blacks and one for whites. I went to the white bathroom because, unlike the black bathroom, it had toilet paper in it and an attendant was assigned to ensure its maintenance. While I'm in the john, in comes a white kid of about eighteen or twenty who works around the studio. I'm finished but I need some toilet paper that's up on a shelf. I open the door and say, "Could you please pass me some toilet paper?" He shoots me a hostile look and says, "What are you doing in here?" I say, "That's not the point at the moment—would you mind passing me the toilet paper?" He says, "Don't you know you're not supposed to be in here?" I say, "I'll discuss that with you in a moment—meanwhile would you mind passing the paper?" He makes some unpleasant remark and storms out, leaving the roll of toilet paper where it's standing on the shelf. I quickly devise a way to reach the paper on the shelf and complete my business, and then I go immediately to the office of the middle-aged, mustachioed Afrikaaner who's the director of the studio activities and explain what's happened. "I would like you to call the young man in.

As long as I'm at this studio I'm going to use that bathroom. I don't want you to fire the boy, but I want him to know that he must absolutely not say a fucking word to me as long as I'm here, and if he uses such language to me again, I'm going to punch him out." The Afrikaaner executive hems and haws, but I insist and he finally calls the boy in and tells him that this charge is being lodged against him and to behave himself in the future. That's the end of it and I return to work.

Dissolve. About a week before we finished, I was walking into the studio one day and this kid was sitting on a wall at the entrance. He spoke to me for the first time since our encounter ten weeks before in the john. "I hear you're leaving next week." I said, "Yes." "What time are you leaving?" he asked in a tone made casual by a friendly smile. The incident in the john was no longer in the forefront of my mind, so I told him when I would be catching the plane and continued on into the studio to prepare for the day's work. But in my dressing room he stayed in my head. Soon I began running that scene down in my mind, wondering why he wanted to know exactly when I was leaving. I got more and more suspicious and finally told Dickie Niaka about it. He said he thought we should discuss it with Canada Lee and with an Indian friend of his who was in the Indian National Congress, who in turn discussed it with some of *his* friends. The Indian activists decided it would be wise to accompany me to the airport, just in case.

On the morning of my departure six of them, including my driver, arrived at the farmhouse in two cars. The leader of the group gave me a .22 automatic pistol with seven shots in it. He said, "Keep this in your hand. If anything goes wrong between here and the airport you may need it." Sixteen weeks in that country—but it was at that moment that the full impact of South African politics hit me. We started out for the airport. As soon as we hit the road that wound for ten miles before emptying into the main highway that would eventually sweep past the airport twenty miles away, a car came out of a side road and started following us. Dickie Niaka stared into his rear-view mirror and said, "Here they come." We looked back and saw this car bearing down on us. Then Dickie said, "Hang on—I'll try to outrun them," and he started pushing. He pushed that car to its maximum. We were doing about 110 miles on that narrow dirt road, kicking up all kinds of dust. Right behind us was our backup car with three of our Indian friends, all armed— and right behind them in a blue sedan were five South African whites, who, it would be safe to say, were also "dressed for the occasion."

The size of a .22-caliber pistol is not very comforting —it looks like a toy. What happens if they catch us? I thought. They're probably carrying howitzers in that fucking car. I hope they don't start shooting at our tires. Dickie Niaka's nerves were good—his hands were steady —and he kept his foot right on the floor, pushing that car until at times it seemed almost airborne. Meanwhile his friends sat calmly with their revolvers on their laps. Yes, I was sweating. We had a good fifty-yard spread on them at the start, but they'd whittled it down, mile by mile, to about thirty yards at the halfway mark. Right within range, I thought, if they wanted to start shooting. Unexpectedly, totally without warning, the narrow dirt road emptied into the two-lane blacktop highway that led westward to the airport ten miles away. Our speed was too great for the sudden right turn, so Dickie Niaka, gambling that there would be no moving objects in that intersection when we hit it, kept the pressure on the accelerator as we sliced across the highway, crashing through a flimsy wooden fence surrounding some farmland that had been plowed for seeding. The bouncing and vibrations were so severe I thought we were finished; the contours of the earth were so rough it would be suicide to continue at our speed—we'd have to slow down. But Dickie Niaka had no such intention. In fact, on top of maintaining speed, he began coaxing the vehicle against its own momentum, forcing it into a wide-arced right turn that cut deep into the barren field, forcing the reluctant car to carve its way through a half-moon back toward the highway we had just swept across. He was driving with a vengeance now; he was in control. The competition was between him and the white South African driving the blue sedan. It was one-on-one, skill against skill, with the white man having no special advantage. Dickie Niaka was like a man possessed as he dueled with a whole system following us in a blue sedan. For the first time in his life, in those brief terrifying moments, with the smell of death in the air, Dickie Niaka was liberated —because he was tasting what it was like to have his destiny in his own hands. He realized that if he lived through this he would never again be the same.

Crashing through the wooden fence again, we hit the highway with tires screeching like wild animals as Dickie edged the nose of our automobile westward toward the airport. While demanding more from the car than it was designed to give, he was thinking: This one the white man must not win.

But the blue sedan kept creeping closer. In the home stretch, about three miles from the airport, they made their move. Swinging wide, they tried to gun by our backup car, but Dickie's friends wouldn't permit it. They started interference maneuvers, weaving to and fro in front of the blue sedan. The Indian friend who had given me the .22 automatic said, "We're almost there—if they don't start shooting I think we've beaten them." Dickie Niaka replied, "Yeah, I think we have." All three cars were practically burned out by now, but the blue sedan didn't give an inch. It pressed its threat to the very gates of the airport turnoff—at which point it reduced its speed suddenly, rolled to a stop, and sat there like an outmaneuvered predator, its occupants watching our two-car caravan disappear into the airport complex. South Africa was like that, dangerous and brutal. But the white man didn't win that one.

On my way back to London where I was to finish the picture, a change of planes in Lisbon necessitated an overnight stay. Arriving at a hotel, I checked into my room and fell absolutely on my face. Fainted—passed out! The bellman, who came to pick up my shoes to be shined, found me and called a doctor. I had welts as big as quarters all over my face and upper body. The doctor said I was living under great stress, great nervous tension. Yes, I was.

10 Juanita

I RETURNED to New York riding a very bad set of emotional lows. The hooks were still in because of Dolores, and although I knew that was finished, I spent weeks positioning myself and planning my days hoping to run into her. But that was not to be—she was gone forever. Her goal was to finish school and pursue what to her mind, and obviously her mother's mind, was a practical and safe percentage for a happy life. And I resigned myself to the residual traumas that were sure to be mine. There would be no escaping the pain. In an attempt to blunt its edges, I tried being a big-time bachelor seeing lots of girls, but Vivian Cervantes was the only one I could trust, and we dated frequently though not exclusively. I bought a brand-new Buick to brush up my big-time bachelor image and tooled around New York with Vivian at my side in search of things I couldn't identify, in places I knew they wouldn't be. Wandering through the nightlife of Harlem, playing poker with my friends, sitting in 42nd Street movie houses or going to the theater, Vivian was always there, helping me through the maze. She remained my number one—until I met Juanita.

A young actor friend, Bill Greaves, introduced me to the cover girl who frequented the fashion and beauty pages of black America's three leading magazines— *Ebony, Sepia,* and *Our World.* This well-known model-dancer with an attention-getting body, a great face, and a clean-scrubbed country smile was the prettiest thing I'd ever seen—she even had Vivian Cervantes topped. Her name was Juanita Marie Hardy. Life and Dolores, having worked me over in the preceding months, had softened me up for the sensational Juanita. Just when my big-time bachelor pose was ready to shrivel and collapse in the heat of the torch I was carrying; just when I wasn't able to deal with the loneliness anymore; just when I knew I *had* to have a steady girl in a steady relationship before

155

I got any further on into the years where being alone was too tough, to say nothing of being unnatural; just when, for a fleeting moment briefer than the swiftness of the mind, all things were equal—I met my wife. After many months of steady dating she became my number one. In the course of a daily conversation I held with myself on life in general and my career in particular, I said: This girl is terrific—she's crazy about you and you're nuts about her—and she can even cook! Since becoming your steady girl she has eased your mind, and a tranquil personal life has to be a hell of a plus considering the total commitment in time and energy the theater demands from those who come knocking at its door. I'm not trying to get into your business, Sidney P., but if I were you I'd marry that girl. At that point the conversation hung suspended, waiting respectfully. Since suggestions of this nature deserved a considered response, I considered. I even mentioned her several times in my letters to my parents. Then I considered some more. Finally I responded appropriately with: Hey, I think I will. And we got married.

Evelyn and Reginald Poitier, with finances being what they were at both ends, couldn't afford to come to New York for the ceremony, which took place in a Catholic church in Harlem. The fact that not one person from my side of the family was able to be present at such an important event in my life spotlighted once again how far I had wandered from the Poitier tribe. Even though we frequently exchanged letters, and there were some telephone calls, I was still a hell of a long way off, in more ways than one, from what used to be home. Evelyn and Reggie's disappointment was eased by the fact that some weeks before they had seen me for the first time in a movie when the local motion picture exhibitor in Nassau invited the whole family to the opening of *No Way Out*. A highly impressive, and for some, an earth-shattering evening that no member of the family will ever forget— not so much because of my presence on the screen, but more because of Evelyn Poitier's response to it. At a moment near the climax of the movie, Richard Widmark hits me with the butt of a gun. Evelyn jumped to her feet in the darkened theater and shouted to me up on the screen, "Hit him back, Sidney! Hit him back! Don't you hit my boy—he didn't do anything to you. Hit him back, Sidney. Hit him back!" The emotions that forced Evelyn

156

to her feet in a darkened theater to give Richard Widmark a piece of her mind embarrassed those in the clan who knew what motion pictures were all about, but to those like Evelyn, to whom it was all a new experience, the movie was an extension of real life and Richard Widmark had to be put in his place. How dare he lay a hand on one of "ours"! Though Evelyn's view of Richard Widmark would mellow over the years, he would never be one of her favorite people.

By the time I paid for the wedding, by the time we moved into a one-family house in Astoria, Long Island, where the owner converted the attic into an apartment with a ceiling so low that I walked around bumping my head every time I stood up straight (but it was kind of cute otherwise, and fairly inexpensive—I think we paid sixty dollars a month), by the time I had bought some furniture, I was broke and had to go to work as a dishwasher a few days after I got married. My best man was an actor friend of mine named Dots Johnson. After the wedding reception, he drove us out to our new home (I no longer had my car—I had sold it) and I borrowed ten dollars from him to see us through our honeymooning in our attic home—or should it be: "in our home in somebody else's attic?" No matter. If we had been in the bridal suite of New York's fanciest hotel those three days couldn't have been happier. On the fourth day, however, I lost ground to a giant machine that spewed out tons of hot dishes and silverware in a steamy madhouse they called a kitchen in a far from fancy hotel on the west side of Manhattan. After three weeks in that kitchen, some friends turned me on to a guy in the construction business who gave me a job as a laborer on a middle-income apartment complex his family was building, and I worked there for several months until the project was completed. Then once again the machines beckoned—but I stood fast. No more, I vowed. I will look for something else—anything else. I must put those machines behind me forever.

But how? My wife's modeling was as sporadic as my acting, bringing in no more than fifty dollars in a good month. In addition, she occasionally performed as an interpretive dancer for ladies' club luncheons, Saturday night get-togethers of various community organizations, or whatever other gigs were available to swell our coffers that extra ten bucks per month. Realistically speaking, our economics, which included the ninety dollars we had saved from my work as a construction laborer, were not much of a barricade against the monster machine. Two weeks of unemployment was about all our rainy-day resources could shoulder and, as we have seen, the monster machine had outwaited me before; she was patient. But no, this time she will wait until she rusts. For I know at last that I'm not destined to spend my life paying court to her.

Still, although I wasn't an economic genius, I had enough money savvy to know that ninety dollars could in no way be viewed as formidable resources, and two weeks from destitution left very little time to accomplish anything. Clearly I had to move at speeds where the margin for error was dramatically reduced and wasted motion could be fatal. At 9:59 on the morning of a Monday, geared up and ready to strike, I stood poised waiting for the signal to fling myself into action. At the stroke of 10:00 the doors of all the casting offices in the combined areas of television, film, and theater flew open, and I was off: charging, blitzing, hounding, haunting, pestering every casting director and/or his secretary listed in "Casting News," the weekly tout sheet of the acting profession. I reasoned there had to be a part in all that theatrical activity that I could play, and if I built up enough points for persistence the job wouldn't have any trouble finding me. Day after day, office after office, I struck. Those offices where there appeared a glimmer of hope I struck over and over in the same day—never losing my smile or the polite "thank you" or the other little human courtesies drilled into me for years by Evelyn Poitier. A pest I was, to be sure. But *likable*. Yet day after day I drew blank after blank. At the end of the first week with nets cast far and wide, I came up with nothing. I had visions of the monster machine patiently keeping count as my days dwindled down. When Monday came again I was out of the chute redoubling my efforts, but nothing shook loose. Likewise Tuesday and Wednesday produced no nibbles, and on Thursday our ninety-dollar savings were invaded and ravaged by the plundering hand of our landlord laying claim to his first-of-the-month rent. Friday came and closed the second week, shutting me out with no alternative but to revise my game plan in light of the fact that another unsuccessful week could lead to catastrophe when the first of the month rolled round again and

I had to face a no-nonsense landlord empty-handed—strange how landlords always seemed to be waiting, like the monster machine, to lay claim to my soul.

What to do? Grab something as a porter or a construction laborer was the safe play to make at that late hour; another week of shouting in the wilderness to deaf ears could be too costly even for one who loves to dance close to the flames. But, hell, I said to myself, you're already in a hole—if you gamble on another week and lose, you'll only be that much deeper in that hole. So what! Nothing ventured, nothing gained. Even if nothing turns up, I'll have made so many rounds I'll be on their minds for years to come whenever they need a young black actor. I choose to gamble on the extra week—and it came and went as unproductively as the previous two. Finally I began to make the rounds to construction sites, looking to be taken on as a laborer. Returning home after my second unsuccessful day of this, I found a telephone message from my agent asking if I'd be interested in playing the Ralph Bellamy part in *Detective Story* at the Apollo Theatre on 125th Street for one week. I collapsed with relief. A surge of hope. With the cupboard at its barest, a nibble. But hey, caution. I mustn't collapse with relief prematurely. I must get a proper reading. Wait for the details from the agent in the morning. Because from the lookout point of desperation, a man cornered by the crush of life is very likely to see a favorable turn approaching when, in truth, only an ironic twist is coming his way. So in order not to anticipate myself into a frenzy overnight, I threw cold water on the possibility and left it suspended the rest of the evening. My wife's delight at the prospect of activity for my dormant skills filled our little attic apartment (where I was still regularly bumping my head). For her it wasn't necessary to wait for verification from my agent. She was a believer, in touch with another source. She knew in her heart that the Maker, in His mercy, arranges for the coming of good things to the deserving. I could only hope that there was no quarrel between them as to my qualifications as "deserving."

The next morning the offer was indeed confirmed as genuine. The details were simple—two weeks of rehearsal at $75 per week, and one week of performances for $150. Juanita beamed a smile at me that unmistakably mocked my lack of faith in her heavenly connections. "I told you so—ye of little faith," was written all over her face. (Could it be—did she really have the ear of a friendly Force?) "I accept," I told the agent. In a few days, with the contracts drawn and signed, I set about learning the play. Rehearsals were a joy. I was happy to be back in action again, and especially so with the group of dedicated black actors who were pouring all their creative energy into our uptown production of Sidney Kingsley's play, giving it a different kind of liveliness from what it had had on Broadway. All in all, and critical reactions notwithstanding, it was an enriching experience doing a dramatic play at the Apollo Theatre, whose audience, since time immemorial, was used to big bands, rhythm and blues, Ella Fitzgerald, Billy Eckstine, and Pigmeat Markham's vaudeville comedy sketches.

Half a block east of the Apollo Theatre, dominating the southwest corner of Harlem's busiest intersection, was the Hotel Theresa. There she stood, where Seventh Avenue and 125th Street interlaced, the premiere hotel in New York City to welcome blacks without reservation (so to speak). That fabulous landmark, and in particular its bar and lounge, was a watering hole whose status reached far down all the railroad tracks of America into the bowels of every colored town from Maine to Florida and westward to the Pacific, igniting the imagination of Mr. Doctor, Mr. Lawyer, Miss Schoolteacher, Mr. Funeral Director, Miss Pretty Girl, Mr. Sharecropper, Mr. Dream Chaser, and countless others for whom a trip to New York and the Theresa Lounge would be a fantasy fulfilled. The sparkle and glitter from the show biz and sports trend-setters who frequented the lounge showered black America with gossip column tidbits, further sharpening appetites for that once-in-a-lifetime opportunity to rub shoulders with Joe Louis, Lena Horne, Dorothy Dandridge, Ralph Cooper, the Nicholas Brothers, Ray Robinson, Lionel Hampton, Count Basie, Duke Ellington, Ella Fitzgerald, Noble Sissle, Bill Robinson, Rex Ingram, the Mills Brothers, and so on.

Now the manager of this hotel lounge and bar was a grossly underpaid, very handsome young man named John Newton with whom I became quite friendly during my weeks of rehearsal and performance in the neighborhood. Having tumbled back into the throes of unemployment, I took to visiting him frequently for breeze-shooting sessions that invariably ended up with us cursing the darkness that surrounded our individual careers, until one day he lit a match. "You know, we should open a restaurant." I said, "Okay, why don't we, but I don't have any money." He said, "I don't have any either, but I tell you, maybe we don't need any money." I said, "That'll be neat. How do we do that?" He said, "I'm good with my hands." His eyes focused momentarily on a distant horizon until the lull in our conversation reminded him that I was waiting for him to come back. Then he went on. "I've been working here at the Theresa Hotel for years already— I can't spend my whole life working here—the pay is rotten and the glamour of this job won't feed my family. I want to be in business for myself. I know how to build —if we can just get up enough money for the first and last month's rent, we can sorta manage our way through to opening day." I said, "You're serious, aren't you?" He said, "I've gotta make a move sometime. And I'm not afraid of hard work." I said, "Neither am I. Let's sit down and put it on paper and see if we can work something out." He threw his open palm at me saying "Deal," we shook hands, and a partnership was formed. Johnny Newton knew something I didn't. He knew that the fabulous Theresa had seen the best of it and was on its way downhill. He was jumping ship. He had an eye for business, that man; he could see beneath the dazzle that a hard economic nut was not being cracked.

By our conservative calculations the minimal requirement for getting off the ground consisted of three months rent to be paid at the signing of the lease, plus a few hundred for obvious things such as license, paint, some lumber, and a down payment for the equipment necessary to outfit a small but classy restaurant. Whoever we owed after that would be paid a little bit here and a little bit there after we got our doors open. We were disturbingly short on essential working capital, but long on manipulative razzle-dazzle designed by Johnny expressly for holding off and shifting people and commitments around until our cash register started ringing in earnest. "I know where we can get five hundred dollars right away," Johnny said. "How are you going to do that?" I asked. "Well, we're going to put in a jukebox and in order for the jukebox people to have a right to put a jukebox in our restaurant they have to give us an advance of five hundred dollars against our returns from the jukebox." "Hey, that's good thinking. You're really sharp. Let's go for it," I said. As proof of our intentions, we presented to the jukebox company a signed three-year lease on the smallest store-front you have ever seen. (We would ultimately be able to serve only sixteen people sitting down, but we antici-pated a hell of a takeout trade.) And true to Johnny's word, they laid five hundred bucks on us against future receipts.

Johnny promptly gave his Theresa Hotel employers four weeks notice and plunged into working eighteen hours a day—nine hours at the hotel and nine hours as the archi-tect, carpenter, bricklayer, concrete pourer, plumber, and all-around miracle worker transforming a shabby little storefront into a petite but classy restaurant. I intensified my search for work in the business while working with Johnny on the restaurant. My wife went to work at Ripley's clothing factory sewing labels into Ripley's clothes for thirty-five dollars a week. That thirty-five dollars was the essence of our income. Juanita was very supportive in the early stages of our marriage, and especially through those depressing, uncertain periods of unemployment. She never doubted for a moment that things were going to get "good," even as I was moving closer and closer to finan-cial oblivion and coming to consider her faith in things getting "good" as the faith of blind ignorance. But she hung in there with her arms wrapped tightly around her convictions. Eventually it would become clear that the secret ingredient in that "faith" was the fact that she was a hell of a lot smarter than I was about many, many things (more about that later).

Johnny and I took his car to the dump grounds in the East Bronx near the Triborough Bridge in the late after-noons. Any kind of lumber or box or wood that looked salvageable, we would pull the nails out of, bring back in the car, and dump in the back of our little store. We used this wood to build our paneling, our counter, and our little kitchen area. He was a genius with his hands, that John Newton. He worked and he worked—and I helped and I helped. We were putting that restaurant together with pure spit, when suddenly a job materialized, a movie called *Red Ball Express* at Universal Pictures, to star Jeff Chandler and Hugh O'Brian.

When the details of the contract that guaranteed me four weeks of employment were finalized, off I went to Hollywood for the second time. As unbelievable as it seemed to me, there was no escaping the fact that I was even more excited the second time around. I was in

Hollywood, and more to the point, I was working in front of a camera. After the assistant director had called for quiet on my first morning of work, I became suddenly aware of something very special happening inside of me. It seemed as if an unknown value had opened up somewhere down in my gut, sending juices rushing to my brain and from there filling my whole body with an exhilaration that somehow appeared to be completely in sync with the gentle humming sounds coming from the activated cameras. Before that morning was over, I realized how much I had missed acting in the movies; I was hooked deeper than I had allowed myself to admit. By the end of those four weeks there was no denying that I had gotten as used to moviemaking as a duck to water. But hard reality forced me to wonder more than once: What happens to a duck when he can't find water? Yet there is always water somewhere, isn't there? Right? Okay, then it is incumbent upon the duck to find some, isn't it? Each payday during the filming of *Red Ball Express,* I funneled money back to Johnny Newton, and then I returned to New York and we opened our restaurant. Business was good, but our debts were such that we were to see no profits for a long time.

Soon after our opening, I was asked to do another film in New York City called *Go, Man, Go.* Most of the money from both these pictures went into the restaurant. With the remainder, Juanita and I moved from Long Island into a very nice apartment for seventy-three dollars a month on 123rd Street in Manhattan, and we took a quick trip to Nassau for the family to meet my new bride. They loved her instantly and showered her with affection. Back in New York she continued working at Ripley's, but now she was pregnant.

Our first child was on the way. The arrival of the first baby was traumatic. While I felt terrific about being a father, it also scared me when I came face to face with the responsibilities of the fact. And I was broke. I had *no* money—and very few prospects of earning any. The uncertainty of the job market, plus my inability to express my fears to my wife, left me in an acutely vulnerable position, and I did a great deal of fretting and worrying that eventually crystallized into an ulcer condition. Juanita? She was happy. She was really the salt of the earth. She had the baby and she took care of the baby. She was willing to work. She was fulfilling what she saw as her role—the role of Wife and Mother that all her life she had seen unfolding before her. For her it was a fulfilling experience, and she was never able to understand my turmoil, why I was so frightened all the time. There was an innocent, trusting openness about Juanita that exists to this day. She has the biggest heart. She'd take in a stray puppy, a stray human being—anybody who needs comforting or mothering can find it in Juanita. She is so trusting that people take advantage of her. I suspect I did too, as it turned out. More times than I can remember, I was driven to think it would have been so much better for her had she met a guy who was less troubled, a guy much simpler and healthier in his head than I was. Poor girl, when she met me I was already a mess, and her goodness, her openness, her loving nature weren't enough to turn me around, to unravel the tangles of my mind.

Beverly was our first child, and I was really scared when she was born. She was beautiful. She had a great big fluffy head of hair and a round face—she was really stunning, that child. She looked like her mother. Juanita fed her all the things that mothers fed their kids and she became a chubby little baby. There were unusual characteristics about her even then. She was a touch inscrutable. You could never read her as a baby. Her typical expression suggested that she knew more about what was going on than you thought she could. But she's a baby, I used to think to myself. She was a very sensitive, introspective, shy and observant child, qualities she was never to lose. But most of all she was our little baby girl. She was a part of me. I remember feeling my manhood surging through my being whenever I held her in my arms or looked down at her sleeping peacefully in her crib. I was thrilled. My pride was such that I would have worked at dishwashing machines all my life to protect her and give her food and shelter. Whether it is an organic condition native to the male of the species or a cultural affect created by the weight of habit over thousands of years, I have no idea. All I know is that the macho mood that comes out in a guy when he looks down at his little kid came pouring out of me. I was plenty glad to be the dad of that particular little girl. Her birth saw a renewed determination on my part to assume responsibility as a father and as a man, however difficult it might be, and with whatever cards I was dealt by life. I swore to see to it as best I could that she have opportunities necessary for a good shot at life.

And then there was a second pregnancy, and a second child. In 1954, Pamela came along—and she was something else, a very different kind of a child. She was more assertive than Beverly, from the earliest; more outspoken. Juanita's father used to call her "Truck," because she was a plump baby, muscular, and she would come rolling through the room. She was tough, straightforward, and forceful. She and her sister, Beverly, during all those early years were just one hell of a new experience for me. I had not observed my father being a father to other youngsters because I was the last—I was being a father by instinct, and screwing up a lot of the time because I didn't know what I was doing. I was making mistake after mistake, but I was there for them in ways that I thought were necessary. Certainly not in all the ways I could have been, had I been better informed, had I had better role models, but I was there as best I could. I enjoyed them a lot, and I had a terribly proudful feeling about being their Daddy. The word "Daddy" held some magical connotations for me.

11 Politics

THE YEARS 1952, 1953, and all but four weeks of 1954 were a dry spell for me in terms of the movies and the theater. Nothing, absolutely nothing. I didn't know exactly why it was nothing, but I had my suspicions; with the racial situation being what it was I didn't need three guesses. During that period I was being introduced to many people who were very politically aware. Among them were a lot of white people who seemed to be strikingly different from the majority of whites I had encountered before. They were friendly and sympathetic on the racial question, when most other people were decidedly not. They seemed more willing to grant me an equal opportunity for economic, cultural, and political expression, with no strings attached. Of course most of those new white people were actors, actresses, writers, producers, directors, and people generally on the fringes of a world bound on one side by the theater, on the other by motion pictures, and somewhere, in the back of the bus, television, in its infancy.

I took care to nurture these relationships because through them I was exposed to new ideas, new concepts, and new points of view on old troubling issues. And in the process of airing these ideas and questions I eventually began—slowly, on a gut level—to develop my own political ideas. I began to realize that politics is an integral part of how we lead our daily lives. It has an influence on everything: education, health, art, economics, the attitudes of one group to the other—it just permeates everything. I began to realize more and more, and in time, shooting the breeze with old cronies about girls and getting laid was replaced by political discussions. My interest in the political views swirling about me in this new circle of acquaintances attracted invitations to numerous homes for dinners or parties or cocktails, all of which had an underlying political motive reaching far beyond eats and drinks. At these friendly gatherings of Democrats, Republicans, Progressives, Liberals, Socialists, Communists, and FBI informers I would always sit and listen. I would join in the discussions occasionally, depending on the extent of my information, but mostly I would listen—I would learn. I would learn about politics—I would learn about America—I would learn about urban life—about all kinds of things that otherwise I wouldn't have been exposed to. On many occasions I would be invited to cells of left-wing political activists who said, "Come and hear what we have to say." I would go to somebody's house and there would be half a dozen or a dozen other people, some of whom I might have seen somewhere before, others total strangers. The talk would be Progressive, Socialist, Communist, or a mixture of all three, aimed at developing new converts.

My initial introduction to politics came at a furious time when a political upheaval of hurricane force was battering the country at large, while slamming itself with particular force at the high-visibility areas of art and intellect, with theater, film, and television absorbing the lowest blows. While that period, known as the McCarthy era, was scaring people in mighty places, I didn't even

166

know who the hell McCarthy was—so removed was I from the mainstream of American politics—he was just a Senator who was white and mean to other white people, especially those who had black friends. But I was to learn in detail about the period in American history that he symbolized. I was to see his hurricane touch down around me, striking friends who were not Progressives, Liberals, or Communists as well as friends who were. Blacks who had white friends were in as vulnerable a position as whites who had black friends. So before I had learned enough about politics to get a fix on McCarthy, I found myself victimized by the indiscriminate gusts from his demagoguery. With a long arm that was never ready to help but always ready to hurt, the Senator smeared and paralyzed much of the area I had by now chosen to spend my life in. Before I could understand any of it, I was blacklisted. I wasn't able to work.

Mind you, I don't think if affected me as much as it did others, because I wasn't working anyway. And I couldn't really say for sure whether it was a blacklist or my black face that was keeping me out of work. I do know that I was considered an upstart, left-wing troublemaker by the hierarchy of the Negro Actors Guild of America. The president of the Guild on several occasions had threatened me about my politics, and later declared me persona non grata at the Guild, informing me that on at least one network I was on a list of unhirables.

During that dry spell of nearly two and a half years I just worked in our tiny little restaurant, plunged into the role of new father, while I took three classes a week at the Paul Mann/Lloyd Richards Actors Workshop and made the rounds religiously and unsuccessfully.

In 1953 I got a call from the casting director at MGM in New York. Since I had visited him many times in search of jobs, he was familiar with my credentials. "You're too old for what I'm looking for, but I wonder if you'll help me out. I'm looking for a sixteen- or seventeen-year-old kid who can play a juvenile delinquent in a picture we're doing called *Blackboard Jungle*." "I'll certainly give it some thought and call you back," I said. A few days later I phoned him back with a list of eight or ten names of teenage black actors. He thanked me and that was that. About a month later he called me up again, saying, "We haven't been able to find that boy yet. We just wondered if you could come down and we could talk about it—maybe you know someone else who might fit the bill. So drop by my office and let's have a talk."

I "dropped" by his office that very same afternoon. Seated behind his desk in a big leather chair, he stared silently at me, nodding his head as if in agreement with some conclusion reached in the not too distant past. He smiled apologetically and said, "I'm sure by now you've guessed that I really wanted you to come by so I could take a look at you—well, now having seen you let me tell you, you don't look too bad. Would you make a screen test for me?" "Yes, sir, I sure will." "Okay, in a couple of days we'll run a test and I'll send it on to California." Two days later he directed me in a short test that was sent to Pandro Berman, the producer, and Richard Brooks, his director, for a final decision. They approved, and I was hired. I flew to California, and went straight to the MGM Studios to meet the fiery Richard Brooks. He was a strong, tough, agile man of about forty-two years who looked and dressed like a bum most of the time because he hated the codes of the front-office contingent. But were those flashes of street survival instinct that dominated his personality in unexpected moments the real Richard Brooks, or were they a meticulously nurtured camouflage that a forceful personality had chosen in order to ward off, and forever frustrate, simple definitions of itself? Puzzlement. Yet could he not be both? Surely no one of us is one of anything. Well, time itself will ultimately render a judgment as to the many sides of Richard Brooks's personality—provided Richard doesn't find a way to frustrate even time's efforts.

"I'm very glad to have you aboard," he said to me with those fierce, penetrating eyes boring into me. "Thank you very much," I said. "While you're here today, drop into Wardrobe for a fitting and I understand the producer wants you to come up to his office. Tell his secretary to give you a revised script. Read it and if you have any questions, let me know." Off I went for a fitting and then to the office of Pandro Berman, the producer. The secretary said Mr. Berman was away from his desk for a moment, but that my appointment was really at the legal department. She gave me directions and I made my way through the maze of corridors to the legal department, where I was taken into the office of a young lawyer fellow who closed the door behind me and got right down to business. "You know we have your name on a list of

168

people whose loyalty is questionable." "Who, me?" "Yes sir, you. And in order to do this picture you will have to sign a loyalty oath." "Me? A loyalty oath? To who? For what?" "It's just a piece of paper that says you have no intention of overthrowing the Government." "I see. Well, let me think about it." "You'll have to sign it before you can start work." "Yeah? Well, okay, I'll have to let you know." I was perplexed. He stood up, extended his hand, I shook it, and I left.

I never went back to that office. I just put it off, because I didn't want to face that. I didn't want to have to deal with whether or not I was going to sign—because deep down I didn't want to sign. I don't want to feel that my livelihood depends on that kind of a compromise. I mean if I'm loyal—and I'm loyal—I don't have to put it on paper. Who the hell am I to overthrow the Government by force or violence? Is the Government going to sign a loyalty oath in terms of *my* rights? I didn't go back and I didn't call. The day came for the start of the picture and I reported for work. All day I looked for that guy to come down or for someone to send me up to his office, but I didn't hear from him all that day. The next day for sure, I thought. But no—no word. In fact I never heard from him again. I thought it very strange, but then I got to thinking: Did they trick me? I know I signed my contract. Could they have slipped that in the contract? But I say no—because by now I can read pretty fucking good. I can tell a loyalty oath from anything else, and I don't remember signing a loyalty oath in my contract. So how come they're not after me?

One day Richard Brooks said to me out of the blue, "You're a good actor and you've had an interesting life." I said, "Oh?" He said, "Yeah. I've read your whole dossier." I said to myself: Oh, shit—what the hell is this? I know what "dossier" means—like I'm some kind of international spy or something. I said, "I see." He said, "Yeah, I guess they asked you all those things up in the office." He didn't give me a chance to answer—he continued with, "Fuck 'em." Such was his attitude about front offices, that guy from the trenches. I believe he knew I was on the blacklist when he hired me. I believe to this day, though I never discussed it with him, that he said, "I want that kid and don't give me all that bullshit that he knew Paul Robeson or he knew Canada Lee." Those were the charges against me. That I knew Paul Robeson intimately—that I knew Canada Lee—and that I used to get up in union meetings in New York and ask for equal rights for black actors. I'm sure he said, "I don't want to hear all that crap, I just want that actor. Get him for me."

Anyway, I did *Blackboard Jungle,* and at the end of that picture, I went back to New York and into another decline. We also moved from 123rd Street to 146th Street and Riverside Drive, where we found a two-bedroom apartment for ninety-two dollars a month. The restaurant was doing quite well, but it wasn't enough to feed two of us, so John Newton and I decided to open a chain of restaurants—once again using spit and glue as our basic materials. In the months that followed, we managed to open the doors of three additional barbecue restaurants. But the price of spit and glue had gone up. The new establishments quickly ate their way through the few thousand dollars I had cleared from *Blackboard Jungle,* and pushed our partnership deeper into debt. Two of the restaurants never found their stride and failed almost before the paint had dried. The third one caught on, not like wildfire, but enough to make our expansion program not altogether a total loss. Of course we licked our wounds over the failure of fully half our budding empire, but at the same time we were heartened by the demonstrated ability of the surviving half to consistently clear its own expenses, which included a weekly draw for each of the partners ranging from forty to sixty dollars per week, with sixty being the exception rather than the rule.

Then one day I got a phone call at the restaurant from an agent named Martin Baum. This Mr. Baum said he was in business for himself with another agent named Abe Newborn and that they were known in the trade as the Baum-Newborn Agency. "Could you come down here in an hour or so? We'd like to see you." Thirty minutes later I walked in to see this Mr. Baum, who said, "Thank you for coming down, Mr. Poitier. Listen, I think we might have a job for you. It's a job for one week down south where an independent producing company is doing a picture called *The Phenix City Story.* They need a black actor and we would like to submit you." "Fine," I said. The producers were across the street in what was then the Savoy Plaza Hotel at 58th Street and Fifth Avenue. I dashed over to see them, they asked a few questions, looked me over, liked what they saw, and gave me a script. "You look fine to us, Mr. Poitier, why don't you go back and have Mr. Baum call us and we'll make the deal with him." Martin Baum was pleased with this outcome and said, "Okay, I'll make the deal, you go ahead and read the script, and we'll let you know when you leave." I took the script home, read it, and took it back the same day and told Mr. Baum I couldn't play the part. "What do you mean you can't play the part?" I said, "Well, there's nothing wrong with the part. The part is certainly a nice part—but I don't feel anything special about it." The part was that of a black father who worked in and around gambling in a notorious town called Phoenix City. The gambling element threatened the black father (for reasons that are now obscure), he ignored their threats, and they killed his little daughter and threw her body on his lawn. There was nothing derogatory in it, I just didn't feel I should be playing parts like that. He was shocked. I was broke and he knew it and therefore he looked at me as if I was crazy. "What do you mean, 'playing parts' like that? It's a perfectly honorable part that pays $750 a week and you need the money, don't you?" "I can't play it." He shook his head in bewilderment, then said, "Okay, I'll try to get you two weeks. I can't promise, but I'll try, okay?" "I can't play it." "What do you mean, you can't play it? That doesn't make any sense!" "Yes, it does. It makes sense to me." We both fell silent for a moment. Then I explained to Mr. Baum that I could only do things that seemed to me to distinguish me from a dishwasher. In other words, if it's just ordinary work with no significance to it, nothing significant or special about it that sets it apart, then I can't do it. I knew precisely what I meant, but he didn't. He looked at me as if I was a nut case, and after I left, he notified the producers that I wasn't available for their part.

But months later I got another call from Martin Baum, saying, "Come in and see me." Now, Baum was a very dapper, elegant, sharp, and imaginative agent, always wheeling and dealing, always moving and tumbling, always in search of the creative element in every deal. There he was in his hand-sewn tailored suit, his silk tie and Gucci loafers, sitting behind a desk in his office that was itself magnificently decked out as befits a new-breed agency on the come. He was shaking his head and sighing in mock exasperation as if we were picking up exactly

171

where we'd left off months before. "You know something —I don't understand myself." "What's the matter, Mr. Baum?" "Here I am—I've got a pretty good business going for myself. Some solid stable clients, some of whom are as hot as firecrackers. I have a partner, we're making money, we're doing very well, yet—for the last three months I can't get you out of my mind. What the hell is this?" "I don't know, Mr. Baum. What is it?" "I called you down here because—I don't have a job for you—I mean I called you down here to tell you to your face that anybody as crazy as you are, I want to represent them. I know you don't have a job and you haven't worked for some time. Now, do you want to be represented?" "I'd love for you to represent me." "Good. I want to represent you. I don't know where I'm going to get the jobs, but I'm going to find something for you." With a handshake we ended that discussion and began a remarkable association that was to thread its way through the succeeding twenty-five years. Some months later, after *Blackboard Jungle* was released and was a big hit, Lauren Bacall is reported to have said either to John Wayne or to the director William Wellman, who was going to make a picture for John Wayne's company called *Goodbye, My Lady,* "I saw a picture called *Blackboard Jungle* and if you need a young black actor, this kid is absolutely terrific." Thanks to Lauren Bacall, John Wayne's company got in touch with Martin Baum, and in short order I was off to Georgia to work for Bill Wellman.

This fellow Wellman was a very talented man with a lot of sensitivity that he constantly disowned. There was a time in Hollywood when tenderness or sensitivity on the part of an artist, especially a director, was considered a disgrace almost. To show tenderness was feminine; if you were sensitive and there were telltale traces of sentiment in your approach to life, you were suspected of weakness, of not being a real two-fisted hard-cocker. William Wellman, like a lot of directors of his time, made many pictures that personified "macho." Bogart "macho," Cagney "macho," Garfield "macho," Robinson "macho." Macho—macho—macho. But aside from his need to camouflage his sensitive, artistic inclinations, I found William Wellman a truly wonderful man. In later years when I began directing films myself, I would come to fully appreciate his remarkable talents. (Yet another such man of the same era was Raoul Walsh, for whom I worked in *Band of Angels* starring Clark Gable.)

Anyway, after finishing Wellman's picture in Georgia I returned to New York with a net salary barely enough to appease my most pressing creditors. I found an unhappy partner complaining that as things stood, most of the work was on him and that he felt the compensation wasn't equitable. "So I'm asking for a dissolution of our partnership. I think if we separate our resources, divide the two restaurants between us—you take one, I take one —I think it will be best for both of us." I had seen it coming but had been reluctant to force it on the table for an airing. He on the other hand had allowed his resentment to fester too long without articulating it. Yet while what he said was not unexpected, his solution was of such a drastic nature that I was thrown off balance, and by the time I had recovered sufficiently to formulate a reasonable response, I found my pride and ego barring the way to any likely compromise. After the breach we went our separate ways as businessmen while keeping in touch as friends. But traveling solo didn't change things for either of us. It was still a grind. Eventually, Johnny Newton called me on the phone and told me he had sold his restaurant. He reminded me in a weary voice that he was nearly forty years old and couldn't see himself scuffling as hard as he had been for too many more years. "Sidney, I'm going back to Pensacola, Florida—I've had it—gonna take my wife, my family, and probably open up a supper club down there. This ain't worth it, man. I'm gonna ease up and cool down."

I have been witness to the naked process of men lowering their expectations in face of mountains that won't be moved, but they were dreamers for the most part, not simple men who are good with their hands and seek no greener pastures than those hands can realistically fashion. To see John Newton, who wanted only a fraction of what lesser men took for granted, lowering the shades at forty saddened me and left an indelible impression on my mind. The best men don't always win. John sold his restaurant, his apartment, his furniture, I wished him good luck, and he took off—got together a little stack and took off. I was left in New York with my one restaurant that was failing rapidly. During its best days the help consisted of one waitress for the day hours, two at night, and one cook. Now in the absence of Johnny's business acumen and sure hand to keep the enterprise afloat, I had to let one waitress go—then another—then the cook. So I ended up doing the scrubbing, making the cole slaw, washing the dishes, and cooking the chicken and ribs, with one waitress handling the service. On a Tuesday when that waitress was enjoying her day off, I opened the restaurant alone at two-thirty in the afternoon. By eight-thirty or nine o'clock that evening I had sold one sandwich and one order of ribs—seven hours, and I had sold $1.50 worth of food. I said to myself: That's it! I very calmly took off my apron, turned off the gas, turned off the electricity, took the $1.50 out of the register, and went next door to a guy who had a little luncheonette/candy store and gave him all my supplies like mustard and paper plates that I thought he could use. I pulled the restaurant door shut, turned the key in it, and said, "That is the last time I'm going in there." I went home and said to Juanita, "I've just closed the restaurant. I can't make it there anymore. I'm going out to get a job. But first I need to borrow some money from someone, just enough to hold me for a week. I'm exhausted—I need a week's rest. At the end of that week, I'll go out and get a job—I don't know what kind of job yet. Maybe I'll get a taxi driver's license. Maybe." "That would be fine, a taxi might suit you better, give you time off to make the rounds and all," she said.

Before my week of rest had flown, however, a call came in from Martin Baum instructing me to rush downtown to the offices of a Mr. Fred Coe in the NBC complex in Rockefeller Plaza for an audition-interview. According to Marty, a young white writer had written a fantastic piece called "A Man Is Ten Feet Tall" that NBC was going to put on television, and they were looking for a young black actor to play in it. Zipping downtown, I presented myself to Mr. Fred Coe and associates, putting my best foot forward. They were impressed sufficiently to hand me a script, saying, "Mr. Poitier, we the producer, the director, and the writer are unanimous in wanting you to play this part. In fact, it may please you to know that the writer, Mr. Robert Alan Aurthur, had you in mind when he wrote this teleplay. So when you read it we hope you will become as excited about it as we are." After thanking them, I headed for the elevator, but I was overtaken by one of Mr. Coe's assistants, who said, "Excuse me, Mr. Poitier, but in the event you decide to work with us on this project, it would be necessary for you to see a certain gentleman in a certain office in the legal department, and it occurred to me it would facilitate things if you could stop in on your way out." The words "legal department" should have sent up a flag in my mind. They didn't. I took the elevator down (or was it up?) to the legal department, where I was ushered into the office of that certain gentleman. He was a very young man, hardly much older than I was. Very Brooks Brothers, this certain NBC gentleman in his gray flannel suit, very WASP and conservative in his appearance. "I understand you're going to play a part for us." "Yes." "You have to sign a small piece of paper for us." "What kind of paper?" "Well, you know there are those who feel that there are some dangerous people in this country. According to our information, you happen to know some of those dangerous people." "Who are these people—these dangerous people—that I'm supposed to know?" "You worked with a man named Canada Lee for instance." "Yes, I did." (By this time Canada Lee was dead.) "You also know a man named Paul Robeson. As a matter of fact, you attended a salute for Robeson held at the Golden Gate Ballroom." "That is correct." "You spoke in a theatrical sketch that was in praise of Paul Robeson." And so he itemized a list of charges against me that questioned my loyalty. He put it to me that unless I repudiated those charges, I would not be able to play the part.

I was torn inside—a mass of ambivalence. I could easily put my signature there, because what is my signature on their piece of paper? I sure as hell could put my signature on that paper, but—there was a morality to it. Yes, dammit, something of a moral nature had been called into question. Although I was an uneducated kid, by and large, I had begun to structure for myself, chisel out for myself, certain values that were important to my life. Now, I was never under the impression that Paul Robeson was a dangerous person. He certainly wasn't dangerous to me and other black people. And never was I under the impression that my relationship with Canada Lee was an un-American activity. How could I not be proud of Paul Robeson? How could I repudiate a relationship with Canada Lee, from whom I had learned so much about life? The advice passed on to me, the fatherly way he took care of me in South Africa—how could I? Three weeks before he died he told me that he wanted me

175

to learn from some of the mistakes he had made in life. In his last weeks of life, because he was broke, that man *walked* in his illness from New York City to White Plains in support of some black people who had suffered an injustice. Though his fires were banked and his energies low, he continued to speak out openly against the way in which most of our country had been responding to the black community, completely ignoring our rights.

And now I was being asked to repudiate that relationship. Torn between my desire to get on with my career and my revulsion at what they were asking me to do, I broke down and cried. When I cry—I get angry. That man was lucky I didn't throw a chair at his head. I leaned on a file cabinet and sobbed. I couldn't control my tears and had to speak through them, saying what I felt couldn't remain unsaid: "Not only is this unfair, but I have nothing but respect for Paul Robeson—and that's the truth. And if you see my respect for him as un-American, then I *am* fucking un-American." Using my shirt sleeve as a handkerchief, I went on. "I worked with Canada Lee in South Africa. I spent weeks and weeks and weeks with that man, and I happen to respect him too. Now you are telling me that my judgment of these men is suspect? Who the hell are you to tell me about them, huh? I'm not going to sign anything—you got that?"

I remember feeling particularly good that I had said my piece. I went home and called my agent, who in the meantime had been informed of the impasse by Robert Alan Aurthur. And then Aurthur, single-handedly, set in motion a colossal effort on the part of the creative forces (producers, writer, director) aimed at bringing about a workable compromise between the network, the advertising agency, and the Philco Company on one side, and me and my agent on the other. Mr. Aurthur said to me on the phone, "Did you read the script?" "No, I didn't." "Please read the script—you may change your mind." "It's not my mind that has to be changed, Mr. Aurthur." "Please, read the script anyway. We're working on it from this end. I've got to have you to play this part. I wrote it for you." I read the script that evening. It was dynamite, pure dynamite—but my position remained unchanged, and a compromise was finally worked out

176

that didn't require my signing a repudiation of Robeson or Lee.

We went into rehearsals with the play, and it was a huge success. Hilda Simms, Martin Balsam, Don Murray, and I played a live, coast-to-coast, one-performance television show on the Sunday evening Philco Playhouse and were watched by millions and millions of people. Halfway through the program I forgot my lines. Just went blank. Don Murray's eyes flew open, I looked into them, and my eyes flew open. Panic! Millions of people looking at me. Time dragged. Blood rushed to my head. Silence everywhere. With its gears stuck, my memory locked and two helpless actors in 5 million living rooms lost rhythm, lost their tongues, were drenched in instant sweat, and were about to go crashing downhill out of control into the waiting arms of raw disaster. Was it the quickness and mental agility of youth that gave wings to my mind for the swift journey back to the top of the scene, from where it could run over the terrain speech by speech in search of the point where my memory had short-circuited, and allow me to regain my rhythm and continue on with the play? Perhaps. Or did the assistant director off-camera, out of microphone range, throw me a cue, a word, a signal, a sentence from the line that was refusing to pass through my consciousness? Perhaps. Time tinkers with facts at the demands of ego and vanity, especially in matters of terror and panic. At any rate, I recovered and pressed on. No one—except the technicians, the director, the writer, and Don Murray—was aware that I had "gone up." The elapsed time was no more than 10 seconds by the clock. The viewing audience received it as a dramatic pause—natural to the emotional content of the scene.

The production was a qualified success. NBC was bombarded with calls from all over the country. Most people were thrilled with the show—others hated it. Philco was threatened with cancellation of many of its franchises because some viewers thought that Hilda Simms was a white actress. (Hilda Simms, as you may or may not know, is a very fair-skinned black actress who played my love interest in the teleplay.) The Philco Playhouse people hastened to explain that she wasn't white, but it made no difference to the hard-core dissenters whose pressure threw an economic scare into the Philco Manufacturing Corporation. This pressure was brought to bear not only because a black actress was thought to be white, but also because the Philco Playhouse producers had the courage and sense of fairness to examine universal human questions in a black show when large segments of the viewing audience were unaccustomed to black shows.

For me it was a personal triumph. First, because it went so well after the near-tragic lapse of memory, and second, because it was received with wonderfully high praise by the critics and by the people in the Industry. In 1975 we did the motion picture version of "A Man Is Ten Feet Tall" and called it *Edge of the City*. There were some cast changes: John Cassavetes in place of Don Murray, Jack Warden in place of Martin Balsam, Ruby Dee in place of Hilda Simms, and Martin Ritt directing instead of Robert Mulligan. Our executive producer was David Susskind, a dynamic, bright, tough, mountain-mover. Along with the author, Robert Alan Aurthur, David Susskind contributed appreciably to the increase of job opportunities for minority actors in New York City.

12 Africa

WHILE WE WERE making *Edge of the City* I had a call from Richard Brooks saying that he was going to East Africa to make a film, and wanted me to do the picture. Martin Baum worked out a salary deal for me that guaranteed $25,000. Rich, right? I got sick just two or three weeks before I was supposed to leave. I woke up one day weak and feverish, grew weaker and more feverish by the hour, until I was a devastated person by the end of the day. The eleven days it took for that fever to break were the worst eleven days I ever spent in bed. I couldn't sleep, day or night, for more than ten minutes at a time, before I was awake tossing and turning, my whole body on fire. Lying there with the most awful illness I had ever experienced, I found myself hoping that something would happen to take me out of the pain. On the eleventh day, my resistance having long been crushed beyond the point of caring whether I lived or died, the fever broke—pow! My wife wrapped me in blankets and I just stayed there on the bed sweating for hours and hours—feeling wonderful as all that poison poured out of me. At the end of it I was weak and had lost a lot of weight, but I was still able to go off to Africa on schedule.

When I arrived in Nairobi, in Kenya, to film *Something of Value,* based on Robert Ruark's novel about a war being waged by an armed guerrilla force called the Mau Mau against the colonial forces representing Great Britain, I was scared. I had been programmed and expertly propagandized by front-page accounts in newspapers about atrocities committed by the Mau Mau guerrillas, not only against the white settlers but against uncooperative black Africans as well. According to those reports, the Mau Mau were some superman dudes wreaking havoc on defenseless white settlers who had done nothing to deserve such barbaric assaults on their existence. Any violent response on the part of the white settlers was amost always in self-defense, according to the newspapers. I was not yet politically aware enough to decipher the subtleties or pay extra-close attention to the fine print; had I been savvy about the politics of race and war and economics, I would have had my grain of salt at the ready every time I sat down to digest a front-page account of the uprising in Kenya. AP, UP, and UPI were clues that would not have gone unnoticed. Associated Press, United Press, and United Press International were the sources, the compilers, the licensed transmitters of information and news to readers, viewers, and listeners all over the world. Did the news service people, the reporters, the people they gathered their information from, the people they sent their information to—did they as a body have an opinion as to which side they would like to see win the war? And if so, how much was that preference influenced by race and economics? The subtle hand of politics was everywhere around the question of independence for Kenya, pressing its palm against the will of the majority and caring little for the moral, ethical, and human values of those who sought to free themselves from the rule of a corrupt minority. Neither the Mau Mau nor the tribe from which they sprang had a wire service, or powerful friends in high places of officialdom, no Western nations willing to sell them guns and very few well-wishers outside Africa itself to applaud their challenge of European colonialism—yet the Mau Mau guerrillas would win the war, because of a fatal weakness in the other guy's politics. More than its lack of humanity, more than its not being representative of the people, more than its being tired, more than its being impotent, colonialism in Kenya was rotten. And as with a fruit when it passes from ripe to rotten, there is nothing left for it to do; its very last act will be falling from the tree.

Upon my arrival in Nairobi I was greeted at the hotel by Richard Brooks, who had seen that a comfortable room was waiting for me and that there would be no problem about my eating in the dining room—blacks had not been staying at the hotel until that time. In making arrangements, Richard saw that every base was covered in order to minimize any difficulty I might encounter.

However, to show how screwed up one can get in misconceptions, there was the question of snakes. I was under the impression that there were snakes in Africa—and there were. I was also under the impression that there were poisonous snakes, lots of them—and there were. I was also under the impression that those poisonous snakes were under my bed. Indeed they were not—but you couldn't quite convince me of that, especially when I was in bed and had turned out the lights. For some inexplicable reason I would have to jump up every hour or so and look under the bed. Where did that come from? Was it too obvious to assume that it arose from the whole mythology of Africa found in Western literature, that characterized it as wild, primitive, infested with dangerous animals, and crawling with poisonous snakes that slip into your bed at night, and all that kind of shit? Yes, too obvious—and it lets off the hook all those dumbass Tarzan movies, and the white hunter Bwana movies, in which lions, elephants, and alligators are always chasing the hapless African gun bearer up a baobab tree, and the most sinister purveyors of African culture, the Jungle Jim–type comic strips that represented the initial exposure of many black American children to "what it must be like in Africa."

There I was in my hotel room in the real Africa, totally victimized by the books I had read, the movies I had seen, and the stories I had heard, to such an extent that

I was too terrified to go to sleep. Mind you, I made sure the door was locked. I made sure the window was closed. I made sure that even the smallest entrance into the room was secured. So, objectively speaking, how was a snake going to get in there? "If he gets in here he ain't going to be no bigger than my little finger, and if I can't handle a little son of a gun like that—shoot, I've got everything under control." In a matter of seconds this earnest attempt to manufacture self-assurance fizzled in the light of my galloping phobia. I got into bed, positioning myself dead center, which allowed me an advantage— if a snake tried to crawl over the side, I would certainly have the jump on him. Every time I approached the bathroom I would yank the door open and peer inside to see if there were any snakes in there. What the hell is this? I puzzled, trying to understand the deep-seated unconscious anxieties that were manifesting themselves in my fixation about snakes. Though I can't swear to it, I believe I finally went to sleep that first night with the lights on and one eye open for snakes.

The day after my arrival, Richard Brooks took me to see the locations we were going to shoot in, most of which were located in a game park not far from the hotel. I saw all kinds of fantastic animals up close—lions, leopards, gazelles, giraffes, wildebeests, and others. Then back to the hotel that afternoon for start of rehearsals. Rock Hudson, the star of the movie, had a very heavy work schedule at the beginning of the picture that didn't include me. During those free days I went around Nairobi exploring and learning about that part of Africa. It was different from South Africa—until sober reflection revealed that it wasn't *so* much different, come to think of it. I spent many days roaming, looking, and listening. And when it came time for me to start shooting, we returned to some of those same areas I had been browsing through. We filmed in and around the Nairobi area for a number of weeks, during which time I received word from New York that my third daughter, Sherri, was born (it was July 1956). Then from Nairobi we moved 125 miles north to the little town of Nanyuki at the foot of mighty Mount Kenya. We stayed at what was then known as the William Holden Safari Lodge, a beautiful, tranquil place nestling in the shadow of the mountain. Elephants and lions could be seen in the still of the night walking around on the lawn outside our windows—it got so quiet out there that if an elephant let go, you could hear it falling on the ground. Needless to say, I was doing my under-the-bed check every hour.

In the course of filming on the mountain, the big day came when Richard Brooks and I had a difference of opinion. We were doing a scene in which I was on the run from an ambush attack in which my wife had been killed by the settlers, but I had managed to escape by running through the woods with our little baby in my arms. The camera was on a dolly and the dolly was on 200 feet of tracks and the tracks were on the road. The script called for me to run through the woods—not on the road, because the camera was on the road and the audience wouldn't be seeing the road in the film, just me running through the woods. I had been told that Mount Kenya was a notorious place for the black mamba snake. I had also been told that the black mamba snake and the green mamba snake were the most dangerous snakes in the world, and that they weren't big ones—they were small ones. Furthermore, it was generally conceded by the local population that there was no way one could recover if hit by one of those. No way!

Armed with this piece of folklore, I go over to Mr. Brooks and say, "You know that I know that you know how much I respect and appreciate you. This is the second job you've given me. The first job was my coming of age, in a sense—without you I wouldn't be here and I'm grateful to you and will forever be grateful to you. However, you are asking me to run through these woods, and all I'm wearing on my feet are a pair of old sandals. I have to run at least two hundred to three hundred feet through the woods, my feet coming down in the grass and the underbrush area where snakes are possibly minding their own business, and here comes this big old foot slamming down next to them. Probably out of self-defense they will take a shot at one of these two feet. Let it hereby be known to you that to demonstrate my appreciation, I am going to run through the woods one time. I want you to have your camera ready and I want your cameraman and your operator to be apprised of the fact that they are going to get *one* shot of me running through there. Don't ask me to run at a certain speed—that's bullshit—I am going to run through there as fast as I can. If you get me —you've got it. If you don't—too fucking bad. Is that clear?" With an understanding nod of his head he said,

My father, Reginald Poitier

My mother, Evelyn

I'm standing in front of what remains of our house on Cat Island.

1943 I was in the Army... and I wore a zoot suit.

Right: My daughters Pamela, Beverly, Gina, and Sherri

With my daughter Sherri

Our home in New York City

Mrs. Eleanor Roosevelt, my wife Juanita, and me. Mrs. Roosevelt is presenting me with the Silver Bear award for *The Defiant Ones*.

Harry and I bail out a group of civil rights protesters who were staging a sit-in at the office of the South African Consul General. At Harry's right is SNCC Executive Secretary James Foreman and in front of him SNCC Chairman John Lewis.

In 1972 at the "Harlem Homecoming" with Brock Peters, Ruby Dee, and Cab Calloway

At the opening of *Uptown Saturday Night* with Coretta King

Below: I'm carrying Anika, Joanna is wheeling Sydney.

With Canada Lee in *Cry, the Beloved Country*, 1952

Go, Man, Go!, 1954

Blackboard Jungle,
1955

Something of Value, 1957

Band of Angels, 1957

Edge of the City, 1957

Above: The Defiant Ones with Tony Curtis, 1958

Right: Porgy and Bess with Sammy Davis, Jr., Claude Akins, and Dorothy Dandridge

Below: A scene with Dorothy Dandridge

Above: Paris Blues with Diahann Carroll and *below* with
Paul Newman, 1961

The stage production of *A Raisin in the Sun*. Lloyd Richards is directing me and Claudia McNeil, while Ruby Dee and Diana Sands watch.

In the movie with Claudia McNeil

Lilies of the Field, 1963

Anne Bancroft presenting me with my Oscar for *Lilies*

Duel at Diablo, 1966

Opposite, above: A Patch of Blue with Elizabeth Hartman, 1965

Opposite, below: To Sir with Love, 1967

In the Heat of the Night with Rod Steiger, 1967

Opposite, above: Guess Who's Coming to Dinner with Spencer Tracy and Katharine Hepburn

and *below* with Roy Glenn, Beah Richards, and Katherine Houghton

The Lost Man with Joanna, 1969

Let's Do It Again with
Bill Cosby, 1975

Directing

"We'll try our best to get it on the first go." I got on my start mark 300 feet down the line, Richard Brooks said, "Roll 'em," and when the camera was spinning at twenty-four frames per second, he yelled, "Action," and before you could say "snake in the grass," my ass was out of there. The man on the camera said, "I don't know if I got him." Richard said, "Sid, I don't know if we got you." I said, "Well, that's not my problem. Listen, you had your shot. That's it." I, in fact, did not run again.

The Mau Mau guerrillas came by two or three times. Nobody saw them; we just knew they were there. They didn't bother us. The local people said they were keeping an eye on us to see that what we were doing would not damage their cause, and once they were satisfied of that, they would be off about their business. After finishing on the mountain, we returned to Nairobi for a couple of days and then flew back to California to finish the film.

The city of Nairobi, the nation of Kenya, and the production of *Something of Value* were all one hell of a learning experience. It is not possible to walk away from such encounters without lessons learned, subtle changes registered, some long-held perceptions altered and others solidified. And because my acting technique was no longer based on shabby and outmoded concepts (thanks to the Paul Mann/Lloyd Richards Actors Workshop), I began to recognize very tiny touches of improvement here and there in my acting—nothing resembling a breakthrough, but a little movement in the right direction.

While in California, I got a call from David Susskind. I liked David and was very pleased to hear from him, and when he said, "Hey, let's get together and have some dinner—do you know a couple of girls?" I said, "Fine," and arranged a date with two gorgeous black girls who were filled with excitement when I mentioned that we would be with a New York producer of television, theater, and films. I picked the girls up and we met David at a restaurant near his hotel. After dinner we decided to go to the home of one of the girls for a nightcap. Mind you, we were all a little smashed already as a result of two bottles of wine at dinner. But the night was young, so we piled into the convertible Oldsmobile I was renting. David was in the back seat with one of the girls, feeling no pain, while I was up in front under the wheel, zipping along, loose and relaxed with a beautiful companion next to me. Mellow and promising was the mood as we cruised along

La Brea Avenue heading south. As we neared the intersection of La Brea and Washington, the traffic signal flipped from green to cautionary amber. In an attempt to beat the imminent red light, I squeezed my foot down on the accelerator, juicing the engine of the Oldsmobile. The car leaped forward, barreling into the intersection, and I had begun my left turn when an empty RTD bus roaring homeward at 60 miles an hour came surging over a rise right at us in a similar attempt to beat the red light. It hit us head-on with a force that folded the Oldsmobile like a crushed paper bag and threw me out of the driver's seat 30 feet north along La Brea. The girl who was sitting in the front seat next to me was thrown across the street to the other side of Washington Boulevard. The other girl and David were still in the car.

When I came to, I looked around. Across the street, some people were standing over the girl on the sidewalk, and there were some other people at the car. I thought David was dead. I thought the girl with him in the back seat was dead. Someone helped me up, and we moved toward my young companion lying unconscious across the street. Dazed and aching, I knelt down to help, moments before she began to stir and moan her way back to consciousness. The man who had helped me to my feet was still at my side. He leaned close to me and said, "I think she'll be all right. Listen, I was driving the bus. There are some people still in your car." We looked at each other, and in a moment of silent absolution, we settled it between us, clearing the air of blame-fixing. Hurrying to the car, we found David and the girl unconscious but alive. Thank God, within a matter of minutes after we extricated them from the wreck, they both regained consciousness. The car was so mangled that the mechanics at the car rental place said it was impossible for anyone to have walked away from that wreck. Yet all four of us had walked away from it, and with no real injury to anyone. Clearly a friendly force was riding with us.

Upon completing the film, I returned to New York with the after-tax remains from my $25,000 salary in pocket, a figure that gave me the pleasurable realization that I was, at last, moving outside the gravitational pull of the monster machine. And of course I hoped that with the concurrence of the good Lord and the salesmanship of an inspired agent like Martin Baum I would break entirely out of its sphere of influence and into an orbit all my own.

Juanita and I, with cautious regard for the uncertainty of the acting profession, took the big step of purchasing a two-family house in a blue-collar neighborhood in Mount Vernon, New York, only a few blocks from our good friends Ossie and Ruby Davis. A substantial down payment equal to nearly half of the purchase price was exacted by the mortgage holders, based on the high-risk nature of showfolks' incomes, and after closing fees, etc., we had very little left. A chancy move, but nothing ventured, nothing gained, right? With our daughters Beverly, Pamela, and Sherri, we moved to the suburbs—to a little piece of America that had our name on it.

Work experiences on the films *Cry, the Beloved Country* in South Africa and *Something of Value* in Kenya had stretched me, fascinated me, scared me, confused me, helped me to define me, and enriched my life in endlessly pleasurable ways, in painfully maturing ways, in joltingly disturbing ways that ripped me from my boyhood moorings and shoved me violently onto the open sea of an adult world.

But there was more to come: *Mark of the Hawk* in Eastern Nigeria, *The Wilby Conspiracy* in East Africa, and beyond this writing—who knows? The old country and I could be meant to touch each other many more times before we say goodby. However, as things stand now, of my four experiences of Africa, *Mark of the Hawk* was the most unpredictable and infuriating, all because of my leading lady, the stunning, sexy, free-spirited whirlwind with the sexy legs, Eartha (one of a kind) Kitt. A small independent film producer seeking to move up to the big time had put together, with blessings and stacks of dollars from the Presbyterian Church, a full-length feature about a labor movement in Africa, a story with strong and healthy religious overtones. His and the church's intent was to release the film commercially, giving it as broad an exposure as possible in the hopes of showing the world the good work the church was doing in this independence-conscious continent. The script wasn't bad, the church was evidently willing to take a bold step, and I rather liked the whole idea, so I said, "Okay, I would like to do it." That Eartha Kitt would be my leading lady sweetened the pot that much more. The young up-and-coming documentary producer, whose name was Lloyd Young, had also written the screenplay, and according to his logic, that made him the best possible person to function as the film's director.

Lloyd Young was an indefatigable scrambler out of Burbank, California, distinguished less for his skills as a filmmaker than for his Quaker-like adherence to honesty and fair play. A contradiction, that Lloyd Young—an exception to the rule. Charm, hard work, guts, tenacity, and a misplaced sense of calling would be an on-the-nose description of this man who could have been excellent in any number of professions but fell in love with one at which it seemed he could be no more than adequate. No matter. Lloyd Young the man scored heavily as a good human being, and that has to count for a lot.

I was already at work in Eastern Nigeria (known for a brief and violent period as Biafra) when Eartha Kitt arrived on location several days before she was scheduled to begin work. Enugu, the capital of Eastern Nigeria, was in every way a small town with visions of becoming a big city. Its commercial district in the center of town was barely three or four streets, made up of ten or twelve buildings dominating an area surrounded by a few dozen small shops and a couple of outdoor markets, beyond which at the outer edges of the town were some very light industries such as building supplies, cabinetmaking, supply warehouses for farmers, a few banks digging in for the anticipated growth of the years immediately ahead, and the government-owned hotel-chalet tourist facility where our film group was housed. The majority of Enugu's population lived up in the hills in shanties and mud huts that overlooked the town below. In the mornings they poured down into the town by the hundreds to work for the middle-class blacks and upper-class Europeans who dominated the economic life of the region and could thereby afford to live in town, and at night they returned by steep and dangerous trails to places a thousand years away.

I had met Eartha before she came to Africa, but never more than to say "Hello," and I could tell when we were introduced on location that she had no recollection of those greetings. One evening after dinner she said to me, "Would you like to go and see what it's like up in the hills?" "Yes, that would be interesting," I said. "Tomorrow. We'll do it tomorrow when you've finished work," said Eartha.

Late the next day we dressed in clothes that didn't altogether erase our Western appearance as we had hoped they would, but were sufficiently muted to make us almost indistinguishable from the people streaming toward the hills and home at the end of a day's work. We rode bicycles through the town to the base of the hill, and continued on foot up the almost vertical narrow pathways threading in random fashion toward the sky. Stepping casually into the flow, we were immediately swept upward by the crowd of homeward-bound workers, and we quickly became excited at the opportunities made possible by our anonymity as we listened to bits of conversations carried on around us in tongues foreign, ancient, and unknown. Reaching a small plateau where the pathways forked into numerous branches, each leading to a different settlement or village, we elected to follow the largest stream of people, who seemed to be climbing onward to the next plateau. We reasoned that they must be heading toward the largest settlement in the hills, which is exactly where we wanted to go.

The next plateau was a revelation. A sprawling, bustling settlement, as old as time itself, abruptly came into view as we climbed the last few feet along the rugged path that emptied onto the flat lands at the very top of the hills. Humming with activity under the crimson glow of a setting sun, that hilltop settlement, that conglomeration of large family compounds, that cluster of "unincorporated villages" African-style, was everywhere preparing to receive its weary breadwinners.

Eartha's face was a wonderment: her wide eyes eagerly drinking in—gulping down—everything; her lips creased in the smile that adds such mystery to her tantalizing rendition of "C'est Si Bon," she whispered, "Beautiful. Isn't that beautiful?" She wasn't talking to me, of that I'm sure; Eartha has a way of being with you and talking, but not talking to you.

Here was a main street made up of market stalls and small shops selling cotton dry goods, vegetables, root medicines, dried meat, etc., etc. But our attention was drawn to the mud hut buildings, the corrugated tin buildings and lean-tos whose various architectural styles might seem to suggest some cultural significance, but really only reflected the economic reality that these were the cheapest materials available to a people who had to catch as catch can. These buildings then were all households, many with individual outside kitchens surrounded by walls woven from straw. Others were serviced by a communal cooking area conveniently located in a cluster of six or eight households. Eartha and I roamed in and out of compounds, strolled through various cooking areas, and came brazenly close to intruding a couple of times by wandering into private living quarters.

When the sun had gone and the sounds of night were tuning up, we stood in a communal kitchen watching a particular African woman stirring the contents of a cast-iron pot with a cooking stick. This woman put me in mind of Evelyn Poitier, and strange yet familiar sights and sounds awakened memories of happy moments between a mother and son on an island both far away and long ago. Meanwhile, Eartha squatted down on her haunches ten feet away and watched that very real African woman who had caught my memory's eye. Studying her intently, Eartha seemed to be looking for clues. It was my guess that she too was reminded of someone—something—somewhere. There she was, an American black woman, watching her African sister standing just ten feet away; yet generations of time and thousands of miles separated them. Eartha watched and wondered, intrigued by the possibility that a bond might exist between them, a bond strong enough to have survived time and distance. Soon the African lady became aware of our presence and returned our stares while trying to read our features in the semidarkness, but the light from her cooking fire wasn't strong enough and she gave up the effort on the likely assumption that we had to be somehow, some way family of a sort. She waved, nodded her head, half curtsied from the knee, and mumbled what we took to be a greeting in her native tongue, before returning to her cooking.

Suddenly we heard drums in the distance exploding into wild rhythms and accompanied by chanting and singing. Eartha stood up, listening intently. She didn't have to speak—I knew she wanted to follow the sound—so we took off in search of the action. A quarter of a mile away we found a group of singers, dancers, and musicians energetically rehearsing for an upcoming performance of some kind. The language barrier, coupled with ignorance of the area's cultural calendar, successfully hampered our efforts to learn precisely where and when whatever they were rehearsing for would take place, but it was evident that Eartha, visibly excited by the raw theatrics unfolding before her, was loving every moment of it. Her body picking up the rhythm, she swayed with the dancers, repeating their movements like a slightly delayed echo, and all the while itching to join those kindred souls who could speak to her in a language her artist's heart could understand. Suddenly, Eartha exploded with laughter as she moved with the music—big, free, and unexpected laughter came rolling up from inside her, telling the world that she was feeling good on this evening in Africa.

Eartha and I worked together for the next days, and then she disappeared. She was told she had a week off according to the schedule, and the next morning she vanished. No one knew where she had gone, and in a few days we became anxious about the unpredictable Eartha returning in time to continue shooting. Rumors and speculations filled the air and intensified, posing real and disturbing questions about her safety. "Did she go back to the States?" "Maybe she's flown to Ghana or the Ivory Coast." "Jesus, I hope she isn't—I mean, I hope she's alive and all right." "Didn't she mention to anybody where she was going? I mean, anything she may have said in conversation over dinner the evening before she took off?" "Hey, come to think of it, I do remember her saying she wanted to go exploring, but I didn't think she meant *now*, or by herself." "Who says she's by herself?" "Eartha? Listen, that lady is a loner and more than a little strange. There ain't no place she won't go if she takes a fancy."

Then, to everyone's relief, Eartha reappeared on the eve of her scheduled return to filming. Her account, embellishments notwithstanding, of how she had spent her week was amazing. She had gone deep into the jungle as a guest of a chief to visit his people, had involved herself in their lives, stayed for a few days, then moved on upriver to random places and other encounters, one of which produced a genuine proposal of marriage from a handsome prince from the Moslem north who had already, by Eartha's observation, seven or eight wives too many. Next, she moved downriver to study the dance and music of the powerful Urubus, who sent her back at the end of her adventures loaded down with gifts of appreciation "for a returning sister out of the Western world."

At any rate, the returning sister, professional that she was, was fully prepared when we resumed filming the following morning. Things are not always what they seem. The mercurial Eartha Kitt in a work situation was as dependable as money in the bank. The fact of her utter professional responsibility was at variance with the gossip column portrait of a volatile sex kitten standing poised and ever ready to scratch out some unsuspecting eyes on a moment's notice or unleash a tongue-lashing of headline proportions, giving rise to the speculation that there might conceivably exist more than one Eartha Kitt. The cattiest observers have speculated that as many as four Earthas may be housed in that one sensual frame. But no one knew for sure, and since I had not met the other three, the Eartha Kitt I was working with was, to put it mildly, more than interesting enough to keep me constantly on my toes.

13 Tensions

JUANITA'S FATHER was an Alabama-born itinerant bricklayer who moved around to wherever the work was, and his family followed him. So they lived in various parts of Alabama and Georgia before moving north to Washington, D.C., and finally New York City. Juanita was raised with all the complications of being female and black that too often result from limited educational opportunities and cause too many girls to arrive at the threshold of their young womanhood suffering from a certain degree of cultural deprivation. From such a beginning, for better or worse, Juanita Marie Hardy met, fell in love with, and married a young man who was far more culturally deprived than she.

What I remember most fondly from the times when our marriage was really working well was the familiness of it. She and her large loving family were a kind of safe, warm place for me. At those times Juanita was indeed a lot of fun for me, given all the mothering that comes with being well taken care of at home, the food, the sex, the other physical gratifications. I don't know how much fun I was to Juanita. I can't imagine having been very much fun at all. I didn't know about sharing—about giving, about being generous with myself and my time and my thoughts. I never contributed to the sharing necessary between two people if they're ever going to develop a good, healthy family life. I was too messed up; I was running too fast by the time we met. In retrospect I realize that if Juanita had been a more urbane sophisticated woman she would have thrown me out early on, or probably wouldn't have married me at all—or gotten an annulment after six weeks of living with such a cultural zombie. But love accounts for an awful lot. And she was always so friendly and sunny; when she wasn't, it was because I was such a downer. I had been revved up to a point where I had to attack the living of life, go after it with an aggression that Juanita was not accustomed to. Partly because of the serenity that was the essence of her personality, and partly because of what racism does to the minds of young blacks, she had, by the age of twenty-two, staked out her perimeters and was content to function within them. When it first dawned on her that she wasn't going to become President of the United States, she was not especially moved to ask why. When I found I wasn't going to be the President of the United States, I wanted to know "How come?" She was clearly content to say, "Okay. Understandably, I don't like what happens to black people in this society, and I'm enraged by the restrictions that are placed upon us by the unjust and insensitive laws of the land. I'll fight—I'll do whatever I'm able to about these conditions—but in the meantime I'm going to try to live my life as best I can." And she set out to do just that. To do "just that" meant getting married, having some children, and being as comfortable as possible while raising those children and getting them educated. Had I been raised in the same milieu, I might have been forced by those same relentless pressures to pull in my boundaries to fit designs that were not in my best interest.

Back in New York with Juanita and the children, I began to become aware that our marriage, while working on some levels, was falling apart in other fundamental areas. By then it was plainly evident that Juanita had no interest in the theater, no interest in films, no interest in learning about either. So there was nothing we could discuss beyond the children and certain aspects of the family's day-to-day living. When it came to my work, Juanita and I were not able to communicate—we couldn't talk for five minutes. As a result, I began to find a certain kind of fulfillment beyond the home. For instance, intellectually I was still a sponge, and very interested in learning new things, exploring new questions and exchanging opinions on any subject that would stir my curiosity. To fulfill those needs I found friends like Julian Mayfield, Bill Marshall, Omar Van Prince, Elwood Smith, Henry Scott, and Vivian Cervantes. Over a period of time I found myself needing more and more intellectual stimulation, and the more I sought it outside my home, the more an uneasy guilt would build up inside me. I wasn't home enough. I wasn't home enough functioning within the family structure—I just couldn't be. I really couldn't. What I didn't realize until later was that a sizable incompatibility existed between Juanita and me. It was so strong and I was so unaware of it—and I suspect she was too—that we just simply tried in our ignorance to remain together as a family. But the basic incompatibility hounded us relentlessly. I began playing golf, and got to the point that I would leave the house early in the morning and play golf all day. Far more important, my children never saw me as I should have been. I was too often angry and uncomfortable. I think I was sensitive to them, and I tried hard to be there for them and do things with them—teaching them to read, teaching them multiplication.

But . . . I ran a strict house—my wife ran a casual house. I was a disciplinarian—my wife was very permissive. I insisted that my children must develop very solid attitudes about responsibility to themselves, responsibility to the family unit, and responsibility to whatever tasks they pursued. That's how I operated, that's what I found necessary for survival, and I wanted to pass it all on to my kids. But I wasn't quite able to, because their mother was from a different school. She would rather do for them than force them to do for themselves. And she had allies —she had her sister, her mother, her father, her brother, and her friends, plus a friend who worked for us as a housekeeper—and the crunch of clashing styles left its mark on me all the more because I wasn't prepared to stay home in defense of my position. As a result, there was tension—a lot of tension.

I believed that children at a certain age should know how to do certain things for themselves; that the cornerstones for responsible adulthood must be laid early in a child's life; that by a certain age, a child should no longer be permitted to skirt any necessary activity purely on the basis that it's "dull and boring." He (or in the case of my children, she) must be taught that every lesson in life does not come in an entertainment wrapper; a child should be trained, as early as possible, to identify boredom, tedium, and dullness as hurdles that have to be worked through rather than reasons for discontinuing something.

My children were born during a time when permissiveness reigned supreme in too many homes in the United States. And beginning in their tenderest years in that environment, their father, the dishwasher-turned-actor, started on a miraculous streak of prosperity. Permissiveness and prosperity were a potent mix in the fifties and sixties, a mix that has left its mark on practically every doorstep in America. Not all bad, certainly, but on the whole a formula too weak to build self-sufficiency of the kind we now find in disturbingly short supply. The need, indeed the necessity, to learn to do things for themselves and by themselves came hard to many of that particular generation. But an encouraging number of them, including my own children, seem to be turning out a shade better than some of us imagined they would. And today permissiveness is not quite as welcome a guest as she once was. Time, we pray, will strip her of her crown and whittle her down to size.

Tensions in the marriage were surfacing more frequently by the middle of 1957. I was more likely to roam around than not. I began to grow resentful that I was growing in one direction and Juanita in another. In trying to talk about it, I suggested that she go back to school as the first step in broadening her interests to include areas outside the home. Little did I realize that I was not only trying to change her lifestyle but trying to alter the woman she fundamentally was. A fool's errand, and a destructive one. "Loving suggestions backed up by friendly persuasion" was how I viewed it at the time, when in reality it was an anxiety-ridden attempt on my part to dictate what her life should be. In this regard, I was about as subtle as a Mack truck in a rose garden. The years of struggle to survive had developed into a psychological burden. I was beginning to display obvious signs of neurosis. Had I been smart enough, I would have recognized them earlier, since most of them stuck out like a sore thumb. Certainly, in my relationship with Juanita there were many, many signals. I was asking too much of myself, too much of everyone around me, but most especially much too much of her.

I had had little or no help with the decisions that had brought me to where I was, and the journey had taken so much energy, so much feeling, had been so complex, so taxing, that it had forced me into an undue reliance on native wit to survive (and I had never been thought rich in that resource). It had required not only above-normal use but on occasion considerable abuse of my emotional apparatus. It had required that I play father, mother, and counselor to Sidney Poitier, and that was a hell of a responsibility. Every time a decision had to be made I had nowhere to take it for an impartial review, or a look at its underside or its far side. I had very little objective input on anything, nothing beyond what I could supply for myself. I was constantly being pressured for a decision, an attitude, or a commitment, and sometimes when I made the commitment, took the position, came to the conclusion, it turned out to be the wrong commitment, the wrong position, the wrong conclusion. I got burned—I got hurt—I lost ground. I didn't have time to do anything except absorb the loss and go on, hoping to register enough of the experience to avoid a repetition down the road. But I was always living so close to the precipice that there was no surcease from responsibility— ever. My wife just didn't understand enough of what was going on inside me to help—perhaps I hadn't been able to open myself to her. I believe the only person who might have been able to help me at that time was the Army psychiatrist who had treated me. He would have understood the kind of pressures that could build up in a young man locked into rat-racing in New York, who twelve or thirteen years before was walking around the sandy beaches of the Caribbean with not a thought in his head.

My marriage continued to deteriorate. Being so tightly strung, I found it easy to convince myself that all of it was Juanita's fault, even that our incompatibility was due to her: were she not as she was, there wouldn't have been any incompatibility, and therefore I wouldn't be so tense and short-fused. It wasn't very often that I envisioned the difficulty as lying with myself. Juanita would have been quite happy to settle there where we were, incompatibility and all, provided I just eased up on her a little and gave her a bit more room to try to enjoy a reasonably comfortable life. She prayed for it. But I was already too far out of sync. I was somehow being pushed to save the world. I was somehow being pushed to raise my black brothers and sisters to the next level. I was being pushed to change the world as it related to me and mine. I was being pushed to do the impossible. I figured that black people just wouldn't survive without me saving them through dealing with the pressures on myself. I didn't think the *world* would survive if I didn't live and develop in a certain way.

And my eye was fastened to the possibility that somewhere in those years my dreams could materialize and I could shoot through a barrier into uncharted waters where no black actor had ever been before. But of course there were two sides to that edge, and I was obsessed with the nightmare of being unable to make the distance and falling off into the realization of my fears. In either case, the years ahead threatened to be costly—but, shit, at the point of no return in what to then had been a hell of an interesting life, all things considered, who was going to quibble about price? Certainly not Evelyn Poitier's little Sidney. Besides, the neurosis, insecurities, fears, doubts, illusions, and other objects of my complaint may have been necessary companions for the completion of my journey. Beleaguered Juanita was very comfortable when I was away, because she had the children to care for and be comforted by, and she was close to her parents and other members of a loving family. If I had just left her alone, she would have had a terrific life—but then along would come the nitpicker. Me. I imagine that every time I called and announced that I was on my way home, she probably said, at least subconsciously, "Oh, Lord, here he comes again." And indeed I would.

I was building up to something. Moving at intense speeds through social and professional levels, and arriving at most of them without a road map, revealing my heavy reliance on instinct, crossed fingers, and good guesses to get through from new level to new level. Sometime I misguessed. Sometimes my instincts were wrong. If they hadn't been subject to an unusually high degree of pressures and tensions, they might have given me better service. The American society at that time, as I began to understand it, was a hell of a challenge. One day it was a teacher, at work with loving patience, the next day a grudge-bearing adversary bent on revenge. I was black in it—I was uneducated in it—I was young in it. I had an additional disadvantage in that I didn't understand all its components. The more I understood politics, the more I began to learn that there were other parts to it and how each influenced the other. Year by year, learning a little at a time, I was able to define the environment in clearer and clearer terms, but I couldn't get a fix on its totality. And the more I learned, the greater the price exacted from me by that environment as we interacted on each other and I battled on stubbornly, trying to put it all together in my head, element by element, until finally I wou'd have an all-encompassing overview of what America was about. Unaware that there was no such view to be had, given the organic and kaleidoscopic nature of human society, I trudged desperately on searching for that illusive "moment of clarity" that I was sure would ease my mind and free me of the unwanted companionship of pressure, insecurity, anxiety, fear, and ambivalence. The answers to my many questions of substance would most assuredly be answered, thought I in my ignorance, by that one glorious "moment of clarity." Am I a black person as this society perceives a black person? Am I smart? Am I honest and fair and considerate and strong and worthwhile? Answers—quickly please!

A long, long time was to pass before, looking back, I would be able to realize that all those early years when I was trying to "make it" in the film/theater world, I was actually living an essential part of the American dream in all its glory, but didn't know it until I was on the other side—where I learned that the dream itself, with its pay-off in money and position, was not necessarily a pleasurable one.

"Making it," according to the American dream's view of the American dream, means being completely relieved of some elementary problems like car notes, rent, food, local bills, clothes, vacation, tuition for the child's school. It also means being able to help a brother and his wife, or a sister and her husband, over a financial hump that would otherwise overwhelm them. And it also means a kind of ego-boosting satisfaction. It doesn't matter what level one sets for oneself—$25,000 could be it in some circumstances, a hundred in others, a half million in still others, even a million in some, then three, five, ten, and so on. It doesn't matter. Once one has "made it," that's all the pursuit is about. That's all the hoopla is about. So the American dream according to the American dream operates on many levels—leaving each individual free to conduct an appraisal of his wants and needs and determine the level he or she should shoot for. (Again, no mention of pain, discomfort, or difficulty.) Is there an end to it or is there only a beginning? A loaded question. But never mind. The end is where one finds it best for oneself, given one's age, one's material, geographic, and, in some cases, racial disposition, to say, "Hey, that's it for me. No more."

And what about those, you might well ask, for whom time is running out and who haven't come anywhere near close to reaching their target level? Who, short of a miracle, will surely find themselves numbered among those many millions who *didn't* make it? Well—according to the American dream, those who never achieve the American dream will one day decide, "Hey, I've spent too many years in constant pursuit and never got close enough for a real shot at a big win, so now with my reflexes slowing and my time running low, I'm going to let the dream go and say goodby. Spend the next ten or twelve years enjoying where I am now, with what I have now." But unfortunately, most of us don't do it that way; most of us never let up until we die. I now know that most of us go to our graves resentful that we got old and had to give up the pursuit of something we were never really able to articulate. With my own eyes I have seen so many of us gathered at the bottom of yet another hill, tightening our muscles and flexing our minds, psyching ourselves up for a dream that is always a couple of hills beyond. Pursuing and assessing our way up those countless hills, with crossed fingers and hope as bright as a young lover's expectations, we continue onward, committed to the theory that one must never say "die." Because wherever there is the will there will always be a hill, and wherever there is a hope there will always be a chance. . . . In my own relentless pursuit of the "dream," tensions built up in my marriage at an early stage and to such an intolerable extent that I was unable to sit still and say, "Enough. Let me explore life where I am because my wife can easily stop where she is and live very comfortably, very nice and very cool. She can raise the kids, reach out for simple needs, and enjoy it all. Except—except for me fucking her over all the time."

Somewhere down the road there was to be some surcease from the tensions, some neutralizing of the anxieties, but not yet. I had more to endure before I got there, and so did Juanita.

14 Survivors

MARTIN BAUM struck a deal with Warner Brothers studios that sent me off to Baton Rouge, Louisiana, to appear in a picture, *Band of Angels*, starring Clark Gable and Yvonne De Carlo. I had a featured role as Clark Gable's son (would you believe), and the film also boasted a rare appearance by Carolle Drake in a featured role. Carolle was married to Billy Eckstine, but they were in a bit of a separation at that time—rumor had it that a lady in Paris was responsible for the friction between them. I think that eventually Carolle won out and old Billy came back home. She was a tremendous woman, that Carolle Drake, not much of an actress but a phenomenal human being—beautiful, warm, and friendly. She had a laugh that would make your whole day brighten. I think it would be safe to say that Carolle Drake would appear on any list of black America's five most beautiful women over the last thirty years, and if you restricted the voting to men of my generation, you'd find Carolle Drake at the top of all of them. And, dammit it all to hell, old lucky Billy Eckstine had her all to himself.

Watching Clark Gable play the principal role in that picture turned out to be a lesson in professionalism. He came to work each day knowing every word of his dialogue—every word. When director Raoul Walsh called for a rehearsal, Gable would play the scene exactly the way he was going to play it in front of the camera. Exactly. Impressed with his ability to commit to memory ten or more pages of dialogue, and on a moment's notice execute them without a single fluff, I set about picking his brain, trying to ferret out how he did it. That

198

he studied his scripts aggressively and that he sometimes put his lines on tape to be played back while he slept was about all he would allow me to unearth. But there had to be more, and I wondered what the missing elements could be. If I hadn't been so young and flip, I would have recognized them easily. I would have seen an old, tough professional who had been pounded into shape by the grueling regimen of the proving ground that was the American film business in the vibrant thirties, where one could learn only by doing—doing—and doing. He could have come (though he didn't) from the rigors of Broadway, the straw-hat summer-stock circuit, and second-rate road companies, as one of the lucky soldiers of the greasepaint army called westward by the powerful, bustling Hollywood that was still years away from peaking, the Hollywood that was both demanding and ferociously competitive, where the newly arriving young soldiers discovered quickly that the ability to live on one's toes was an absolute prerequisite to becoming a survivor. These were the elements I was too unseasoned to recognize, coming to Hollywood as I did years after they had stopped making old pros like Clark Gable. In fact, *Band of Angels* brought us together quite late in his career, when he was already suffering from a kind of palsy. His head and hands would shake involuntarily almost all the time, but when the cameras turned they would stop. He managed to control the shaking throughout a scene, and then he would release whatever mechanism he had been calling on and go back to shaking. It was not too noticeable—you had to be close to him to pick it up—but he was definitely afflicted with a malfunction in the nervous system.

The director, Raoul Walsh, was also a survivor and, like Gable, a model no longer in production. He had one good eye and wore a black patch over the one not in service. He had a very deep voice, rolled his own cigarettes, and wore cowboy boots. And he knew all there was to know about film at that time. To my experienced eye he seemed to work instinctively, never giving the kind of attention to detail that the other filmmakers did. He would say, "All right, guys, bring me my actors." When we were assembled he would address us, his attention focused on the rolling of a cigarette. "Actors, you know what you're doing here. So let's rehearse." While we were rehearsing he was still not looking at us—he was probably trying to figure out where he was going to put the camera. Lighting up his cigarette, he would say, "All right, you guys, let's shoot it." And we'd shoot it. Once in a while he'd turn his back on us and go walking away somewhere, and I'd say to myself: How can he know what he's getting on film? But apparently he knew what he was getting on film. Either that or he had arrived at the point where he was just bored to tears and didn't care and the stuff turned out okay in spite of him. I didn't know. I was told at that time that he knew so much about what he was doing that the chances were he was just a walking genius about film and didn't have to go through the gyrations and pretensions that most directors go through nowadays—myself included. But as I got older and took a second look at the man through the body of his work, I found him one of the giants of the game. *Band of Angels*, however, turned out to be a disappointment, far below the norm for both Gable and Walsh. Maybe I had caught the aging director at a time when he really was "just bored to tears."

Some months later, John Cassavetes and I were teamed up again by a British producer in a film shot in its entirety in the British Virgin Islands. I was to play a robust West Indian lover-of-life in a creampuff featherweight of a story about a boy and a girl who fall in love and decide to build a house on a beautiful isolated island where no one else lived. They get involved with me—the robust West Indian—because I have a boat they need to move their marital bed to what the lovers call "Our Virgin Island," which, you may have gathered by now, is also the title of the movie. Then again you may not have gathered it, since the film was not destined to gather much attention to itself.

Well, with that behind us, let me hurry onto the further background of what was to prove the most dangerous crossroads in my career. The lovely Ruby Dee was in this picture, and so was Virginia Maskell, a wonderful British actress who played the romantic lead opposite John Cassavetes (she died—very young—a few years after making the picture). We all lived on an eleven-acre island in the British Virgins called Guana Island. An interesting little hotel built on the highest point on the island was the film company's home for the entire eight weeks of filming. The hotel provided motorboat transportation to and from the uninhabited island locations necessary to the film. There were no telephones on the little island, but since we had to send our film over to St. Thomas every other day by boat to be shipped to London for processing, phone messages that had accumulated in St. Thomas would be delivered to us on the return trip. Midway through the film such a message came to me from Martin Baum, saying that Sam Goldwyn wanted me for *Porgy and Bess*. Further, there was a definite offer of $75,000. A lot of money.

In my judgment, *Porgy and Bess* was not material complimentary to black people; and for the most part, black people responded negatively to that American opera, although they stood ready to acknowledge and applaud the genius in the music. Taking a boat to St. Thomas and a telephone, I told my agent I was not interested in playing *Porgy and Bess*. With appropriate emphasis I repeated my position—"I have no interest at all, so please pass that on to Sam Goldwyn"—then took the boat back to Guana Island.

While I was finishing the picture, some other people were busying themselves with my life. My agent worked in association with another agent in California, a lady who had been involved in some of my other pictures. She knew Sam Goldwyn. Mr. Goldwyn, one of the most powerful men in the history of Hollywood, had said to her, "I want that boy to play Porgy in *Porgy and Bess*." Now she was in the agency business, and that business was subject to the pressures of powerful Hollywood producers. It is my impression that she said to him, "Sam, if you want him, I'll get him for you." I'm sure she sold me to him not knowing that I had a considerable aversion to *Porgy and Bess* because of its inherent racial attitudes.

When I got back to New York, I found to my surprise that I had been for the previous two weeks the center of a brewing storm. I had said to Martin Baum that I wouldn't do *Porgy and Bess* and so the California lady agent had been forced to say to Sam Goldwyn, "I'm trying, Sam, but I can't get him to change his mind." The press got wind of the situation. There was a columnist in New York named Leonard Lyons (now dead) whom I liked very much. He said in his column that Ralph Bunche and many other important black people were prevailing upon Sidney Poitier to change his mind and play *Porgy and Bess*, a classic, for Sam Goldwyn. Following that, and the resulting barrage of press hoopla, the issue flared into the open, placing Goldwyn and myself in very difficult positions. He being the big man in Hollywood, how could he absorb this little actor saying he didn't want to work for him? On the other hand, I was suddenly under pressure from all the power he could muster, with the assistance of Leonard Lyons, who was a friend of his, and Ralph Bunche, who was a friend of Leonard Lyons, and all kinds of other people who began calling me and saying, "What is this about Sam Goldwyn? Why won't you do *Porgy and Bess?* We think it's one of the best operas ever written and it's won this kind of award and that kind of award." I was being nudged hard because Sam Goldwyn's nose was publicly out of joint.

My agent in New York said to me, "I have a feeling we've been put in a bind. Goldwyn wants us to come out to see him." I said, "I don't want to go see him. I don't want to do *Porgy and Bess. Porgy and Bess* is an insult to black people and I ain't going to play it and that's all there is to it." But Martin Baum was troubled. He pondered for several moments, circling the impasse, before a heavy sigh revealed how deeply frustrated he was at our being caught in this dangerous, sticky, no-win situation. Finally he cleared his throat and spoke again in a voice noticeably flattened by the absence of its usual buoyancy. "Do me a favor—Goldwyn says that Lillian, our agent out there, said to him that you will play the part. Now the fact he was told that—someone misrepresented themselves to him. Goldwyn says he wants you to come out and have a little talk with him, and after, if you don't want to do the part, he can walk away from it and you can walk away from it, and then it's over. But he feels that since you've been misrepresented to him, he thinks you should come out and explain your position."

I smelled a trap. I gave it a lot of thought. My alternative was to say, "Screw Sam Goldwyn." Then he would be told, "Sidney Poitier doesn't even want to come and see you," and in a town like Hollywood that was not good politics. I decided to go and explain my reasons to him; however difficult they might be for him to buy, they were my reasons. I was sorry the agent had presold me—she made a mistake and stepped out of line, but that's the way it was. Martin Baum and I went to California. When we were met at the airport by the lady agent, I tried unsuccessfully to hide how really upset with her I was. Then she didn't even know where Goldwyn lived. After we checked into a hotel, she took us to a house that belonged to the big wheel at Columbia Pictures, Harry Cohn. His wife, Joan, responding to the ringing of the bell, leaned out of a second-floor window and said, "Yes?" The lady agent looked up and said, "Oh, my God, Joan—we're supposed to be at Sam Goldwyn's house." So at last, with instructions from Mrs. Cohn, we drove to Mr. Goldwyn's residence. It was, as I expected, a fantastically beautiful house with a croquet court on the grounds, a swimming pool, and all the rest of an American dream as fully realized as you could ever ever hope to find.

The butler who lets us in says, "Mr. Goldwyn will be down soon," and within a few minutes a very solicitous, absolutely charming Sam Goldwyn appears. After an un-hurried moment of handshakes, smiles, "Hellos," and "How do you dos," we all sit down. Now I am smart— I am aware that one must be quick, charming, and in-gratiating while doing everything one can to neutralize the other guy. I am smart enough to know that this is the way one does business in circumstances like these, so I'm determined to keep my eye on whatever lies behind the pleasantries. Sweetness and charm be damned—I'm not going to be distracted! Besides, two can play the game of sugar and spice, and if push comes to shove, I will bury him in the stuff before I allow myself to be moved one fraction of an inch from my position. Martin Baum simul-taneously sets the stage and eases into the role of referee by briefly recapping the step-by-step events that have led to our stand-off. Sam Goldwyn, whose steady eyes have locked in on me throughout Marty's narration, thanks him for refreshing our memories, thanks the lady agent for helping to arrange the face-to-face meeting that he hopes will resolve the problem to everyone's satis-faction, and then hits me hard with a flurry of compli-ments about my work in those pictures he's seen me in, ending with elaborate predictions about the wonderful impact I'm on the threshold of making, not just on the film industry but on America at large, to the benefit of myself and all the people I represent. I thank him, but he's scored no points with that, since such an opening was not unexpected. Handing me the floor, Martin Baum asks me to: "Tell Mr. Goldwyn what your feelings are about the *Porgy and Bess* project. As I told him on the phone, and as our presence here substantiates, we all agree that he is entitled to hear your objections to this project directly from you—because of the mixup, Mr. Goldwyn feels that he is entitled to a personal explanation."

I open with a few sizable compliments of my own that may or may not have found their mark, and then gently but firmly state my case. At the end of which I stroke him once more with a well-deserved compliment for having produced the post-World War II classic *The Best Years of Our Lives*. Then I pass him the floor.

Sam Goldwyn thanks me for the last compliment and I can tell he knows it was genuinely meant. That unnerves me because I see in a split second that Sam Goldwyn is razor sharp. In that brief instant he lets me know he's quite able to separate the bullshit from the real. He bears close watching, this fellow, so stay on your toes, I think to myself.

After a few editorial remarks concerning *The Best Years of Our Lives,* Mr. Goldwyn levels those steady eyes on me and says, "I understand how you feel, Mr. Poitier, but I disagree with you—this is one of the greatest things that has ever happened for the black race." He wins his first point right there with such an outrageous bullshit statement. I look in his eyes for a twinkle, on the chance he's kidding. There's nothing, not a twinkle. He believes every word he's saying. Or is he even smarter than I thought, and is just playing with my head? Testing?

The statement hangs there in the silence of a pause long enough for him to smile like a poker player sitting on a straight flush. I answer his smile with a smile of my own that can very easily be mistaken for a frown, knotted brow and all. He gets my message, and like a good poker player chooses not to invite a further challenge. Instead, he allows the smiles to cancel each other out. Score one for me. He presses on with the genius of Gershwin, the worldwide popularity of the opera itself, the critical acclaim it's reaped for itself, and the many artists who have performed it over the years. I tell him that this is all probably quite true from his point of view, but I can only look at the material from *my* point of view, and from my point of view it simply isn't what I want to do. We go round and round for ten minutes with no advantage gained on either side. Then, suddenly, Mr. Goldwyn shifts gears and introduces a new strategy that takes me by surprise. He says, "Well, the bottom line is I can't force you to do anything you don't want to do. If I did, you wouldn't be of much value to my production. So I wish you would give it more thought. Don't make up your mind at this very minute—when you leave my house I want to feel that you will at least give it some more honest thought. Man to man, that isn't asking too much, Mr. Poitier, is it?" I jump suspicious immediately. That man knows something—I can feel it. The tactical switch is too smooth. Can there have been some understanding between my California agent and Goldwyn? Can it be he really *is* sitting on a royal flush? Something is up, because he sure is acting as if he's got me in the bag—yet I haven't given him any indication that I'm open to any negotiation on playing the role. "Mr. Poitier, leave with that attitude—just relax—give it some thought. Maybe when you get back to New York your agent can call me and tell me that you've—well, just think about it. You're a great actor and you could be fantastic in the part of Porgy." I give him the frown-smile, thank him for the audience, and we go.

Back at the hotel Martin Baum said to me, "While we're here we're going to see a man named Stanley Kramer." Immediately the name jumped to my mind as the producer responsible for the film *Home of the Brave,* and for the black actor James Edwards getting his start in films. So on a sunny afternoon we drove to Stanley Kramer's studio, tucked away almost unnoticed on a side street, a mere block and a half away from the mighty complex that was Paramount Pictures Studios. Kramer was a lively, outgoing man, just itching to address head-on those issues other producers were inclined to dance around. I liked him right away, from the very first moment we met. He had handsome boyish looks, a sturdy frame of medium height, and a tart sense of humor that all too frequently radared in on painful truths. "I've got a couple of writers who've turned out a script I want you to read. I think it's powerful, but I don't want to talk about it anymore until you've read it. Then we'll sit down. I believe you'll find it interesting and refreshing." I thanked him very much, adding not only how pleased I was to meet him but also what I—and a lot of other blacks—thought about *Home of the Brave.* It pleased him no end to hear he was well thought of where I came from. "Read it and we'll talk again." That was it. The meeting was over.

Back at the hotel I read the script immediately. It was an explosive piece of work that left me in a state of sweaty-palmed excitement. It was called *The Defiant Ones*. Eagerly I phoned Marty Baum's room. "This I gotta do. This is a picture!" Suddenly the buoyancy was back in Marty Baum's voice. "Marvelous—I'll call Kramer immediately and set up an appointment. Leave it to me."

Stanley Kramer invited the two screenwriters to sit in on our next meeting, and we talked about ideas for changing things here and there to strengthen the overall piece. The two writers, both white, wanted to know how I felt about the relationship between the two men from different racial backgrounds who were the principal characters in the script. After about an hour Kramer said to me, "Listen, kid, I want you to play this part. Do you want to play it?" "I would love to play it." He said, "Okay, it's a deal. Now—I hear you've got a problem with Sam Goldwyn." Oh, shit, here it comes, I thought. "No, I don't really think I have a problem with Sam Goldwyn."

Stanley Kramer hesitated as if an exact choice of words was necessary at that delicate point. Taking his time, he strolled over to his desk and stood behind it, lightly tapping his knuckles on its surface as the silence swelled. Planting the palms of his hands on the top of his desk, leaning in for emphasis, he looked directly at me and said, "Well, let me put it to you this way—it would be very difficult for me if Goldwyn assumes, and I believe he does, that he has a deal with you. That might preclude my being able to use you in this picture. What I mean is, it would be difficult for me in terms of union regulations and business protocol if there is indeed some kind of deal. You must understand I don't care what your problem is with Goldwyn—it's none of my business and I'm neither pro- nor anti-*Porgy and Bess*, I have no interest in the material—but I genuinely have to be concerned if Goldwyn brings any action against you. Otherwise I can find myself stuck and unable to proceed with my picture until such time as an action against you is clarified. In other words, if you can get from Goldwyn an absolute release from the promise he says he's been given, then we've got a deal." "Great. Then we don't have a problem as far as I can see," I said, rising from my chair. "The ball is in your court," said Kramer, escorting us to the door. "You'll hear from us, Stanley. We'll get right on it," chimed in Marty Baum.

Walking to our car, I said to the California lady agent, "Call Mr. Goldwyn now and tell him I have thought about it again and I'm not going to do *Porgy and Bess.*" Now whether she called him or not I don't know, but word got back to me in the afternoon that Sam Goldwyn was going to hold us to the promise made to him by her, and fully expected her agency to deliver me for his picture. Suddenly, with his Mr. Nice Guy façade no longer tactically advantageous, Sam Goldwyn freezes firm and the screws begin to turn.

Okay, I've got a part I'm crazy about and I'm in a box. But I've been in boxes before, right? Fair enough. Good. But—a hot question surfaces in a corner of my mind—is this a box that the white people have been designing for me for weeks? Or, if all of it wasn't, how much of it is? To this day, I lean to the theory that some of it was predetermined, because I refuse to believe that Goldwyn didn't know about the Kramer project and know that I would flip for it. I'm also sure that my agents knew I would flip for it. In other words, I think I was manipulated. As smart as I thought I was, that time the white folks were smarter.

As phase two of the Goldwyn plan bore down, my agents, playing as agents do, said, "Well, we want to do what you want to do. If you want to say a final 'no' to Mr. Goldwyn and take your chances, we'll go along with you. We just want you to understand what his power is like in this town. He is one of the biggest, most powerful studio heads in the business and if he chooses to, he can blackball you so you'll never work in a studio again or as long as he's a power in the Hollywood community." I was stunned for several moments, simply unable to envision anything beyond the blackballing of the little black boy. Just like that, a crisis not of my own making had loomed, threatening me with this awful choice, with my whole career in cold jeopardy facing the alternative: survival in the film business or death in the film business.

I can't walk away from this situation without a commitment to one or the other of two hard, hard choices. If I refuse to do *Porgy and Bess,* the town is going to know that I messed over Goldwyn, in which case, as I've been amply warned, the unwritten laws governing behavior in these situations will unquestionably wipe me out. But the other side of the coin, how can I do *Porgy and Bess* when I don't like it, don't want to do it, and have declared publicly that I have no intention of doing it? I'm stuck —I'm boxed—I've been outfoxed—but I'm still smart, and I know that I'm not about to allow myself and my career to be snuffed out at this point. I've come too far —I've begun to accomplish too much.

As I saw it, in my career there was a real beginning for a breakthrough—not only for me, but for other blacks in films. Suddenly decisions of a very political nature were on my doorstep. Was it important to carry on? Was it important for *me* to carry on? Naturally I felt I had certain things to offer, since I had begun to work with some regularity and had generated what I thought to be good vibrations spreading around the industry. *The Defiant Ones,* speaking directly to the point of how black people want to see themselves on the screen, would be a hell of a shot for us. And the role of Cullen would represent for me and other black actors a step up in the quality of parts available to us, and at the same time afford the black community in general a rare look at a movie character, exemplifying the dignity of our people—something that Hollywood had systematically ignored in its shameless capitulation to racism. A thorough scrutiny of the politics behind this issue led me through some sober, serious thinking and forced me to face an unflattering, unpleasant, and unavoidable fact: I was not smart enough in this situation to have what I wanted when I wanted it; therefore I was doomed to get scorched. There was just no way for me not to get burned a little if I wanted to come out on the other side; like it or not, I was due to give up some blood. Well, I thought, so be it. But first things first.

We went to Kramer and made a good deal pending the satisfactory resolution of the Goldwyn mess before going on to see Goldwyn. Flanked on one side by Marty Baum and on the other by the lady agent, I marched into Sam Goldwyn's palatial office, where he was triumphantly awaiting our arrival for the signing of the surrender. As he stood there playing the good host and gesturing us to be seated, I noticed that the smile had returned to the victor's face. But still, no twinkle in his eye. I chose to stand, and comfort was out of the question in the light of what I was about to say. "I know that I'm caught in a bind—I want to do Kramer's picture. I know you know about the Kramer deal. I understand that you're not going to let me off the hook from the promise my agent gave you. If that is correct, then I'll do *Porgy and Bess*." He said, "I don't want you to do *Porgy and Bess* unless you're going to do it the best way you know how. It's no good me spending all this money if you're not going to come in with team spirit and a feeling of participation." I replied to the victor, "I am a professional actor, Mr. Goldwyn, and I will do the part to the best of my ability —under the circumstances." Then in a conciliatory tone he said, "Well, Mr. Poitier, welcome aboard. This is going to be a great, great moment. I think we should sit down and prepare a joint statement for the press. But don't you worry about it—your agents and my press people will work something up and show it to you before it goes out." I wasn't savvy enough then to know how those things were done. The press release in its final form was not to my advantage in the slightest—it was all to Goldwyn's advantage. I got screwed again and there were reverberations in the black community.

I wasn't too worried about that except from one quarter. By then I had become extremely good friends with Harry Belafonte. I had developed a relationship with him that I felt was worth protecting and respecting, and I found it most difficult to explain to him why I had elected to do *Porgy and Bess* after all. He was as fair as he could have been under the circumstances, but I didn't convince him that I had to do *Porgy and Bess* so that I could do the other picture. He didn't buy it—he would have preferred me to just walk away from the whole thing. But he was, as he has always been, fair enough to say that he honestly didn't know what his responses would have been if he were in the same position. He just wished I hadn't done it, and could only hope that he would have had the strength not to do it. That bothered me for a long time, but it didn't damage our relationship, which was an enormous revelation to me. Harry is a hard friend when he's a friend—he's vast and tight and there. We've had our ups and downs, as you'll find out, but there isn't in the whole world better material for a friend than that man.

I went back to New York for a while trying to adjust to how I was going to play a part I didn't want to play, then after a couple of months returned to California to start the Kramer picture. I went through wardrobe fittings and other preliminary activities for *Porgy and Bess,* but primarily I was there to begin shooting *The Defiant Ones.* I met Tony Curtis, and he was terrific. He was full of life—bubbly, bubbly all the time. In recent years this town's not been too kind to him, but it hasn't killed his spirit—he's still bubbly. He'd have every right to a trace of resentment. He poured a lot of his time, his energy, his talent, his personality into this community, he was a big part of Hollywood's last twenty-five years, but this town ain't too cool with you when you're in the afterglow of your stardom. To me he was wonderful coming out of the gate and he hasn't changed even a little over the years. His very first kindness to me was when he said to Stanley Kramer, "Listen, I don't want to be on the top of the picture by myself. Why don't you put Poitier up there with me?" He insisted that I be given co-star billing for the first time in my career, saying, "What is this? Put him up there too!" And in those days getting co-star billing above the title was difficult.

Well, we went to work for Stanley Kramer, who, like Richard Brooks, was his own man in a company town. But unlike Richard, whose hard-as-nails, street-brawling, rebel image might have been a façade behind which several other Richard Brookses may have been living out sensitive lives, Stanley Kramer was exactly what one saw: aggressive, liberal, intellectual, a loner. He was very bright—one of the brightest men I ever knew—and he was very, very socially conscious at that time. For Richard Brooks and Stanley Kramer, differences of approach and style obscured the fact that they were traveling companions on the same highway heading for the same sunset, because they had both looked the same world in the eye and said, "You're not quite structured the way I like, and here comes a little energy to move you around a little."

Filming *The Defiant Ones* was a memorable experience mainly because of Tony, Theodore Bikel, who played the southern sheriff, and Ivan Dixon, a talented black actor whom I had encouraged to come to California with me and try his luck. The Kramer company agreed to take him on as my stand-in on the picture. His wife and my wife, having become fast friends in New York, joined us in California for the duration of the film, bringing both families with them, and we settled comfortably in two rented houses in Altadena. Ivan was a truly talented actor whose potential was never realized. Part of it was his own fault and part of it was the industry's fault—the industry wasn't ready to cultivate two of us at the same time, nor did it have the psychological wherewithal to absorb two of us at the same time. Yet—had he been more of a tough, hard-driving, go-getter personality accustomed to smashing down doors, the industry might have—just might have—looked up and paid more attention. With one noteworthy exception (*Nothing But a Man*) the industry was to pass this gentle, easygoing actor by. Happily, they would rediscover each other when the actor Ivan Dixon moved over for the triumphant arrival of the motion picture director Ivan Dixon.

With *The Defiant Ones* in the can, I reported to the Goldwyn lot for a get-acquainted gathering of the principal actors over refreshments in Mr. Goldwyn's private office. Dorothy Dandridge, Pearl Bailey, Sammy Davis, Jr., and Olga James were among those present. I did not meet Diahann Carroll at that time. Not long after that first get-together, there was a fire at the Goldwyn Studios in the wee hours of the morning and some of the sets for *Porgy and Bess* burned down. Gathered in Mr. Goldwyn's office once again, the actors were told of a five- or six-week delay in the start of the picture, and agreed to adjust their schedules to keep themselves available. It was then I met Diahann Carroll. Her hair was covered by some material she had fashioned into a headdress the color and shape of which enhanced her already striking beauty —allowing the slightest suggestion of a smile to immediately transform that arresting face into poetry. Or perhaps it wasn't the headdress—it's more than likely that the source of her magic was that her mouth was so perfect. Yes, hers was the mouth I had been looking for all my life. But when we were introduced the earth didn't move. She simply said, "Hi," I said, "Hi," and that was all that passed between us that day. Yet thoughts began bumping into each other in my mind, stirred up by the prospect of working closely with this woman who had such tempting lips. Since mystery can either frighten or fascinate, and since there were such traces of it in the air around her, I wondered what the world was like behind that magic smile. But patience, I warned myself, slowly, slowly, there will be plenty of time.

211

Jackie Robinson and his wife, Rachel, longtime friends, joined Juanita and me and Martin Baum and his wife, Bernice, on a vacation trip to the Bahamas. After a few days of not having as much fun as we thought we would have, Jackie and I, both subject to impulsive actions, came up with the idea of moving on to Acapulco for the remaining ten days of our vacation, and off we went.

The next day, while Acapulco and our wives are roasting under a relentless afternoon sun, Marty and I are beating the heat with a refreshing swim forty feet off shore in the sky-blue waters still cold enough to be invigorating. A solitary lifeguard, engrossed in a girlie magazine, was perched on top of a wooden lookout tower enjoying his fantasies. Like two carefree adolescents joyfully skinny-dipping in a water hole, we're splashing about, clowning and laughing, and after a great fifteen minutes we head for shore. When we'd first entered the water, we were surprised to find that the beach didn't gradually descend into the sea, but rather—at a point where the water was only knee deep—simply disappeared from under our feet, falling straight down a sheer wall of sand to the bottom of the sea, about fourteen feet below. Beyond our initial surprise, there seemed to be no reason for concern.

But now we're heading for a different kind of surprise as we breaststroke our way back to shore. A severe change, having to do with temperature and current flow, had taken place on the bottom of the sea while we're swimming, and a few feet from the vertical wall of sand, a turbulence from the bottom starts pulling at our legs. We panic and begin swimming harder, but we make no progress. Then a tide comes along, not a tide on the surface of the water, but a raging thundering wave swelling up from the floor of the sea and slamming itself against the wall of sand before exploding upward and over onto the beach in a mighty rush of foaming waters. The momentum of that angry wave yanks us free of the undercurrents pulling at our legs and flings us violently onto the beach. Relieved at feeling sand under our feet, we instantly begin wading through the receding water on our way to highground and safety, up toward the ridge where our wives are sunbathing.

Then it happens. With reverse momentum, the receding waters start pulling us back toward the sea. In panic we claw at the sand with our hands, trying desperately to plant our feet against the pull of the ocean. But outmatched and terrified, we're sucked back to the edge of the wall and pushed fourteen feet down to the bottom into a churning undertow that twirls us around like rag dolls in a washing machine for seven or eight seconds until an incoming wave, thundering along on the floor of the sea, smashes into the wall of sand, reversing the momentum, and pushes us up again. We don't make it. We're pushed back down along the wall of sand to the bottom of the sea, back into the turmoil of the undertow. More scared than either of us has ever been in our lives, we hold our breaths and pray that another wave will toss us up again—one more chance, please, God.

The seconds tick away, oh, so slowly, before the next wave comes smashing into the wall, pushing us ahead of it and once more onto the beach. We waste no time checking on each other—now it's each man for himself. With every ounce of strength we can muster, we start wading toward the shore, hoping to gain as much ground as possible before we have to make another stand against the outgoing tide. Running, wading, clawing, scrambling with the tide, we get as far up the beach as we can before the moment of truth—and then, digging in and bracing ourselves, we cry and pray—and I'm sure I'm calling for my mother. The tide reverses, causing billions of grains of sand to swirl around our legs and out from under our feet, loosening our grip on life. With every ounce of strength left in us, we try not to give ground, but there's to be no holding against that tide. It has come to take us down for the last time, I think, and it crosses my mind that the bottom of Acapulco Bay is a strange place to meet death.

While holding on like mad to two handfuls of sand and being pushed back toward the sea, I begin to scream for help. Marty begins to scream for help. We scream for our wives and we scream for the lifeguard who's up on the tower reading his dumb magazine. He doesn't hear us. Since there's no one else within hearing distance, the sea, in the absence of any human witness, pulls us back into itself and down we go for the third time. And then, amid the violent turning and twisting in that undertow, a peace and serenity start to come over me, and I think: Oh, my God, has my time come—is it to be here? Is this sense of well-being your way of easing me through that final barrier? Lord, I ain't ready to die here—I am simply not ready—I am certainly not ready to die here. I pray during the seven or eight seconds that experience had taught us is the approximate interval between waves: "O Lord, don't let the wave be late. If we're forced to breathe down here, it will be all over. Let it come on time, please. Father, don't let it be late. A few seconds off the mark and we'll be done for." Suddenly the wave, arriving with no time to spare, smashes into the wall of sand and jettisons us up to the surface and onto the beach. Making a split-second check to see if Marty Baum has made it up this time, I find him ten feet away, half-conscious. The man has started to take in water—he's coughing from having tried to hold his breathe beyond endurance—and he's turning blue. Now I have to scream for both of us—Marty no longer has the strength. I scream and scream and scream.

Finally that dummy on top of the tower looks up, sees the situation, and starts coming down. But he's coming down at a rate that says clearly: Oh, shit, why do you guys have to interrupt my reading? He's sauntering over ever so slowly and I'm screaming, yelling, struggling to hold on, and as he struts casually across the sand, Marty Baum and I are swallowed up once more by the sea. But this time I know somebody is coming, so I've got to hang on. I get tossed forward and backward and twirled and spun, but I hang on and wait—it's like an underwater sand-storm down there, you can only hold your breath and close your eyes, you don't dare breathe until you feel you're up on the beach again. With my consciousness fixed on my last view of the lifeguard strolling in our direction, I manage to hang on until the next wave brings me up. With almost no strength left, I'm too weak to do anything more than look over to the lifeguard, who's standing in the water waiting for Marty. Which is really all for the best, because Marty can't possibly manage—he's almost gone. When he comes up this time the guard grabs him, and apparently he's had special training so he knows how to hold the victim and himself against the pull of the tide and he's able to drag Marty up on the beach to safety. In the meantime, I've gotta go down one more time. Well, let me tell you—that peaceful feeling which floods you when your muscles are no longer able to come to your aid is extraordinary. You've fought all you can with the last gram of strength left in you, and at the point when you can absolutely do no more, you find yourself crossing over into a place where struggle is no longer necessary and all you need do is relax. I decide that if I get tossed up again, and if that lifeguard is there, that will be my only shot, but other than that—there isn't anything I can do about it. "Lord, I hope I've had a good life if you're calling me home this early, and I hope your assessment will be that it's been a worthwhile life." I worry about my children because they've been constantly on my mind each time I've come up and gone back down. I worry about how they'll get their education—how they'll manage—will their mother be able to get a job and continue to make a home for them . . . and how will my family react back in Nassau when they hear I've drowned . . . all this is going through my mind, but I'm still holding my breath. And I'm turning blue—you may not be able to visualize it, but take my word for it, I'm turning blue.

Finally, I get tossed up for the last time. There is a pair of Mexican legs in the sand. Someone grabs hold of me and I grab hold of him and I hope he knows what he's doing—because it's going to be me and him *up* there, or me and him *down* there. Well, he hangs on to me for dear life and after the water has receded he drags me up and drops me by Marty, who by now is coughing and choking. We lie there side by side, and our wives come dashing over in response to an alarm sounded by the lifeguard and soon a doctor arrives and we are declared okay.

And we weren't okay twenty minutes before we began laughing and telling jokes about it all. Lying there on the sand, Marty Baum, the confirmed wisecracker, couldn't resist the rich opportunity to fire off a half-dozen irreverent one-liners about this chillingly close call that had brought us to within a hair's-breadth of the kiss of death. Mind you, the jokes were funny, very funny. But I guarantee you there was no sacrilege in our laughter. Tears we had shed aplenty, and genuine prayers for mercy had filled our hearts while nature held our fragile existence in the balance for an absolutely critical moment before she ordered that dumb lifeguard to look up from his girlie magazine. Yes, our laughter expressed our deep and profound appreciation for the precious extension of our lives. A reprieve had been granted, and we knew it.

215

15 Porgy and Otto

ORIGINALLY it had been announced that Rouben Mamoulian would be the director of *Porgy and Bess,* but a disagreement developed between him and Sam Goldwyn, and Goldwyn went into the marketplace for a new director and came up with Otto Preminger. When I reported to the studio to honor my contract, the wardrobe I had been fitted for months earlier was ready, the sets had been rebuilt, the music had been prerecorded, the production machinery had been meticulously primed, the principal actors were all present and accounted for and ready to begin the intensive week of rehearsals that would precede the start of filming.

Everyone in the case anticipated some difficulty with Otto Preminger because of his notorious reputation for being harsh on actors; we had all heard the many stories about him chewing up actors and spitting them out. And there was supposed to be a ritual that occurred on all his films: somewhere between the beginning and end of a production, someone from the cast or crew would be picked absolutely clean in the presence of his fellow workers. This time who will it be and when will it come? Mr. Preminger had worked with blacks before. Having made a picture with Harry Belafonte and Dorothy Dandridge called *Carmen Jones,* he was not entirely new to us as a group, and word came down suggesting that he was a liberal on the question of race. And it was soon established that he *was* indeed a liberal when it came to racial questions, but he was also a tyrant whose monster within surfaced frequently on his bad days. At our first meeting I looked for telltale signs to confirm the presence of furies lying dormant somewhere in the strong, muscular, baldheaded director. Unless I missed something, no sign appeared, he was as charming as a minister, and checked out normal—he was sweet, kind, loved to tell stories, laughed a lot and was fun to be around. During rehearsal time he never once raised his voice, and was very patient and considerate with each actor, even those who were slow in getting to what he was attempting to convey. All went very nicely indeed.

With a week of productive rehearsals behind us, we started to film *Porgy and Bess* on location in Stockton, California. Since I was not in any of the location scenes, I remained in Los Angeles working at the studio on synchronizing my lip movements to the prerecorded songs of Porgy, which of course had been sung by someone else. In due course the company returned to the studio and began shooting the interior scenes. It happened, I think, on the first day I started to work. Otto Preminger jumped on Dorothy Dandridge in a shocking and totally unexpected way. She had done something that wasn't quite the way he wanted it. "What's the matter with you, Dorothy?" he exploded at her. "You're supposed to be an actress. Now what kind of an actress are you that you can't do such a simple thing?" I thought: Well, he's a little irrational now and it looks like it's not going to be a smooth day, but I never anticipated events moving so quickly to the next level. After a brief pause during which he seemed to be calling his monster to heel, he said, "All right, we're going to do it again and I want you to give it to me the way you did it in rehearsals. Okay, let's take it from the top." Dorothy Dandridge, visibly shaken, started the scene again, hoping to recapture the missing ingredient and save herself from further embarrassment. She hadn't proceeded very far before he exploded again. "No, no, no—what's the matter with you? You can't even do a simple thing like that? That's stupid, what you're doing—you don't have any intelligence at all. What kind of a dumb way for a girl to behave! You don't even know who Bess is. You call yourself an actress—you get paid to perform, not to do stupid things." And on he went. Well, I heard it—watched it—analyzed and categorized it—because one day sure as hell my turn was to come.

Nobody went to Dorothy's defense. The rationale was, since he was not abusing her physically, since his attacks remained verbal, no matter how brutal, it was still an "artistic dispute" between the director and his actress. Totally unable to defend herself, Dorothy Dandridge fell apart. Nowhere in her anguish was there enough venom to dip her dagger into. There she was, that delicately beautiful woman whose appearance suggested many more things than her personality could deliver, stripped naked. Unable to call on the strength of character that her elegant carriage implied; unable to summon up that survival sense essential to the secure person she wanted people to think she was; unable to strike back, because her defense mechanism was that of the prey, and the predator had selected her, staked her out, marked her for the kill, then struck without warning. On that day I learned that the serene look Dorothy Dandridge always wore only served to mask the fears, frustrations, and insecurities that were tumbling around inside her all the time. Fears about herself as a black woman—just those were enough to overburden her sensitive personality. And she also had fears as an actress, because her tools were admittedly very limited. A great deal of her desirability as an actress rested on her appearance, and she knew it, but she couldn't find much solace in that because she knew that while appearance might get you a job, it's skill and craft that enable you to keep it and get you considered for the next job. I think that these contradictions—the appearance of serenity, the visage of a self-assured lady, accompanied by the absence of any real foundation underneath it all to fight the world with —made her the most vulnerable member of the cast. Otto Preminger smelled this, and she became sacrifice number one.

It wasn't long before my turn came. It happened on a day we were filming "Bess, You Is My Woman Now," one of the highlight songs in the opera. As Porgy with shin shoes strapped on my lower legs, I hobbled about the set singing (lip-syncing) my heart out to the tempestuous Bess whose ineffable beauty had electrified the gentle, love-starved crippled beggar and marked him for tragedy by flooding his drab life with exciting promise. I had come as close to perfection as hard work could get me in timing my lip movements to the words of the song as they had been prerecorded by a professional opera singer; I had no intention of giving Preminger an excuse to question my professionalism or my lack of preparation or my ability to play this part, so I was super— super—ready. I was deeply concentrated, and working my way through the song quite well, when something I was doing fell short of the mark for Otto Preminger, who instantly bellowed, "What's the matter with you?" Mind you, the entire crew was assembled for this scene and he was sitting on a camera crane very high up, almost in the rafters, so when he spoke to me he was speaking in the presence of several hundred people. I did not respond. He went on, "Don't you know how to sing the song? Didn't you study the lip sync? Don't you understand this man's attitude toward what's going on in Catfish Row? This is the woman you love! You've got to *feel* it, and make the *audience* feel it." I said, "Yes, I understand that." He said, "Well, what are you doing this stupid thing for?" I didn't respond, but something deep down in me moved. I knew that he had just about threaded the needle. If he said one more word—it didn't matter what it was, if he just said "but"—we were going to be on. I waited. The cast and crew froze. "All right, everyone, we'll take it from the top once more. Let me know when the playback is ready." The tension eased. Cast and crew, breathing easier, scurried about taking positions in preparation for another take. Preminger hollered down to Leon Shamroy, his cinematographer, "Leon, if you have to trim any arcs do it now." An unnecessary instruction, since Mr. Shamroy's assistants were already fiddling with the interiors of the gigantic lamps. With actors in place and every department ready, the cameras rolled once more.

About halfway through the first minute of the song, an angry voice came piercing down from the rafters. "Cut—cut—cut! Mr. Poitier, you call yourself an actor? What kind of an actor are you, Mr. Poitier?" I said, "Mr. Preminger—" He cut *me* off: "Don't talk, I am the director here. I will tell you what kind of an actor you are. You don't even know how to play a warm scene—a warm scene with the woman you love. That's what you are. An actor who doesn't know what he is doing. What am I dealing with here—children?"

So—not only had the needle been threaded, but the knot had been tied and a stitch had been taken. I reached down behind my right ankle, began to unstrap one of the little shin shoes that were part of my costume, and got the shoe off while he went on ranting. "This is what I mean about doing your homework. After all the rehearsals we've had, we can't afford to have people come in here at the moment of truth and not be able to do what I want

219

them to do. It's going to take forever to make this picture, and we don't have forever. We have nine weeks, so you've got to pay attention to what I tell you." I loosened the other shoe, slipped it off, and stood up. At which point he noticed that I had stepped out of character. "What are you doing?" I said, "I'm going home." He said, "What do you mean—you're going home?" I said, "I'm going back to my hotel." He said, "You're crazy. You can't go back to your hotel. Put on your shoes—we're going to shoot the scene again." I said, "No, we're not." He said, "Mr. Poitier, do you know what you are doing?" I said, "I am going back to my hotel." He said, "You are making a picture." I said, "No, I'm not." He shouted down to his assistant director, "You must call Mr. Goldwyn. I don't understand this," and then he turned back to me. "Poitier, don't walk off the stage." I said, "By the way, my hotel is the Chateau Marmont on Sunset Boulevard. When you have time you can come over there and apologize in person—after which I will consider coming back and resuming where we left off. Good day." I got in my car, drove to my hotel, and lay down on the bed.

Soon the phone rang—it was Otto. "Sidney, Sidney, Sidney, what is this? You can't take a little joke? What's the matter with you? We're friends. I talk to you and you get mad and go home—that's no way for friends to behave. Look, I think we should work out an understanding—you do your work as an actor, I'll do my work as a director. If there is something I want to say to you, all right, you and I will talk it over." I said, "I don't mind talking it over with you, but I don't want you shouting an instruction at me in front of three hundred people and not giving me a chance to respond to it. I'll come back if you give me the respect I think I deserve. Then I'll certainly be in a position to give you the respect you think you deserve. Otherwise, we're not going to be able to work together." He said, "Don't worry about that, we are going to do very well—very well."

I returned to the studio and, needless to say, he and I became very good friends. Never once throughout the film, and I worked my tail off for him, never once did he raise his voice to me again—ever. Of course, he raised it to a lot of other people, that's the way he was, but nevertheless I believe that Otto Preminger—and this is from personal observation—I believe he is one of the best producers Hollywood has ever forged. He is a *great* producer, and it would be wonderful if he would just produce films, because he has excellent taste and know-how acquired over dozens of productive years. At this stage, I don't think he should waste his precious time *directing* anymore.

16 Diahann

DIAHANN CARROLL AND I had not been working together more than a few days when I realized that I was unusually interested in the lady. It was somewhat beyond the interest normally generated by an attractive, sensuous, sexy-looking woman. It was more. She was unique. She carried herself with admirable flair and style. She was beautiful—thin, but well defined; great, great, great face with its fantastic cheekbones and dark mysterious eyes. She moved with a rhythm and at a pace that tantalized; she seemed both confident and inviting. She had perfect teeth, and skin whose brown was somewhat deeper than the color of a peach. Her hands were strong delicate-looking hands, or delicate-looking strong hands, I don't remember which. They were feminine but sturdy, and they reminded me of a piano player's—but then I'd never seen many female piano players. In short, she was hard to ignore.

So I invited her to dinner. She wanted to know why I wanted to go to dinner with her. "Because I think it will be pleasant for us both. I am married and I know you are married and that's our mutual protection. All we'll be doing is having dinner together as fellow workers would, since fellow workers need each other's company from time to time. I'll be serving in place of your husband and you'll be serving in place of my wife, just for one evening. We'll talk to each other about our absent loved ones and we'll eat. What's so difficult or wrong about that?" She said, "I'll think about it." I said, "Okay, I'll check with you a little later on."

Diahann had a girlfriend-roommate, a traveling companion, named Sylvia, who was very close to her. I believe that in her deliberations she checked to see what Sylvia thought of the idea, and of me. Remember, Diahann was not then and is not now one who needs the concurrence of anyone else in her decisions—still, she wanted to know what her very good friend thought of my intentions. Apparently girlfriend Sylvia thought I was a nice guy, and I think that was just a corroboration of what Diahann thought, because my reputation at that time wasn't bad. I was considered a pretty nice guy—on the whole. Later that afternoon when I asked her if she had reached a conclusion she said, "Yes, I think it will be all right for us to have dinner." I said, "Would you like to go to the Beachcomber?" She said, "That will be fine."

We both had apartments in the Chateau Marmont Hotel, I on the third floor and she on the first. On the evening of our date I descended the stairway to her first-floor apartment, rang the doorbell, was admitted, and then was kept waiting twenty-five minutes while her friend poked around in a last-minute check-out of me to see if she could spot any lust or lechery lurking behind my boyish smile. But except for a mental asterisk to keep an eye on me, she gave me fair marks.

The Beachcomber was a very chic Polynesian restaurant in those days, and its imaginative lighting and décor formed an appropriately romantic setting for our first date. Diahann was beautiful, intelligent, witty, sophisticated, and feminine. I was relaxed, and pleasantly surprised to find myself at peace with the world. The exotic and deceptively potent drinks with innocent-sounding Polynesian names—drinks guaranteed to warm the blood and loosen the tongue—had subtly begun to take their effect. We talked about Monte Kay, her husband; about Juanita, my wife; about my children; about her parents and her sister. We also talked about our work. I was very impressed, and I could see even then that much lay ahead. Yet I was not one to move too quickly, especially with women close to my dream—as she was. And I wanted her to take note of how well I was behaving myself. So after dinner I just took her home and deposited her at her door and went up the stairs to my apartment.

During the following weeks I saw as much of her as she allowed. We went out to dinner again, to the movies, a couple of visits to night clubs on Sunset Strip, and best of all, there were evenings when we would study together in her apartment while her friend Sylvia fixed dinner for the three of us. While taking full advantage of each opportunity to learn everything I could about Diahann, I was carefully monitoring my behavior to make certain it was ever gentlemanly and free of those on-the-make ploys her friend Sylvia was on the lookout for.

One of the first things I learned in those early weeks was that Diahann Carroll was an independent woman who shifted emotional gears quickly. From getting angry quickly or hurt deeply, she would always come bouncing back a little wiser and a little stronger. She would laugh and she would cry and sometimes both at once. Yes, she was volatile. I quickly learned how volatile one night when I said something she didn't particularly like and she picked up a brush and threw it at me. She didn't throw it at me teasingly—she threw it at me to crack the old skull open. Luckily, I was fleet of foot and ducked in time to save my skull—I learned then and there what kind of temper that child had. But that was the least of what I learned about her. She was one of the brightest women I had ever known. Though she was what one might call politically unhip, she was sharp and knowledgeable in most other areas far beyond the needs of casual conversation. She was articulate in expressing her feelings, her convictions, her likes and dislikes—as well as those fears and dreams that usually lie beyond the reach of words.

Monte Kay, her husband, came to California to visit her, and I was introduced to him. I found him what I had expected to find him—very gentle, unassuming, quiet, introspective. Much, much more aware of the world than his laid-back quietness would suggest. By the time Monte's visit was over, I found myself thinking about Diahann a lot more than I should have, and within a week of his return to New York, Diahann and I both recognized that something was taking hold between us. Frightened by the prospect of being overwhelmed by what we were feeling, she elected to cool it down—tried to back off, gather her thoughts, and catch her breath. But it wouldn't let her. A struggle developed as to who controlled whom.

Independent people fear the loss of control more than anything else, and she really fought against it. And I, no less independent, was forced to reflect on the complications that would ensue if we were to lose control of what was taking hold between us and find ourselves in its power. I mounted some resistance to that galloping fever of the heart, and joined (but not wholeheartedly) in her efforts to slow it down before it became impossible to handle.

We both lost. Halfway through the picture, we fell in love. One night we took a walk up the hill from the Chateau Marmont Hotel. We knew during that walk that we had to find some answers, had to make some decisions fairly quickly. By the time we had reached the top of the hill and discussed our situation and hugged and kissed and gazed into each other's eyes and looked over the flickering lights of Los Angeles, both of us trying to talk at the same time and all those dumb things you do when you're in love, we had resolved nothing except that we were in serious trouble. And on that note we walked back to the hotel and into our respective apartments.

Toward the end of the film, Pearl Bailey and Louis Bellson invited me to a picnic party at their ranch in Victorville. I went solo. Diahann's husband, Monte, was in from New York on another visit, and they came too. Even though nothing had happened between us that could be considered a serious compromise of our respective marital bonds, we had decided it was unfair to Juanita and Monte not to tell them of the emotional complications that had developed. Diahann was especially concerned about Monte's trust in her: she felt that the honest and respectful thing to do was to tell him. It was decided that she would do that as soon as she could, possibly on their drive to Victorville. He loved her, he was very solicitious whenever he was with her—and apparently he was having such a happy time that she couldn't bring herself to hurt him on that Sunday afternoon in the desert.

But Diahann did a crazy thing on the way back to Los Angeles. I left Pearl Bailey's ranch heading for Los Angeles. Diahann and Monte were right behind me. Once I arrived at the main highway that ran adjacent to Victorville, I really took off, trying to put some distance between us, but she wouldn't allow it. She kept pace with me and stayed right on my tail. I stretched out, pushing to 90, then 95, then 100, 105 miles per hour. She was right behind me all the way into town and when I asked her the next day what was the reason for that suicidal exhibition, she said, "Well, if you were going to go, I was going to follow you." I said, "That doesn't make any sense." Then she said, "Actually, I didn't know the way back so I had to follow somebody."

The relationship thickens and by the end of the film, I'm locked in and so is she and we both know we have a hell of a problem to deal with. I have a wife and kids in New York and she has Monte and the marriage and her parents and her sister and her career. She says she's going to tell Monte when she gets home to New York and whatever happens—happens; he's a decent man for whom she still cares a great deal and he deserves to know the truth. My thoughts are pretty much the same with regard to Juanita, so we go home determined. Together we take a night flight from Los Angeles, holding hands all the way across country, and arrive in New York at six o'clock the next morning. Someone picks her up and whisks her toward Manhattan and the difficult responsibility she must meet when she walks into her West End Avenue apartment. While my taxi rolls through Queens and across the Triborough Bridge heading for Mount Vernon, where we're living at that time, my mind is full of all kinds of weird things—most of which can safely be described as guilt things. Because Juanita's been expecting me, she's in the midst of preparing breakfast when I walk into the house. There, in the kitchen, before the children get up, I have to tell her what's happened in California. I remember her face, how deeply shocked she was. She couldn't believe it. She says, "How could you do that?" Which stirs my guilts—because how could I? I say, "I don't know how I could do it—it happened—it happened in spite of my not wanting to hurt you." Quite quickly she begins edging toward the theory that it's all Diahann's fault. I try to dissuade her from that and remind her that these things are never one-sided. She starts to cry. Her father had died not long before, and she starts to sob and say things about her misfortunes—her father is gone, and now somebody is trying to steal her husband. . . . It was a terrible morning for her—and for me it was one of the worst I have ever lived through. Mind you, *one* of the worst; I have several more to come. That was the *first* "worst" one.

The children start to move about and she pulls herself together and says to me, "What do you want to do?" I tell her, "I genuinely don't know. I could move out if you choose." "Do you want to?" she asks. "I don't know at this time. I don't feel that I want to, but I don't know that I want to stay—or should stay—and if I stay how long should I stay? I just don't know." She says, "Why don't you try to sort it out and we'll talk about it tonight." I go to bed, but I can't sleep, and that night we talk about it again. And again. A pall is over everything, and especially for her.

Things stayed under that cloud for a long time. In Manhattan, Monte Kay, who is not a violent man by nature, had an explosive reaction when Diahann told him about us. I think what saved the moment for them—and for us —was that at least we were honest. We had brought it out, right up front, and there we all were faced with it. Hindsight will reveal that moment to have been the most opportune for me to press for a separation from Juanita, but I couldn't do it. I was trapped—trapped by my children. My father, Reginald James Poitier, had woven that trap for me many, many years before. I remember an evening in the Bahamas, after my sister Teddy had been physically assaulted by the man in her life, when my father found it necessary to make a speech to those of his sons who were still living at home—Reginald, Carl, Cedric, and me. I was the baby of the family and barely in my teens, but I remember every word. "There's something I want you all to remember. Never, ever beat on a woman. If you ever find that you must beat on a woman then you must leave her. Because if you have to beat on her once, you will have to beat on her again. There is no life for a man who has to reason with his woman through his fists." For emphasis, while pausing to let the message sink in, he stared intently into the eyes of each of his sons as if he were hammering the value of his words into our subconscious. Then referring indirectly to Teddy's two children, whom he had taken into his house after she and her husband had broken up their home, he continued, "And another thing you must learn—always take care of your children. Under no circumstances, ever in your life, must you allow yourself to neglect your children. Take care of your children before you put food in your own mouth. Take care of your children before you do anything else. That is a law of life. You understand?" We all nodded our heads. I was sitting on an old battered steamship trunk in which my mother kept incomplete pieces of a china set, carefully wrapped in brand-new colored bathroom towels she had bought ten years before and never used because "They're too pretty to use—some day, when me and your father build another house." (Not so strange when you realize that never in her life to that day had she ever had a bathroom in any house she owned or rented.)

Her two Sunday dresses and a shawl given her by her husband were folded neatly on top of the towel-wrapped china, and on top of them was a pair of high-heeled satin shoes she was reluctant to wear for fear her neighbors would think she was putting on the dog, and dozens of other precious items were lying secure in the midst of a generous amount of camphor balls, standing guard against the intrusion of moths and mildew. I sat there on top of my mother's memories, wide-eyed with fascination as my father's words penetrated deep inside me, where for better or worse, a part of his philosophy set its hook.

Those words began to waken in me on that morning when I told my wife I was involved with another woman, and they came surging up with a vengeance that evening to jam my thoughts whenever the possibility of leaving my children was verbalized, creating what was to become in time a conflict of such proportions that I can hardly describe it. The children were very young and I was very much in love with them and furious at our inability as parents to find a comfortable or reasonably pleasant ground on which the marriage could unfold itself, at least to the advantage of the innocent. Fostering a resentment through all those years and not being able to communicate with Juanita or she with me, except on the most elemental level, I instantly became angry at the slightest reminder that she was quite content while my needs were going begging. Why couldn't she develop a meaningful interest in my work so I could have someone with whom I could intelligently discuss all my never-ending problems? Why were so many of my most vulnerable moments endured without a reassuring touch? Admittedly, among my needs were some even I could not articulate and which Juanita would be at a dead loss simply trying to understand, much less serve. But dammit, they were not all complicated Freudian puzzles, some were genuine honest-to-God needs, and an effort should have been made. And then there are certain needs that are hard as hell to confront, because of the difficulty of pinpointing their origin. I didn't have the education, the experience, the know-how to pinpoint them—to put labels on them—to hold them up and say, "Hey, you, what are you all about? Why are you so strongly in my head at this time?"

Looking back, I wonder how much better I could have done, given who I was and where I came from. I was still living by trial and error—by instinct. I was living by a body of reactive mechanisms I had accumulated in my strange, overcrowded existence. There I was in my thirties and had been through several lifetimes already. And I was in a mess—in a real mess. On the one hand I had found a woman who was in tune with my needs, a woman who I believed would satisfy both my mind and my body. On the other hand, I was married and had children who my father said I must protect and never leave. The storm began—the storm began. The questions surrounding that dilemma matured into a popular topic with Juanita's friends and Diahann's friends and Monte's friends and my friends, with Juanita's friends trying to talk some sense into me on her behalf. That didn't help, except to aggravate the situation. Two sets of active characters in two different camps set the stage against which my relationship with the wonderful Diahann Carroll spun itself into being across two continents, many countries, and dozens of cities over nine bittersweet years. Regrets? Yes, I'll have a few.

17 A Raisin in the Sun

THEN FATE, juggling events at her discretion, interfered to bring me surcease from my problem for a moment or two. Philip Rose, an old and dear friend, was smitten by a play written by a friend of his and an acquaintance of mine named Lorraine Hansberry. I had heard talk of her being a gifted writer who was in the process of writing a play, but I knew her only as a politically aware, contemporary black American who was fairly close to Paul Robeson—one of those young people very much in his camp. Robeson was an enormous inspiration to us all. Philip Rose's enthusiasm over her gifts and his eagerness to produce her play were well founded. I was overwhelmed by the power of the material and told Mr. Rose I would be happy to play in it. Set in the 1950s, the drama concerned a black family on Chicago's South Side, headed by a very strong matriarchal figure who, widowed by an industrial accident that replaced her husband with a ten-thousand-dollar insurance check, struggles to hold her family together in the face of her son's fierce desire for recognition in a white man's society, her daughter's identity crisis, her daughter-in-law's unwanted pregnancy, and the problem of her grandson's future. The playwright's fix on the black experience was truly uncanny. She designed a plot structure and characters so refreshingly real that just reading her play, *A Raisin in the Sun,* was an uplifting experience. Philip Rose's production went into rehearsal on December 27, 1958, under the direction of Lloyd Richards with a cast that included Claudia McNeil, Diana Sands, Lou Gossett, Lonnie Elder, Ivan Dixon, Ruby Dee, and Glynn Turman. We rehearsed in New York, then went on the road for our first performance in New Haven. That evening, after a ten-year absence, I stepped out on a stage in the company of some heavyweight actors and actresses with material of substance in front of at least a thousand people. The immediate raw nakedness of being on a stage is very different from standing in front of a 35-millimeter Mitchell camera. A camera hums softly while it's watching you; an audience breathes, it coughs, it shifts about in its seat and whispers to itself while it is watching you. I had forgotten how unpredictable that classic one-on-one between audience and performer can sometimes be. At the end of the first act I took stock and to my surprise found that while I was very nervous, I was not intimidated, nor was I encumbered by the awkward tightness that ten years before used to interfere with the full use of my body. By the time the curtain came down on the third act, I had discovered that, one, we were on to something very special with that play, and, two, that I had learned some useful things about my craft in the long absence. It seemed the additional ten years of life had left me a little wiser in the use of my tools. From New Haven we moved on to Philadelphia, where we were an instant success. In the light of our excellent reviews there, the management wanted to go directly into New York, but there were no theaters available. I, alas, didn't think the play was being performed as effectively as it could have been, which got me into a lot of trouble with Lorraine, Phil, and Lloyd Richards, who were happy with the production the way it was and were quite prepared to "lock it in" at the level of the Philadelphia appearance. I honestly thought the play wasn't yet working as well as it should be before we bared ourselves to New York in that "do or die" performance in front of the critics.

We had to go into Chicago for some weeks before a theater loosened up in New York, and opening night in Chicago turned out to be phenomenal for everyone, but especially for Claudia McNeil, who played the mother. In Chicago I was not on speaking terms with Lorraine, who was understandably happy because her play was doing so well and couldn't grasp why I was dissatisfied. The reason was complicated. I believed from the first day I went into rehearsal that the play should not unfold from the mother's point of view. I still believe that. I think that for maximum effect, *A Raisin in the Sun* should unfold from the point of view of the son, Walter Lee Younger. (Yes, I played Walter Lee.) Because Claudia registered so powerfully in the play and because the audience responded so wonderfully to her *and* the play, the producer, director, and author were all satisfied. And yet I kept insisting that the mother shouldn't be the focus of the play.

They accused me of "star" behavior. Of wanting to be the top dog on stage. The simple truth of the matter was that if the play is told from the point of view of the mother, and you don't have an actor playing the part of Walter Lee strongly, then the end result may very well be a negative comment on the black male. They didn't agree, and before we stopped speaking to each other over the issue, they argued with me for hours. They professed to be at a loss as to the underlying reasons for my feelings about the image of the black male. But I was in the dark every bit as much as they were. My feelings were real and strong, but I had no idea where they sprang from. Were they a reflection of my parents? My self? Were they political? Yes? No? Maybe? With no adequate response at my fingertips that would dispel their confusion, or arrest their suspicions, they went on to accuse me of (among other things) being unreasonably sensitive to this issue for unattractive and selfish personal reasons. But I still saw it that way, and I had an ally—the talented, highly intelligent Ruby Dee. We decided on an approach, and conspired to keep the strength in the character of Walter Lee Younger, which meant my playing *against* Claudia McNeil, who is a tower of strength as a

stage personality. I had to change my whole performance to prevent the mother character from so dominating
the stage that it would cast a negative focus on the black
male. But the excellent reviews in Chicago hardened
management's resolve to "put it to bed." After all, what
strange kind of nut must I be to keep quarreling with
success? By the end of the run in Chicago, management's
position was: All Poitier is thinking of is that he's the
star of the play and Claudia McNeil is getting all the
audience's response.

But how could that have been? Wasn't I more secure
than that? Didn't I receive marvelous reviews everywhere we went? Didn't I get terrific responses from the
audiences too? Indeed I did! Then their stinging accusa-
tions were obviously not true—unless, God forbid, I
was miles and miles off base, completely out of touch
with my ego and therefore blinded to the merit of their
argument. Heavenly Father! Could I be that far out of
touch? You're damn right I could. I wasn't exactly what
you could call a Rock of Gibraltar at that time in my
life, and besides, they were very bright people, Lorraine,
Phil, and Lloyd. Yes, they might be right—even then I
recognized that there could be honest differences of opinion and judgment. But however much I leaned in the
direction of objectivity, trying to give them the benefit
of every doubt, I still was aware of the whiff of gold in
the air. That intoxicating element was quietly orchestrating management's sharp responses to my specific challenge, as if it were an unholy threat to a bonanza whose
aroma was already creeping over the horizon. And to
management's not unreasonable desire to keep the play
running forever had to be added the fact that I was committed to remain in the play no more than six months.
Claudia McNeil had a "run of the play" contract, and
they had seen by Chicago that she was going to be a big
part of the future commerciality of the play, whereas I
was leaving in six months to fulfill motion picture commitments. (One of which was to be a picture with
Diahann Carroll in Paris; as you can see, the Poitier-
Diahann Carroll relationship was just beginning to heat
up.)

One night before we left Chicago, Ruby Dee and I
sat over drinks and analyzed the way the Walter Lee
character should appear to the audience. He could appear as a weak man overwhelmed by his mother—in-

capable of engineering his own life, which he has based on dreams that exceed his skills; in other words, a weakling who doesn't deserve very much attention. Or he could appear as the average man with an average potential and average dreams, who fails to achieve them only through a combination of misunderstandings in his own family and the racism of his environment—a man who winds up bested not because he is incapable but because circumstances conspire against him—a far cry from a weakling who is reaching beyond his grasp.

Anyway, the play opened in New York with me playing it the way I wanted to play it, and it was an enormous success.

The Barrymore Theatre was a place of magic that opening night. As the curtain fell at the end of the third act, the audience came to its feet in a standing ovation that brought tears to the eyes of our cast. That audience, many of them with tears streaming down their faces, stomped, howled, and screamed with joy. Finally, the thunderous applause took on a rhythmic clapping and they began shouting, "Author, author, author." Lorraine Hansberry was standing in the audience with members of her family, and Ruby Dee told me to go and get her. I jumped from the stage into the audience, took her by the hand, and led her up onto the stage, where the audience and her actors continued to pay her the tribute she so very much deserved.

The experience of being a big hit on Broadway is so thrilling it can never, even from this distance, be fully captured in words. We were an event! We were *the* play to see that season. Night after night people from all walks of life came to pack the Barrymore and get caught up in a powerful evening, Laughing and crying and being moved before springing to their feet at the final curtain for that soul-satisfying standing ovation that has to number high among the best moments in an actor's life. Black people for the first time came to Broadway in unprecedented numbers; the majority of them had never seen a play before. Blue-collar workers from Harlem and Brooklyn; sleep-in domestics from the suburbs; professors; doctors; numbers runners; hairdressers—they all came to see Lorraine Hansberry's black family from the South Side of Chicago.

The breach between me and the management continued unrelieved for a number of reasons, not the least of which were my complaints about unprofessional behavior on stage during performances of one actor who, for reasons that remained a mystery, would make subtle changes in performance style that would weaken the effectiveness of others' performances. Management, still suspecting that ego was the root cause of my earlier complaint, concluded that the new charges probably had no basis beyond my ego's addiction to the occasional stroking.

Lorraine and I barely spoke for years after, until, with her health failing, the time came for us to put aside petty things. When guards are down and weapons laid aside, the distance between argument and gentle discussion can be a short and simple step, and so it was with us in that New York City hospital room where she was confined during the advanced stages of her illness. We talked about her work in progress, my activities, politics, racism, Africa, and the general state of the arts from our people's point of view. She spoke simply but touchingly about the direction her life would take if circumstances were otherwise. Even before her illness, it was clear that Lorraine Hansberry was orchestrating her life toward more involvement, more activism. The only subject we did not touch on was death. There was no need to.

DIAHANN AND I were unable to stay away from each other. But it was getting very difficult for her with her parents—her mother especially. So much so that her mother came to see my play. I came out of theater after a matinée performance and this very nice lady said, "Hello, do you know who I am?" I said, "No, I don't, but I do know that you are a lovely, lovely lady, *that* I know." I figured, I'm going to charm this lady to death. She said, "I'm Diahann Carroll's mother." Well, I choked —I choked. She had come just to check me out. And also to pass a certain word on to me, like: "Whatever it is you have in your head, you had better find some way to arrive at a logical and acceptable conclusion quickly."

That was my first exposure to Diahann's mother. There were to be many, many more. She was an attractive, reserved, cultivated woman in whom I could occasionally see the source of Diahann's arresting sophistication. She never once verbalized her opposition—she stayed out of our relationship as far as her contact with me was con-

233

cerned. Whenever we saw each other she was solicitous and kind to me. But I think she really nailed me to the cross in her dealings with her daughter. Diahann's father, on the other hand, was my kind of guy. He was tall, open, and friendly, and I think he liked me. To this day I think he looked on me with a great deal less suspicion than his wife did. But Diahann was much more responsive to her mother than to her father. Much, much more. She was more concerned with what her mother thought. And therein lay one of our great difficulties. Many times without her articulating to me what she might be afraid of, I could tell, I could deduce, that it was her mother's reaction to whatever was happening.

At the end of my six months on Broadway I reported to Hall Bartlett in Hollywood for his production of *All the Young Men* starring me and Alan Ladd. It was a remarkably uneventful experience, except for some blisteringly cold months in Montana and Oregon. A considerable amount of my salary was spent in dozens and dozens of hours on the phone with Diahann, whom I missed more than I can tell you. During that separation and for the remainder of that year, my continued inaction in regards to my foundering marriage deepened into a paralysis, while Diahann and her husband tried to heal the rift between the two of them. Those efforts resulted in several genuine attempts by the couple to work through their difficulties. And while those earnest tries were eventually unsuccessful, she in the meantime became pregnant. An unexpected event? Perhaps, but surely an added complication, especially at such an emotionally delicate time. But, not so exactly. Both Diahann and her husband, as best I could tell, were delighted at the prospect of becoming parents, the state of things notwithstanding. My feelings about that matter? Well, they were predictably mixed, but not so subjective that I missed the fact that the event would introduce a sober pause of some months' duration, and possibly bring about some not altogether unwelcome relief from a variety of pressures that sometimes seemed unrelenting. During the spring and summer of 1960, with time to think and reflect in an atmosphere of partially reduced tension, my thoughts ran toward the possibility of repairing the damage in my own backyard. But because fundamental contradictions can be obscured by wishful thinking only for short periods of time, here, too, failure was to be the reward for such efforts as were made. With the coming of the fall, Diahann and I, thrown once again into a work situation, were soon to gravitate to our familiar position in that same old push-pull struggle between opposing forces.

Paris Blues was the name of the picture, a United Artists production starring Paul Newman and Joanne Woodward and featuring Diahann Carroll and Sidney Poitier. The script was a one-dimensional concoction of expatriate jazz musicians living and working in Paris. A second-guesser, speaking after the fact, said it should have been Joanne Woodward and myself, and Paul Newman and Diahann Carroll, as love interests; such unconventional pairings at that time would have made a considerable impact in the business. Then, too, it was rumored (possibly by the same second-guesser) that the original idea called for exactly that kind of imaginative casting, and that United Artists and those responsible for the film felt it would be too revolutionary and backed off, leaving the creative forces no way to raise the material above the level of the commonplace.

Juanita came to Paris with the kids, and we stayed at the Georges Cinq Hotel, and I was miserable. She, having a greater capacity for joy than I, was not nearly as down. On the contrary, she found the newness of Paris stimulating. A rural, down-home, southern, irrepressible quality was one of the simple blessings God laid into the personality of that fortunate woman. I even tried to psych myself into a more pleasant frame of mind with: How come you're not happy, Sidney P., with all the opportunities floating around you? In fact, how the hell dare you wear such a troubled look? For instance, you're staying in the best hotel in town, in the center of Paris, your children are with you, you're working on a film, doing what you know best how to do, you can take short trips to other countries, you can eat in the best restaurants, go to museums, you're in good health—hey, what the hell else is there? But try as I might, I wasn't able to cure my sour disposition. If I had had a smattering of Juanita's capacity for joy, I would have sat right down and counted those blessings until I came up smiling and feeling a lot better than I was accustomed to. But that was not to be. I was to go through my days and nights in a kind of agony.

During a talk I had with Juanita before she went back home with the children, I suggested to her how much better it would be for her if she would just let me go. She replied that such an act on her part would allow me to leave without the responsibility of my guilt; she had no intention of doing that, and I could forget any thought of her letting go that easily. "If you're going to go," she said, "you are going to go without any help from me. You will have to be responsible for that move all by yourself." (Has she been talking to my father? Isn't she playing a perfect variation on notes he set down a lifetime ago?) "My responsibility is to keep this family together," she said. No, that woman was not as unhappy as I was; she was not pleased about the turmoil I was in, but she was not so unhappy. At least she had survived the trauma of knowing that a strong emotional pull existed between Diahann and me. She wished it weren't so, but she had lived with it, and for the moment she had every intention of continuing to. "I'm not going to send you off with my blessings, you can rest assured of that," she said, and I didn't much like her for it. Nor was I favorably disposed to my father, who struck the first blow as I sat there on my mother's battered trunk.

Juanita left for New York. One day as the film drew to a close, Paul Newman and I toyed with the idea of staying in Paris. He liked that city very much and said, "Why don't we take apartments here? We can work out of Paris as easily as anyplace else." Savoring the sweet brief fantasy, I said, "Might be the solution to my problem." But of course we were only playing fantasy games. When the film finished, we all returned to New York.

With the release of each of my fifteen films, my name had become increasingly familiar to filmgoers, and by the end of 1962 there was developing in Hollywood a historymaking new attitude countering the long-held conviction that the appearance of blacks in other than menial roles would offend the movie industry's principal constituency. The realization that year by year more and more white Americans were willing to pay their way into a theater to see entertainment about blacks or involving blacks would encourage most of the studios to make minor alterations in the rigid and generally insulting policy for dealing with America's black citizens. Though history will accurately acknowledge my presence in those proceedings, my contribution was no more important than being at the right place at the right time, one in that series of perfect accidents from which fate fashions her grand designs. History will pinpoint me as merely a minor element in an ongoing major event, a small if necessary energy. But I am nonetheless gratified at having been chosen.

In 1961, at Juanita's insistence, we moved from Mount Vernon. A maneuver that would not, in the end, put the distance between her and our problems she had hoped it would. Once more we moved, Juanita, myself, our daughters Beverly, Pam, Sherri, and the newly arrived baby, Gina. With material goods and psychological burdens, we moved to a house on a hill in a newly integrated part of Westchester called Pleasantville.

DAVID SUSSKIND, who produced the film version of *A Raisin in the Sun,* encouraged me to learn how things were really done on the inside of the film business. "A whole world of commerce exists behind that camera, Sidney—you should learn about it. Learn about the *whole* business. It will be your best insurance against sitting at home waiting for the phone to ring." Although my relationship with Stanley Kramer had allowed me a behind-the-scenes look at how deals were put together, I never paid much attention to what were the important ingredients of a successful deal until Susskind put the bee in my bonnet. Recognizing the value of his advice, I immediately adjusted my focus to include that all-important world behind the camera. To much of the film industry I was still a curiosity after twelve years, but at Columbia, Fox, Paramount, United Artists, and MGM, I was considered a part of the working core of Hollywood artists. At those studios I was allowed to gently pick the brains of some of the most high-powered executives. Over lunch in private dining rooms, or in exclusive front offices where the important decisions were made, those men of power and influence would patiently explain to me how motion pictures, functioning as an industry, are on the whole subject to the same sound business practices that are the foundation of success in other American industries. Among the friends I had gathered at those studios through my twelve years were those I found willing, and in some cases eager, to work on behalf of minorities whenever it was possible to do so.

Let us not forget that the exclusion of blacks and other miniorities from films during that period, with myself behind the most notable of the few exceptions to the rule, was institutionalized. No one in Hollywood walked around reciting the need to exclude us from films. It had been done for so long that it was a mindless, unconscious perpetuation, firmly built into the fabric of the industry. So the people who were not helpful to us were just simply operating on what was the normal value system, while those who helped us were men and woman stepping out of the parade. And in some cases they took very real and considerable chances with their own careers.

One of the pictures I made under those circumstances was a Stanley Kramer production called *Pressure Point* in which he had me play a black psychiatrist. The film starred me and Bobby Darin. Casting me this way was an absolutely revolutionary idea for Hollywood, and more to the point, Kramer gave artistic control to a young unknown director named Hubert Cornfield. Kramer was in the habit of taking these kinds of chances precisely when his reputation could have done quite well without them, but with his maverick nature he persisted. I am convinced, knowing him as I do, that he did what he did because he *had* to do it. It wasn't because he was trying to make a lot of money—obviously a picture about a black psychiatrist treating white patients was not the kind of sure-fire package that would send audiences rushing into theaters across the country. But Kramer had other gods to serve, and he was faithful to them.

18 Death

FROM THAT MAGIC MOMENT in his boyhood days when a farmer's sensitivity blossomed within him, Reginald James Poitier understood in his heart the fact that there is a cycle to each and every living thing. He understood, acknowledged, accepted, and respected that most basic law of nature. Late in 1961, after hard work, poor soil, and an indifferent tourist economy had weakened him in the struggle against Father Time's final assault, I received a call from Nassau asking me to hurry to his bedside. The spread of arthritis in his aging joints was only one of the many relentless pressures on his hard and challenging life, maneuvering him into a wheelchair from which he methodically put his life in order and proceeded to oversee his departure from this world. In his seventy-seven years he had seen enough. He had laid eyes on the children of his children's children. And on mornings more numerous than most men could hope to witness, he had watched the sun come up to warm the earth. Not wanting to leave too many things undone, he called in a young lawyer friend and, under the pretext of engaging him to search out a title to some land on Cat Island, he casually dictated a two-page will. That young lawyer was unaware that Reginald was preparing to let go. He seemed full of life and told several funny stories that had the young lawyer responding with a few funny stories of his own, not realizing that those relaxed moments represented the farewell exchange between him and his client. My father's plan was foolproof in that it was imaginatively designed to avoid detection for the seven days necessary to make his plan irreversible when finally uncovered.

From years of habit, my mother's instincts picked up something—some vibration, a vague uneasiness—despite her husband's smiling attitude of buoyant well-being. She knew there was something in the air trying to be said—why else would her tried and true instincts be alerting her? You don't live with a man more than fifty years and not know when a smile is a fraction too broad. Or when he is protecting you from something—or something from you. At times like these, she would usually wait for clues from her reading of his actions, clues that would lead her eventually to whatever unspoken things were churning inside her husband. But not this time, for her husband was outfoxing her.

On the morning after he dictated his will, Reginald Poitier stopped eating. A simple act, unexpected and to the point. As usual, Evelyn Poitier fixed his breakfast, delivered it to him on the porch where he was in the habit of taking his meals, then returned to her household chores, leaving him as he preferred to be, alone on his porch catching the summer breeze. The scavenger dogs of the neighborhood were swift and effective accomplices; they devoured every scrap of food thrown to them from his plate. Except for the interruption of a grandchild

darting across the porch in play, or looking up in acknowl-
edgment when a passing motorist of his acquaintance
honked a friendly hello, or when neighbors stopped in
front of his gate to bring him up to date on community
gossip, he spent the last few months reviewing a life that
he knew was drawing to a close. Anchored to his wheelchair in the solitude of his porch, he went back in time
again and again to relive those moments which, in his
judgment, made his seventy-seven difficult years of life
unquestionably worthwhile.

He was sure Evelyn would understand his behavior
when it was all over. And five days was as far as he could
get into the ritual of orchestrating his own death before
the rapid deterioration of his vital signs led her instincts
to uncover that powerful unspoken commitment of her
husband's. A doctor was quickly called, with emphasis
on "emergency," and Reginald Poitier was hospitalized.
The scavenger dogs were displeased, but the end to which
they had lent themselves as co-conspirators was in sight.
My father was past the halfway mark in his effort to
reach his final life goal.

As I approached the end of the first-floor corridor in
Princess Margaret Hospital, I saw a group of family
members and friends, some with eyes swollen from tears,
huddled in low and solemn conversation as they kept vigil
outside the closed door of his room. After hugs and whispered greetings, I entered the room and closed the door
behind me.

My mother looked up warily from her chair at the
side of his bed and managed a weak smile before struggling to her feet—"My son, my boy." We fell into each
other's arms and she immediately began patting me on
my back. "Oh, my son, my son, your father is going
away, your father is going away." Pulling from our em-
brace, she turned me toward the bed, saying, "Come,
talk to him." My father's eyes were closed and there
were tubes in his nose and a needle taped to his arm.
As I looked on his thin and sallow face, I realized that
this was the very first time in my life I had seen him
without his fighting spirit. Leaning down toward his left
ear, my mother said, "Reggie, Sidney is here—Sidney
is here." He tried to open his eyes, but the effort was too
great. His lips struggled to stage one of a smile. Two of
the fingers on his left hand quivered for recognition. I
picked up the hand before I spoke. "Papa? Papa? Can

you hear me?" The answer came through his hand in the form of an almost imperceptible squeeze. "We don't want you to go away, man, we want you to get better. You've got lots of living yet to do." He squeezed my hand again, but that reply ignored my words and only conveyed his appreciation that I had come to see him before he departed. I looked at my mother, hoping she would offer some guidance as to how I should proceed, but she only stared back, watching, as her dying husband and her last-born son struggled for contact during that purest of moments. I instantly realized she was hoping for a spiritual touching between my father and me. Nevertheless all I could say to a dying father were things that would only be of interest to a father who wasn't especially anxious to die. Whereas his mind was locked and sealed against persuasion. Yes, Reginald Poitier was in every sense ready to go.

But I wasn't ready to let him go. Although I felt fearful at death hovering nearby, waiting to take charge, I nevertheless articulated my resentment at its presence by only speaking to my father about the wonders of life. "I want you to get well so you can finally come to New York and see for yourself what a fabulous city it is. America's really a great place, you've got to see it, and millions of people there know your name now. I'd like for you and Mama to take a train ride across the country to see how big it is, and maybe visit some of those fantastic farms in the Midwest. You know, man, they have farms out there—some of them are as big as all of Cat Island—just one farm. Sometimes they have them bigger than Cat Island—and the soil is rich, you can grow anything in it. You just spit out a seed and the chances are it will take root."

My mother watched and listened as I continued to defy death by singing the praises of life. Of course, it's very likely that both death and my mother were old hands —wise in their respective ways to the frailties of the human heart—who could see behind my defiant words a frightened little boy whistling past the graveyard.

Two nurses entered my father's room and conducted a brief check of his vital signs and the life-support systems feeding him oxygen and glucose. Satisfied that all was as well as could be expected, they offered a few words of encouragement to my mother and elicited a promise from me to autograph the two pieces of blank paper, one of them placed on the table near the bed before leaving the room. Returning to my father, I attempted a bit of humor: "Man, if you would only open your eyes and take a look at these pretty girls you've got running in here to flirt with you—why, you'd be out of that bed and on your feet in a minute." He almost hit stage two in his attempt to produce a smile. By squeezing my hand he let it be known that he approved of my salute to the rascal in him. In the silence that followed, my mother took his right hand into her hand and stroked it gently, saying, "He waited for you to come, son. Now he has seen all of his children—he can rest now." And a short time later he died.

On the morning of the funeral, after respects had been paid by the hundreds of people who filed by the open casket, the sons of Reginald Poitier cleared the room of all but the immediate family, setting the stage for Evelyn to say her last goodbys to him surrounded only by the children they had brought into the world. My brother Cyril said, "Mama, it's time for us to walk him to the church." Evelyn Poitier rose from her chair, stepped over to the coffin, and gazed down at the face of her husband. After a long silent look, she said to him, "Oh, Reggie, don't worry about me. It won't be long now. It won't be long now."

That did it. Those few simple words of love and promise, of goodby and appreciation, were all it took to shatter my resolve not to cry at my father's funeral. Trying to hold on to my composure, fearful that a loss of control would see me flying off into a million pieces, I fought to slam shut a floodgate of tears. I blinked my eyes and gritted my teeth and dug my fingernails into my palms and tried to think of anything other than the majestic eloquence of that semi-illiterate island woman whose fighting spirit still endured, even though she was no longer afraid of either life or death. My father had been lucky—a lesser woman would have buckled under their hard existence.

One of my brothers went to the door and called the undertaker into the room to close the coffin. With his wife directly behind the coffin, Reginald Poitier's body was "walked" to the neighborhood Catholic church by his pallbearer sons, Cyril, Redis, Carl, Reginald, Cedric, and Sidney.

Two weeks later, my brother Cedric would die, and my

family was to walk him up along that same route, to that same church, for a final service before laying him to rest next to Papa.

Evelyn Poitier lost two of her men within two weeks, one to the attrition of old age and the farmer's puritanical abhorrence of being useless, the other to accidental asphyxiation by carbon monoxide on an evening when alcohol had dulled his senses. But, "Oh, Reggie, don't worry about me. It won't be long now. It won't be long now." In fact, it will be barely two years before she joins him.

19   Academy Award

A BOOK CALLED *Lilies of the Field*, written by William Barrett, was brought to the attention of theatrical agent Fred Ingels, who thought it ideal material for a motion picture. His most important supporter was the accomplished director Ralph Nelson. Together, with strong assistance from Martin Baum, they brought the magic of that little book to the motion picture screen.

It was not easy. Fred Ingels quit the agency he was associated with and went to work for Marty Baum, taking his client Ralph Nelson with him, and thereby setting the stage for the miraculous packaging of *Lilies of the Field*. United Artists Corporation displayed very little faith in the project: they offered Nelson and Ingels a mere $250,000 for the entire production. Moreover, they stated that if Mr. Nelson had any difficulty completing the film with that amount of money he would be held personally responsible for all overages encountered.

Ralph Nelson's faith in the material was strong, and in support of his judgment he put his house and other worldly possessions on the line as collateral to insure United Artists against loss. He knew he couldn't hire me to play in that picture—my salary at that time would have taken more than half his budget to pay it—but he came to me anyway. "What do we do?" was the question before me and Martin Baum. At that point in my career, Martin was functioning in such an unbelievably effective way that I was not about to question any aspect of his dealmaking; I just assumed that he would never authorize the drastic cut in salary that would be required for me to play in a picture with such a low budget, no matter how much I liked the script.

But he said, "Hold on now—not so fast—take it easy. Just back up and hold your horses for a minute. I'm pretty close to an approach on this thing. Let me sleep on it one more night." By the next afternoon he had worked out a formula that would allow us to proceed without the damaging effect a cut in salary would undoubtedly bring to our bargaining position throughout the industry. He said, "Here's how I believe we can save this project. You take a small salary and, in addition, take a piece of the profits. It operates like this: Instead of taking the $150,000 they can't afford to pay you, you'll take $25,000 or $30,000, plus ten percent of the profits—if the picture works. With $250,000 as the negative cost, the picture has to break into profit at seven or eight hundred thousand dollars. Now if it grosses three or four million dollars, you'll get ten percent of a lot of money." Because Marty knew more about dealmaking than I did, and because I trusted him completely, I said, "Well, let's go." And we did. We made the deal with Ralph Nelson's Rainbow Production Company, flew to California, and immediately began rehearsals. At his hilltop home in Beverly Hills, in the prime of his productive years, Ralph Nelson initiated the gamble of his lifetime with an unauthorized rehearsal with his principal players around his dining room table. The ludicrous, punitively low budget grudgingly allocated to the project by United Artists left no margin for even the slightest error, thereby making success virtually impossible for anyone other than an ingenious, imaginative, creative, and highly disciplined production manager working closely with an inspired, committed, experienced director who believed so much in himself that he never once gave serious thought to the possibility that he and his family might wind up sleeping in the street. Production manager Joe Popkin and director Ralph Nelson were such a team. Fired by the challenge to do the impossible, they worked night and day for weeks before coming up with a shooting schedule so tight, so meticulously assembled, it was rumored they had put it together with a stopwatch. That schedule called for us to shoot the entire film in fourteen days. And indeed, we traveled from California to Tucson, Arizona, made the picture, and were back in Los Angeles at the end of two weeks. Five weeks from the day I left I was back in New York. By contract my name would appear above the title of the picture in the position of the star. But I knew and Joe Popkin knew that the real star of *Lilies of the Field* was the man whose creative force, whose integrity and professional commitment, husbanded the entire project into being, Ralph Nelson.

The picture opened and did remarkably well. By the end of the year the picture was considered so good that, to my real surprise, I was nominated for an Academy Award. Well, I didn't pay that much mind, over and above the thought that such a nomination could be good for my career; I was very aware that I was in a field with four other nominees whose performances in their respective pictures made each of them an almost unbeatable competitor. There was Albert Finney, whose *Tom Jones* was a much bigger success than my picture was—it was just about universally accepted as the picture of the year. There was Paul Newman's dynamic performance in *Hud,* there was Rex Harrison's highly praised work in *Cleopatra,* and there was Richard Harris's electric impact in *This Sporting Life.* Understandably, in such company I was considered the dark horse, so to speak.

I accepted an invitation from the Academy of Motion Picture Arts and Sciences to take part in the presentation ceremonies in April primarily because Diahann and I felt it would be good for black people to see themselves competing for the top honor, especially since we as a people had not been that close to an Academy Award for some time. Second, I thought it was a good career move to be present. Winning was the least of my expectations—entirely out of the question. Well, almost. In the odd reckless moment since learning about the nomination, I did fantasize a bit, but what the hell, that's only human nature. Anyway, in the late afternoon of the Day, Diahann, helped by our old friend Frank London, dressed me in my rented tuxedo and fussed nervously over my appearance as she prepared to send me off to the ceremony at the Santa Monica Auditorium with Martin and Bernice Baum.

My going alone was a decision mutually arrived at out of consideration for our delicate situation. In her caring and loving way, Diahann was utterly supportive. In fact, years later she would help me to correct my faulty memory by reminding me of the pride she felt in our having made such a mature decision in the interests of vulnerable loved ones on both sides of our togetherness. Sitting silent and alone in the limousine as it wound its way to Marty's house, my attention focused back over the many crises we had survived in order still to be together on that afternoon of April 13, 1964. I lingered over something that had tested us both not long after we returned to New York after falling in love on the set of *Porgy and Bess*. I had told my wife about her, she had told her husband about me—and he had responded violently and moved out of their apartment. She said to me that it was necessary to her as a person, and that it would benefit our relationship, if we both met Monte and discussed what had happened and what was happening so that he would know he was not being abused in any way. She felt he was entitled to this because he was so deeply involved. I had never done such a thing in my life. I had never gone to a man and said, "I have to sit you down and tell you that I'm involved with your wife." But she insisted and I admired her for it, and loved her even more, because putting such painful cards on the table had to be tough for us all, but most of all for her.

Diahann makes the appointment with Monte and we meet in the cocktail lounge of a hotel. Monte is already there when we walk in—sitting, waiting. He stands up as we approach, and I see that his face is grim and stern. Having met him before, I say, "How are you?" and he answers, "Fine." I say, "This is very difficult for me, but I guess it's necessary. It's necessary because Diahann thinks it's necessary that you be told what our intentions are. I find it admirable but a little touchy." He says, "I see." I say, "Whatever objections you may have—and I'm sure there are many—I want you to know that we intend to try to have a life together. Because of that we're here to tell you those intentions up front, so that you can raise whatever questions you may have in your mind and take whatever course of action you find you have to." He says, "Have you moved away from home?" I say, "No, I haven't yet, but I fully intend to." He says, "When?" I say, "Soon, I hope." He says, "But you don't have a date." I savor that one. I take my time, because this is a very intelligent man and given a chance he will pin me in a corner and I have to avoid that, no matter what. I say, "Hold up a minute—hold up a minute—I didn't come here to go into that." He said, "Why not? It affects me. I have a right to ask." I say, "I don't see how my date for moving out of my house affects you." He says, "Well, I'm out of my house, aren't I?" Needless to say he's gaining on me. I say, "In time—I'm working on it." He says, "I see." Which is enough to leave the question unresolved, but with the moral burden unquestionably on my side of the table. After a pause he says, "Tell you what I'd like to do. I'd like to talk to my wife for a little while." I look at Diahann and she says, "Fine," and I say, "Okay," and we arrange to meet somewhere else later on. I left, admiring the straightforwardness of the man. He was not crazy about me, to say the least, but there was no nonsense about him. There was a serious question before us and he handled it with directness and sensitivity, and I was impressed.

Things moved on from there, and eventually Monte went to Mexico and got a divorce. And by the night of the Academy Awards, I was at least out of my house. But alas, I was still in conflict. At that time in my life I was being hammered into shape by all kinds of forces, and our relationship was one of them, but we had moved on and things were much better for me, sitting in that limousine, than they had been that day in the lounge of a hotel on Seventh Avenue. As the car zipped through the streets of Beverly Hills I happily concluded (once again) that Diahann Carroll was worth all the pain and the heartaches.

After pausing to pick up Marty and Bernice, the limousine raced on to Santa Monica, and soon after we took our seats, the audience in the jam-packed auditorium settled into quiet, the lights dimmed, and the ceremony began. As I sat there watching it all unfold—from the first award to the second, and so on—moisture began to accumulate in the palms of my hands. And as they got closer and closer to Best Actor of the Year, my anxiety mounted until it was unbearable. I noticed that there was a television cameraman walking up and down the aisle searching out the people involved in a particular category. His procedure was to cut immediately to the winner and capture his or her reaction before he or she jumped up, then cut right away to the four losers. I thought: Oh, my God, here I am a bundle of nerves—I've got to collect myself and be in control when Albert Finney's name

247

is called. I knew that Finney wasn't present, but that someone was on hand ready to stand in for him. With Finney not present, the camera would probably take a quick glance at the person designated to receive the Oscar for him, then, sure as hell, they're going to focus right on me to see what my reactions are going to be—then move on for the reactions of the other three. Or the four of us in some other order. Well, I tell you, I was sitting there being ripped up internally. But outside I was just too cool for words. I was smiling and applauding the winners in the other categories as they came up to receive their Oscars. And when the people who came up to present awards would make their obligatory cute remarks, I smiled at almost all of them. I was really being what I would like people to see me being if they shot that camera on me suddenly.

Time passes—category after category. Envelope after envelope is opened and winner after winner scrambles to his feet and rushes to the stage. We get closer and closer. I am absolutely beside myself with nervousness. I begin making promises to myself in my mind. I say: I can understand that this is an important moment and I have to be here and in fact I want to be here for what it means to us as a people, but I'm never going to put myself through this shit no more—never again under no circumstances am I going to come here again and put myself through this. By the time we arrive at the two or three categories preceding the best actor category I'm so nervous I begin to sweat. And about then the thought hits me: What if some miracle's about to take place, what would I say if I ever got up there? The odds against the miracle suggested that I not waste my time composing an acceptance speech but—but what if? Anyway, it's always been my credo to be prepared whenever possible. Besides, if this was the night for the longshot dark horse, I was not going to get up there and look dumb. The first thing they were going to say was, "Here comes the first black actor to win the Academy Award and he can't even say nothing—dumb—dumb!" Well, there I was switching from no chance at all to writing my acceptance speech! Presumptuous? Maybe. At any rate, safe was decidedly better than sorry, so I foraged through the bins of my mind in search of the appropriate words. Think, Sidney, think, time is of the essence! Whatever I say must be the truth first, and it must be something intelligent and impressive that will leave the people in that room and the millions watching at home—leave them all duly and irrevocably impressed with the intelligence and decorum of one black actor, Sidney Poitier.

After building and discarding a series of opening sentences, I happened upon the phrase, "It has been a long journey to this moment," and immediately nailed it down as the most symbolic, lyrical, and illuminating line possible. A really super, neat phrase, I thought, in a moment of self-congratulation, before I pressed on in search of an appropriate follow-up. I remembered that other people were thanking those who had helped them and I thought now who helped me? Without effort the names began to come. First of all my agent. Most people don't thank their agents. They thank their director, the writer, the producer, and the studios, but they never seem to get around to their agents. But my agent was the most important person; without him I wouldn't have done the picture. Then other people and other sentences came to mind, giving me more than I could remember without writing it down. I went over it and over it and over it, and over it, and as the time came closer, I knew that I would never need all this silliness I was memorizing. Nevertheless I kept running it down, over and over, quicker and quicker, until it was time for the best actor award.

There it was. The emcee introduced the presenter, and Annie Bancroft walked onto the stage to thunderous applause. A cameraman ran up the aisle to the row where I was sitting and trained his camera on me; another cameraman dashed into position and pointed his camera at the person waiting to receive for Albert Finney. On stage, Annie Bancroft read the list of nominees and was handed an envelope. I tell you, I will never have butterflies in my stomach as I was having at that moment. I was so nervous I couldn't raise my hand up to wipe the sweat from my brow because I didn't want people to detect the volcano that was bubbling inside, and I was sure it would be conveyed in that gesture of raising my hand. So I sat there with my smile. I remember distinctly that my smile froze after a while and I could neither unsmile nor widen it. I was just stuck there with a lot of teeth exposed— just stuck. A hush fell over that huge audience as Annie Bancroft opened the envelope. My mouth went completely dry, and it was only with effort that I was able to pull back my lips from my smiling teeth.

Annie Bancroft pulled a card from the envelope and said, "The winner is Sidney Poitier." I was about to start the obligatory face-saving applause that custom demands from the losers when it hit me. Aiiiiee! It's me—it's me! I won! I won! I flew to my feet. The place broke out in deafening applause. I finally pulled myself together enough to rush down the aisle. Well, I want to tell you, as I rushed down the aisle I was so flushed with the moment, my nervousness, my anxiety, my happiness, my enthusiasm, all of which so overwhelmed me, it was hard to keep from fainting. I ran up on the stage and looked out at those thousands of faces and suddenly forgot my speech. Fortunately for me, they were still applauding. The applause continued for an additional five or six seconds, just enough time for me to pluck from my mind the opening line to a speech I had never seriously thought I would be called upon to deliver. As the applause died down I was ready. I began, "It has been a long journey to this moment . . ."

I walked offstage and was directed to the pressroom, where damn near every newspaper in the world was represented. I went through all kinds of picture taking and stuff and stuff and stuff—it was bedlam—it was madness, but I was exhilarated by it. I was happy for me, but I was also happy for the "folks." We had done it. We black people had done it. We were capable. We forget sometimes, having to persevere against unspeakable odds, that we are capable of infinitely more than the culture is yet willing to credit to our account. I was filled with good feelings on that marvelous evening. Marty and Bernice Baum joined me in the pressroom, from where a barrage of security guards steered us safely through hundreds of enthusiastic fans milling outside the stage door and in the parking lot. Safely in the limousine, we headed for the celebration party at the Beverly Hilton Hotel. As soon as I possibly could, I called my children in New York and was told that my daughter Pamela had burst into tears of joy and collapsed to the floor when Annie Bancroft called my name. The four girls were so excited—they were still awake at three in the morning.

While celebrating that evening, I paused somewhere in my merrymaking to count my blessings. And not the least of them was to have the privilege of sharing the evening with loved ones like Diahann and Frank, who were watching it back at the hotel, my children in New York, Marty and Bernice, and the many other people around the world.

But a private sadness haunted the celebration and left a place unfilled inside me because I was unable to share it all with the one person most responsible for my being there. Evelyn Poitier's life had come to an end some weeks short of that April evening. She died January 18, 1964, at the age of sixty-eight, after confiding to my sister that she wasn't feeling too well and asking her, "Would you fix me a cup of tea and bring it in to me? I'm going to lie down for a while." In the few minutes it took my sister to brew a cup of tea and take it into the bedroom, our mother had slipped quietly away to join her Reggie. A swift and dignified departure was granted her by a merciful heaven. No time to say even one last goodby. But then, in her last moment, she may have thought that goodbys were not all that important in her case, because, after all, her children knew exactly where she was going. She had promised her husband it wouldn't be long. Yes, that evening belonged more to them than anyone else. And most especially to Evelyn. But they were gone.

I never got to show them the America I had come to know. Reginald never saw the vast stretches of Midwestern farmland that ran on endlessly for hundreds of miles with soil rich enough to grow millions of tons of golden wheat. In fact, Miami was as far into America as his life had reached; he never came north. During his last ten years of life when his energies were low and the gap between our two worlds had widened too much for him to hurdle, I, the last of his sons, presented him with his final grandchildren. With time at a premium in those sunset years, he contented himself with having us bring them to see him as often as possible, and in those short visits with them, he carved out an imprint of his existence on the walls of Beverly's and Pamela's memories. Sherri and Gina were too young to retain much more than a few strands their subconscious minds might, possibly, have tucked away.

No, Reginald never made it north; he never laid eyes on gigantic and awesome New York City. But Evelyn did. She came in the early fall of 1960 for a week's visit. Not the least among her many reasons for coming (at

Juanita's strong insistence) was to talk some sense into her son—who, she had been told, was neglecting his children something awful and ignoring his marriage vows. Staggered and disoriented after a week in that strange new world, Evelyn marveled at the rituals that existence in New York required. Her fighting spirit tried to pick up the rhythm of the big, brash, brazen city, but it wouldn't give an inch. She never got in step, and was ruffled by the impolite and impersonal nature of that mess that called itself a city. She might have squared off for a longer fight if she had still been the tiger of her early years; instead, she spent her time collecting impressions of the city, of me, of Juanita, our relationship, the children, all to be taken back for Reggie to "see" what was going on up north.

One afternoon in Pleasantville, Juanita arranged for a group of women of my mother's age to come and have a get-acquainted afternoon over tea. Ossie Davis's mother was present, Juanita's mother was there, and two other women. Juanita, being unaware of the extent of Evelyn's shy nature, designed the afternoon in the hopes that it would make Evelyn feel at home. Neither Juanita nor I had the presence of mind to realize that we had brought Evelyn together with strangers from an alien culture who themselves were being asked to entertain someone with whom they had nothing in common beyond skin color and the title of grandmother. Definitely not enough to make for relaxation and ease on Evelyn's side of the match. From the outset, after the introductions and the first cup of tea, Evelyn found herself on the hot spot with a stream of questions coming her way about her children, her grandchildren, recipes for West Indian dishes, religion, and her husband. She sweated and squirmed under the concentrated attention of the four strangers who *thought* they were simply trying to be nice, until she could stand it no more and picked up a *Jet* magazine, opened it, and presumably became instantly absorbed in it. With a face characteristic of an involved reader, Evelyn appeared preoccupied with the magazine. When she glanced up to see if the other women's attention had indeed shifted away from her, Evelyn found them all staring at her as if she was crazy. She smiled at them and went back to her "reading." Evelyn, you see, was near-sighted, and the magazine was upside down in her hands and she didn't know it.

When she wetted her fingers with her tongue and then proceeded to turn a page or two, her guests thought surely she was cuckoo. How were they to know she was merely taking refuge from their overpowering warmth and their too generous attention?

A few days later, I sat silently by her side while she stared thoughtfully out on the seven rolling acres of land on which our house stood in one of the choicest sections of Pleasantville. She was making a mental record of the grounds, the trees, the stream, and the apple trees that were still heavy with fruit. After a long time she stirred, took a deep breath as if shifting tracks mentally, and looked at me in silence as a smile gathered in her eyes before cracking to the surface at the corners of her mouth. The barest movement of head followed—it might have been a nod or two. If so, I felt it to be one of approval. Satisfaction perhaps. She patted me on my knee and her eyes wandered back to the Westchester countryside before she spoke, more to herself than to me. "I want Reggie to come and see this property." He never did. And on that most important evening of my life, one that I very much wished Evelyn could see, she too was gone. Because they, my father and mother, Evelyn and Reginald Poitier, were no longer with me, the historic evening of April 13, 1964, was, in the final analysis, an imperfect night.

IN THE CAREER HEAT created by the Academy Award, I was offered a Columbia picture, *The Long Ships*, costarring with Richard Widmark. It was to be shot on location in Yugoslavia. In the meantime, Diahann became a big hit starring in a Broadway musical called *No Strings* with music by one of her favorite composers, Richard Rodgers. With her career going so well and my publicity following the Award, external pressures on our relationship developed rapidly. And because of my relationship with Diahann, I was being pot-shotted at a little more frequently by some black newspapers. I chose to remain above that storm, which wasn't easy, knowing as I did how relentless the black press can be. I hoped my going to Yugoslavia for *The Long Ships* would ease those pressures somewhat. But out of sight wasn't necessarily out of mind, and I continued to be a target. However, I stuck firmly to the hard and fast rule I had made some years before, which was never to allow myself to be sucked into a public defense of my private life.

Anyway, off I went to Yugoslavia, not at all pleased at leaving Diahann behind but comforted by the realization that she was busy at her work and raising her lovely daughter and loving it. Alas, Belgrade was without doubt the worst place I have ever been to make a movie. It was just awful. In the most casual encounters, a pervasive hostility was always ready to chase the sunshine out of an innocent smile. No, that city was not nice to me, and were it not for a social club and canteen attached to the American Embassy whose facilities were available to visiting Americans, and where I was warmly welcomed, the experience might have been intolerable. Maybe I tried too hard to like the place. I could have been insensitive to nuances and unknowingly worked over some of its cultural subtleties with a sledge hammer. I did make a vigorous effort at trying to keep my first impressions from throwing themselves into concrete too quickly, but in the end I just didn't like Belgrade. For one thing, many of the Ethiopian students studying there were under such fierce racial harassment that a great number of them asked for permission to leave Yugoslavia and go to West Germany to continue their studies. It seems that there was a resentment on the part of some Yugoslavs because the African students were brought in on scholarships and given subsistence allowances. But most of the African students felt that this was just an excuse for the venting of an innate racism. Anyway, some of whatever it was spilled over on me during my stay there, which turned out to be a total of fourteen weeks. A previous contractual agreement required the producers to release me for two of those weeks, so that I could return to the United States to play a cameo role in *The Greatest Story Ever Told*, and those two weeks back home were a powerful breath of fresh air. And once in a while, in search of a holiday from my off-key relationship with Yugoslavia, I would fly from Belgrade to Paris for the weekend. For one such glorious weekend Diahann arranged to be absent from her show and flew to Paris to be with me. We packed a lot of living and loving into that weekend before going out to Orly airport together for separate planes back to our jobs in New York and Yugoslavia.

That trip back to Belgrade on an Air France jet was

when I stopped praying on airplanes. For years it had been my habit, after strapping myself into my seat, to say a little prayer just before the plane began taxiing down the runway. I would say, "Dear Lord, please ride with us to our destination and help us to return safely to the ground." The plane would take off, fly to wherever it was going, come in for a smooth, safe landing and at the moment of contact with the ground I would say, "Thank You, Lord, for riding with us safely." I did it every time I got on a plane, but I always felt guilty because I never seemed to call on the Lord except when I was in a potentially dangerous situation. And as that guilt intensified through the years, I started thinking of myself as dishonest and hypocritical. I mean, where was my awareness of God when I was having a good time? I could imagine Him saying, "Oh, for heaven's sake, here he comes—he needs a favor again." So, finally, I said to myself: That is a hypocritical relationship to have with God or Jesus, that is unhealthy—calling on Him only at these times makes me an opportunist in the relationship. A user. So I said: I have to stop doing it, because I'm only doing it out of fear. And if I can relate to God only when I'm afraid, then we must be in a relationship unworthy of us both. I'm gonna quit praying on airplanes.

I get on that Paris-to-Belgrade plane, strap myself in, and consciously prepare myself to fight the urge. Needless to say, the neurotic energy feeding the urge is the idea that this particular plane is going to crash as soon as it gets up high enough to. The plane lurches forward for its takeoff run and I try desperately to steel myself against my fears. By way of consolation I tell myself: Sidney P., in every life there comes a now-or-never moment, and you will be a better man once this plane has touched down. It doesn't help. The more the plane picks up speed rushing down the runway, the more I'm tempted. I think: Well, I'll say one more little old prayer just to get me over this trip, a last one—I'll start being brave on my next trip. But I fight it. Finally the plane lifts off and climbs up into the clouds, and I tell you I sit there motionless in the grip of a paralyzing fear that is systematically squeezing beads of cold sweat from every pore in my body.

Our first stop is Munich. From Paris to Munich I'm expecting the plane to fall out of the sky at any moment. It doesn't. Arriving at Munich, we touch down without incident, ending the first phase of my cold-turkey cure. After a half-hour layover, we take off for Zagreb in Yugoslavia. On the flight to Zagreb I don't pray going up and I don't pray coming down. We take off from Zagreb for Belgrade, and again I don't pray going up or coming down. By the time I get to Belgrade, I'm cured of my opportunist habit. And I say to myself: If I'm going to develop a healthy relationship with Him, I must from this very moment be cognizant of God at good times as well as bad—during the calm and during the storm. As a result, I still pray; but I don't pray only in adversity.

20 Analysis

IN 1961, desperately needing someone to talk to, I placed a call to Harry Belafonte. That phone call led me into psychoanalysis. Although Harry was busy with a blazingly successful career in music at the same time I was hopscotching from film to film with hardly a breath in between, we found time somehow to stay in touch and even grow closer. Mind you, at the heart of our relationship was still the competitive energy that had made its presence felt from the moment we first met, threatened, and challenged each other under the stage at the American Negro Theatre in 1946. While we soon came to admire each other, and over time grew to love each other, we each remained a bit wary of the other, with Sidney trusting Harry only on alternate days—and vice versa (of course). So strong was that undercurrent of competitiveness between us that for many years people far from our lives reported having picked up ripples or sensed vibrations that caused them to wonder about "those two West Indians."

Yes, it is true. We have been tigers at each other's gates for more than thirty-three years. But it is also true that our friendship has endured in spite of this. Or, on second though, maybe *because* of this—by somehow bending that competitive energy to its own use. Anyway, whatever the ingredients of its survival, it can safely be said that between us has been the genuine stuff from which the best of friendships are made. In these many years I have watched the man mature in many ways. I've seen him suffer much, I've shared some of his suffering, and in some measure, I'm sure, I've caused some of his suffering. I love him because he has the capacity to persevere when life's obstacles have flung him down time and again with such force that most men would think twice about moving on. And if my survival or my family's depended on a single friend, I know that I could call on any of his resources and would not be at the barricades alone (of course I'd have to find him first). Without question, the most attractive quality in the man is his ability to follow through. I mean, you could knock him down a hundred times, but if there's an ounce of strength left in that West Indian frame of his, he's going to get up and keep going.

Now, since I am aware that the above comments will not completely escape suspicion, let me say to those readers who have no intention of swallowing a one-sided view of the man, brace yourselves: He can be the worst S.O.B. that God ever created. Harry Belafonte will do you in, up, down, and crossways in a minute. You've got to be terribly special to him to be excluded from his guillotine when he's out for blood. But if he's there for you, he's there for you all the way.

Which brings me to that awful period when he suffered through a divorce from his first wife in order to marry Julie. At that time I think he was struck a series of low blows from many quarters, including some sections of the media—black and white. At times it appeared to be open season on him, and not the least among the reasons was his divorcing a black woman to marry a white woman. The rumor mill, gurgling overtime with ugly and uncool hearsay, was in perfect unison with a handful of press people who were having their own special field day at his expense. It all added up to a very bad time for Mr. B. But he absorbed it, and he never let anybody see him crying. He stuck with the woman of his choice and, incidentally, she with him; because it wasn't very easy for her either—not by a long shot. But they stuck to each other, shared the pain, and survived the whirlwind.

Time came when I found myself going through similar pains with my wife and Diahann. I knew I was really at the crossroads when I discovered that there was more pain than joy in my average day and the source of the pain was inside me. Although, to be truthful, both ladies were pouring oil on the fire—both of them. (Well, who can blame them?) I called Harry and said, "B, I'm in trouble. I can't resolve some problems and I need to talk to you." At that time he was appearing in Miami Beach at a hotel called the Fontainebleau. He said, "Come on down. I'll get you a room and we'll kick it around." So I took off for Miami Beach. His wife, Julie, was traveling with him, and I explained my distress to them. They were familiar with most of it, of course, but they weren't aware of the extent of my inner conflict. I finally said to them, "Look, I've really got to have some help." Harry started to tell me about his analysis. I knew he had been in psychoanalysis for some time, but I had never got into any discussions with him on its merits—either for himself or for others. I didn't want to pass any value judgments because I never felt that *I* needed it, and would probably have jumped very quickly to the conclusion that *he* didn't need it either. But now I was being forced, in the absence of any viable alternative, to search for scraps of relief in the most unlikely places. Harry confessed to being, on occasion, all but paralyzed by an inability to cope with the avalanche of pressures, crises, guilts, rages, and fears that often come crashing down on survivors of failed marriages. He recalled the emotionally excruciating time when he was bedeviled by too many indications that his career was being shaped by the unsteady hands of men of little vision. He spoke candidly of the high-visibility interracial relationship that had succeeded his dead marriage, and went on to reveal how living in a spotlight, subject to the scrutiny of a curious public, generated its own set of bewildering problems. My attention became arrested, and I listened attentively as he told me about those things that had set him in search of someone to talk to. Julie then mentioned that she too was in analysis, and I thought to myself: Isn't that something? These two articulate, dynamite people who seem to be on top of everything in their lives, who seem to have somehow put it all together, are sitting there telling me that portions of their lives are plagued with difficulties so great they can't handle them and have had to seek professional help.

That revelation, that sharing of their very private selves, endeared them to me even more. Julie is a remarkable woman. She not only recognized the complex relationship between Harry and me, she also respected it. She knew that each of us had come a long way from the same start marks deep inside ourselves. She knew that Harry's background was very much like my background —both of us West Indian, both poor on the streets of New York, and both catapulted into some kind of notoriety and prominence. We alternately prospered and suffered through the fifties and sixties with roughly the same enemies at our heels. Yes, and she was well aware that there was more than a modicum of the killer in each of us. It was she who suggested that I not go to Harry's doctor because that might complicate the situation. Besides, if Harry's doctor was on his toes, he certainly wouldn't want to be seeing both of us at the same time. She suggested that a more neutral selection would be her own doctor, whom she glowingly described as "an especially terrific analyst, the ideal person you should see now that you've arrived at the place where you feel you need to talk to someone." "Cool," I said, committing myself. "I think I would like to go. I want you to call him and make an appointment for me—just allow me a few days to get back to New York and I'll be ready for him."

"Wait a minute," Julie said. "It's not a 'him,' it's a 'her.'" Stiffening, I said, "Back up a little bit— you mean I'm going to have to go in there and be talking to a woman?" "Yes, you are," she rejoined, "and what the hell is wrong with that?" I said, "Jesus—Julie, you mean I'm going to have to tell that lady about me and all the things that bother me and stuff and stuff and stuff?" "You're damn right you're going to go in there and tell her. She's a doctor. What's wrong? Women aren't supposed to be doctors? Are women doctors supposed to have only women patients? What kind of attitude is that?" Caught without an intelligent reply, I stared for quite a while at this longtime supporter of equal rights for women, only to have her stare back at me unblinking, ready for a fight. And then I smiled and backed off, knowing that to lock horns with her on that issue was a waste of time. I wasn't going to win. "Okay, I'll go and see her." Julie took a moment to unruffle her feathers and relax her fighting stance before saying, "Anyway, the chances are, my doctor won't be able to see you on a regular basis because she's a terribly busy lady who is also involved in teaching psychology at Columbia University and has hours at a hospital, but if she gets an idea of what your situation is, she might be able to suggest someone who could take you on." "All right, that will be okay with me. Call her," I said, hoping her very busy woman doctor would waste no time in referring me to a not so busy male analyst.

Back in New York I told Diahann what my plan was, and her reaction was encouraging. I also told Juanita, but she didn't think that it was a good idea, or necessary. As far as she could see, all I needed to do was get rid of Diahann and there wouldn't be any problem left—it was as simple as that.

I arrived on time for my appointment at the Fifth Avenue office of Julie's doctor, and was greeted by a mature white woman. Protestant, I think; very together. In the first few moments, I got the impression that she had her life pretty well organized. I liked her. But the shock of the century came in discovering that she was the brightest mind I had ever met up to that moment. The moment I entered her office I looked around for a couch, but reluctantly, because it would have embarrassed me to have to lie down to talk to that lady. She offered me a chair instead and opened up the conversation by asking how I thought she could be of help to me. I said, "I'm hoping that after I've explained some of the difficulties I'm wrestling with, maybe you can suggest someone who could help me unravel these very complex threads in my life." She said, "Good. Why do you think you need someone to help you with these threads?" I said, "Well, because . . ." and I got into it.

Usually you get fifty minutes; I'm into it for over two hours, running my mouth while she's taking notes. Finally, after well over two hours, she says, "We haven't gotten it all down yet, but I've got to stop, I have other patients. How about meeting again another time?" Sure as you're born, I'm back there for a second visit, and again we go over the clock. I'm running my mouth and she isn't doing anything but taking her notes and saying an occasional "umm-hummm," which lets me know she's still there. I'm there with my eyes closed, because after a while when you go into it you close your eyes—I do anyway. At the end of it she says, "All right, I think I understand. Will you give me a week or so and I'll try to line you up with someone? I'm unable to take you myself because my schedule just isn't flexible enough."

A week later she hadn't been able to line me up with anyone and asked if she could be given an additional week; the person or persons she had in mind were themselves overloaded, and it wasn't possible for them to take me at that time. At the end of the second week she asked me to come and see her. "I've been unable to fix you up with anyone I feel would be good for you to work with. In the meantime, rather than leave you without any attention at all, I'll take you on a catch-as-catch-can basis until such time as I'm able to set you up with someone else. Is that agreeable to you?" "It certainly would be," I responded. By then I definitely liked the way she operated; and also I liked the fact that I seemed able to talk very easily with her. She gave me three or four appointments over the next couple of weeks, and soon I was being jogged way down in my psyche and subconscious where things shameful, disturbing, volatile, and fearful had been packed so deep that they were mercifully out of my memory's reach. Suddenly I was being put back in touch with them for the first time since the impact of the initial experiences. Not with any depth of understanding—just the general realization that on the other side of the conscious mind is an active, seething world of forgotten elements influencing virtually every decision made up top on the conscious level.

During those early weeks, I spent every session slouched in a chair with my eyes closed, talking about whatever came to my mind. When I finally started lying down on the couch, it was a hell of a lot easier. Especially when I started going over all the childhood relationship things I could recall—my mother, my father, my brothers and sisters, what I did as a child on Cat Island, what I liked and disliked, whom I liked and whom I didn't like, who liked me, who didn't, and why they didn't. Slowly but surely the analyst was getting a fix on me. But, fascinatingly enough, I also was getting a fix on me. As I talked out these things, I started to "see" me. Flowing out of me, my words free-associating, came a series of glimpses into the early life of a little boy as he really was before he grew old enough to censor out the painful

261

parts. I was seeing for the first time a kind of whole Sidney.

I was seeing resentments I had held deep down in me against certain people. For example, my mother—I never had any resentments against my father, probably because I hadn't spent that much time with him. In those patriarchal days, my mother carried the biggest burden in all things relating to the children. Not only did she have to work in the fields, cook, clean, change diapers, and take care of many other things; it also fell to her, when the time arose, to tend the sick and see to the burial of the dead. I was constantly within her jurisdiction, because my old man was taking care of the tomatoes or packing them in crates to send them away or getting the bat shit out of the caves to put on the tomatoes to make them grow.

I remember resenting my mother because of her lack of gentleness while dressing me when I was small. She used to starch my shirts and pants so heavily they would be stiff as plywood after ironing. In helping me to dress, she would force the shirt down into the pants, then button the pants, then blouse the shirt out over the pants. Well, it was not easy to blouse a stiffly starched shirt, and my mother would jerk me around indiscriminately in the process of getting it done. And each time it happened, I remember wondering why she had to be so rough. Being a little boy, I of course wasn't knowledgeable enough to understand that the woman had all kinds of frustrations, and that this activity may have been one of the modest outlets she may have had for some of them. However, with the doctor's help, I was finally able to look at that directly and, thirty-odd years after it happened, say out loud, "Dammit, I didn't like that."

Another high-priority resentment I was able to put into words was my mother's habit of slapping me on the back of my head. I vividly recalled her doing that with enraging frequency, and though I was tiny and new to the world then, I remember setting it down as a humiliating and hostile act. In most cases she was angry at something unrelated to me, but I was always convenient, and so was my head. In those days the expression was, "I'm going to box your ears." Well, it wasn't my ears that got boxed—it was the back of my head—and I ha-a-te-d it! So much, I can't begin to tell you.

While looking at those early resentments, I realized the

262

key to my being able to explore my consciousness with that woman doctor: she never once passed a value judgment on anything I said. Which meant that I was free to open up more and more without fear of ridicule as I inched my way closer to those crucial areas that were infested with all manner of things uncomplimentary to my self-image. Once in a while the doctor would ask a leading question to keep my roll going. "What did you feel?" "Why do you think that happened?" "What do you think?" But she would never label anything, good, bad, or indifferent. From the minute I could see she was not going to be judgmental, I was free to uncover some of the many things I wouldn't ordinarily expose to anyone's judgment, out of my deep-based fear that only a putdown could result.

At the end of my first four visits, I was hooked on psychoanalysis: I could see where it made sense. I caught in those visits fleeting glimpses of something—something familiar—that seemed to suggest there was more to me than I was in touch with. Previously unknown bits of my personality, revealed in the momentary flashes resulting from the small amount of exploring we had done, released an enthusiasm in me over the possibility that there might be a whole "me" buried underneath there somewhere, a "me" I was determined to excavate.

Finally, the doctor said that she hadn't found anyone else for me, and so would continue to squeeze me into her schedule as best she could for a while. Well, "a while" wound up to be nine years of psychoanalysis with that lady. Let me tell you, I saw Sidney Poitier in total, got to know him, and I rather liked him. In fact, I was proud of him—he was worth the time and the effort and the energy to get to know, despite the fact that he was afflicted in the extreme with his anxieties and tensions and ghosts of times past; programmed by past situations so that his reactive mechanisms responded to present-day situations as if still in the past. (We call that "neurosis.")

Except for the occasional interruption necessitated by my professional commitments, I saw that lady analyst four to five times per week, year in and year out. Five intensive sessions over a single week worked very well for me in many ways, not the least of which was that they served as an escape valve for the pressures that were building up. Diahann by then was also in analysis, and, fortunately for our relationship, we were both making progress. One of the bread-and-butter interruptions that took me away from my sessions was the MGM production of *A Patch of Blue,* produced by Pandro Berman and starring Shelley Winters and me, with featured roles for a young actress named Elizabeth Hartman and my old friend Ivan Dixon. It was a small picture, shot on the MGM lot in Culver City on a six-week schedule at a relatively modest price, but it was an instant success and returned a more than handsome profit. It also marked my third time in the employ of producer Berman (*Blackboard Jungle* and *Something of Value*), all with satisfying results. I considered him my good-luck producer. Shelley Winters made a strong contribution to the success of that picture through both her performance and her box office strength, which was quite hearty. In fact, she was much more of a favorite with movie audiences than was generally realized, but the overall success of that picture was due, however, to the fact that the artistic reins were in the capable hands of a fine director named Guy Green.

Another interruption sent me off to London for a co-starring role with Richard Widmark in producer/director James B. Harris's sea saga *The Bedford Incident*. Again, the part I played in that Columbia release was not specifically written for a black actor. That happened through the good graces of Mike Frankovich, who as head of Columbia Pictures was determined to help bring about reasonable representation of America's minorities on the motion picture screen. With James Harris feeling the same way, there was no hesitation between them over my being hired to play the newspaper correspondent aboard the Navy submarine destroyer the *Bedford*. The reins of a major studio were seldom to be found in the hands of men with such a sense of fair play. That action by Frankovich and Harris again allowed America to see a black actor in a part that obviously could have been played by anybody. And at the same time, it caused people in the industry to ponder the nature of the move—some to raise their eyebrows in disapproval, others to vigorously applaud it as a step long overdue.

My career was continuing to build in ways that would be advantageous to the black community and to other black actors, but that advantage was not yet manifested in tangible terms. It would be eventually—but not yet. It was still just Sidney Poitier out there; however phenomenal his own career was, it wasn't being reflected by the inclusion of other blacks in the film business—an occasional part, yes, but not on anything approaching the level where I was operating. I was now viewed as a fixture in the film world, but my fellow black actors, almost to a man, were trapped in a drought of inactivity and unemployment that sapped and embittered whatever satisfaction they may have derived from the success of a single one of us.

Martin Baum heard of a producer who was about to make a film called *The Slender Thread*. He read the script and found a part he thought I could play, although again the part was not designated for a black actor. Through a determined effort, Marty sold the producer, who in turn sold the film company, who in turn gave permission for Sydney Pollack to hire me to play that part opposite Anne Bancroft, Steven Hill, and Telly Savalas. So off I went again to face the cameras—this time in Seattle—leaving my analyst, Diahann, my children, and Juanita behind in New York, where the web of confusion would presumably spin at less than half speed until I returned. *The Slender Thread* experience gave me great satisfaction. Annie Bancroft was simply fantastic, and Telly, of course, is an infinitely better actor than *Kojak* allowed us to see (alas, *Kojak* may have completely submerged his large talent; its imagery is so indelible in people's minds).

Following each movie I returned to New York. I lived in New York. New York was my home now. And New York was where my troubles were. Come to think of it, I don't know why I kept rushing back to New York— I've never had so many bad times waiting for me in any one place. In New York I had the lovely Diahann Carroll *and* the sweet, beautiful Juanita Poitier; and I had my kids; and I had myself in the middle of them all. On the other hand, I had my doctor. New York was also where the public wasn't being too cool with me, and the press was on my tail. Maybe I was rushing back to New York because I needed the pressure cooker. Then again, maybe it was the seductive "good life" of California, which has been known to strike terror in the hearts of certain New York actors who fear being trapped into artistic prostitution by the permissive pleasures and values of what they call "a tempting cultural desert." Though I was one of those purists who secretly found much to admire in the cultural desert, I was nevertheless terrified by the prospect of moving to California and then never getting another job in the film business.

The thought of moving out there never came to mind without firing off a spirited conversation between me and myself on the subject of the very well-known black actor who no longer is being asked to work. How would I manage? Suppose I have no funds to support myself and my family—what do I do then? I would have to go out and get a job-job. So? It's been done before—what's wrong with that? Well, it won't be too easily digested by my considerable ego, to have been pretty big in the picture business and then wake up one morning and go out to wash dishes or park cars. Not that I wouldn't go out and wash dishes and park cars just because I've made a few movies—I certainly would do it for my kids any time. But I don't have to do it in the same town where I've been a successful actor. If I fall on such hard times, better that I'm in a city like New York where anonymity isn't so hard to come by. Makes sense—I can certainly get lost in New York. I can take myself an apartment in Brooklyn or the Bronx, grow a beard, and go to work every day as a dishwasher and not run into more than a dozen people during the course of a year who'll say, "Hey, ain't you the guy who used to be in the movies?" The slightest flirtation with the notion of availing myself of the pleasures of the cultural desert invites that recurring nightmarish conversation between me and myself, holding me to the rule I had made years before: Never move to California until such time as you're not dependent on work in the film industry to feed your family. So back I go to New York City, under the gun of the agonizing entanglements of my personal life.

While psychoanalysis was stimulating and in some cases liberating during those introductory months, it gradually deepened into another dimension where any given session could produce devastating surprises that were poles apart from the nice and charming revelations I had grown to expect from earlier encounters. But it no longer mattered whether sessions were good or bad (or good *and* bad)—I was depending on them more and more. Sometimes it was hard to talk because I was getting into parts of my past that were so stress-producing, so anxiety-triggering, that I became uncommunicative and just plain afraid to look under the stones and find parts of myself I wasn't proud of. Some sessions were brutal—absolutely brutal. I would say, "What the hell do you know? Why am I talking to you? What do you know? You're white—you're a woman—you're older than I am. You didn't live any of these things"—any kind of evasive tactic. My doctor would simply answer my question with a question. "Why shouldn't I know about these things? Why would being white preclude my understanding? Why would being a woman not entitle me to grasp the matters we're dealing with? Do you know why you're resenting me at this moment?" "Yeah, I know why I'm resenting you at this moment—because you're a busybody. You're asking things I've already told you about. Why should I repeat them for you? Is there anything new to you in all this?" "No, there isn't, but why are you so upset?" "Look, let's go on to something else." "If you like." She'd say this in a simple accommodating tone with no trace of any personal reacting she might be having. After a giant pause, I'd say, "Look, let's not go on to something else. Let's stay right here but—let me think about it before going on."

On a bad day, those fifty minutes seemed like an eternity. She had a clock in the room, and sometimes I would lie there in silence, monitoring the minutes as they ticked away like months. And the bad days were frequent. Yet each torturous moment I was fully aware that I couldn't lie on a foam rubber couch five times per week saying, "I'm in love with a woman who is terrific for me, I have ties that are very emotional with my wife, ties that are very emotional with my children, a strong sense of unfairness to Diahann," and acknowledge my crippling inability to resolve these conflicts short of terrible pain on all sides, without at least being somewhat willing to look unflinchingly at some scorching truths. Yet fearful that those truths would singe the ego if examined, I became uptight, silent, and sullen. Most men find it difficult to focus when they're staring straight at their personal deficiencies. They're reluctant to look at their weaknesses because they're being asked to acknowledge parts of themselves they dislike, and above all, they don't want to hate themselves. But my doctor would bring me right back to my shortcomings, however much I tried to get away from them. She brought me back to them in very subtle ways, and she kept bringing me back. If not in the next session, then in the next, or somewhere not very far down the line, we were back to questions that had been left unresolved because I couldn't bear to examine them before. She would lead me back time and again to face a difficult issue and keep me at it as long as I could stand the heat. Yes, on the whole it was painful. But eventually I would come back to it—four days later, or two weeks later—with a little more understanding. Because standing above and beyond all the pain and distress was the realization that I was finally getting in touch with myself; and the solid contact I was making brought me more and more understanding. In session after session we would concentrate our attention on some aspect of my childhood, my adolescence, my young adulthood. Day by day bits of information out of dark corners of the past were helping me to understand how I had come to be. I had to look at, review, and dissect many of those things that seemed so unbelievable in my life, episodes I was afraid even to mention to people because I assumed they would be horrified, or raise an eyebrow to say, "Is this kid putting me on? Is he really nuts?" Relunctantly, and against substantial resistance, I was brought to a point on that foam rubber couch where I was able to see (through squinting eyes), and talk about, the multitude of certifiable acts in my life that more than justified a net being thrown over me—from wrecking other people's cars in order to learn to drive, to the outrageous things I had done in an Army hospital. I quivered with uneasiness at the thought of what a perfect candidate I was for a mental institution. But over and above the unease I realized that an important unfolding process was slowly taking place, and so I stuck with it. Because— it was I who was unfolding.

And psychoanalysis is not a one-way street. While I was getting to know myself I was also getting acquainted with Diahann. I had held images in my head of the people who were important in my life—parents, wife, children, girlfriend. All were stable fixtures in my mind until psychoanalysis started spotlighting the fact that the images one holds of people are quite often far from the reality of those people's lives. Often the image is flawed in ways we aren't able to see—and don't want to see; seeing and accepting those flaws might interfere with the way we use that image to accomplish something important to us—maybe interfere with our image of ourselves. In getting to know Diahann, the first thing that started coming across to me was her strength, and how it exercised itself on our relationship; and then her weaknesses, and how they alternated with her strength to influence certain things in her life and the lives of people she cared about. I came to realize a loyalty in her that was admirable. And then in one particularly revealing session, a red flag went up drawing my attention to something that neither Diahann nor myself had been conscious of: some of the blame we had been placing on my marital situation did not really belong there; our difficulties were partly personality differences. It was an important discovery that deserved exploration, but I sidestepped it, making only a brief mental note and hoping the doctor wouldn't nail me down to the base of that red flag. Because when you're in the kind of emotional, romantic state in which Diahann and I were cocooned, you tend to mount massive resistance to any suggestion that your union isn't exactly made in heaven. The doctor didn't press. Maybe because there were red flags all over my life, or possibly she had in mind a more appropriate moment in the future to bring me back to that very pregnant spot. In the meantime, left to ourselves Diahann and I chose not to examine that dangerous bit of wisdom. We simply didn't want to. Things were too sweet—when they were sweet.

But of course they weren't always sweet, and therein lay the rub. There were fights, big ones. I should have gotten a clue when she threw that brush at me at the Chateau Marmont Hotel, I should have known then that this child was going to have the last word whenever she could. As it turned out, she went on to become a formidable collector of last words. But I didn't mind that too much; in fact, I rather enjoyed it. The fights were satisfying—frustrating, but also satisfying. I clearly got some strange sort of satisfaction out of being so frustrated, and she must have had similar pleasures, or we wouldn't have fought so much for so long. And so it was that in those early years while I was learning about us both, she was in another part of town on another foam rubber couch learning about us from another point of view. In time her patience grew short and she joined a chorus of her friends who were screaming at me, "Now listen, you either do it or get off the pot—is that clear?" And finally, after years of analysis had eased some anxieties, yanked some fears and phobias out by their roots, and cauterized those psychological nerve ends that specialized in sparking emotional distress, we decided to get married. She made a public announcement to that effect which evoked a hurricane-sized sigh of relief among her supporters, the force of which threatened more than a few of them with lung collapse. And then she accompanied me to Mexico, where I got an overnight divorce.

Back in New York we found a terrific Riverside Drive apartment, signed the customary long-term lease, and in joyful collaboration with her decorator, she set about putting the premises in the sumptuous condition her exquisite taste insisted upon. Then—just as it seemed that our cherished dream would, at last, come to fruition, the bonds of love, need, and devotion began to unravel. We had agreed that just the two of us would live in the apartment for the first six months, and have the beautiful child born to her and Monte stay with her mother and father in Yonkers, a distance of twenty minutes from Riverside Drive. It was a decision arrived at partially because I was traveling a lot and due to leave momentarily for filming in Utah while she was busy between her professional life and the pulling together of what was to be our future home; and partially because she feared her ex-husband might make things difficult if we were not married and the child was living with us. The idea of six months on our own also grew out of my strong desire to throw myself into neutral and float free for a while now that all the preliminary steps had been taken, which seemed to me a perfectly reasonable yearning. In front of me a giant step was waiting to be taken, and I felt the need for a moment of pause before stepping right out into marriage again. Diahann had agreed and promised to make all the necessary arrangements to facilitate the undertaking—a nurse to live in at her mother's house while we were away; a housekeeper with child-caring experience in the apartment on Riverside Drive where the baby would spend some time every day we were in town. And she was already submerged in samples and patterns, and surrounded by carpenters, upholsterers, electricians, painters, and all the other skilled hands needed to transform an empty apartment into a comfortable home for three—or more.

Meanwhile I went off to Kanab, Utah, to begin filming *Duel at Diablo* with James Garner and Bibi Andersson. Midway through that film Diahann flew in to spend a few days with me. It wasn't a good visit. There was something on her mind. Our togetherness was at a distance; we were not quite in step. When irritation flared and things got worse following my attempts to probe for the source of the trouble, I backed off and gave her time, thinking that if I was patient she would share it when she was ready.

She returned to New York, and on a day I shall never forget, she telephoned to tell me the deal was off. She said she could not put her baby up with her mother—she had talked to her doctor about it and discovered she was conflicted about the decision, and after agonizing over it for a long time, she had decided once and for all that she was not going to do it. Instantly feelings of anger and betrayal flooded me from head to foot. My skin grew hot and a ringing began to sound in my ears. I could smell my own blood in the caverns of my sinuses, and my heart began slamming itself about at double speed inside my chest. Because I knew that an incalculable loss was coming my way. With fury crackling through the long-distance wires we had a tremendous fight—or prehaps it was a summing up. Though words of eloquence can often flow from anger, that was not the case at my end of the phone because anger of a certain force invariably tends to tie my tongue. Although to this day I cannot recall with complete accuracy what I said, I am confident that what I *felt* made itself unquestionably clear. She had first asked me to talk to Monte—which I did. She had asked me to move out of my home—it took me a long time, but I moved. She asked me to get a divorce—I got on a plane, went to Mexico, and got a divorce. I made one request—to give me six months; let's get an apartment and live together for six months so I'm not jumping straight from one marriage to another, while your parents happily look out for the baby. But the one thing I asked of her, she couldn't do. That triggered my rage. And I felt justified. But was I? Couldn't there have been feelings of at least equal intensity on her side— feelings of anger and betrayal pushing *her* heart to double speed and filling *her* nostrils with the smell of her own blood? Was it possible in my anger to ignore her very very genuine love for her child? Or her frustration at the length of time I had taken to free myself in the final giant step.

But whatever the betrayals and justifications, no deliberate choice or whim of fate could have singled out a more inappropriate moment for our relationship to com-

271

mence unraveling. Through years of stormy, unruly weather, willing ourselves to stay afloat in defiance of wave after wave of unfriendly pressure, moving on inch by difficult inch, we had arrived at the very edge of the safe harbor we had yearned for. And there, at that perfect place, for reasons known and unknown (some will forever remain a mystery), we foundered. As our long-distance fight bristled between Utah and New York, we said things we didn't mean—and things we meant, we didn't say. Strange, isn't it, how love sometimes fights its way through the dangerous uncharted forest of life to the edge of the clearing, only to wither in the first light of success. Were we afraid to win? If our love couldn't survive prosperity, what did that make us? And sitting heavy in our hearts during that final goodbye fight was the most unsettling fear of all, the one lovers most often are too proud to acknowledge: How will I deal with the emptiness, the loneliness, the powerful feelings of abandonment when you are no longer there for me?

Bad times of a special kind came upon me the moment we hung up that night as I searched both for the reasons we had fallen apart and the reasons we had fallen apart at such an inappropriate moment. Psychoanalysis offered several insights, one of which might eventually prove to be accurate: that Diahann and Juanita were, for me, two halves of a perfect whole. Home, hearth, and children gave Juanita such strong appeal, while the excitement of a cultivated, glamorous, and talented lady suited the restless side of my nature. Yet who can say for sure that I would have fared better if I'd found the perfect combination of these qualities in a single person? Would such perfection in one woman have driven me through the furnace and tried my soul as happened when my ideal "whole" was represented by two independent halves? But enough of this futile effort— if there are answers, how important are they now? For those who are interested, here is a clue: When I was finally able to obtain my Mexican divorce I remember feeling liberated—but from what? From an unhappy marriage surely, but also, I suspect, from one independent half of a two-sided whole. If the whole is dependent on the existence of two independent halves, then liberation from one half weakens the need for (or the dependency on) the other half. End of clue. But not the end of the relationship. Diahann and I would have more to say to each other. Much more. Through the next couple of years, mostly over Ma Bell's telephone lines, we helped each other through those lonely, empty times that hovered around us, especially at night. The fact that we continued to fight was incidental. Of primary importance to both of us was the need to help each other through our period of letting go, because as intelligent people, we both knew we were too weak to let go "cold turkey." We supported each other long enough to gain our legs and then, with deep regret, we walked away.

A long lease on a twenty-ninth-floor penthouse pad in an integrated high-rise on Manhattan's west side in the sixties symbolized the varied and, in some cases, radical changes my lifestyle had undergone in the preceding five years. Unattached, with my bachelorhood visibly established, I loafed around that comfortable two-bedroom apartment in the sky, far from happy, but not altogether sad, reviewing the pluses and minuses, wandering off into the solitary game of woulda, shoulda, coulda, and fighting the urge to run back into warm, safe corners of the past. Though my standard of living seemed a light-year's distance from my earlier years in the big town, I kept a curious fix on the hard fact that Harlem was still no farther than a ten-minute subway ride away, and however many new changes might come and new friends and fresh ideas, sadly some dear old friends and a few priceless values would be lost, stranded forever on the other side of bridges burned. On especially cloudy days, I was reminded over and over that life can be a bitch on any floor. For me much had changed besides my address, standard of living, and marital status. In those turbulent years of the mid-sixties, change and the fear of change were in evidence everywhere, clinging to the nation's consciousness like static electricity to a wool blanket, and my high-rise penthouse apartment did not remain out of reach for very long as the civil rights movement, Martin Luther King, the Student Nonviolent Coordinating Committee, Freedom Riders, Stokeley Carmichael, sit-ins, and long marches through danger zones like Mississippi were galvanizing and forcing a reluctant America to take an unbearably painful look at itself—and evoking frequent violent spasms of rage and guilt. As a supporter of the civil rights struggle, I found myself participating most frequently by making appearances on behalf of those on the firing line. I went from street corner rallies to picket lines to fund-raising events in the homes of wealthy white sympathizers to light arm-twisting of the studio heads in Hollywood for financial support for Martin Luther King, to a dangerous mission into the backwoods of Mississippi with Harry Belafonte to deliver a vital package to Stokeley Carmichael and other leaders of the Student Nonviolent Coordinating Committee. No, the times were not conducive to loafing around in a penthouse apartment in the sky—too much needed to be done down in the streets of the nation.

Harry and I were then living just four blocks from each other, and I was a constant visitor to his home, not so much because of our friendship, but because his home was a beehive of civil rights activities. Civil rights leaders, moderates, radicals, hardliners, planners, strategists, fund raisers, were coming and going nearly all the time. So it was no surprise when he called one evening and said that he wanted to talk to me about something important that had to be done in Mississippi. "What is that?" I asked. He hesitated, then said, "It's an emergency. I've got to go down to Mississippi and I want you to go with me." "To Mississippi?" "Yup." A pause swelled, then, "What the hell for?" I inquired. "I don't want to go into specifics on the phone. But there are some people down there who are in very desperate need of something, and we have to take that something to them." What could this "something" be? I wondered to myself. Am I being asked on the spur of the moment to run guns into Mississippi? Or smuggle in an atomic bomb, or a little vial of poison? Or was Harry's occasional tendency toward dramatic flourishes overstretching an otherwise routine situation, purely for effect? On any question other than civil rights, possibly, but on matters concerning that burning issue I knew, better than most, that he would never play games. Which only meant that he was dead serious about us going down to Mississippi. I hastily ran down in my mind all the obligations I thought I had for the succeeding days, in order to come up with something legitimate and acceptable to both of us that would keep me from Mississippi. Unfortunately, nothing surfaced. "Listen, you need me, I'm there—of course I'm there," was my somewhat less than enthusiastic response. "Okay," he said, "I knew I could count on you." "When are we going to leave?" I asked. "Tomorrow." "Tomor-

274

row!?" "Tomorrow," he said simply. "Okay," I whispered with resignation.

The next afternoon on the way to the airport, he said, "I've just been on the phone with Bobby Kennedy [then the Attorney General of the United States]. I asked him to alert the FBI in Jackson, Mississippi, that we are arriving there and will be going from Jackson to Greenville." He told me that he suggested to Bobby Kennedy that in light of the very real possibility that our presence in that area might cause some hostility or even violence, the FBI should keep an eye on our movements—just in case. "Now tell me why are we going there? What's this 'something' we're delivering?" "We're delivering money. Lots of it, to the civil rights workers in Greenville. They need it. They need it for bail money, they need it for court costs, they just need it and they need it now." "But why are *we* going to take it? Where is the wisdom in picking two highly visible guys to play anonymous couriers? Or is there more to this than meets the eye?" Harry took his time before saying, "Our presence there will be a very forceful morale booster for a lot of kids who have been in that area all summer—kids who have been there six months and some have been there two years, and they generally don't get visitors, especially two guys who are involved in the struggle, maybe not as deeply as they or on the frontline like they are, but certainly involved in the struggle on many levels and many ways. It would be good for them to see us." "That's reason enough," I said.

The airport at Jackson, Mississippi, was a big, busy, up-to-date facility. Walking through the terminal toward the baggage claim area, we tried to read "FBI" on every face we saw. If they were there, they didn't make themselves known to us. The interior of the terminal was like any other large overburdened American airport, and we felt only mildly uncomfortable. Nobody was overtly hostile to us, and a pervasive civility seemed to lie over everything. Yet beneath all the seeming order was the undercurrent of the times. Arrangements were made by Harry's office for a charter plane to take us from Jackson to Greenville. Later that evening, while walking in the dark away from the commercial activity of the big planes to a far corner of the airfield, we came upon a little plane. A beat-up little old raggedy-looking plane that must have been older than both of us put together. We looked at each other but said nothing, assumed that the white pilot's interest in staying alive equaled our own, climbed aboard that contraption, and took off into the darkness.

About ten o'clock that night, after a bouncing, stomach-churning, treetop skimmer of a flight, we began our landing approach to an airport that matched my imagery of Mississippi. Except for a couple of lights, we couldn't see the airstrip, and there were no lights in the shed that passed for the passenger terminal. We came down on a runway that was terribly short, and taxied up to the shed, where six civil rights friends in two cars were waiting in the dark to greet us. As we stepped off the plane, Stokeley Carmichael's voice came cutting through the darkness with words of welcome. Following embraces with old friends and handshakes with new acquaintances, we moved briskly to the cars. Stokeley divided the group into two, and Harry and I squeezed into the back seat of his car. As our car started its motor and turned on its lights, with dramatic precision, another vehicle directly across the field from us turned on its lights. Everyone in our car took note of it. Nobody said anything for a long time. As we backed out to head our car in the direction of the highway, the headlights on the mysterious car began to move. All we could see was just those two great big headlights. They started to move counterclockwise with the intent, it seemed, to intercept. At which point Stokeley said, "The Klan." Harry said to Stokeley, "What's happening?" Stokeley said, "They probably know you're here and they've come to start some trouble. But don't worry—if they've got cannons, we've got cannons, so be cool." He went on to explain that they had programs mapped out for their survival in case they were attacked on the road, and the lonely stretches of roadway outside of town were where the Klan usually mounted their ambush. As Harry and I sat on that back seat squeezed between experienced Klan fighters, communications between us consisted almost exclusively of an elbow nudge to the ribs indicating: Did you hear that? The Ku Klux Klan tried everything except gunplay to wreck our little caravan, but Stokeley Carmichael and his people, old hands at a dangerous game, delivered us in one piece to the center of the tiny black community.

Entering a local dance hall that had been rented for the evening, we found it jammed with black and white civil rights workers who had gathered in anticipation of our arrival. Amid cheers and applause we were hustled up on the stage and given a rousing introduction by Stokeley Carmichael that included a matter-of-fact mention of an "escort into town provided by the local nightriders." The gathering thanked us for coming and we thanked them for doing what they were doing, we sang songs, we danced, we drank, ate chicken and spareribs and toasted to the future, until about one o'clock in the morning, when we were taken to our quarters in the home of a local black resident who was sympathetic to the activities of the civil rights movement and close to the Student Nonviolent Committee and its leadership. It was the home of people of modest means. Neat, clean, simple, and plain. After dumping our stuff in the bedroom we were to share, we went into the kitchen for a meeting with those leaders responsible for the voter registration drive and were brought up to date on their activities in that particular county.

It was inspiring to see the hopefulness of those fearless, committed youngsters. Like a spark from the dynamic Kennedy syndrome that was sweeping the country, it illuminated all their political undertakings. We in turn gave them a brief rundown on what was going on in New York and on other fronts of the Movement. After saying good night to our friends, who promised to return the next morning to take us to our plane, we went to our room and started preparing for bed. There was a window in the room that looked out on a side street, a part of the yard space, and beyond that another street. I saw someone walking stealthily in the darkness behind the chicken coop. I said, "Hey, B, there is someone out there." He said, "No." "Yes." "Who?" "How the hell do I know? But there is someone out there. I just saw them." "You're just seeing things." "I am not, man, I saw someone out there behind that chicken coop." "We'd better close the window." "We'd better close the window *and* try to find out who the hell that is out there." We went into the kitchen —there was nobody there. We woke up the man who owned the house. He in turn got on the phone and called our friends, who hastened to reassure us: "Be cool—not only is there one guy out there, there are four guys out there, and each one of them has a shotgun. And they will be out there all night. Their job is to see that you get a good night's sleep." Well, that was at once comforting and scary. Because if they had put four friendly shotguns outside our windows, it means that there is a very good chance that they may have to

277

use their shotguns and if they have to use their shotguns, it means they have to use their shotguns to protect us—and if they are using their shotguns to protect us it means somebody might be coming after us—shooting, and if somebody is coming after us shooting how the hell can we have a good night's sleep—especially with no shotguns of our very own?

Returning to our room, we tried to sleep but couldn't. Instead we drifted into conversation, but every time we heard a twig crack outside we would stop talking and listen—listen for the next cracking of a twig. In between the twig crackings and other odd little sounds that would suddenly break the silence, we chatted back and forth across the room.

During those very tense hours Harry's way of dealing with anxiety was the telling of weird, funny, spooky stories that had me falling out of the bed laughing. About 4:00 a.m. that morning we heard a car pull up outside. "Did you hear that?" Harry asked. "Yeah." "What do you think?" "I don't know." I eased over to the window, pulled the shade apart, and took a peek. There was a car. I looked around the yard—my eyes went immediately to the chicken coop—I didn't see any activity over there. I said, "Lord, if those brothers are sleeping somewhere . . ." The car just sat there and we just sat watching the car and looking around for our guards. After a while we grew impatient with the vulnerability of our situation and discussed the merits of borrowing a shotgun from the owner of the house and walking on over to that car and finding out who the hell was in it. At that moment some slight movement around the chicken coop caught our attention; our guys were on the case. Relieved, we settled down and waited for the next move, shoot-out or stand-off. An endless ten minutes passed in silence before the car's engine jumped to life, the lights sprang on, and the machine slowly rolled away. At about 6:00 a.m., with the coming of dawn, the crisis was over and our four shotguns disappeared. Later, over bacon and coffee, we were told that the mysterious car was never out of their cross hairs, not even for a moment. After breakfast we went through the town very briefly to see what it looked like, and then we headed for the airport. Sure as hell there was that little old raggedy plane waiting for us. We said goodby to our friends, got on board, and flew back to Jackson. From there we caught one of those big, safe-looking numbers and flew back to New York. So ended our overnight flight to Mississippi.

THE SECOND HALF of the 1960s was also crowded with a profusion of career activities. Columbia Pictures' president Mike Frankovich and Martin Baum brought me together with a book that had struck the fancy of a host of filmmakers including Carl Foreman, Jack Clayton, Harry Belafonte, and others of considerable weight, but the film rights to which, for a variety of reasons, had passed from one famous hand to another without results. Eventually, when Columbia Pictures came into possession of the rights, Frankovich embarked on a personal crusade to bring the book to the screen. It was not easy even for the president of a motion picture studio. In the opinion of many of his associates, the contents were too soft, too sweet, too sentimental, and most of all too special because the setting was England and all the characters were English school children, their teachers, and parents. American audiences, it was thought, would find little or no interest in a situation and in characters that were seemingly so far from their own cultural milieu. The name of the book, of course, was *To Sir with Love*.

But Mike Frankovich refused to let the book pass from his hand to yet another. Even after several false starts at putting the necessary ingredients together had failed, he hung on tightly to the simple little story of a Guyanese teacher and his band of incorrigible East End students. Finally, Frankovich and Martin Baum found the key: James Clavell, himself a novelist, who was captivated by E. R. Braithwaite's book agreed both to write the screenplay and direct the picture. When my name was added to the arrangement, one would reasonably expect the green light to flash on, but—no such luck. So little was thought of the commercial possibilities of *To Sir with Love* that an offensively meager "take it or leave it" budget was offered. Eventually, Clavell and I worked practically for nothing in order to accommodate the tight economic parameters of the six hundred and forty thousand dollar budget after Martin Baum devised an ingenious deal that gave Clavell a huge percentage of profits and me a healthy percentage of the gross. Columbia responded enthusiastically to this proposal because I believe they really expected a very small gross, while profits were almost out of the question. It took a lot of give and take, a lot of stubbornness, and no small number of minor miracles to get that simple little story before the cameras at a studio just outside of London.

The first time I met the young actors who were to represent the East London incorrigibles, I was hard pressed to imagine them being anything other than real delinquents. And having never heard of a person named Lulu, I found myself marveling at the chubby, pixieish youngster with that bubbly quixotic cheeriness that forced one to take notice of her. When I discovered she could sing and dance too I was saddened at the thought of such a delightful and talented youngster going to waste on those mean deprived streets of East London. Little did I know that, with her little round face and her sparkling talent and energy, she was well on her way to becoming a national treasure. Moreover, my own tone deafness robbed me of any pleasures I might have derived from her musical talents, which are considerable (I am told). Nor did another teenager, Judy Geeson, impress me as being more than a cute little brat in pigtails. That impression held until one evening when I was taken out on the town by Judy and others from the "classroom crowd" for a heavy night of discoing at a place called Tramps, then one of London's most fashionable points. Those kids could really boogie. I didn't do a good job that evening of upholding the legend that all our people got rhythm. "On top of being tone deaf, he can't dance a lick," seemed to be the silent, collective comment on their disappointed faces. (My personal—highly objective—opinion of my dancing tells me that it's not so much hopeless as out of date. What's more, I'm not really tone deaf; the world is just full of other people singing off key.) Anyhow, Judy Geeson that evening was a perfect hostess, displaying all the charm of a young lady honed in the social graces. And if Judy and Lulu were not, as I had thought, delinquents right off the streets of East London, then Christian Roberts was farther yet from the vicious, nasty, trouble-making class leader he played so strikingly in the film.

Slowly, as the weeks rolled on, I got to know them all for the people they were rather than the characters they represented, and let me tell you they were a microcosm of the United Nations. Mother England and the Commonwealth were amply represented among them and I wondered what was going to happen to them after the film was completed and the filmmakers went away. The racial minorities such as the Pakistani, the Malaysian, the West Indian, the East Indian, the African, and the Chinese will unfortunately find very little opportunity for career building as actors and actresses in England, and the fact that a surprising number of them were born and raised in England added a touch of irony that I discovered was not lost on any of them. One young Englishman of brown skin invited me to his neighborhood to see a play written by a minority playwright that was being presented by the ethnic theater group of which he was a member. While the production was praiseworthy and the work by the cast quite professional I couldn't help thinking how frustrating it must be for them to be pouring themselves into a life of theater in a society where the dominant culture has no interest in, or little use for, their creative output. No, England in that respect was rather not very much better or worse than America.

The subsequent great success of *To Sir with Love,* to my mind, can be traced to two outstanding contributions: the inspired direction of James Clavell and the excellent performances by every member of the "classroom crowd," each of whom gave, in the best tradition of the professional actor, a little bit more than was asked of him. I would like here and now to say a heartfelt thank you to my "classroom crowd," wherever they are in life.

On my return from England, I reported to Stanley Kramer for another Columbia picture called *Guess Who's Coming to Dinner.* When that script was ready and the contract set, I flew to California for a get-acquainted dinner at Spencer Tracy's house. A dinner that was cooked by Katharine Hepburn.

Let me tell you it was some evening. Spencer Tracy was an intellectual, an extremely well-read man who knew a great deal about a wide variety of things. When the delicious meal was over and the after-dinner drinks had been served, Miss Hepburn encouraged Mr. Tracy to entertain us with some of the classic stories he had a reputation for spinning. They were delightful stories, beautifully told, but more arresting than the stories was Miss Hepburn's reaction to them. Although she must have heard them dozens of times, she listened to each one with wide-eyed fascination, as if she were hearing it for the first time. It was heart-warming to see how much affection flowed between that man and that woman. He treated her with an offhand appreciation, but at the same time he obviously loved her. "Oh, Katie, just shut up and let me tell the story," was one of the ways he showed her who was boss. And I got the impression that was the way she liked it. I was profoundly impressed with their relationship: they put me in mind of Evelyn and Reggie. In the course of that evening I fell in love with the two of them.

As actors, well—I tell you they were giants. It wasn't easy for me to work opposite them. I wasn't able to get this out of my head: I am here playing a scene with Tracy and Hepburn! It was all so overwhelming I couldn't remember my lines. With the other actors I was fine. The long, tough father/son scene with Roy Glenn, in which I had pagelong speeches to make, went smooth as silk without a hitch—no stumbling, no bobbling, we sailed right through it, and it turned out to be a terrific scene, a highlight of the picture. But when I went to play a a scene with Tracy and Hepburn, I couldn't remember a word. Finally Stanley Kramer said to me, "What are we going to do?" I said, "Stanley, send those two people home. I will play the scene against two empty chairs. I don't want them here because I can't handle that kind of company." He sent them home. I played the scene in close-up against two chairs as the dialogue coach read Mr. Tracy's and Miss Hepburn's lines from off camera.

Because Spencer Tracy was in ill health, Stanley Kramer worked him only an average of two to four hours a day, that was it, and he would seldom keep him after lunch. The plot resolution at the end of *Guess Who's Coming to Dinner* required the Spencer Tracy character to deliver one of the longest speeches ever written for a modern American film. It amounted to a soliloquy several pages long, and Spencer Tracy never fluffed a word. Like Clark Gable in *A Band of Angels*, he was letter-perfect every time. The two of them were from the same school, trained as actors to exercise discipline over their tools. Every person on the sound stage that afternoon became engrossed with Spencer Tracy's character as that remarkable actor did his job. With unbelievable skill and finesse he dotted his *i*'s and flicked his commas, and hit his periods, and touched down lightly on his conjunctions on his way to making magic.

We, his fellow actors in the scene, began falling under his spell until he had succeeded in converting all of us, one by one, into a single captivated audience. It was hypnotic watching that man pick up the pace here—slow it down there, take a pause here, smile there, roll a word here and break up another word—take one single word and break it up into two or three parts—all of it making sense—all of it believable. It was like watching a ballet. I remember wondering: How in the world did that man develop such control? (Mind you, at the time he was sick.) There was applause when he finished. Everyone marveled at the execution.

Most of all Katharine Hepburn was there. And I somehow had the feeling she was always there. Soon after the completion of *Guess Who's Coming to Dinner* Spencer Tracy died. Not knowing that his last picture would turn out to be one of his most successful.

21 Discoveries

In the Heat of the Night was produced by the Mirisch Brothers for United Artists release. While its script was being developed, there were long and heated exchanges over content. Stirling Silliphant's screenplay was good, although I have heard him say in later years that he didn't care for it because it was not an honest portrayal of blacks. But I think he was reflecting the revolutionary changes America had gone through since he wrote his script, and so in some way he was apologizing for something he couldn't have helped. At the time he wrote the script, most of America was where he was, and to my mind it was a very forward-looking piece of material; naturally, there were things in it that black people would have preferred to see more of, but on the whole it was revolutionary as mass entertainment. Anyway, Stirling, Walter Mirisch, and I worked through the differences— Mirisch then and always a first-rate human being, in the class of the Kramers, the Richard Brookses, and the Ralph Nelsons.

We began the picture in a little town just outside St.

Louis called Belleville, Illinois, the town where tennis star Jimmy Connors was born and reared. We were housed in a little motel in Belleville, and from there we would travel deep into Illinois to the kind of rural community we needed for the filming. From Norman Jewison's direction I learned many things that I stored away in the back of my head just in case—who knows—you never can tell. That man Jewison has a very good eye that accounts for the unusual number of beautiful touches to be found in his films. Largely because of him, *In the Heat of the Night* was on the whole a very good experience for me. Rod Steiger was a product of the Actors Studio, and his approach to his work fascinated me. His preparation period for a scene was astonishing in depth. First he explored everything objectively. Then he made subjective everything he found in his objective exploration. In this final process, he would zero in on his character in such a way that for the entire period of making the picture he would speak in the same cadence. Even sitting down at dinner in the evenings. On weekends when we ventured out to a movie or dinner, or when we sat around the motel just running our mouths about various things, he would remain completely immersed in the character of the southern sheriff—he spoke with the same accent and walked with the same gait, on and off camera. I was astonished at the intensity of his involvement with the character.

I have never worked with a good actor from whom I didn't learn something useful, but Rod Steiger taught me something invaluable: I had been a-c-t-i-n-g! Pretending, indicating, giving the *appearance* of experiencing certain emotions, but never, ever, really getting down to where real life and fine art mirror each other. Performing well-written scenes from *In the Heat of the Night* together with Rod Steiger and Lee Grant was an illuminating experience, and finally what Lloyd Richards and Paul Mann tried to teach me at their workshop throughout the early 1950s was starting to fall into place. Throughout the making of that film I sensed that I was on the threshold of discovering what acting really was. I always knew that first-rate actors had exceptional gifts, but I also knew that an exceptional gift, in and of itself, did not necessarily a first-rate actor make. It was essential that his gift be subject to a technique, a learned procedure, a discipline, in order for him to constantly function at close to his best. I had fumbled about for years trying to find that "learned procedure," that "discipline," and I knew how difficult it was to put together all the pieces of an effective technique. Thanks to fine actors like Steiger, Grant, Ruby Dee, Brando, Alice Childress, Frank Silvera, Spencer Tracy, and the many others who over the years slowly led me into the light, I was closer than ever to not only being able to recognize the fine line that separates high-quality "indicating" from first-rate organic acting, but closer also myself to successful performances on that side of the line where the real pros worked. While I wasn't home yet in the truly professional sense, I was a long way from those early times back in the theatrical woods when I was told by fellow inexperienced actors and by some not very good drama teachers, "You have to take diaphragm lessons. You have to be able to speak from your diaphragm so that you can be heard up in the last row of the theater. You must learn to bring your voice from the diaphragm, push it up, squeeze it out so that it will resound into the audience."

Well, I almost squeezed myself to death trying to be heard in the balcony. I'm serious. I was constipated during half my performances. My stomach was always in one of those Canadian isometric exercises. I mean it was like a knot, I developed such muscles around my diaphragm from *squeezing* everything out of me all the time. Other widely held attitudes with no real basis in fact were slipped to me as gospel from the actors' Bible, such as, if I was playing a tough guy, I was to remember that all tough guys walked tough, talked tough, breathed tough, smelled tough, *spit* tough. That forced me into caricatures you would not believe. To play a tough guy I would go around with my hands ready to strangle somebody, my mouth twisted; I would lower my voice and really be breathing fire, you know what I mean? Well, I looked ridiculous trying to play a tough guy. Not that I *couldn't* play a tough guy—but I was under the impression that in order to be the tough guy, you had to create that tough guy out of external appearances. When I began to learn what acting and life are all about, I began to realize that some tough guys look very feminine, that some are skinny and not particularly tall and not particularly strong, and some of them have voices that are kind of tinny. Some of them, if you were to assess them on first impressions, look like priests, others like file clerks or service station attendants, or bookworms. I wince when I think back to the times when I was playing tough guys and squeezing my diaphragm. I must have looked something awful up there on the stage. But in the beginning there was no one to tell us that acting at best was a complex, yet simplified, way of reacting to life's circumstances, and that human beings off the stage spend a large part of their lives doing just that. Things might have been otherwise for many talented but inexperienced young actors who have dropped by the wayside if someone had told them that the emotional elements making up human responses are basically the same in every personality, and have been for millions of years. Why could we not have been told that human beings are multitalented in their ability to respond? We do it with anxiety—because we want something to happen, or we don't want something to happen. We do it with nervousness—physical and emotional—because we become overwhelmed by anxiety from the anticipation of something happening or not happening. We can respond with fear—or a mixture of fear and trepidation and some happiness. A little joy, a lot of joy, other forms of pleasure, or fear of those joys and pleasures. Loneliness, boredom, frustration, self-pity, embarrassment, shame, love, hate, shyness, low self-esteem, exaggerated high self-esteem, the fear of rejection and the fear of dying.

In the absence of a guiding light, I moved blindly, with misconceptions pointing the way, and as a result, I was too many years in coming to understand my craft. But I finally discovered that there was essentially no difference between actor and audience; neither is a stranger to the experiences of life. I am broadened as an actor the moment I realize that when people sit in a theater and watch an actor expressing feelings similar to their own, we, the audience, can tell if the actor is really experiencing those emotions or if he's faking them. Deep down inside, where we've had these same experiences and same responses, we know whether he is interpreting them in a genuine way, or just play-acting.

Okay, as new discoveries slowly lifted my veil of ignorance, dispelling myths and erasing misconceptions, acting became for me something else; a new concept was dawning. When a character walks on a stage, that stage becomes a representative setting—a home. the exterior of a building, an open field, an office, a schoolroom, something. You're not coming onto that stage as an actor walking into the set from backstage. No—when you enter that stage, you are a person with an immediate past coming from a definite place. Example: If the play begins as the farmer walks into the kitchen for his lunch it is a certain time of year. Is he coming from planting or harvesting? Is he coming from clearing the land? Is he coming from weeding? Is he coming from watering his flock? And what are his economic, political, and social circumstances? What is the situation of his family? All of these things must be understood and accepted by the actor so that when he walks on the stage he is a farmer rather than an actor playing a role. He must bring on the stage with him the whole of that character. To the extent that he is able to do that, to that extent, the audience will respond: Terrific, fantastic, good, not so good, fair, or awful. So acting is a reactive progress; when that man walks onto that stage into that setting, everything he sees will entail reacting. He doesn't have to act, he will only need to react as he feels the farmer would to what happens to him, to his experiences. Acting becomes both experiencing and reacting.

Neither of which is possible without that third all-important and seldom understood, fundamental ingredient —*listening*. America gets a kind of uniform professionalism from 90 percent of her actors, any fifty of whom, in the same age range, can play the same part and you would hardly notice any real differences. But bring along one or two organic actors who are really gifted and it is an entirely different play, an entirely different evening—magic is made. They are, almost always (like Steiger, Pacino, Hoffman, De Niro, and Brando), the best listeners. In any response there is a rhythm, but the rhythm is inexplicably wound up in what you have heard. The actor cannot produce an honest rhythm unless he hears what is said to him. Not only must he hear what is said to him, but he must hear the emotional content of what is said to him. The actor who is not listening will answer in a rhythm that is not harmonious with the question. Moreover, the rhythm of the question has contained numerous subtle nuances, including revealing insights into the questioner, over and above the literal face value of his question. But if the actor hasn't really *heard* the question, yet goes ahead and answers it anyway, the rhythm of his response is going to be seriously off kilter, as he remains oblivious to the many hidden motives and meanings that may be lying undetected beneath an apparently simple question.

Well, I don't mean to try to write a textbook on acting as I came to understand it—I only want to suggest the kind of thinking and the kind of work I was coming to, which was crystallized during the making of *In the Heat of the Night*.

During the filming of the movie in Belleville, Illinois, I met a woman—from Chicago. One night at the motel I received a long-distance call from a lady who said to me, "I've been thinking that I would like to meet you, so I decided to call and introduce myself to you. I'm interested in the kind of person you are and thought the best way to be in touch was simply to find out where you were, pick up the phone, and call you. My name is Michelle Clark." I said, "Well, that's terrific. How are you and what do you do?" She said, "I work for an airline and I'm studying communications. I hope to be an anchorwoman on television." I said, "That's neat." At that time there were no black anchorwomen on television—there were women and there were blacks, but none of them, to my knowledge, were in the anchor position. "I would like to come down to see you," she continued in her self-assured feminine voice. I replied, "First let's talk about it for a while." I wanted to get a view through her conversation of what she was like. I quickly discovered that she was a terribly bright, up-front lady who wasn't into game-playing. She said, "You want to know what I'm like. You don't want to commit yourself to a visit from me until you can figure out from what I say what I look like and what you're letting yourself in for. Well, I'm beautiful." She told me she was 5 feet 8, or 8½ (she in fact was taller, over 5 feet 9), and that she was brown-complexioned. "I have high cheekbones, my face is fairly small and narrow, and my smile is captivating," she continued. She's a really interesting kid—right? "Well, do I come down and see you?" "You bet your life you're coming down and see me." So I booked her a room for the night and she flew into Belleville.

She was exactly as she said she would be—all of it. A beautiful woman with an open, straightforward, and to-the-point personality. After that introduction we stayed in touch. In time she would fly to California and New York to see me on a fairly regular basis, always returning to Chicago, where she was enrolled in night school. Her strong urge for self-improvement impressed me and put me in mind of the years I had behind me. Finally, with a hard-earned degree in her pocket, she moved to New York. We were able to be together a lot more often. While it was nice to have her close by, I was nevertheless determined not to get involved on a one-to-one basis. I hadn't recovered sufficiently yet, and just didn't have the resources to deal with such a relationship. I was still phasing out of the previous nine years and needed most of all to flow free for a while. Michelle said she understood that —but she really didn't, and there was a subtle kind of pressure toward more one-to-one and less free flow. But being as smart as she was beautiful, she kept the pressure subtle, just enough of a gentle reminder to keep me aware of what her long-term interests were.

One day I got a call from her saying she had got a job as an on-camera person in Washington, working for a major network. She was off on the first leg of her lifelong dream. We promised to visit with each other as often as possible, I wished her luck, and I promised to be there when and if she needed me. From the very beginning of her new career, Michelle's potential was strikingly evident to all who saw her. In that first year she was embraced by the people of Washington and was well on her way to becoming a fixture in its television circles. Then—she left Washington on a quick trip to Chicago. Landing on a bad winter night in Chicago, the plane crashed. Michelle was gone. A terrible loss for everyone who knew her.

All my friends who died too young came to mind as I tried to puzzle out what was clearly not meant for me to understand: was there a blueprint from the first moment of creation so irrevocably exact that it itemized the eventual existence of a passenger plane destined to fall from the skies over Chicago's airport? If so, then was the passenger list a hard fact even way back then? And if, as some schools of thought suggest, there is no blueprint and there never was, did Michelle Clark have an honest-to-God choice as to whether she should take that particular flight on that particular day? Where are those answers? Maybe Michelle knows them now. And understands. Perhaps ignorance is a kind of protection for those of us who are left behind to grow old. Yet we cannot help trying to puzzle it all out from time to time, searching vainly for something that never comes. . . .

FOLLOWING *In the Heat of the Night*, I directed a play on Broadway, *Carry Me Back to Morningside Heights*, starring Cicely Tyson, Lou Gossett, Diane Ladd, David Steinberg, and Johnny Brown. It was written by Robert Alan Aurthur, an old friend whose teleplay "A Man Is Ten Feet Tall" and screenplay *Edge of the City* gave me roles that added immeasurably to my career. But luck deserted us on the stage. The play didn't work—not on any level. The critics dumped on the writing and the direction, but most of all, the direction. *Carry Me Back to Morningside Heights* lasted seven performances and left me severely bruised by the pounding administered by the critics. Clive Barnes of the *New York Times* said, "The kindest thing I could do to the play's director, Sidney Poitier, would be to avoid mention of his name."

With the full weight of the failure pushing my shoulders to the ground, I slunk away to the Bahamas to lick my wounds, but a mere sip from the cup of self-pity cleared my head and forced me to realize how much wiser the experience had made me; it taught me to never again lose sight of how much I have yet to learn.

Back in New York, I went to work for ABC Pictures Corporation on a big-city love story, *For Love of Ivy*. It was made from my own original idea about a successful gambler who runs an illegal operation and is blackmailed into dating a maid who threatens to quit her job because no eligible black men are available in the lily-white Long Island community where she works for the twenty-year-old blackmailer and his mother, father, and sister.

At the end of that film I began moving about, floating free, in a restless sort of way. I had a bachelor friend named Terry McNeeley who owned a successful cocktail lounge called Terry's Pub on 97th Street and Columbus Avenue in New York City. There, late one night, we sat at an out-of-the-way table with another bachelor friend, Doug Johnson, and hatched vacation plans for the summer of 1967.

Terry, a former liquor salesman, had eventually put together a business of his own that became the "in" place for the sophisticates of Harlem. Doug was a tall, handsome actor. He had come to my attention through his sister, who for many years was my secretary.

I needed to get out and away, and Terry McNeeley and Doug Johnson, themselves itching for a change, readily agreed to go in search of new adventures in corners of the world they had only read about. So the three

New York bachelors headed for Europe. First Paris, then Rome, Madrid, Barcelona, and Majorca. The Barcelona/Majorca trip with those two guys was one of the eight wonders of the world. I had never seen two men with more ferocious sexual appetites. Terry McNeeley, who was to die at the age of forty-six, was the kind of guy who, if you looked at him as one man would look at another, you had to assume there wasn't a woman in the world who would consider him twice. Merely to say that he wasn't handsome would have been a compliment to the man. He had a bulldog face, and a kind of rough-hewn masculine aura that bordered on the crude. His knowledge of the world around him was meager; in fact he knew very little about anything. Except sex. He was a walking hard-on. The man was enriched with a sperm production system that had to be a scientific phemonenon. And Doug Johnson was not far behind. And me—I was floating free.

There the three of us were in Majorca, and Majorca's population that summer of 1967 seemed to be made up mostly of beautiful women from Scandinavia, England, North Africa, the United States, the Caribbean, South America, even from Spain itself. Apparently summer after summer they came to that sun-drenched jewel of an island to live it up or down or through. Now, McNeeley had no fear of rejection. I don't know whether he threatened them; I don't know whether he relied on the power of his charm (to my mind, an unlikely possibility, since I was convinced that the man had no such charm); I don't know whether he cultivated pity in them. I haven't the faintest idea what his secret was, but I bore witness to the fact that he scored and scored and scored and scored.

We stayed in Majorca about a week and got out a couple of days before we meant to because one day while we were strolling down the main thoroughfare, McNeeley struck up an unsteady conversation with a young lady who spoke very little English. She was Spanish. From her he learned about the location of a private discotheque frequented mostly by Spanish people, a place for the local society set. She volunteered that she would be there that evening, whereupon he asked her if she would honor him with a dance if he happened to show up, and she said she would. Just before going about her business, she gave him a lingering come-on smile that virtually assured his turning up.

It has been said that Majorca has more discotheques than Los Angeles has cars. Well, about eleven-thirty that evening we stepped into what was generally believed to be the best in town. As soon as McNeeley's eyes adjusted to the lighting, he scanned the premises like an airborne hawk and in a matter of moments zeroed in on the señorita sitting in a booth with a large party of local young people. She stood up as she saw him approaching, for she knew he was on his way to lay claim to the promised dance, and she, a woman of her word, was ready to oblige. We watched him monopolize her dancing time for the better part of an hour. Knowing his track record, we just supposed the child was a goner. And so it was that while the night was still young, McNeeley and the young lady disappeared.

Later, we rendezvoused in a late-snack place and in walked McNeeley with a very unusual tale. He hadn't scored, he said, and the young lady was a virgin. He had every intention of scoring, but it was going to take another day or so. He had learned somewhere that Spanish culture placed a high priority on virginity. He had also learned somewhere that a Spanish girl who finds it difficult to ignore her pleasurable yearnings, while at the same desiring to arrive at her wedding night with her highly prized purity unstained, can have her cake and eat it too—so to speak. And since he had long been an accepted master at eating other people's cake, Terry McNeeley had in his arsenal a blueprint tailor-made for the Spanish virgin. The next morning, armed only with the outward sprigs of knowledge he had yanked from Spanish culture, McNeeley lured the young lady first to an elaborate lunch, then to his room in the hotel.

She is the daughter of one of Spain's top military men, and she and the family are in Majorca for their customary two months at their summer home. She is engaged to some kid back in Madrid, and is going around the discotheques in Palma with her brother or a cousin or some "safe" escort approved by the family. Someone who works in the hotel had seen her entering McNeeley's room and clocked her, and to his mind she's stayed in there for an indiscreet length of time. He passes that information on to the family, and the family calls her to an accounting. She in turn doesn't tell them exactly what's happened, but does tell them there was a man in that room. Prompted both by the family's need to protect its good name and the culture's insistence that honor be defended, a lightning-quick response in the form of a visitation from three very serious-looking guys follows. We have strong suspicions they are from the police. Luckily McNeeley is sitting in the lobby when they go over to the desk and ask, "Who is room number so and so?" At which point McNeeley comes upstairs to us and says, "Fellows, I have a feeling that we ought to be on the next plane to Paris." Doug and I pack, and about an hour after those official-looking visitors sniff through McNeeley's room and leave, he goes in and packs, and we're on the first available plane to Paris. . . .

Roaming around Europe and along the Mediterranean Coast with McNeeley and Johnson was not all raucous, erotic, hedonistic fun—at least not for me. In my quieter moments I grieved over my troubled and far from fulfilling relationships with my daughters. Through the preceding tumultuous years, they had reached their teens. Among increasing tensions and strains we had somehow managed to hang on to each other—even though I had been, as long as they could remember, the hardliner in the family and was not popular as a disciplinarian, especially since their mother's progressive attitudes on child rearing were easygoing. They nevertheless wanted me around —they wanted a family. However, as is typical in a broken marriage, sides had been taken: Mommie was always there and Daddy was not. They were convinced, as was their mother, that I was the culprit. Their feelings were unmistakably with her, and their wish was that I would "cool it," then everything would work out, and the family unit they wanted would stay intact. When they were teenagers they became very vocal in expressing their disapproval of my not being at home, a disapproval fueled in my absence by an awful lot of propaganda that swirled around them about my not being there to do what I should have been doing. It pained me that, so early in their lives, they were being called upon to deal with the neurotic problems of fractured loyalties. Although they were squarely on their mother's side, they desperately wanted to maintain a relationship with me, and it was difficult for them. They were unavoidably cornered into feelings and conclusions because I was never quite able to communicate to them—or, more to the point, I was reluctant to communicate to them—the true facts of the matter; I was everything but helpful. Primarily because I didn't want them to be a part of the dispute, I side-stepped and skirted the issues with such regularity over such a long period of time that they became completely confused about the problems between their mother and me.

Undoubtedly a full explanation was in order. No question. But I wasn't able to give it to them. I rationalized my failure to honestly open up with my children by telling myself that not a hell of a lot would be accomplished if I *had* itemized the specifics, because they were too young to understand where I was coming from and because there had been such thorough home-front propaganda. I also clung to the lame notion that despite the reserved, subdued manner in which they related to me, we still had lots of fun on a certain level. In my psychoanalytic sessions, I was talking my head off about the problem, the triangle, and other matters. But I was still not yet able to lay it on the line with my kids, even though I could read in their faces how painful it was for them to have this kind of situation hanging over them all the time, the possibility that their parents might break up. Their mother doesn't want it—their father wants it—no, he really doesn't want it, but—he wants it—is it really another woman or is it that my father and mother are unable to get along even if there's no one else in the picture? They simply wanted me to come back home after I'd left, and when I was still at home they wanted their mommie to be happy. In some fantasy way they determined that if I made her happy, I in turn would be happy.

Their teenage years, outside the rigamarole that entangled their parents, were otherwise normal teenage years.

Beverly became a bookworm who couldn't resist anything from romantic paperbacks and general textbooks to African politics and culture, all of which had an enhancing effect on her general education. Pamela, on the other hand, got hooked on show horse jumping and went into it with such determination that by the time she was fourteen she had become a fantastic rider who had won dozens of ribbons at horse shows in Connecticut, New Jersey, and New York. My concern that her intense commitment to that hobby during her crucial teen years would be at the expense of *her* general education produced several confrontations between us. But no amount of threats, bribery, hard-sell, soft-sell, or lectures could wean her away from her romance with horses—until, inexplicably, one day she abruptly closed out that phase of her life and without a backward glance went on as if she had never even *met* a horse. In the beginning we hoped she had met something better than a horse—maybe a nice teenage boy. But no, teenage boys were still close to the bottom of her "things of interest list"; she had simply grown sick of horses. The stubborn determination that infuriated us so during that "romance with horses" has turned out to be a plus factor as she struggles in her adult life to survive a world that she and many of her peers were not properly prepared to deal with. Her strength now seems to renew itself year by year as she wages a fierce and sturdy fight to make up for lost time. At her core she is well equipped for survival, I am firmly convinced.

Sherri, who is almost completely deaf in one ear, was also dyslexic, and unfortunately we didn't realize any of this until she was almost ten. Both conditions, understandably, created massive problems for her during her school years. She was the child I feared for most. How would she manage in this complex modern world was the worry constantly gnawing away at the back of my head. As a little girl she was forever being overwhelmed by the school work required of her, and consequently was often held back while her classmates moved on to higher grades; but in the face of crushing difficulties there was always that tangible *something* in her personality that made her invincible. Nature clearly made adjustments. Today she is the most delightful person, daily showering an abundance of humor and love on her family and friends. This child whom I worried most about has, to now, wound up with the best fix on life—another indication of how nature tends to store her jewels in the most unexpected places.

Then there was the baby, Gina. She was an affectionate child whose laughter was infectious from the beginning. At first, of course, she didn't know anything about anything, but in time, with all the residual wash-off from the older kids, she too became aware of Daddy's peculiarities. "If he would only come to his senses and stop messing around." Most of Juanita's fashion-model beauty was passed on to Gina. From a breathtakingly beautiful baby she grew into an attention-getting adolescent, and on to a head-snapper by her mid-teens. Unlike her mother she did not go into modeling, but took up karate and became an expert—I have never ceased to wonder why. (Was it an outlet for pent-up aggressions she had skillfully kept out of view? Or was it merely an exercise for weight control? Or was it . . . ?) All her life she has worried about the well-being of others, and for precisely that reason I am never too concerned about how she will manage in life. (At present she is in her second year at university and is heavy into campus politics.)

Yes, in the wee hours of the night in European and African hotels whose names I've long forgotten, while McNeeley and Johnson were fast asleep or busy with un-mentionables, I rummaged through my mind, spot-checking, examining the teen years and the preteen years of my children. In each case there was lots of love, and lots of confusion. They had sympathy for their mother, and they had prayers for me to stop being whatever they heard I was being.

My oldest daughter, Beverly, and I became estranged when she defied me by getting married at the age of eight-een. Luckily for her, the young African student she mar-ried is a super guy with mountains of determination; he finished his education and became an engineer. They live in Dallas, very happily, with two children—so that mar-riage turned out very well. But it started off awful. She decided to get married when I decided that she was too young to get married, and I did not go to her wedding. That was my expression of my disapproval, and as I heard later they had one hell of a nice wedding without me. Our estrangement really started sometime before the marriage when I was still trying to lay claim to a father's rights, while she, being the oldest, was the first to crack under the family schism. I was telling her she couldn't do certain things without parental approval. Well, she didn't think I had the right to lay down any such laws to her anymore. She took the position that I had forfeited a father's rights by my behavior, and I in turn was saying that she was go-ing to be my daughter as long as she lived and that she'd better not forget it! The result was we didn't talk to each other for a while, but once she was married and into her own life—it took about two years—we began to seek each other out and then began to talk. Finally she was on the road to being her own person with sobering adult re-sponsibilities. Eventually in an atmosphere of painful give and take, we began to bridge our differences, and slowly, over a long haul, we made such steady and solid progress that by the time she had made me a grandfather for the first time, we had become very good friends.

The brilliant work of my psychoanalyst, Dr. Viola Bernard, helped me to understand the necessity of maintaining contact so that my children will always know that I am there for them. My relationship with all my children had to go through a kind of catharsis, a reevaluation, and some confusing stages, but at the root of it all was my determination that they know that I was there for them. With the doctor's help I found it absolutely essential that I maintain contact so that when the day came for them to assess the relationship between themselves and their father, they'd have ample reason to say, "Hey, but he was there for me." I may have been living in the city, I may have been working in California or traveling in Africa, but I was there for them. I was never more than a phone call away and they could reach me day or night. If they wanted to discuss something, go somewhere, needed help in decisionmaking, I was there and I was ready. What I couldn't do as a father was be happily married to their mother.

22 Joanna

AFTER TERRY, DOUG, AND I returned to the United States, I was summoned to California for a conference at Universal, where Robert Alan Aurthur was putting the finishing touches to *The Lost Man*. In the offices of the producers, Bob Aurthur, wearing twin hats as writer-director, presented his finished script for final approval with a long list of casting suggestions attached. Before the producers and I went off to read that final draft, we held a discussion on casting possibilities, most of which were centered on the selection of the ideal leading lady. She had to be, among other things, white, beautiful, young, sympathetic, and last but not least, must have a sophisticated upper-middle-class bearing. Using Bob's suggestions as a nucleus, we added scores of other names until we had a very long list headed by the likes of Joan Hackett and Katharine Ross. But nothing was decided.

A few days after that meeting, Bob's wife was thumbing through a copy of *Vogue* and noticed a picture of a striking Parisian model on the cover. She said to her husband, "Would you look at this face? She looks very interesting." He said, "Boy, that is some face." After studying that picture and other pictures of the model he eventually said, "I would like to see this girl—let's find her." He notified the casting office at Universal, and the search was on.

It turned out that the *Vogue* girl was an actress working in Paris by the name of Joanna Shimkus. Immediately the producers agreed to bring her over so that we could meet her, check her facility with the English language, and see if everyone found her as impressive in person as she was to Robert Alan Aurthur on the cover of *Vogue*. Well, I wasn't too keen on her coming. The truth is, I wasn't that bowled over by the cover, not by a long shot. (Rest assured she will never let me forget that minor indiscretion.) Besides, I didn't know anything about her work as an actress. While the studio was arranging for her to fly over, I was pressing hard for Joan Hackett, who I thought would be just terrific. Joan invited the director and me to her home for lunch, and gave us every opportunity to talk her into our movie, but we failed. She was a very cerebral lady who measured the artistic purity of our script against the artistic purity that characterized her work as a distinguished American actress, and our script fell short (we like to think by not too much). However, she laid on a memorable lunch.

So Joanna Shimkus arrived in California and the producers asked if I would join them for lunch in the studio commissary. I agreed very reluctantly. She was chatting with the producers at a table near the far wall of the commissary when Bob Aurthur and I walked in. After quick introductions, we all sat down and plunged into crosscurrents of that special kind of nonspecific chatter that serves as a scrim behind which, almost always, people can be found secretly sizing each other up. At once I grudgingly acknowledged that she was the most refreshing thing I had ever laid eyes on. I guessed her to be twenty-four years old. She was serious, bright, open, innocent, worldly, and beautiful. Quick as you please, she displayed a mischievous disrespect for the rules of the picture business. She gave less than a damn about the fact that the producers wanted her to do a screen test. As soon as the wind of their intent wafted across the table, she sliced cleanly through the nonspecific chatter with, "I'm not going to take a screen test." The scrim fell away and the nonspecific chatter tumbled to the floor like so much dust. How dared this little Paris model with only a few obscure European films to her credit, who by no stretch of the imagination was anywhere near being a star, big or little—how dare she! The little Paris model-actress was clearly running against the usual scenario. Every up-and-coming performer in the world knows there is solid advantage in showing respect for tradition when established producers hint at the need for a screen test; the proper response is, "Yes, sir, of course I certainly would love to test. Thank you."

The beautiful Paris model pressed on against the grain with, "If you want somebody to do a screen test you will have to get someone else." She seemed genuinely unconcerned that she was setting the torch to a bridge she hadn't even crossed yet. Then for good measure, she added, "You know I didn't want to come here in the first place." At that point my ears perked up. I thought to myself: What manner of child is this? Words that would ordinarily offend came at us in accent-free English bearing not even the slightest trace of hostility or defensiveness; on the contrary, they struck us all as being honest, simple statements of her feelings. At the age of twenty-four, unlike most young adults, she had not yet allowed self-censorship to calcify at that crucial spot inside herself where feelings were transformed into words. By the end of that lunch, the producers and director were captivated by this girl of a different rhythm.

It turned out that she had indeed come to California reluctantly, being quite content to divide her time between Paris, where she worked, and London, where she was near the man in her life, who also happened to be a successful motion picture producer. Universal Studios had prevailed on him to lend his influence on their behalf after their initial attempts at persuading her to come were unsuccessful, and he had sent his secretary along as a traveling companion for her. After lunch, the producers asked if she would stay around for a few days, and she said she would. In our casting discussions later that afternoon, Bob Aurthur said, "I want her—that's the girl I want." I was still not crazy about the idea, but my resistance had weakened somewhat since I'd met her. One of the producers said, "She seems okay to me. I don't see any reason for her to test. Besides, there's already a lot of film on her we can look at, and we already know her English is excellent." (Until she arrived, they didn't know she was bilingual, having been reared in English-speaking Canada.) With the producers and the director convinced that she was it, I acquiesced and fell in line, and the little Paris model was confirmed to play opposite me in *The Lost Man*.

During a casual conversation I held with her a few days later when she came to the studio for a wardrobe fitting, tact permitted me to express none of the negative feelings I'd had about her getting the part. In fact, I'm afraid she walked away with the notion that I was all for her getting the job. "Is there anything I can do for you while you're here?" "You could tell me what's worth seeing in the theater, or if there's an interesting museum." I told her what was going on in town, and got tickets to a Bill Cosby concert for her and her traveling companion. The day after the concert we saw each other again at the studio and another casual conversation followed, in which she said, "We're leaving tomorrow, stopping over in New York for a bit, then on to London. Thank you for the evening you arranged—the concert was really enjoyable." "Well, that's interesting, I'm going to New York myself [which was true]. How long are you going to be there?" "Just a day for a little shopping." Now I don't know what made me do it, but I went on, "What hotel are you stopping at in New York?" She said, "Well—I'm going to be at the Lexington Hotel." I said, "I see." She said, "Why?" I lied, "Oh, I don't know, since you're coming on board with us, I guess the company would like to send you some flowers." She didn't say it, but I could see she was thinking "bullshit."

The next morning we both took off for New York on different airlines, and later that afternoon I sent a bouquet of flowers to her hotel and waited until after they had been delivered before calling her up, sure she'd be duly impressed. I invited her to dinner and she said, "Fine." We went to a favorite French restaurant of mine, and over a marvelous dinner, through chitchat and small talk, we began feeling each other out. I suspect she was interested in figuring out what kind of guy she was going to be working with, while I had entirely other things in mind. Remembering to be careful not to exceed the natural limits of first dinners, I proceeded with the gentle approach of an experienced player—testing, checking, a subtle question here, a bit of information volunteered there, always looking for an opening. But the little Paris model wasn't allowing any. In the course of the evening she asked, "Have you ever been to Paris?" I replied, "Oh, yes, many times. Paris is my favorite city." An opening at last, I thought. Rushing to make the most of it, I said, "In fact, I think I'll be in Paris soon and if you're going to be there, it would be really nice to see you. How would I find you if I happen to come?" She took time to play with her dessert spoon, then curled her lips and looked directly into my soul before saying, "Well, if you're there—we'll see." But she didn't give me her address or phone number in Paris. I took her back to her hotel and the next day she flew off to Europe.

The word "surprise" would not cover all that went on in me ten days later when the phone rang and it was Joanna, calling me from London. "I remember you said you were going to be in Paris, and I wondered if there was any way I could reciprocate your kindness to us when we were in New York. I'll be leaving for Paris in a few days and if you're there in the next few weeks and you don't know anyone, maybe I can be of some help. By the way, I got your number from the director." "Oh, that's fine, I'm glad you did. And it's very kind of you, because I really don't know anyone in Paris [lies]. Anyway, I'll be at the Hôtel de la Trémoille this coming Friday." "Good. Then I'll give you a call." Before that phone rang, needless to say, I had no intention of being in Paris on that coming Friday, but I picked up the phone again, called my travel agent, and asked him to book me to Paris on Thursday evening and make a reservation at the hotel.

A few hours after I arrived at the de la Trémoille, there she was. "Well, then, what can I do for you? Do you want to go to the Louvre? Do you want to go on a sightseeing tour?" I said, "First of all why don't we have some lunch?" She said, "Okay, where would you like to meet?" I said, "Why don't you pick me up here at my hotel—or I can come and get you at your place." She said, "No, I'll come and pick you up at your hotel in an hour."

301

Well, after hanging up I scurried around trying to decide how to interpret the situation. Was it a thinly veiled opening she was allowing, or was she merely showing kindness and consideration in return for the way in which she had been received in the U.S.? Either? Neither? Or a bit of each? I didn't want to make a bad move, so I decided to lay back and stay cool and wait for other signals. In the meantime, the child was on her way over to the hotel and I wasn't even dressed yet after the nap I'd been having when she called.

And then the bell rings at the front door of my suite. Not realizing I've been daydreaming for so long, I go to the door, open it, and there she is. And there *I* am—in my pajamas. The strangest look comes over her face, and it's saying: Uh-oh! What is this? What have I gotten myself into? This man is taking an awful lot for granted, or I must have misunderstood something. I read every word of that in her face. So I say, "Hi, come on in." There's the briefest moment of hesitation as she runs that down in her mind. She seems to be asking herself: Will there be any opportunity for retreat after I've made that first step into his apartment? Her eyes dance briefly the should-I-or-shouldn't-I shuffle. Finally, deciding to give me one more chance she takes a deep breath and steps into the room looking very elegant, yet dressed very simply, and I say, "Oh, my goodness, why don't I order something here while I get dressed," and I take her into the living room. She says, "Well, I thought that we'd go out, but that's all right if you—" "Well," I interrupt, "it will give us a chance to talk and while the food is coming, I'll get dressed." She gives me an okay that lacks conviction.

When I come back out of the bedroom—dressed—we begin to talk, and I soon sense a shyness in her that puzzles and surprises me because she's been a public figure for quite a while, has made seven or eight movies, and is one of the top models in Paris. Over lunch at Universal Studios she was anything but shy, and I had no recollection of shyness surfacing over dinner in New York. Then why suddenly in Paris? I wonder. But then again—why the hell not? Who said she couldn't be lots of other things *and* shy too? If discomfort, apprehension, suspicion, and a sense of caution are surfacing in her as she sits in a hotel room with a stranger of questionable motives (here please note how my psychoanalysis comes galloping in to rescue me from a narrow view) she is also very sensitive, quick of mind, vulnerable in some ways, and yet tough enough underneath it all to put up a good fight for her survival if the need should arise. A breakthrough for me —and I'm proud of myself for being able to view "the little Paris model" as a whole human being with a complicated personality rather than (only) as a sex object. Yes, I liked that. And yet my "questionable motives" were in no way altered. Psychoanalysis knows better than to stand in the way of natural laws, and I'm still out there, looking for openings.

After lunch we went to the Louvre, and that was a marvelous experience. Having been there so often, she knew the museum intimately and the guided tour she gave me was as expert as I could have gotten from any of the official guides. It was really a wonderful afternoon. That evening we went out to dinner at an elegant discotheque on the Left Bank, and after dinner we worked out on the dance floor for a couple of hours, then traveled on to another place for more of the same. About 2:00 a.m. I took her home to her apartment. Striding along the hallway toward her door, with each step taking me closer to the moment of decision, I began priming myself to break into my "get inside the door" song and dance if needed. Arriving at the door she turned to me and smiled—I smiled back. An awkwardness hung in the air for a moment, only to dissolve in the silence of the morning while we stood there grinning at each other like counter-punchers each waiting for the other to telegraph a move. Finally she said good night and started fishing for her keys. I jumped into my routine. "It's been a wonderful day and I thank you for it, but the night is young—there's so much we have to talk about and since my time is limited here in Paris and I won't get to see you again until we start the film . . ." She located her keys in her bag, looked at me a second, then took a deep breath and was about to speak when my long experience detected an edge—she had wavered ever so slightly somewhere between the look, the pause, and the deep breath. So I pressed my advantage. "Besides, we've hardly talked about the script or the characters we're going to play," blah, blah, blah . . . "Well, it is late, you know," she said. "Yes, I know." "Aren't you tired from your trip or do you sleep well on airplanes?" "No, I'm as fresh as a daisy." Turning to the door, she stood before it motion-

303

less as if it were an altar, again thinking—should I? Shouldn't I? Then she inserted the key, negotiated the lock, and invited me in.

Her three-room apartment offered a wealth of information about her personality. The ordered state of things suggested discipline and organization, while a combination of workmanship and quality characterized every object in the place, leaving no doubt that cultured and expensive tastes had engineered these elegant surroundings. In her sitting room/bedroom I saw what for me was a first—an enormous comforter made of fur. "My goodness, that's attractive. It's real fur, isn't it?" "Yes, it is. I got it at a place called Hermès." I stayed as cool as if she had said Woolworth's, but in the privacy of my hip pocket my wallet shuddered. Hermès! Jesus! That thing must have cost five thousand dollars, I said to myself behind my cool smile; exquisite merchandise to be sure, but Lord have mercy, those numbers are heavy, especially for a little boy from the tomato fields of Cat Island where a hundred dollars per year was an income goal a family seldom reached. I changed the subject and felt a sigh of relief emanating from my hip pocket. Shifting to small talk on a less traumatic subject —the sky-blue waters of the Bahamas—my eyes hop-scotched around, reading everything the apartment could tell me about its occupant that might aid my program when the time was ripe. Then came that lull in the conversation during which we stared back and forth at each other until the silence became charged with something promising, at which point my experience in such matters told me we were at the absolutely ideal point for me to make my move. And just then, to my great surprise, she made *her* move. Let me tell you, the little Paris model let it be known very quickly and quite forcibly that it was nice for us to be getting to know each other because we were going to work together, but "please let's leave it there." With that jolt she put everything in perspective. Until that moment my focus had been on her attractions as a woman and I hadn't recognized the very generous human being who had to employ her wits to stay in control of her life while trying to stay afloat in the modeling/movie business in the most seductive city in the world. And since men on the prowl more often than not tend to reduce generous human beings to one-dimensional objects, little Paris models have an awfully big job trying

304

to captain their lives through a sea of attitudes that deny them their full selves, to steer clear of the huge surpluses of dishonesty, deceit, and deception that lie at anchor in the dark behind a thousand cool smiles, and, most galling of all, to set their course according to moral standards laid down by the very male dogs who roam about at night undermining those very standards.

In addition to feeling properly and understandably ashamed and shitty, I also felt particularly stupid for misreading the young lady and trapping myself in an awkward situation. Still, I thought, it could have been worse. She could have let me get farther out on the limb before she sawed it off. At any rate, I decided to ease up right there because the last thing I wanted was for her to think it was my style to come on too strong. Hoping it wouldn't be too noticeable, I switched gears from the pursuer to the person only interested in being friendly on the work level. Yes, I had overestimated my game. I had hit my approach shot and she had lobbed it back over my head, forcing me to turn around and run it down behind the baseline, where I then elected to stay and keep a closer eye on the ball.

A few days days later, I left Paris for the States. I didn't see Joanna again until she arrived in Philadelphia to start work on the movie. She was escorted by the English producer she was seeing at that time, and when she introduced me to him in the lobby of the Warwick Hotel, he seemed to be a very pleasant chap. After we started to work and she was comfortably settled in, he returned to England. Gradually, day by day, Joanna and I became more aware of each other in areas beyond our work, and by the time we were halfway through the picture I found myself always wondering where she was. Later I learned that the same thing was happening to her. There it was. That familiar signal. It couldn't have been clearer, and having seen it before in my life, I had grown to recognize its message: PROCEED WITH CAUTION, TREAD LIGHTLY. BETTER STILL, STAY RIGHT WHERE YOU ARE AND REASSESS THIS WHOLE THING BEFORE YOU TAKE THE NEXT STEP, WHICH MIGHT BE OVER A CLIFF. But I paid no heed. We started having dinners together for the purpose of discussing the script, and invariably wound up talking about our lives, and the lives of those persons who were an important part of our lives, and where we came from, and where we wanted to go. Her producer friend's decision to fly in from London for a few days' visit threw her into a state of conflict. She began to cry a lot, and he didn't understand why. Being a solicitous and considerate person he didn't probe, but nevertheless I think he was intelligent enough to know that something was happening on an emotional level that she wasn't able to talk about. He evidently loved her very much, and whatever her problem, he accepted that she would have to struggle with it as best she could until she was able to share it with him. He left, we finished our exterior work in Philadelphia, then we returned to California for interior filming at Universal Studios. By then, our relationship had strengthed and deepened, and Joanna found herself right in the middle of a situation where her fate and her guilt were playing tug of war inside her. I was renting Billy Daniels's house in the Hollywood Hills, and we had dinner there almost every evening. A lot of tears were falling in her plate, and I knew where her pain was coming from. I knew the territory well. And yet I couldn't really help her; sympathize and hold her hand was all that I could do.

Then one day I tried to do more: "Okay, I don't want you having to go through these conflicts. Besides, I've just recently come out of a hell of a number myself, and my wounds are still much too fresh. So—why don't we just cool it?" She said, "Probably that would be the best thing." Her producer gentleman came back and they attempted to sort out their lives, while I figured that in order to help myself through the succeeding weeks, I needed some company. I got in touch with someone who lived in Europe, and she came over as my houseguest for a time. It was awful, just awful. After ten miserable days she went away. And two weeks before the end of the film, Joanna's friend also went away, leaving us utterly vulnerable to reignition from any of the thousand sparks that seemed to dance around us whenever we came near each other. By the beginning of the final week, it happened. Once again we became really tight, yet we still didn't want to be too close, because there were too many ramifications, too many unresolved questions, and I still hadn't had my fill of floating free. Finally, and mercifully, the end of the movie came.

I zipped on to New York, where I got out my old telephone book and called up every number I had in it. For the next few weeks I was like a drunken sailor or a bee

306

in the botanical gardens. After trying unsuccessfully to wipe out New York, I thought it best to get out of town, so I headed for Nassau to cool out my head and look in on a house I was in the process of having built there. I lazied about the beach, visited the building site, slept late, and generally did nothing of importance until the phone rang on Christmas Day. Joanna was at a party in London where she'd run into mutual friends, Quincy Jones and his then wife, Ula, and their presence flooded her with memories she couldn't shake off. She asked them how I was and one thing led to another until she picked up the phone and called all the way to the Bahamas—to wish me a Merry Christmas, she said. I wished her a Merry Christmas too.

And then—I don't know what made me say it—I said, "Why don't you come down to the Caribbean?" She said, "When?" I said, "Now." She said, "I can't get a plane now." I said, "Tomorrow." She said, "You're crazy." I said, "I guess I must be." She said, "Where, in Nassau?" I said, "No, let's meet in Puerto Rico. Sammy Davis, Jr., is there and I promised I'd come down and spend a few days with him, so why don't we meet in Puerto Rico?" She said, "Okay." I hung up the phone and asked myself: What have I done now? What have I done???

Whatever it was, it was done. I flew to Puerto Rico and she flew from London, and when she got to the San Juan airport, I was there, anxiously waiting to see her. We checked into the hotel where Sammy was appearing, and I spent some of the best days of my life. From San Juan we flew by helicopter to another hotel at Fajardo, where we had an even more glorious stay. If all the honeymooners who represented a sizable percentage of the hotel's guests were enjoying themselves half as much as we were, then Heaven was surely smiling on their union.

One lovely summer morning, the owner of the helicopter service arranged to have one of his machines drop us off, with a picnic basket, on an uninhabited island with a fantastic beach. We swam, ate, snorkled, collected shells, and strolled around in that ideal setting until the helicopter returned to pick us up just before the sun went down. That blissful day reminded us that we were within a stone's throw of any number of Caribbean islands Joanna had never seen before, so on we went to Barbados, Saint Vincent, Grenada, back to Barbados,

307

then to Antigua before finally heading home to New York.

While gazing out the plane window as we streaked toward J.F.K., I realized that for the first time in my life I was with a woman whose presence seemed to calm the turbulence in me rather than challenge it to battle. I was aware that ours was still a young relationship, but I was pleased to note no trace of any "unspecified conflicts" lurking on the periphery to keep me forever on guard and in a fighting frame of mind. Sitting there beside her, I reflected that through the five months we had known each other, there had not been one fight between us—unquestionably a record for me. During that time I had been introduced to a compatibility the likes of which I had never before known in my life. Never. It was Puerto Rico where the first realization came that I was in love with this woman. No doubt it happened on that little uninhabited island where we had spent the day alone. Sitting 38,000 feet above the clouds, looking back over the territory we had covered in five short months, I had to look the fact straight in the face and say, "Okay, she has me."

THROUGHOUT OUR STAY on the islands—from Puerto Rico to Barbados to Saint Vincent to Grenada and back —Joanna was making occasional calls to her agent in Paris, because she was due back at a certain time to begin a picture in France. Each time the agent would frantically remind her that she was way overdue, that the picture was scheduled to start in a very few days, that the producer-director was going out of his mind wanting to know where the hell his actress was. To which she would reply, "Never mind where I am. I'll call you tomorrow." "You're going to lose the job," the agent would warn. "Okay, I lose the job." "Where are you? Why don't you come back?" "Look, stop playing games. You know where I am. I'm down in the Caribbean and I'm fine, so just stop worrying and I'll call you in a couple of days." Calling as promised a few days later, she found the pressure intensified. The exasperated agent said, "You know, your friend from London is also aware that you're in the Caribbean. And he knows whom you're with in the Caribbean. He's been calling frantically here to the Paris office to see if we have a fix on you, he says he's got to talk to you." Back in New York, she called

Paris and told them she would be there soon. Through delicate negotiations, the beleaguered agent managed to put the project back on track. She also called her producer friend to tell him she would be stopping in London, and if he would like to talk there was something she would like to tell him. During their brief but painfully difficult meeting in London, she told him she was sorry to have caused him pain but there was a new situation in her life that she was going to pursue. Crossroads and final encounters are places where human courage is most severely tested. When and if we pass through them, we are never the same again.

Joanna went to Paris and started her movie. From Paris the company went to the south of France for location shooting in and around the tiny community of Les Baux. Three weeks later, I went down there to spend a week with her in a truly incredible hotel whose ten or twelve rooms made it the smallest I had ever seen, and hardly the place where one would expect to find a three-star restaurant. When Joanna went to work in the morning, I would lie around this miniature hotel eating myself fat. Then, before returning home, I asked her if when the picture was finished she would give up her apartment in Paris and come directly to New York. She said, "Yes."

Between working with writer Ernest Kinoy in New York on the screenplay for what would eventually be a film called *Brother John,* riding herd on the construction company in Nassau who were way behind schedule in the building of my house there, and helping Joanna in her hunt for a suitable New York apartment, I had little time left during the spring of 1969 for much else. However, in those busy months I did manage to introduce her to family and friends in the Nassau of my childhood, including of course the sky-blue waters and fantastic beaches that make the Bahamas unique. By summer, things had settled into some kind of order, enabling us to take a much-needed four-week vacation in North Africa before Joanna reported to a London studio for filming D. H. Lawrence's *The Virgin and the Gypsy.* I stayed with her in London as long as I could, and her picture was progressing satisfactorily, but she would come home most evenings distraught and crying a lot. It wasn't until I saw the finished picture that I understood why. She is a very private person. *The Virgin and the Gypsy* required her to come very close to some secret parts of herself emotionally, and it was difficult for her. It was probably on that movie that she decided she was not going to continue acting. Being a private and shy person, she found it too much a process of exposure. Acting was always felt by her as an uncomfortable intrusion, an invasion of her most private self. But as soon as the picture was finished, her mood changed, and she was fine again.

In the meantime, my friend Terry McNeeley and I browsed around London, sleeping late and waiting for his girlfriend, Dolores, who was working, and Joanna to come home after a hard day's work. Since doing nothing all day was not our style we decided on a quick trip, and off we went to Paris for a few days. I was quite happy to relax while my woman was making her picture. I was completely satisfied with my life with her, although I hadn't too much enjoyed sitting around the house waiting for her to come home from work—not a wholly unexpected attitude, in light of the brainwashing job my patriarch of a father had laid on me. But I was content. McNeeley, of course, was another matter. He found—and I don't know where, so don't ask me—a young lady he called "Flaps." He rang my room one morning and said, "Listen, I have someone down here I'd like you to meet." I said, "Who is it?" He said, "Let's just say I call her 'Flaps.' " I had my breakfast and sauntered on down to his room. McNeeley opened the door in his shorts. I walked in and there, under the covers, was a young lady with a big smile on her face. I said, "How are you?" She didn't answer and he said, "She doesn't speak English." I said, "Oh—bonjour." She said, "Bonjour, comment allez-vous?" I said. "Très bien, et vous?" Suddenly, McNeeley, who had been studying French but still wasn't too cool in the language, started talking to me in English, quite confident that the young lady wouldn't understand a word he was saying. "I ain't never had no poontang in my life like this one." While he was talking to me, he kept a broad smile on his face so that if she tried to read what he was saying, it had to seem very pleasant and innocuous. "This bitch is pure stallion. Almost killed my ass last night. I have been humping all night long, do you hear me? Now let me tell you why I call her 'Flaps,' " he said through his fake smile, while the bright-eyed young lady looking on from the bed was trying to interpret what was being said. Turning to the bed, he said, "This child has lips on her like the flaps on an airplane." "Come on, McNeeley, this is embarrassing, man—you sure this young lady can't understand English?" "No, this child don't understand nothing." He broadened his manufactured smile, winked flirtatiously at the young lady, then queried, "Do you, baby?" She simply looked at him and smiled back. "You see what I mean? Come closer, let me show you these flaps." "No, man, don't do that!" "I want you to see these fucking flaps, man. You won't believe it." He rips the covers off the lady. Now at this point you've got to figure that number one, McNeeley has to be the crudest man in the world. Number two, he has to be the biggest, most unregenerate, fascist, sexist, chauvinist bastard ever. And yes, you're right. No defense, however inspired, could prove otherwise. But—he must also have been something else that I have never been able to fathom. Something the naked young lady who couldn't speak English must have understood intuitively, or why else would she be loving the experience so? As far as I could make out, she thought he was sensational. He proceeded to point out the "flaps" to me. I said, "McNeeley, I got to go." He said, "No, man, stick around—stick around." I said, "No, I've got to go—I'm too embarrassed. I'm embarrassed for the girl, I'm embarrassed for myself and I'm embarrassed for you. How could you do this, man—this is very uncool." He said, "Listen, P, she loves it—she loves it." I said, "McNeeley, I think you've stepped over the line here, I'm going to leave." I tried in my awkward and insufficient French to apologize for my friend, but she said, "Oh, no, no, no. It's all right. Terry is crazy, but he's fun." Her characterization of him as crazy led me directly to wonder if I was in the presence of two of a kind. Because as always with Terry McNeeley, it turned out that if you were going to nail him for chauvinism, you were going to have to nail *her* for something too—how about a happy accessory, enjoying the exhibition every bit as much as he was?

My friend Terence McNeeley lived fast, died young, and I miss him. On that morning in Paris he still had five precious years to his name before taking his leave from us in a manner that befitted his lifestyle.

23 The Bahamas

WHEN THE HOUSE in the Bahamas was finally finished, we gave up our apartments in New York and the three of us—myself, Joanna, and my housekeeper—moved to Nassau. It was delicious, a real respite from pressure, a haven where the bridge was drawn up at night, leaving cares and woes to perish at the gate. Living in Nassau was wonderful for both of us, and we loved it down there—at first. Alas, unless your Paradise is mostly in the mind, where imperfections need not be acknowledged, it is subject to the laws of reality, and in time will pale and wither as all things must.

In 1967 the Bahamas changed hands from a minority white government that held both financial and political control to a majority black government that won political control through free elections while leaving financial control exactly where it had been for hundreds of years, firmly in the hands of the minority white community. Nevertheless, political power in the hands of the black majority was a victory of massive proportions considering the shameless chicanery and dirty tricks the incumbents used, on top of trying to intimidate segments of the black labor force with economic threats. The men most responsible for our Herculean victory were Lynden O. Pindling and an elderly associate of his named Milo Butler, a man who will be remembered by most Bahamians as the father of black political awareness in their country. Both men took important positions in the new government—Lynden O. Pindling as Prime Minister and Milo Butler as Governor General. Pindling, the young and very astute politician, had studied law in London and then became involved in Bahamian politics, rising rapidly to the leadership of the Progressive Labor party. It had been a long difficult struggle for the young lawyer and his mentor. I remember times when those two lonely political soldiers would stop at my apartment in New York for dinner during their innumerable trips to London where they ceaselessly petitioned, nagged, encouraged, seduced, shamed, and embarrassed the British government into grudgingly granting independence to the Bahama islands. I was very close to Pindling in those days. I understood what he was struggling for and was in complete sympathy with that struggle. He was the only hope we had at that time, and he was politically responsible enough and intellectually sound enough to be able to maneuver the black community's fledgling political consciousness into what was needed to achieve its goals.

In 1967, while helping out with a little campaigning on his behalf in the days before the crucial election, I was told that the party organization was facing a crisis brought on by the fact that an intricate transportation system, expected to move a critical number of people from outlying districts to the polls, was about to break down: the expected arrival of some walkie-talkies from America to coordinate the plan had failed, through either negligence or sabotage. The Progressive Labor party felt it absolutely necessary to have a heavy turnout and had instructed their transportation coordinator to have the system in working order on the morning of the election come hell or high water—no ifs, ands, or buts. The coordinator invited me to a strategy meeting with his staff on a Saturday night, and said, "Sidney, we need your help. We've got to have half a dozen sets of walkie-talkies here on the island by tomorrow." "You've got to be joking! By tomorrow? No chance—this is Saturday night—everything is closed everywhere." "We've got to have them. We've got to." He said it simply, but I knew he meant it. "Okay," I said, "if you've got to have them—I've got to get them. Take me to a phone."

I call Harry Belafonte in New York: "Harry—I need half a dozen sets of walkie-talkies. Let me tell you that it is absolutely essential, a matter of utmost importance, that I have them on this island by tomorrow." After a pause, he says, "You been drinking?" "Not a drop." "Hell, I can get the Empire State Building down to you quicker than I can find walkie-talkies this time of night on a Saturday." "B, you've got to give it a try." Another pause. "You serious?" "Yes, I am." "Okay, you got it. I don't know where I'm going to get them but you don't have to say anything else. You'll get them." Hangs up the phone, and do you know, the next day those walkie-

313

talkies are delivered to me in Nassau? From Saturday night to Sunday afternoon he got me those walkie-talkies. Later I learned how. Grabbing a phone book, he started out by first matching up names off the white pages with similar names from advertisements in the yellow pages, then started calling those people at home and finally, through bits of information obtained from those who didn't slam the phone down in his ear, he was led to a man who dealt in the merchandise we needed. But the man lived out of town in another state. Harry persuaded this man to come into town on Sunday morning at seven o'clock, open his business, and sell six sets of walkie-talkies to someone who reminded him vaguely of a "familiar Calypso singer." Then with the equipment in his hot little hands, he rushed it to the airport and got the Pan Am people to break tradition, rules, and regulations (maybe he sang them a song or slipped them a record or something); he had them put that stuff on a 9:00 a.m. nonstop flight and deliver it off the plane directly into my hands. And with that essential ingredient in place, the Progressive Labor transportation system worked like a charm on election day, moving the voters from outlying regions to the voting places and back to their districts.

It was a euphoric moment when it became clear that we had won the election. The excitement was electric—the outburst of happiness and joy I witnessed that evening in Nassau brought tears to my eyes. At my hotel the next day when it was announced that victory had been secured, an American journalist said to me, "You know, there was a time when there were flowers everywhere in the Bahamas, but the last ten or fifteen years there haven't been any. Do you think the flowers will come back now?" And I said, "Yes, the flowers will come back." And these remarks were symbolic of all the good human things we black Bahamians felt the previous administration had been negligent about.

In the years that followed, the changing of the guard proved itself a healthy experience for the nation and did great and wonderful things for the black community. My own greatest expectation, however, was that after the new government had settled in there would emerge a strong and consistent energy toward cultural development. Understandably, it could not be of very high priority in the beginning, because there were other matters that required more immediate attention (such as restructuring the edu-

314

cational system). But I had hoped that culture would not be too far down the line. We were a simple hard-working people, deserving of many more cultural outlets than we had ever been allowed, and I was certain that our first all-black government would, as quickly as possible, do whatever was required to launch the country in that important direction. Well, between the big victory in 1967 and the time a few years later when I arrived in Nassau to live, there were few indications that any new cultural awareness was in the making. There were three little-theater groups struggling against community indifference for survival, and occasionally Bahamian artists would brave the general indifference and present themselves in concert (usually in the convention hall of a tourist hotel), hardly ever attracting enough of an audience to cover their expenses. It was disappointing to see the lack of support they were getting, both from the government and from the public. It soon became clear that there would be no cultural growth until the government encouraged it, and yet the government gave it only lip service. I, among others, was discouraged. And then one day I suddenly understood: the men who ran the country were themselves culturally deprived and had been all their lives. That was why they had no appreciation of the importance of a cultural life to their constituency.

At about the same time I started taking notice that our politics were small-town politics—you're-either-for-us-or-against-us politics. But hadn't we just emerged from years of that? Either you were for the white folks or you were for the black folks; and when the black folks won the election, it got reversed: if you're not for the black folks, you're for the white folks. Now we had an intra-black situation—if you're not for the Progressive Labor party, you're against them. Everything was thought of in that kind of sharp contrast. I thought it was unbecoming, but I never interjected myself into such squabbles. I had enormous faith in Pindling's ability to move the country eventually to a place where blacks would have solidified their gains, settled into firm control of the country's political life (as well as they should, being the overwhelming majority), and started meaningful movement toward a more equitable distribution of the nation's economic power. But in the meantime I saw so much mediocrity! I had thought once that white folks had a monopoly on mediocrity when it came to governing black people, but I found that the white folks had no lock on those skills. Yes, I thought that the country was becoming politicized in a negative way. But as Pindling once said about me when asked his opinion about certain comments I had made, "Mr. Poitier is a wonderful actor, but he's no politician." I suspect that there's a great deal of truth in that.

Be that as it may, Nassau was slowly turning out to be the place to which I could never "go home again." It disturbed me deeply that there was no cultural life expressing the history of the people—absolutely none. I did see wood carvings, but they were imported from Haiti to sell to tourists in the Bahamas. With the exception of the straw industry in which Bahamian women fashioned highly artistic designs of pocketbooks and baskets from straw, there was no handicraft activity of any consequence. It was tourism, so enormously successful over so many years, that had contaminated—diluted—debased —the shape of all things cultural in those islands, until there was no longer any real semblance of a Bahamian cultural identity. People even danced to Bahamian musicians playing other people's music—Jamaican music or American artificial calypso music; tunes from the American hit parade or the American "soul" top ten.

At the same time I was finding both the black and the white people of the country self-indulgent for the most part. Especially the middle-class blacks and whites. There were far too many people in the middle-class black community doing everything they could to differentiate themselves from the grass-roots black population. On the other hand, most of the white middle class was trying to differentiate itself not only from the grass roots but also from the *black* middle class. The grass rooters of the Bahamas are a simple, easygoing people who have survived more than a hundred years of insensitive, heavy-handed, colonial rule. Like semiliterate and uneducated people in other parts of the world, they have had to scratch their existence from land that was sometimes parched, or from an ocean that was often angry, yet the Bahamian grass rooters were luckier than most of their fellows the world over. Beautiful beaches and phenomenal weather were proof enough that nature had at the dawn of time smiled on the place that was to be their home. Through Reginald and Evelyn Poitier, two typical grass rooters who scratched their way through life and death there, I will always have unbreakable ties to the country, and will visit it whenever I hunger for the ways of my childhood. But I must not tarry too long, or my temperament will surely find too many things that need changing. Yes, the likelihood is that I will forever be a visitor to the Bahamas—and that's cool with me, because my life is elsewhere now.

There came a morning when out of a dark suspicion I held deep within myself, the question arose: When you first moved back to the Bahamas, were you seeking some kind of refuge from the world? The answer was instant, loud, and clear: You're damn right I was. But it was too late—my interests and obligations were already international, I was no longer a Bahamian only. To submerge myself in a modern Bahamas that was irreconcilably at variance with the islands of my dreams was a fool's errand, a waste to all concerned. Well, maybe this little boy Sidney P. is very much alive inside of me as I near the age of fifty-two, and hopelessly disappointed to discover that everything, including himself, has changed.

In 1974, I moved with my family from Nassau to Beverly Hills and have not returned since. But the sand and the sea have been crowding my mind of late, leading me to suspect that a visit is somewhere on the horizon.

24 Harry

AT LUNCH ONE DAY during the filming of *The Lost Man* at Universal, agent Freddie Fields, president of Creative Management Associates, unveiled an ingenious idea he and his partner David Begelman had devised for putting together a motion picture company with Barbra Streisand, Steve McQueen, Paul Newman, and myself. It was to be called the First Artists Corporation. The two agents envisioned a company owned equally by the four artists (all of whom were connected in some way with the CMA agency): each artist would make a minimum of three films during a six-year period. All the elements in the plan, including a reputable distribution company, had meticulously been set in place, following months of hard work by Fields and Begelman. They waited for the main ingredient—the agreement of the four actors. From an economic point of view it seemed like a good deal, but the main advantage to us over and above financial considerations was the complete artistic control we would have provided we made each of our films for $3 million or less. As long as we stayed within those bounds we could make any film we wanted to. Even while it was obvious that a $3 million limit would force us into highly conservative budget practices, we nevertheless thought that artistic control was more than worth the inconveniences and frustrations normally associated with tight budgets, especially since the plan allowed each of us to retain our nonexclusive status, leaving us free to continue making pictures elsewhere. A very attractive setup, I thought, and there over lunch I gave them a positive response and promised them a final "yes" if and when a unanimous response was obtained from the others.

At about that same time my nonexclusive status enabled me to enter into a deal with Columbia Pictures according to which I would produce and star in two films for them to distribute. When the First Artists agreement was finalized, I found myself with firm commitments to make five motion pictures in six years. As a result of the Columbia deal, I was reunited with Harry Belafonte, with whom I had not been on speaking terms for about two years as a result of a fight in Atlanta, Georgia. Therein lies an interesting tale. We were very close to Martin Luther King, Harry much closer than I—he and Martin were like brothers. I never sought to be that close and seriously doubt that I ever could have been, even with maximum effort on my part. Between Harry and Martin there was an almost visible electricity, and a mutual respect and admiration that gave their robust friendship a flavor that at times seemed almost mystical. I was at Martin's disposal whenever I could be of help in raising funds or lending my name to his activities, but I never propelled myself into that inner circle, partly because I didn't want it to appear that I was competing on any level with Harry for Martin's friendship.

Harry at that time was deeply involved in the civil rights movement on every level. Especially with the Student Nonviolent Coordinating Committee and Martin's

Southern Christian Leadership Conference. When Martin was killed, Harry was in charge of certain aspects of the funeral arrangements. Arriving in Atlanta, I called him for instructions, and he told me to come to a meeting later that afternoon of people from Martin's organization and supporters from around the country, to make last-minute decisions about the funeral and activities surrounding it. At that meeting held in Harry's suite, one of the questions on the table was whether or not to hold a rally in Atlanta Stadium on either the evening of the funeral or the evening before the funeral. It struck me as not being a good idea. Besides the obvious monumental problems involved in properly organizing such an event even during the best of times, the massive organizational efforts necessary for the funeral itself made it to my mind a highly impractical idea. In my view, the strain of pulling so many things together in such a short time could prove counterproductive to the real reason we were in Atlanta—to pay tribute to the man and lay him to rest. After articulating my opinion I found that it was directly opposite to Harry's, and while this wasn't the first time we had been on opposite sides of an issue, this was far and away the most sensitive disagreement we had ever had. The time could not have been more inopportune for two old friends to cross swords. Julie Belafonte was very vocal in her support of Harry's position. With blazing ferocity she lit into my position with an attack that was obviously directed at me personally. But my view was my view, so I held my ground; I felt that a demonstration was not appropriate at that time, and made my feeling known to all concerned. I had challenged Harry in the presence of those with whom he was deeply connected; in sensitive matters they were closer to him than to me. The damage was done.

It might have been better if we could have gone into it privately between the two of us, but there was no time for that; quick decisions had been called for from a group in which each person was free to make suggestions and air his thoughts before casting a vote. The upshot of the discussion was that we didn't hold that function in the Atlanta Stadium. But Harry's organizational skills and the energy of his group contributed largely to the farewell to Martin Luther King that illuminated the dignity of his life. A warrior of justice had walked briefly in a troubled land, seeded the minds of men and women with new visions of themselves, and changed the course of history.

The true extent of Harry's anger at me was lost on most of those present at our meeting, partly because it was upstaged by Julie's wrath and partly because he is capable of a peculiar response when he gets angry at someone he cares about. Rather than fly into the expected rage, he reverses and elects to back off, saying simply, "Hey, if that's the way you want it, that's cool." But you can smell his disappointment at times like that, and I just knew I had hurt him awfully; and Julie had seen that hurt in him and known who was responsible for it.

After that day in Atlanta, Harry didn't speak to me. Mind you, I don't know that it wasn't my place to pick up the phone and make sure that he wasn't interested in speaking to me; I just supposed that he wasn't. Now, with hindsight, I feel I should have called him and said, "Listen, we had a little thing down there in Atlanta, and I was probably wrong as hell, but let's talk about it." Unfortunately, that was never the way we dealt with each other. Our pattern was to carry our little festerings inside until they wore out, and as a result this time we didn't speak to each other for damn near two years. Come to think of it, I don't know how it was possible for Belafonte and me to live near each other in New York City, rallying around the same causes we had always rallied around, and not bump into each other—not once in all that time. Yet that's exactly how it happened. With a little help from our friends, we were never invited to the same place at the same time.

I think that whatever hostility existed between us had spent itself about four months after we had our little episode down in Atlanta, but we were two proud West Indians. I remember thinking: I'll be damned if I'm going to pick up that phone and call Harry Belafonte. And I knew in my bones that he would die before he picked up the phone and dialed me. In the meantime, friends and acquaintances were asking, "What the hell is the matter with you and Harry?" I would say, "There's nothing the matter with me—it's what's the matter with him." And he'd say, "Me? Hey, there's nothing the matter with me— it's what's the matter with *him*." Which was, of course, a clear signal each of us was sending to the other: I'm cool

—so any time you're ready to make up you can find me, and I'll come and *maybe* apologize. You know where I am, but you'd better give me a clue that you want me to do that. But a couple of Christmases came and went with no such move being made. Stubborn pride is a quality West Indians tend to husband far beyond any reasonable usefulness it might have.

Then one day, out of the blue, my phone rang and it was Harry, saying, "Sidney?" I said, "Oh, hi, B." He said, "How are you?" I said, "I'm fine. How are you?" He said, "I'm fine." I've hardly ever been on the phone with him when he didn't open the conversation with a little joke of some kind. "P, did you hear the one about—" and true to form, as if the past two years had never happened, he proceeded to lay a very cute joke on me. I don't quite remember what it was, but even if it wasn't cute I would have given it more laughter than it might have deserved because I was so glad he called. "The reason I called is I have a script that I want you to read. It's in very bad shape, but the essence of the story is there. I think it's an important story and it should be told. I'll send it over to you if you'd care to read it." I said, "Send it." He said, "Okay. Let me know what you think."

He sent the manuscript, I read it, and I was genuinely impressed: *Buck and the Preacher* was a beautiful story about black people in the 1800s. I called him back and before expressing my interest I asked him what his relationship was to the material. He said he owned it and if I felt disposed to it, we could co-produce it; if not, he would let me have the idea because he simply wanted to see it made and: "Since you have the outlets to have it translated into film, you can have it if you want it—just reimburse me for what I've already laid out. Also I would like to play the Preacher, but that isn't necessary either. Give it some thought. . . ." I said, "There's nothing to think about. You've got a deal. You play the Preacher—I play Buck—and we can co-produce. There's no need to discuss who gets what from it—no financial terms—we'll just go fifty-fifty down the line, across the board, all the way." "Are you sure you want to do it that way?" I replied, "Yeah, let's do it that way." And that was the way we did it. And now we were talking again. It was such a relief—for both of us. In the succeeding weeks our phones were ringing off their hooks. If he didn't call for twenty-five minutes I would pick up the phone and call him. Two foolish old friends were back in stride.

We hired a writer and started planning the production of *Buck and the Preacher*—a film in which Harry was to prove to the world that he is one of the best character actors in the business, which is irony of a peculiar sort, considering his matinée-idol appearance. I have always suspected him to be many, many more times effective as a character actor than as a leading man. A powerful and luminous energy materializes and strikes magic whenever he is forced to reach beyond the obvious. The same thing applies to Paul Newman, also a much better character actor than leading man. Any assessment of these two artists would be inadequate if it didn't acknowledge the fact that the commercial direction their careers took, however incredible the success in each case, was not necessarily toward the most effective use of their creative powers. (I'm sure they will read this with a great deal of interest on their way to the bank.)

And how did we resolve our differences over the Martin Luther King thing? I think they were never really resolved. Basically I believe I was wrong—if not in my challenge, in my timing, primarily because I should have understood how particularly devastating Martin's death was to Harry. Out of concern for him, and if I had been on my toes, I would have handled it differently. Looking back through the haze of the intervening years, I see more clearly and am presently inclined to take all the blame for that painful two-year rupture. (There, Mr. B, I've said it and that's about all you're going to get on that question. If you want more—write your own book.)

While Harry was supervising preproduction, I went off to northern California to film *Brother John,* the first movie in my two-picture deal with Columbia. The idea for *Brother John* came thundering into my mind one quiet evening while I was fueling my imagination with collected fragments from my checkerboard life. After the initial flurry it produced in me, I tried to file it away in the back of my mind for future consideration, but it wouldn't stay back there—it kept coming to the forefront of my thoughts as if by its own will, forcing me to give it more immediate attention. The strange, fascinating tale of *Brother John* haunted me until I committed myself to seeing it come alive on film.

The picture was about an observer from another world who walks the earth meticulously recording his impressions of the human condition—impressions that will ultimately determine whether mankind is worthy of salvation. I along with dozens of creative people poured a great deal of time and loving care into an unusual motion picture that audiences everywhere chose to ignore. I believe there are three or four people who thought it was a terrific movie, bordering on the classic. But what the hell do they know? I had formed my own company, E & R Productions, and produced it and I starred in it but didn't direct it. I was very interested in directing, but I had no intention of directing my next picture, *Buck and the Preacher*. After Harry and I got a good working script from Ernest Kinoy, we hired a line producer named Joel Glickman, and the three of us then went about trying to nail down a top-flight director. None of those contacted were interested, primarily because most top directors are men who want to make their own films; they are reluctant to hire themselves out. But finally we got a positive response from an accomplished director named Joe Sargent. I had known him many years before, when he and his wife were two of the really good people of the old days in New York. The bulk of his work was in television, though he did have a few features sprinkled among his credits. But his work in television had been quite distinctive. After running two or three of his shows, we were convinced that he was the man for the job. Following a get-acquainted-again, feel-each-other-out meeting, during which we talked a lot about old times, we hired Joe Sargent and headed for Mexico to make our film.

Our hand-picked American crew was fleshed out by additional technicians from Mexico City, as was required by that country's unions, which brought the full strength of our company to well over a hundred people. We housed everybody within the confines of the city of Durango. Producer Joel Glickman's first job was to find several hundred extras, half of whom had to be black. It would have been prohibitively expensive to transport them from the United States, so he set out to find them in Mexico, and indeed he did. From a black American expatriate community in and around Guadalajara, he recruited at least a hundred, and to those he added blacks from Cuba, Brazil, and other Spanish-speaking countries in South America who had immigrated to Mexico. Our principal players were Ruby Dee, Cameron Mitchell, Harry Belafonte, myself, and Julie Belafonte, who played the wife of the Indian chief.

Joanna and I had rented a house that belonged to a local businessman, and he left us his housekeeper and cook, which helped to make it quite a comfortable stay for us—domestically. We started shooting the picture and the first day went all right—we thought. There were questions in my mind about Joe Sargent's selection of certain shots, but my feathers weren't ruffled too badly. I assumed he knew what he was doing—he's a man of excellent taste, with a good camera eye. The second day's shooting was not an improvement on the first day's. From the third day I began to notice a pattern, and Belafonte began to notice the same things. We decided that maybe we should have a talk with Joe. From that talk it became clear that we were seeing the film from two different points of view. Joe's work was very professional, with much artistic merit, but it was not moving in the direction we had hoped for. Strong emphasis was not being placed on certain values dear to Harry and me.

After the first week of shooting, Harry—visibly distressed—came to my house one evening, after we had seen the dailies, and found me deeply concerned as well. He said, "We have to make a change." I said, "I think we have to, yeah—but to whom? You know how difficult it was to get a director in the first place." Harry said, "Yeah, but we can't go on like this." I said, "Okay, the best we can do is to ask Columbia to find someone, tell them we have an emergency and ask them to get cracking and get someone down here as quickly as possible." "No." "What?" "No, we won't call Columbia—you have to take over the directing of the picture." "Look, Columbia won't stand for that, and besides to direct and act in the same picture at the same time my first time out would be too much of a job." "P, we are in one hell of a bind at the moment. Man, you have got to do it. If we tell Columbia we're not getting the kind of film we wanted to get from the director we hired, they'll want to close down the production. They'd rather take a loss of four or five hundred thousand dollars and close us down, because a four-hundred-thousand-dollar loss is a hell of a lot better than a two-million-dollar loss. If we go to them on that basis, the chances are they're going to panic and say, 'What the hell is going on down there in Mexico?' and they're not going to be favorably disposed to your directing the picture, so don't tell them until you're already directing it."

In the long pause that followed I may have seemed to be digesting everything he'd laid on me, but I instantly knew there was much validity in what he said. Partly because he is a good businessman, partly because he has a flair for grace under pressure and partly because the damned circumstances didn't leave us with another alternative anyhow. I told him I would think about it and let him know the next morning. I discussed it with Joanna, and she thought that since Harry and I were responsible for the film, we ought to go in the direction he was suggesting. She then asked, "Do you think you can handle the directing as well as the acting?" "I don't know, but I can't live with the kind of film I'm getting from the other director." "Well, then," she said, "that answers itself." The next morning I told B, "Yes—I'll give it a shot." Joe agreed to step down. He was paid as per his contract, and he returned to California. On the day he left, I took over the production by putting on a hat I had had no intention of wearing for at least another three or four years.

Once more I am in that familiar place. The testing ground. The furnace. There I am playing the principal part of a cowboy. Okay? Well, besides the fact that I can hardly ride a horse, I have hundreds of extras waiting to be choreographed, half of them speaking no English. At least seventy-five members of the crew, and an untold number of townspeople, are waiting anxiously for the words to fall from the lips of the new director. And if that isn't enough, how about a cast of professional actors —my peers—waiting, watching, to see me do or die on a bright sunny morning in the Mexican countryside? The toughest scene in the movie is waiting to be staged.

The scene took place in an Indian village where Buck and the Preacher were taken before the Indian chief and his wife with the entire village looking on. I sat down, closed my eyes, and mapped the scene as I felt it would unfold naturally under these circumstances. When I was ready I said, "All right, I would like to have the actors, please." They all gathered. I placed them all where I wanted them to be, and explained to each of them why I wanted him or her at that particular spot. Then I began moving them around according to whatever it was each character was after. It took me about forty-five minutes to properly choreograph and rehearse the sequence. Then I rolled my cameras for the first time. I want to tell you, after three or four takes of that first scene, a calm came over me. A confidence surged through my whole body. Somehow I knew from the way I had staged that sequence that it would work. Yes indeedy, it would work. And I, as green as I was, had a touch for this new craft I had been courting from a distance for many, many years.

B, who always had confidence in me from the very first time I had revealed to him my strong interest in one day directing films, was very happy. As the day progressed I rehearsed and photographed several more scenes with actors, horses, extras, wagons, and weapons all awaiting my instructions before springing into action. When I finally said "print" on each of those sequences, I felt in my bones that on the screen they would look realistic and make sense. When I returned home that night I was a wholly different person from the fellow who had left that morning. Joanna beamed when I told her of my good day—she had prepared a special dinner "fit for a debuting director." Two days later we assembled in a projection room in downtown Durango to see the first day's work. It was all there.

In the meantime we had placed a call to Columbia and very carefully revealed that due to irreconcilable artistic differences, we had found it necessary to release the director, and that I was now directing the picture only for a few days, until such time as they were able to send down another director to relieve me of the responsibility. Reassuring them that no time was being wasted was intended to soften the shock of the switch, because in the picture business wasted time is wasted money. The person making the decision as to who would be sent down, and whether we would be allowed to continue until the new director arrived, was Stanley Schneider, a son of Abe Schneider, the chairman of the board at Columbia Pictures. Stanley was a tough couragous man, a decision-maker, and fortunately he liked us. He said Columbia would have a director down to us in a couple of days. Well, three days came and went with no one showing up.

Finally we got a call saying that two executives from

the studio in California—Peter Guber from the creative side and Johnnie Veitch from the production side—would be coming to assess the situation and report back to the New York office. By the time they arrived I had a week's work in the can, and I knew that what they were really coming down to do was to look at my work and report back to Columbia. Obviously they couldn't find a director to their liking who was willing to take over, so it was go with me or shut the production down. Mr. Guber and Mr. Veitch went into that projection room in downtown Durango and looked at my film. John Veitch, on whose back the production department at Columbia securely rested, was impressed. The young Peter Guber, who knew more about the artistic side of motion pictures than most professionals twice his age, concentrated on every foot of film as intensely as if his life depended on his not missing one frame. Later, on location, he said to me, "You know something, I think you should continue to direct the picture—that's what I'm going to tell Stanley." Johnnie Veitch said, "The stuff looks good to me, looks professional, we're on time, we can't have lost any time, I believe everything I see on the screen—and I'm going to recommend that you continue." Guber said, "Would you be interested in continuing?" Well, what a question. "Of course." And that's how it happened. I got the green light.

After completing the film in nine weeks, we returned to California. I had to report almost immediately to the Mirisch Company for the start of *The Organization,* for which I acted during the day. I was editing *Buck and the Preacher* in my spare time at Francis Coppola's Zoetrope Studios, with the crackerjack editor Pembroke Herring (through five pictures over eight years he was to teach me all any director needs to know about editing films). When *Buck and the Preacher* was completed, with all of the finishing touches added, I sat and watched it from beginning to end. Afterward, in the privacy of my heart, I questioned the validity of those "irreconcilable artistic differences" that had served as the basis for Joe Sargent's removal from his job as director. The question arose when, after seeing the film, I suspected that the technical work I had done was not superior to Joe's work, and in some instances was clearly not as professional. With the specter of opportunism threatening to cloud the issue, I decided to clarify for myself the unvarnished truth about "those artistic differences." I was prepared to acknowledge

327

any personal opportunism that may have provoked our actions against Joe. But I perceived that there were indeed differences in approach, differences fundamentally deeper than anything technical: important ethnic qualities were essential to give dimension to the character of the screenplay. Harry and I wanted black people and minorities in general to find in *Buck and the Preacher* a certain substance, a certain nourishment, a certain complement of self. We wanted black people to see the film and be proud of themselves, be proud of their history. However dishonest, unpleasant, and inhuman had been the depiction of that history by those white men who had written most of the history books that tell us about ourselves, we wanted this film to say: Hey, look, there were those of us, and not just a few, who were people of great courage, of great stamina, of great personality, of great conviction. People who should be a powerful influence on our sense of ourselves.

Joe was taking the film in the direction of a well-made entertainment film, a typical American Western, but our picture had to be more than that. There was a relationship between Indians and blacks that had never been explored in any film, and we were determined to make sure that in our film, that relationship was projected in the way it actually had existed. Our picture was not an outgrowth of our imaginations; only its dramatic structuring was. The story was of a group of black people in the late 1800s who left Louisiana in pursuit of a promised land far to the west, where no man would be their master. The forces that drove them, the commitments that enabled them to endure the hardships on their way and to persevere even in the face of death—this was the substance of the film. And these were the kinds of values that Harry and I wanted to communicate to our constituency through our film.

So there it was, our true intention. As artists we wanted to make a loving comment about the people we represent. The way we see it, given the nature of our history in America, it is quite appropriate for us to compliment ourselves from time to time just for surviving. And almost always surviving with dignity. That is what the film is about.

The Lost Man was not a successful picture by a long shot. It lost almost everything they put into it. But I came out of that experience richer because I had the occasion to meet and work with one of its producers, Melville Tucker. I was impressed with his integrity. Although I made a picture for him that didn't make any money, it didn't affect our relationship. He was as caring, as concerned, and as interested an anyone you might find who has your best interests at heart. Melville Tucker and his wife, Earlene, are both white Americans—I think WASPS. His politics, I must say, are a shade right of center, while mine are considerably left of center. He is Germanic in his adherence to detail and discipline—it is enviable how meticulously he wraps everything up, with no loose ends. He is refreshingly honest and hard-working, and impressively knowledgeable about picturemaking.

Mel and I became good friends. Some two years after *The Lost Man,* after many, many years of being a part of the hierarchy at Universal Pictures, he was let go in one of their reshuffles and was about to go into independent production when I thought of him as the kind of guy I would like to have produce for me. Joanna said, "Why don't you approach him?" I said, "All right, I will." He said, "I'd love to give it a try." In 1971 he joined my company Verdon Productions, Ltd., at just about the time I was looking for a decent piece of material to honor my first commitment to the First Artists Corporation. We commissioned a rather touching script called *A Warm December,* and it accomplished what I wanted it to, making a comment that needed to be made. Hollywood had produced no love stories for blacks, not really. *A Warm December* was commissioned with that in mind. It is the story of a successful black American doctor whose wife has died and left him with an eleven-year-old daughter; he goes to London on a vacation with his child and falls in love with an African princess.

We shot the film entirely in England. After the principal photography was finished, I was exhausted from the combination of acting and directing. Joanna and I went to Spain for a week's rest. When Mel and I had a final print to our satisfaction, we returned to the United States and delivered it to the First Artists Corporation.

The picture didn't do any business. It came at a time when black exploitation films were in full swing in the United States—a particularly distressing time for me: I was persona non grata among certain militant elements in New York and elsewhere, but especially in New York.

It started after my most successful movies—*To Sir with Love, In the Heat of the Night, Guess Who's Coming to Dinner.* No other black actor anywhere had near my level of success, and in the community of black actors recentment was developing. I had the number-one picture in the country and the number-two picture in the country and the number-three picture in the country all in one year, and most of my fellow black actors couldn't get a job. I was earning hundreds of thousands of dollars while a discouragingly small number of my black colleagues were lucky if they connected with a three-hundred-dollar-a-week gig.

I was a perfect target, and I was aware of it, but there wasn't anything I could do. I could have ended my career, but what would that have accomplished? It wouldn't have got them hired. To tell them of the countless times I had confronted studio people and extracted promises from them to do something about hiring black actors would be of little comfort, since they had seen no tangible results. Worst of all, with the sharp instincts of hungy outsiders, they knew a naked truth about Hollywood: the motion picture industry was not yet ready to entertain more than one minority person at that level. I knew it too, and couldn't fight that.

Regularly I reminded our few friends on the "inside" that we were so starved as a community, we would be happy to see ourselves on screen even in the smallest of parts, as long as there was a quotient of dignity attached to those parts.

That was not to be. Almost all the parts, both big *and* small, remained white. And it was clear that the few black faces passing across the silver screen were not anywhere near enough to assuage the frustrations our people had felt for so long.

25 Black Films

THE FIRST SHOT came at me after I had enjoyed a dozen years of a press that was more often favorable and fair than not. Even for my pictures that didn't work, I generally received very good personal notices. Then Larry Neal, a close friend of LeRoi Jones, saw a screening of *The Lost Man* and said to me, "You're heading for big trouble. Black people aren't going to like that picture."

He was right. At about that time Clifford Mason, a writer who dabbled at playwriting in community theaters, got an assignment from the *New York Times* to write an article on me. It was called "Why Do White Folks Love Sidney Poitier So?" It was the most devastating and unfair piece of journalism I had ever seen. When I read it, I said to myself: This definitely signals a bad period for me. On that Sunday morning I was convinced that the brick-by-brick growth of my career was complete—it had peaked, and there was no place to go but down. In that article Clifford Mason ripped to shreds everything I had ever done. He ripped up *In the Heat of the Night,* and the character I played in particular, to show why white people thought I was so terrific, why they made me such a "big star." Then he went on to destroy *To Sir with Love* and *Guess Who's Coming to Dinner*—and then he went further back into my career and proceeded to skin me alive retroactively. I was an "Uncle Tom," "a lackey," "a house Nigger"—current terms for a lot of people, including some highly visible blacks who were perceived as not doing whatever they did in a way to win the applause of all their fellow blacks.

I didn't know who that man was, that Clifford Mason. But he scalded me awfully. I got on the phone that very day and began asking around about him, but I couldn't assemble more than a sketchy portrait from the fragments of information I was able to obtain. The following week, a tough one for me, I received an invitation from

Roger Therman, a young man I used to know at the American Negro Theatre. He asked me to come and see a play he had directed at a high school auditorium in Harlem.

Would you believe that Clifford Mason is also there to see the play? And would you also believe that I am sitting right next to Clifford Mason? I don't know that at first, because I don't know what Clifford Mason looks like. I'm sitting there in the first row of the packed room waiting for the curtain to go up when the man sitting next to me leans over and says, "Hello, you don't know who I am, do you?" I look at him a moment, then say politely, "No, I'm sorry I don't." He says, "My name is Clifford Mason." Instantly a bell rings, but I'm cool. I say, "Oh, I see," and that's all I say. I turn my attention to the program to see who's in the cast and stuff. Mind you, that isn't really what I'm doing. I'm trying to collect myself. He says, "Did you read my article?" And I want to say: Yes, mother-fucker, I read your article. Instead I say, "Oh, yes, I did." Period.

The play begins, and it's quite an interesting show. Whenever he gets an opportunity, he leans over to make some kind of comment. My response is cold. Intermission comes, and I decide I'd better get up and move away from that man, because there's something about him not quite right. Whenever I'm at the theater it's my habit to go outside or into the john during the intermission to get away from autograph seekers. That night I don't make it to the john. I settle into signing, and suddenly a voice over my shoulder says, "Don't push, ladies, just take your time. He's going to sign them all for you, so don't get excited. He's going to sign them all."

I look around and there's Clifford Mason. Now, I have to suppose that the man is touched, or else he's playing a game. If he's touched, I'm simply going to cool out on him. If he's playing a game, cooling out on him will allow me to analyze his ass. Meanwhile he's taking the papers or programs, passing them to me for signing, then taking them back for redistribution. The bastard is orchestrating my fucking autograph signing! Okay, the lights begin to flicker and we go back for the second act. At the end of the play, having no desire for further conversation with this strange man, I go over to the guy who'd invited me, tell him I'd enjoyed the play, and split.

The next Sunday afternoon, Nigerian musical artist Michael Olatunji gives a concert at Town Hall to raise funds for a civil rights organization. I go, and there's Clifford Mason again, and again he makes himself known to me. By this time I know a little more about who Mr. Mason is. He's a playwright—of sorts. He's worked on radio as a kind of announcer on a small station. By this time I've realized that the article in the *Times,* aside from being an expression of his own feelings, is a career opportunity for an up-and-coming writer of sorts.

What I resented most about Clifford Mason by the time of our second encounter was his laying of all the film industry's transgressions at my feet. Let me say here that I respected the rage and hostility of my fellow actors against the unfairness that, first, kept them out so long and, second, when the door did begin to open, showered so many opportunities on one person, in the tokenism that my presence was. They were trained, they were skilled, those actors, and with only a handful of jobs to be scrambled for, they had to watch one guy wind up getting all the real opportunities. They were right in being angry, and they had to have a place to dump their anger. And I had my share of weaknesses, God knows—I had surely made mistakes aplenty. But I stood ready to fight Clifford Mason's or anyone else's attempt to charge me with even a fraction more of them than in my opinion I deserved.

Hollywood had not kept it secret that it wasn't interested in supplying blacks with a variety of positive images. In fact, in only a few isolated corners of the industry could one find committed souls who could be classified as interested in supplying blacks with a different image from what they had been accustomed to. Thanks to that handful of committed souls, the image of the black man just scratching his head was changing. A black man was put in a suit with a tie, given a briefcase; he could become a doctor, a lawyer, or a police detective. That was a plus factor for us, to be sure, but it certainly was not enough to satisfy the yearnings of an entire people. It simply wasn't. Because a people are a community, and a community consists of bus drivers and laborers and street sweepers and dentists and schoolteachers and hustlers and prostitutes and students and ordinary workers—people, people. They fall in love, they have problems, they have children, they live, they die. Where was that kind of representation on the motion picture screen for blacks? It didn't exist. The closest Hollywood came over a twelve-year period was the one-dimensional, middle-class imagery I embodied most of the time. Although I and our handful of friends in those isolated corners "inside" Hollywood considered it a step forward, it was not a step that could in any way alleviate all the frustrations of the past decades. I understood the pain of the victims, and the pain of their friends. I also understood the value system of a make-believe town that was at its heart a racist place.

My unique relationship with each of the sides of the problem trapped me in one hell of a dilemma, because I also knew some facts that rage and frustration couldn't care less about. I knew that however inadequate my step appeared, it was important that we make it. From one step would come another step, however overdue, and every new step would bring us closer. The dilemma for me was that there was nothing I could do in quick relief for the guy who works in a factory, who's married to a good wife who doesn't look like Denise Nicholas or Dorothy Dandridge but who loves him and has given him a couple of fine kids with whom they have a very good black family home life, the likes of which he wants to see reflected on the motion picture screen when he plunks down his three or four dollars.

I couldn't do that for him because I was not in control of the film business. I was not even in control of my career in the film business beyond making a decision to play or not to play in a given piece of material. Furthermore, nothing in the material from which I had to choose had anything to do with the kind of family life thousands of such guys lived. More than a few of the selections I made were merely the best of a bad lot.

Clifford Mason's article started a kind of deluge. The *New York Times* published several more articles in which I was dumped on. Sometimes I wasn't even the subject of the article: a piece about Fred Williamson had a headline in bold type: "Don't compare me with Sidney, his pictures don't make money any more." I was aware that the *Times* Sunday entertainment section often gets somebody to write an article on a director or an actor that might be controversial and uncomplimentary. After they print such an article, they allow the person about whom the article is written to respond. And so they fill space for free, at the expense of that particular artist.

As a faithful reader of the *New York Times*, I watched these Letters-to-the-Editor exchanges, during which for five or six weeks that poor director or actor would really be throttled. Probably no clear-cut verdict can be given on whether this practice constitutes a cheap-shot habit or a good journalistic ploy to fill space. But given a choice, those of us who have been stung by the Sunday theatrical section will opt for the cheap-shot habit, even while we prize our home delivery subscriptions to the good old *New York Times*. I was sought after to respond, and I thought about it. But as much as I wanted to reply to Clifford Mason, I decided not to. In no way was I going to let them sucker me into that. (The only satisfaction I ever got vis-à-vis Clifford Mason came a few years later, when across my desk one day came a play he had written. In my view it was totally inept. And I just loved reading that play.) It seems that the fact that I didn't respond triggered further attempts to provoke me. In any case, the negative mentions kept coming, but I kept firm against drawing myself into an exchange.

At about the same time, the black exploitation films really began to take hold in America. Finally some elements in the industry were beginning to view the black community as a viable audience unto itself, one hungry for entertainment in its own image. Suddenly the realization that there was money "across town" waiting to be made set in motion a flurry of activity for black actors and actresses unprecedented in an industry that long ago had built racial exclusion into the rules of its game. They gave us *Shaft* with Richard Roundtree, *Slaughter* with Jim Brown, *Super Fly, Cotton Comes to Harlem, Three the Hard Way*. Fred Williamson began doing his numbers, and between him and Jim Brown a new kind of hero was born. Their "macho" films were quite unlike mine. Generally these black heroes were seen beating up on white Mafia guys; it was a "get whitey" time—which certainly added immeasurably to the popularity of their films. I know because I was there at the box office putting down my three dollars to see Jim Brown and Fred Williamson do their stuff. Yeah—I, too, enjoyed seeing the black guys beating up on the white guys for a change. It was delicious. And not only did I like watching the revenge syndrome at work, I also liked watching my fellow actors at work. Suddenly, after too many years of little more than Sidney Poitier films, came a profusion of movies with black stars, male and female; macho guys and beautiful girls. It was terrific, and the response at the box office was tumultuous. My own career went into a decline at that point, and I recognized that there would be no reviving it for a while. A shift in the tide had taken place, and I would have to wait until the exploitation films had progressed to a level of greater substance before I could again be part of the filmmaking process in relation to blacks. So I went into a kind of retirement for a year. I didn't announce it formally, but went on down to the Caribbean and just cooled it. I bought a boat and a lot of books, and I sat around enjoying my family, my house, my boat—and my Sunday *New York Times,* which kept me abreast of the wildfire spread of the black exploitation film, that yardstick against which I was clearly able to measure my own decline. The unavoidable comparison between me and my work on the one hand, and the new-wave offerings on the other, produced some negative comments about "Sidney Poitier and his films" from time to time, but hey, I could take it. I didn't particularly relish it, in fact I hated it, but I could take it. (Or was that simply the way bruised egos tend to make you feel? After all, what was so hard for me to take under the circumstances? By any fair assessment I was still in residence at the top of the mountain. Could I have grown too accustomed to my perch at the top of the world and been spoiled rotten by it all? A sober thought, with more than a little validity to it. But alas, there on my island retreat with my house and my boat and my Sunday *Times,* it never entered my mind. Through it all, I managed somehow to keep suffering.)

Having slipped into a kind of twilight zone, I chose to stay away from my fellow actors unless and until I received an invitation. It's long been common practice for "at liberty" actors to visit the set of friends who are lucky enough to be working, but there had been such a chasm between my career and those of most of my black colleagues that I would never go visiting them at work unless invited. When Ossie Davis was directing *Cotton Comes to Harlem* in New York, I stayed away from his set even though it was populated with actors I started out in this business with, and with whom I was more than casually acquainted. I stayed away from the sets of all those movies because I didn't want any of my colleagues to feel apprehensive about my raining on their parade.

One day I happened to be on a plane with Jim Brown heading for California from Atlanta, where we had been participating in something concerning Martin Luther King, when he came over and sat down next to me. At that time he was at the height of a career that was going extremely well for him. In fact, he preceded the black exploitation films by a beat or two as a result of his appearance in *The Dirty Dozen*, which was followed soon after by *100 Rifles* and *El Condor*. He had gained his feet quickly in this new career, and his impact was strong. Sitting there next to me on that plane he said something that made him a guy I would like forever. He said, "A lot of things are happening now, and a lot of us are working. I just thought I'd stroll up here and say 'thank you' for the contributions you've made to us all having a little piece. I just want you to know that it's appreciated." He got up, shook my hand, and went back to his seat. That made my day. A man of few words who never bit his tongue, that was big Jim, a Prince of many colors. That was the way he was and that's the way he is. But that was not the way it was with most of my other actor friends. Somehow I got the impression that the threat of Sidney Poitier could only be allayed properly if it could be fixed so that he never worked again. I got those vibes from a lot of quarters.

During the period of the exploitation films I went to see each and every one of them as they came out. In the course of my four years in the Bahamas, they were the most popular movies being shown in the islands. You ain't heard nothing yet until you hear a theater filled with a Saturday night audience of blacks talking back to the screen, telling Jim Brown and Fred Williamson what to do with the Mafia heavies. I preferred the drive-ins, where it was easier both to enjoy the films and to study them as product. After the passage of a year or two, it began coming to me slowly that the producers of such films were making a mistake—a mistake which, in the final analysis, will have to be borne by the black actors and actresses who at that time were jubilantly approaching the light of day after languishing so long in the shadows. My understanding of the film business told me that the producers who were making black exploitation films were not interested in much beyond the buck; past the point where that buck stopped, there wasn't a genuine interest in the black audience as such. A healthy interest in the black community would have required a noticeable shifting of emphasis in the content and intent of such films, yet I noticed a dangerous disregard of the hopes and aspirations of black people. I reluctantly arrived at the conclusion that the black exploitation filmmakers, seeing the overwhelming response to the revenge syndrome, elected to use that one-dimensional theme as the dramatic frame for almost all the films they would make for black consumption. They seemed to feel that as long as Fred, Jim, and Richard went on beating up and subduing white crooks, that would continue to serve as the strongest ingredient in a successful film; if in addition, the women were beautiful, sexy, good with a gun, and terrific in bed, they had an unbeatable "money in the bank" combination that black people would never weary of. Not one among these producers, to my knowledge, cared to think otherwise. After all, one of the principal rules of the Hollywood game is to never, never monkey with success.

Had they taken time to look beneath the surface, they might have discovered that the appetite they were banking on would be satiated quicker than their greed, that the macho street dudes beating up on redneck racists and gangster crooks in the "get whitey" formula would be applauded, hailed, enjoyed—but just for a short time. Because that was not what black people were all about. The pleasure they derived from seeing their actors function on that level was only a momentary satisfaction. They knew their actors had a bigger responsibility than that and anticipated them going on to represent the community on levels more important to its existence. They saw the other thing as a nice introduction, a wonderful way for their actors to open up their involvement in film—but not as something to go on repeating forever. As producers of exploitation films continued to invest money in the same kinds of material, the black audience continued to patronize their fare; but gradually they began to develop the same kind of dissatisfaction with those films as they had felt toward some of my own films. Which is to say that neither the exploitation films nor my films were sufficiently about them, sufficiently representative of what in fact they were. Hollywood was still wide of the mark in relation to their dreams, their aspirations, their frustrations, the things they lived with every day. Over the years, as disappointment went on thinning the enthusiasm of black audiences, the exploitation film began to show unmistakable signs of wear at the box office, a condition that prompted more than a few producers to prepare jumping ship, with remarks like, "Well, the black audiences are no longer interested in seeing black films," or "Hey, there's no money to be made in the black community anymore—they're not coming out to see movies that have been tailor-made for them." And at the same time, those black actors who were aware of the state of things were themselves making a mistake. They weren't coming to grips with the fact that the man—the white producer—wasn't really servicing the needs of the community they represented. There were those among them with the requisite talent who should have moved quickly to learn the tools of the producer's trade, so that they could begin to produce their own films that would be closer to the needs of the people of their constituency.

Now let me hasten to add that anyone with even a layman's knowledge of the business would recognize that for black actors to become producers was easier said than done. Blacks functioning as producers, entrepreneurs, and packagers in the American film industry? Admittedly a very long shot, with crushing odds against the outcome. But when the stark alternative is just standing around helplessly while a meaningful start fritters away to nothing, then the stakes involved warrant—no, demand—that one hell of an effort be made toward moving the mountain.

Most of the exploitation movies were made by whites far more interested in making money than in any other consideration. So when the money was no longer to be made with the kind of films they had been producing, it was easy for them to drop everything and go across the street to start making pictures servicing the general American community with white films, leaving a cadre of black film actors and personalities with no place to go—no films to work in. Now I must say that it came quicker than anyone expected it would. The expectation on the part of most of my colleagues was that the trend would last at least five or ten years, and that out of it would eventually grow the kind of black filmmakers who could take things to the next level. Well, it didn't last that long, and when it disappeared, there disappeared with it the fledgling job opportunities it had brought only a few short years ago. And in the meantime, the black audience didn't go away. They were still there—wiser, sharper, more articulate in announcing their needs, and more ready than ever to be lovingly ruthless with the actors and actresses who represented them whenever those actors and actresses failed to come up with things that were germane to their lives. They expressed that ruthlessness simply by tempering their support of such films. But they were still there, and they were still in need.

As the black exploitation filmmakers began dropping out, the black performing personalities were left without an "initiator," a head, a source capable of "putting a package together." With that being the case, all those displaced performers were reduced to sitting at home and waiting for the phone to ring, or for a heaven-sent new producer to come along and say, "Hey, let's make such and such a picture for that audience and let's use such and such an actor and such and such an actress." Those performers who didn't anticipate these conditions are to be excused, naturally. But those whose eyes were on the ball, who had the necessary requirements for learning the skills of "putting the package together"—raising the money, producing the picture, and ultimately walking away with the profits—they should be held responsible in part for missing what might have proved to be a pivotal opportunity. After all, isn't it likely that things would be appreciably better today if we had five or six functioning black producers among our hundreds of unemployed performers?

As the exploitation films declined, I felt that the black audience was owed a new set of quality actors. Mind you, I was not eager to die gracefully away, but dying away I certainly could have endured if it had meant seeing a new set of artists come along. I only hoped that they would be better than my crop—that their skills be sharper, and that *their* dedication, aided by youth and determination, would bring about a new period of film activity for black audiences and artists alike. Well, that may yet be, but in the meantime we are in a state of limbo. I'm surviving because I'm not waiting by my telephone for someone to call me. There are fewer and fewer people out there who are going to call me, and most of my black colleagues are also not going to receive many calls. The number of jobs available to us all is woefully small.

But hold—let's pause right here and put things in their proper perspective before what I'm suggesting gives a wrong impression and creates unnecessary mischief. From the time I started in this business until now an appreciable number of jobs have been available to black actors and actresses. The very fact that there exist Fred Williamson, Jim Brown, Calvin Lockhart, Cicely Tyson, Paul Winfield, James Earl Jones, Richard Pryor, Richard Roundtree, Bill Cosby, Denise Nicholas, John Amos, Isabell Sanford, O. J. Simpson, Terry Carter, Diana Ross, and many others speaks eloquently to an increasing involvement over the years. The very number of us who are now working from time to time proves that there has been increased opportunity. But with that increased opportunity came a proliferation of new actors. Black people in Florida, Mississippi, Kansas, Pennsylvania—from hundreds of towns in dozens of states—saw Jim Brown, Poitier, Pryor, Roundtree, and James Earl Jones working, and said to themselves: It looks as if there's an opportunity for me in the film business now. I can do it at least as well as those guys, so why don't I take a shot? That army of hopefuls, unaware that they'd been victimized by their own fantasies, set out after their dreams on one-way tickets to that gold mine of a suburb near the City of Angels called Hollywood; or for those who wanted to hear the sound of applause ringing in their ears, the Big Apple and Broadway. The resulting influx of us over the years quadrupled the number of black actors on each coast, and if we now compare our overall number to the availability of jobs, we have to conclude that the present situation is somewhat bleak. Back in the days when I first stepped on a stage we had about a hundred black actors stubbornly braving the odds in the desperate scramble for whatever few jobs were available in any given season. Now that fifty of us are likely to be working, there are thousands of black actors. The proportion is a little crazy.

Fortunately for me, I was not at the mercy of the marketplace, having formed my own production company, with guaranteed financing as a result of my deals with First Artists and Columbia. This allowed me to create my own employment, whereas in the absence of those agreements I might have found myself twiddling my thumbs through most of the last seven years. Which is not to say that I didn't receive offers during that period, but the eight or ten scripts that did come my way were without exception the kind of material I preferred not to work with. Such scripts came from producers who felt that having a certain actor might enhance their project, giving it a kind of legitimacy—a legitimacy that I must say few of them deserved. Never once did they consider that the actor himself might have a need to be enhanced by whatever material he associated with. Okay, how does one get to develop one's own company, and through it make one's own films? Well, if you've read this book from the beginning you know by now that first of all you have to be damn lucky. Foresight is not necessarily the chief factor, while the stroke of good fortune that positions you in the right place at the right time is essential. Of course it helps a lot if you're someone who hates sitting around waiting for your phone to ring. . . .

An excellent example of luck at work can be seen around my circumstances after *A Warm December*, the first picture I made for the First Artists Corporation. When it was clear that the picture would make no money I went to the company and said, "For my next picture I'm going to need approximately two million dollars." They had no alternative but to give me the money, because of our contractual agreement. Needless to say, the three men at the management helm of the company tried to talk me out of it; they were afraid that after *A Warm December* didn't do so well, maybe the second one would also go down the drain. They said to me, "Why do you want to make this new picture? This *Uptown Saturday Night?* We frankly don't think it stands a chance." I said, "Because." They said, "But why?" "I just want to make it. I think it's going to be successful." "Look, we're sorry to have to say this, but we disagree with you." "Well, I'm sorry that you're sorry, but I want to make this picture." They spent hours trying to talk me out of it.

Somewhere late in the second hour of this discussion, as I realized how they would relish any tiny legal loophole that would allow them to write me off, I suddenly knew I was at the crossroads. I knew that with *Buck and the Preacher* struggling to break even and *A Warm December* making no money, if I didn't make that new picture —if I didn't continue to generate my own employment— I could segue into oblivion in a couple of years. And that would be the end of a career. Recognizing that my survival as a movie actor rested exclusively on my own initiative, I said to the First Artists people, "Look, whether you like it or not, my contract calls for you to give me up to three million dollars to make a movie. I intend to do this picture, so let's not create a problem for each other." I had them on paper and they knew it. That document, free of tiny loopholes, could be traced back over the years to the day when my "good fortune" thrust me at the right time (the most successful point of my career) to the right place (in the commissary at Universal Studios) where I received the invitation to join as a full partner in the formation of the First Artists Corporation.

The management people wished me well after okaying the money, and I went off and made my picture. When it was done I invited them to come and see it. They in turn invited the Warner Brothers people who were our distributors. Ten minutes into the picture the head of the First Artists Corporation at that time, one of the fellows who had put it all together, fell asleep. He was sitting there in the first row—my picture had been running barely ten minutes, and it was nine o'clock in the morning—and he started snoring. But I was cool, even though he slept through the whole picture. At the end of the screening the lights went up and an awkward silence prevailed for a while because nobody knew what to say. They didn't know whether they liked it or didn't like it— maybe because it was about black people and, moreover, about the kind of black people they hadn't seen much of. To his credit, a man named Ted Ashley (the head honcho at Warner Brothers), looked at me and just asked professionally, "What are your plans for the picture in terms of underscoring and source music?" I gave him an outline of what the music would be, and touched on other post-production work that had to be done. After a short pause, he said, "Well, I don't understand all of it—I'm not as familiar as I'd like to be with the milieu—but I wish you luck with it and thanks for letting us see it."

Now there is a man I have subsequently grown to respect highly: a straightforward, to-the-point guy. The rest of the crew didn't say a fucking word. Ted Ashley was the only one to make a comment, and he was honest enough to say what he meant and considerate enough to wish me luck. After that they left, but about a minute after they'd cleared the room, Leo Greenfield, then a wheel in the Warner Brothers distribution department, came back in, looked me straight in the eye, and said, "I'll tell you what I think about your picture. It's going to

343

be a hit. It will do at least nine or ten million dollars. That's what your picture is going to do. With the exception of Ashley those guys are too fucking scared to pass a comment, because they don't know . . ." He then walked out of the screening room.

Well, he was dead right. And that should give the black filmmaker an indication of what he's up against. When he starts making films for the black community, he'll have to go to the white banks or white distribution companies or white studios to get his financing, and all of them are principally interested in making money—that's what they're in business for. Of course they want to do it with a certain kind of distinction, and of course they would like to reap a certain kind of prestige, but the bottom line is money. If they don't understand where you're comin' from artistically or don't see obvious signs of commercial vitality in your material, it will be damn near impossible to get money from those areas. And since in most cases the black filmmaker and his constituency remain unfamiliar, even discordant, oddities, he must husband his strength and deepen his resolve to be ready and prepared for that day when a stroke of "good fortune" comes his way. Until then he should remember that learning the rules will crack a nut and when a nut has been cracked you have beaten the system.

The success of *Uptown Saturday Night* told me that black people wanted to laugh at themselves and have fun. They were weary of being represented on the local screen by pimps, hustlers, prostitutes, private detectives, violence, macho men, and dirty words. They wanted to have good, clean, family-type fun, and my recognition of that hunger committed me to a try at fulfilling the need. To that end, Richard Wesley, the screenwriter of *Uptown Saturday Night,* Mel Tucker, our producer, and I fashioned a movie from bits of miscellaneous materials my wandering mind had accumulated over time and tucked away in its underbelly. We called the film *Let's Do It Again.* It starred Bill Cosby, myself, Denise Nicholas, John Amos, Lee Chamberlin, Calvin Lockhart, and Jimmie Walker. The First Artists Corporation under new management (Philip Feldman) was superhelpful—gone was the negative second-guessing of nervous administrators. I was earning my keep. When *Let's Do It Again* turned out be be twice as successful as *Uptown Saturday*

Night, it created in me a deeper faith in my own judgment of what an audience would like to see. (Hmmmmmm, had I just taken the first step toward that fatal trap that beckons irresistibly to successful, cocky, overconfident directors?) The picture also had an appreciable crossover success: a substantial number of white people in the United States and elsewhere went to see it, which resulted in its being relieved from a financial dependency on the black community alone. Whereas a well-supported picture in the black community will gross seven or eight million, we did fifteen with *Let's Do It Again.* Which proves that it's possible to attract the attention of the general audience to a film about blacks—difficult, yes; impossible, no.

For an American motion picture that costs under eight million dollars to be successful in this country and the world, it has to do close to three times its negative cost to break even, and so a three-million-dollar movie has to have a nine-million-dollar return in order to get out of the red. Now a nine-million return from a constituency of 220 million Americans and hundreds of millions in Europe and other parts of the world is not out of the ordinary. But if you are a black filmmaker who has made a black-oriented three-million-dollar film, the percentages change. With black people making up 10 or 11 percent of the United States population, we are speaking of a constituency of approximately 25 million people. Twenty-five million people are not as useful a base for a film's domestic success as 220 million; therefore, the black filmmaker with his three-million-dollar movie has to hope for crossover help from beyond the racial fence if he is to reach the break-even point. And let me tell you from personal experience, that can be one hell of a stretch.

Understandably then, in the context of the business as I understand it, the black filmmaker is inescapably dependent to some extent on the white audience if he is to reach his nine-million break-even point with an average film, and that is a difficulty, because usually the black film doesn't appeal to the white audience. White people in America and Canada will go to see a black film if it is about an aspect of life that interests them and if it is populated by black performers who command their attention. But if the film is only about blacks, with no strong Caucasian context, white people are not going to support it. That's the way it is, and it's not altgogether unnatural, is it? And I don't believe that this is a matter of racial prejudice, certainly not to any significant degree. If most of the black audience doesn't go to see most white films, it's because they know that they're not going to find representation in those films. In Los Angeles and New York there are Spanish-language films. Such films depend almost exclusively on people from the Spanish culture for their support. And the majority of people in America don't go to see French films; they don't go to see English films; they don't go to see Australian films; they don't go to see Indian films. People go to films more often than not looking for reflections of their own lives, for something familiar. And that means that in the U.S. a white filmmaker has a natural audience of some 200 million people; we've only got 25 million or so. And on top of this, the inflationary spiraling of the costs of filmmaking has an adverse effect on everyone's future efforts. In the early seventies, for instance, we made *Buck and the Preacher* at a cost of two million dollars. It could cost almost twice that to make the picture today. And that kind of cost increase can be fatal, especially to the black filmmaker with his smaller natural audience. Therefore, it is imperative that he find a way to beat the increase in costs, and to be able to do that, the filmmaker must, first, obtain the concurrence of the unions and, second, have the ingenuity to create professional, quality shows for unbelievably low prices. What the white filmmaker will do with three million dolars, the third-world filmmaker will have to accomplish with a hell of a lot less. That will be his only chance of staying in this business—if he ever makes it in.

Adding the knowledge I had accumulated in my many years as an actor to the experience gained from directing four movies gave me credentials enough to be considered a professional at putting a film together and getting it into the theaters. But for the black filmmaker, acquiring credentials is not a simple matter, and getting films into the theaters is a very, very complex procedure. Aspiring filmmakers, black or white, should be aware that the casualty rate is numbingly high, and at the outset of their journey—before commitments are made or that first step taken—they should be warned that to be a born survivor is essential for the path they have chosen.

So let us ask the question bluntly: What are the real no-bullshit chances of a nonwhite in a risky, high-stake, cutthroat game such as this? The answer is: lean. At best. But so what? Those who would be frightened away by that assessment will never take the first step of the journey anyway, after recognizing that only survivors need apply.

So for those who are here because they have to be, let me repeat—your chances are lean. But your dream is still possible. There are ways. It calls for expertise in cutting costs, it calls for a detailed understanding of what unions will permit and what they will not permit, it calls for an in-depth knowledge of the marketplace, it calls for knowing what you should realistically expect by way of return on your investment, and it requires you to know if and when to lay some of your upfront costs on the gross of the films, allowing you to put as much of those precious budget dollars on the screen as possible. Example: If the actor you want comes with a $50,000 price tag that's too much of a strain on a fragile budget, then pay him out of the gross receipts after the film has been released. If you need five such actors and you don't have the $250,000, pay them out of the distributor's gross rentals. If those actors agree (and many of them will), you'll have added some box office luster without any additional financial risk. Remember, the audience couldn't care less how much your film did or didn't cost.

Speaking of audiences, most black filmmakers dream longingly of that vast potential audience in Africa, South America, and the Caribbean who will one day stand three abreast and a mile deep in queues waiting to see their films. Unfortunately, most of those hundreds of millions of people live in economies where they pay as little as twenty or thirty American cents for admission to an as yet limited number of movie houses. In time, as the standard of living increases, there will be more of a return on films in those areas, but for the immediate future the black filmmaker's number-one asset is going to be the black community in the United States, and he must therefore pay particular attention to their needs and interests. He must also remember his dos and don'ts. Through union requirements, habits, and other rituals that have no relation to artistic necessity, Hollywood has grown accustomed to sending a filmmaker to downtown

Los Angeles or downtown anywhere with forty-five crew members, eighteen pieces of vehicular equipment, and an attending group of supporting management workers who work for half a day and get two minutes of film at a cost of fourteen thousand dollars or even more. A minority filmmaker, working on a thin margin, must find a way to go downtown—or anywhere else—with a single cameraman and two assistants, two sound people, his actors, and his imagination. With those ingredients, if he knows his game, he can return with the same amount and quality of film as the other guy, because any camera picks up only what is exposed in front of it—it will not pick up the forty-five crew members. If you need to create a daytime effect, don't shoot until the sun is shining; then hop in your car with the six or eight necessary people, photograph your sequence, and come away from a half day's shooting with a total cost of no more than about a thousand dollars. If a beautiful home is required as a setting, find a family with a lovely house and ask to rent it for the days or weeks necessary to your schedule. If no such family can be found, then find an empty house and dress it with rented furniture. It may cost you eight thousand dollars a month, but to build such a set on the stage of a Hollywood studio could cost up to a hundred thousand dollars. These are exaggerated examples of the direction most young black filmmakers are going to have to go if they're interested in surviving in this very precarious ocean called Hollywood. Yes, it's going to be difficult. But it can and must be done, because the white filmmaker is not going to make more than an occasional black-oriented film, especially since it's been proven that there aren't easy dollars sitting around in the black community waiting for him to go after. In fact, his reluctance is likely to harden.

We're going to have to make most of our own films. I think we should no longer expect the white filmmaker to be the champion of our dreams. The only kind of help we should ask for is perhaps a bending of the rules whenever possible as far as financing is concerned. But we should be our own prime movers. We have to be. Otherwise the guy who is going to do it for us is going to do it from his point of view. It's going to be his film. It's going to be his comment. And if past experience is any teacher, we can't be looking to him for a reflection of ourselves.

Now before moving on, let me alert the minority film-maker to what I see as a golden opportunity up ahead, and implore him to be ready to take full advantage of it. Stunning new technology is going to make a radical impact on the ways Americans receive their entertainment; in a few short years this new technology will make it possible for the American family to have entertainment and cultural activities of its choice delivered into its home via tapes, disks, cables, satellite scramblers, and numerous other as yet unannounced systems. This new technology is even now being referred to as the basic "hardware" in the new American/European/Japanese electronics industry; and this revolutionary "hardware" will give rise to a need for a great variety of unlimited "software"—entertainments, cultural activities, sports events, educational material, and so on. It has been my experience that the black community has a very strong desire to see itself reflected in ways more in tune with its indigenous culture. Our black community in America represents a billion-dollar consumer market, and "software" producers, unlike many suburban theater owners who are afraid to book black-oriented movies out of fear that too many black patrons might scare off their white clientele, will be rushing to service the taste of so formidable a dream of a market. So, black filmmakers, potential creators and producers of "software," be ready, stay alert. Don't let "the man" beat you on your own home ground. If you do, the chances are you'll find yourselves locked out, again.

26 Marriage

IN 1976, with Harry Belafonte as best man and Julie Belafonte as bridesmaid, Joanna and I got married at our home in Beverly Hills. Shortly before noon on that sunny January 23, we became husband and wife, with loads of friends and family present to share that wonderful moment. During the ceremony my mind kept flashing back to 1969—to Sammy Davis, Jr., Quincy Jones, and a wonderful adventure on the high seas around the Bahama islands, out of which, it could be said, the midday activity of January 23, 1976, very likely had its genesis.

In 1969 I invited Sammy Davis, Jr., to come down to the Bahamas for a vacation. Throughout our friendship of many years, I had always thought that Sam worked too hard and too much. From my observation, he was heading for a breakdown of some kind, or at least some serious stress-related problems. He loved his work a lot, and depended on it for more than just artistic expression or creative satisfaction; often he seemed to be depending on it for a sense of himself—almost as if without his work he didn't exist. And that, I thought, was dangerous. So as a concerned friend I decided I should speak to him about those matters, and in so doing I found myself inviting him to come way to the Caribbean for a vacation. To my delight he accepted. I then said to him, "However, you cannot come unless you leave your entourage behind—just you and a lady." "What are you trying to say, P?" "I'm saying you'll have to manage without your tape recorders, without your radio, without your telephone, and without your movies. You are going to have to deal with Sammy on a very personal and primitive level." Again to my delight he replied, "Hey, man, I'm ready for that—I'll be there, my brother. You just have some greens and hocks ready when I arrive."

Later, Joanna said to me, "Why don't we invite Ula and Quincy?" Quincy Jones and his wife, Ula, were also very good friends—in fact Ula and Joanna had worked together as models in Paris—and they were enthusiastic about coming. Our plan as we outlined it to our guests called for us to cruise the islands of the Bahamas for ten days on a private yacht. Immediately after my stint as a presenter on that year's Academy Awards show, I rushed to the L.A. airport with Joanna and the Joneses, and we all took a redeye special to New York where we rendezvoused the next morning with Sammy, his beautiful young actress friend, and two last-minute additions to the group, Terry McNeeley and his lady, Dolores.

Arriving in Nassau, Terry and I went directly to the docks to reconfirm our reservations for the use of a boat named *The Conky Joe*. Built for comfort and kept in excellent shape, that 60-foot dream of a yacht had three cabins, a lounge, two bathrooms, and an enormous deck area for dining, dancing, sunning, or whatever, but she was one cabin short of accommodating our group. Upon deciding that four couples wouldn't fit into three cabins very comfortably, I thought it best to order an additional boat—the same size, the same make, in effect a sister to *The Conky Joe*. When the others came down to the marina later that afternoon, they oohed and ahhed at the sight of *The Conky Joe* and became as excited as kids at Christmas when we told them that boat number two was steaming in our direction from Miami that very minute.

Everybody, that is, except Sammy's date, who seemed a bit subdued. Or is preoccupied a better word? During odd moments when she would brighten, we could see that she genuinely wanted to be with us; then without warning she would grow pensive, slip back into a haze, and stop focusing on what the group was about. Everyone noticed it, but since we didn't understand the situation, no one made any comment—we just hoped that whatever it was would work itself out so that we all could have a nice, pleasant, productive vacation. But forty-eight hours later, just as we were about to take off, she informed Sammy with many apologies that she wasn't going to go. The suggestion was that she was heading back to a longtime relationship with someone else about whom she was having an internal tug of war. Crestfallen, Mr. Davis took it as well as he could and resolved to go on without her. Sammy being Sammy, he worked feverishly to impress us that he was fine, but we knew it was bullshit and suffered with him silently. Later, as the group sat around exploring the pro and con possibilities of a ten-day trip with Sammy being the odd man out, Joanna said to Sam, "Why don't you call Altovise?" (Altovise Gore, the lead dancer on the Sammy Davis show, had an enormous affection for Sammy, and Joanna knew she had high hopes of being his number one dancer in more ways than one.) The group thought it was a great idea and Sammy agreed. He called his office in New York and told them to find Altovise and invite her to join him for our cruise. By the end of the day, Sammy's office hadn't located her, so we extended our departure time to the following morning and spent the evening close to the phone. The next morning after breakfast, with no word of Altovise, we sailed out of Nassau harbor with Sammy leaving instructions at the airport for a private seaplane to stand by to fly her out to the boat! Late in the afternoon as we cruised through the breathtaking Exuma Keys, we got a call on the ship's phone saying that Altovise had arrived at Nassau airport and been placed on a seaplane heading toward us. About an hour later a seaplane buzzed our two boats and landed in the middle of the ocean. In the middle of the ocean—are you listening to me? When Altovise Gore stepped out of that tiny seaplane into the little dinghy we sent to pick her up, passengers and crew from both boats broke into applause. First of all, the girls were happy that Altovise, no stranger to any of them, had joined us. Quincy, Terry, and I were happy that Sammy had company. But listen to me when I tell you that Sammy Davis, Jr., was the happiest person in the fleet. Altovise Gore was a special kind of special. She made the difference, and it showed on Sammy's face. The mind-blowing image of two yachts in the ocean, the spectacular arrival of a seaplane out of which steps a black woman to enthusiastic applause *from* the world's greatest entertainer, all added up to a clear signal that a great adventure had gotten under way.

To spend the night we pulled into the protected harbor of a relatively uninhabited island called Norman's Key. The next morning the men decided to go fishing. But in order to go fishing we had to get bait, and in order to get bait we had to take a dinghy close to the shore and dive for a shellfish called conk, which gets smashed out of its shell and its meat pounded into a soft fleshy bait that Bahamian fishermen consider ideal. We kissed the girls goodby and set out to scrounge a dozen conks as a prelude to some serious deepwater fishing. While Captain Brownie and I were wading around in five feet of water looking for conk, Quincy Jones, who cannot swim, was sitting in the dinghy. Terry McNeeley, who cannot swim, was also sitting in the dinghy. Sammy Davis, Jr., bless his courageous soul, was wading in water up to his neck, right alongside Captain Brownie and me, looking for conk. But he too cannot swim. Every now and then one of us would spot a conk lying there quietly on the bottom, and Captain Brownie or I would dive under for it. As we walked along, the floor of the sea became porous and a little rocky. Sammy, wading along enthusiastically, would cast an occasional eye of disdain at the non-swimming impotents sitting helplessly in the dinghy—Sammy who in his swimming trunks looks like a nine-year-old kid with spindly legs and a distended stomach. "Hey, Captain, there's another one," he'd shout, and Captain Brownie would dive down for the conk.

Suddenly, as the three of us are walking along, Sammy Davis disappears. We look around and there's no Sammy, only some bubbles coming up. A moment later Sammy comes popping to the surface, trying to wipe the water out of his eyes, and then he is on his way down again when Captain Brownie grabs him. Sammy says, "Captain Brownie—Captain Brownie—I, I, I stepped in that hole—I stepped in that hole or something—I can't swim, you know—I can't swim, you know???" Captain Brownie says, "I got you, Mr. Davis—I've got you—I've got you." So we climb back into the boat, Captain Brownie, Sammy, and me. We didn't want to take any more chances. I mean, that's a valuable piece of property that slipped out of sight there. You can imagine the headlines: "Sammy Davis, Jr., disappears in a hole—in five feet of water!" I thought: Jesus, how will I explain that to the Los Angeles *Times?* We sat Sammy in the boat, gave up on the conks, and just went fishing.

The next day we pull up anchor and head for Georgetown, the capital of the Exumas four hours to the east. After we explore the town—three or four small hotels, a couple of guesthouses, a supermarket, and a few .bars —the girls decide to nap while we elect to have another go at fishing. This time, Captain Brownie buys our conk bait from a local fishing boat. Nonswimmer Terry McNeeley is now gun-shy. He is not about to go out in that little dinghy boat anymore, and he announces without the least shame that he intends to stay aboard one of the big boats with the girls. But when I come up on deck, there's Sammy ready in his swimming trunks—wearing Gucci slippers and carrying a Gucci bag. And in that Gucci bag he has his tape recorder, he has his cigarettes, his gold lighter, and whatever else Sammy carries in his Gucci bag. Sammy and Quincy and I climb into the dinghy with Captain Brownie and head toward the ocean to bottom-fish. After circling for about ten minutes, we find the reef the Captain's looking for, but before dropping his anchor he places a small glass-bottom bucket into the water, then looks through it to see what kind of fishlife is going on around down there. Each of us takes a look through the bucket, and the water's teeming, and I mean *teeming*—everywhere we look, nothing but fish. With rising anticipation we bait our hooks and throw our lines out. Mine doesn't get ten feet under the surface before zap! I've hooked one. Then Captain Brownie gets some action, a few moments later Quincy hooks into one, then right away Sammy connects. For Sammy and Quincy this is the first time in their lives they've had this experience, and they're going absolutely crazy. Quincy is saying, "Oh, God damn you, I've got you now, you son of a bitch." He's laying street talk on this fish in the water that's struggling for its life. "Okay, you dirty dog, come on up here. Q's got you now, you mother." Well, as soon as Quincy big fisherman Jones gets his fish in the boat he doesn't know what to do with it. He will not touch the fish. I have to put down my line or Captain Brownie has to, just to remove Quincy's fish from the hook.

Now Sammy, hooking into a fair-sized one, decides he's going to outdo Quincy in talking up to a fish. "All right, you dirty dog, I've got your tail now—you grabber, I knew I was going to get you, I just knew it—you come messing around with my bait, this is Sammy Davis, Jr., you fool! Didn't they tell you down there that this is Sammy?" Finally, he gets the fish out of the water and into the boat—a nice three-and-a-half-pounder, and it's jumping around on the line. And suddenly Sammy loses his gusto—looking at the fish *he* doesn't know what to do with it. He says, "Captain Brownie—Captain Brownie! Will you get this thing off my line?" In the meantime, Quincy has rebaited his hook and he's back in the water with his line. In no time flat, something hits that's bigger than a three-pounder—a Margaret fish or a small gruber—something about six or seven pounds. Quincy fisherman Jones screams, "Oh, my God, I've got a whale—I've got me a whale!" and he opens up reading the riot act to the fish, challenging it to try and get away. "Ahh, you greedy son of a bitch, you just found my line was down there and you just figured old Q don't know what he's doing out here—ain't that right? Well, let me see how you gonna get off that hook! Come on in here, you dirty rat!"

At which point he's having so much fun that his foot slips on some of the shellfish slime on the floor of the dinghy and Quincy fisherman Jones falls out of the boat.

Now you have got to get the picture. Quincy cannot swim, and Quincy has been talking nonstop about the dangers of sharks in those waters, because we've passed a lot of sharks just zipping around. Well, Q is now falling out of the boat, and half-way out of the boat, I can tell across Quincy's mind runs all the things we've been saying about those sharks—how vicious they are, how dangerous it would be to get into the water with one of those merciless bastards. And as the image of the sharks begins to cross Quincy's mind, something utterly, utterly miraculous happens. To this day, I think it's an impossibility, but I was there and I saw it. Quincy Jones hits the water and bounces back into the boat. Q hits the water—he's three feet from the boat when he lands in it —he hits it and bounces right back into the boat. So don't tell me that fear doesn't motivate people; fear will move many mountains, my brother. And when he gets back into the boat, Quincy Jones, a man of dark-brown complexion, is damn near as white as a sheet.

While Captain Brownie and I are trying to console Quincy, Sammy is finding the whole incident absolutely hilarious. He's beating his feet on the bottom of the boat, clapping his hands, laughing—and while he's laughing and pointing at Q, Sammy Davis, Jr., also slips on the slime covering the floor of the dinghy. But Sammy doesn't fall out of the boat. Sammy's Gucci bag falls out of the boat. And as the bag falls out of the boat, Sammy gets stone quiet. And as the Gucci bag begins to sink, all Sammy can find to say is, "Oh, Lord, my Gucci's gone—my Gucci's gone!" At that point it's my impression that Sammy and Quincy have had enough fishing for one day, so by mutual consent, we pull up anchor and head back to the big boat. There we find Terry fishing from the bow, using salami for bait. I say, "McNeeley, what are you doing?" He says, "Well, *I* eat it. I don't know why *they* don't eat it." Oh, yes—yes, indeed!

After a few days in Georgetown we head for Cat Island, the place where I spent my early years. (With the exception of a two-hour visit accompanying Lynden Pindling on a whirlwind election tour, this was my first trip back since the age of ten and a half.) A few hours out of Georgetown, across the tongue of the ocean, Cat Island first appears as a faint uneven interruption on the horizon, much as Nassau first appeared to me thirty years before, while traveling with my mother in the opposite direction. My subconscious, abnormally burdened by years of demanding service as an emotional and psychological burying ground, gives way. Random thoughts flying about like sparks touch on certain truths, giving them momentary illumination. In one of them, I see a ten-year-old boy inside a forty-one-year-old man, heading home for a reunion with people, places, and things he has kept faithfully alive in his daydreams over great gaps of time and space. In another of those truths, the forty-one-year-old man can be seen hoping, against his better judgment, that this island world has not changed —because he fears having to share the disappointment of the youngster within. With my center divided between man and boy, I grow fidgety from conflicting expectations and decide on a nap as the best way to handle the rampaging anxieties threatening to envelop me.

Finally we arrive at the settlement of Arthur's Town on Cat Island. I come up on deck and step ashore into the past. Immediately I head for the unpaved ocean-front road that leads to where I used to live. I move along that road, gawking at the surroundings, trying to get my bearings. Everything seems vaguely familiar, yet in another sense nothing seems familiar at all. Much here is not really as it has been etched all these years in my memory. Skeletons of houses that have long ago fallen into ruin stand before my eyes in stark contrast to the reflections in my memory, in which they still stand sturdy and alive, life humming all around. The ten-year-old inside me is becoming disturbed by a growing awareness that the world he has frozen into place through thirty years has in fact not been preserved at all, but ravaged severely by weather, gravity, and time itself. With confusion fermenting in the mind of the youngster within, we continue walking, searching for what used to be his family's home. Abruptly we come upon a graveyard and a church, both once part of a single complex entirely enclosed by a stone wall. The wall is still there, but now it's no higher than the thigh of the man the little boy has grown to be. I know exactly how things ought to look— after all I've had solid proof for thirty years that when I last walked past that wall, it was only by leaping into the air that I was able to grab a quick glance over it. Standing there a grown man, 6 feet 2¾ inches tall, I know it is the same place. Yet the youngster within me is wondering if it really can be. The church is a small building, and the graveyard has fifty or sixty stones in it. The youngster within? Well, he's not at all sure, not at all.

Joanna and our friends, not knowing the history behind any of the relics their eyes are gazing on, nevertheless sense the battle of two worlds fiercely contending inside me and remain respectfully silent while patiently walking behind me in a cluster, like some kind of backup force. I move down that ocean-front road closer to what used to be, until at last we come upon the place where I had once lived with my mother, my father, my brothers and sisters. I don't recognize it. The house is nearly all gone, except for a few feet of ragged wall still standing at two corners of the foundation. The kitchen, having been built from straw and palm leaves, has been obliterated. The tomato shed where Evelyn and Reggie packed their tomatoes is gone; again, just the foundation is left. I walk up to the remains and look through windows that are no longer there. Turning away from the house, I look for the stone oven where Evelyn used to bake her bread. No trace of it remains—the spot has been commandeered by weeds. But for a moment, standing there—for a flashing second—I think I can still smell the bread. I also hear sounds of chickens squawking, laughter from the house, a mischievous voice saying something; my sister Teddy, maybe. From what's left of our house I walk out to the waterfront and look down to the spot where they used to throw me in, to teach me how to swim. From the waterfront I go searching for the old house where I tried to seduce Lurlene. Not a trace remains—that spot, rich in history, has been cleared to make way for a number of little bright-colored houses, one with a Vespa scooter parked in front. From there we continue on to the graveyard where my grandparents on my mother's side are buried. I can't find their stones, but, strangely, their faces come very clearly to my mind—clearer than at any other time since I was a kid. Heading west from the graveyard, we stop for one last look at what had been my family home, and standing in the center of the ruins, just about at the spot where I used to sleep when the house was alive, I try to imagine how much headroom was under that house when I tried to seduce the chicken. Judging from the scale of the foundation around me, it must have been very shallow under there, so I must have been a smaller than average nine-year-old. Near the schoolyard and the playground I go into people's homes and ask if they remember

357

my family. Some do. A few even remember me. They don't know I'm an actor because they've never seen a movie. Some of them want to know where I'm living now. I tell them California. They've never heard of it—and what do I do in that place? I just tell them I work there, and that sometimes my work takes me to various places. When a few insist on knowing the type of work I do, I never go beyond saying, "Well, I work at some entertainment business," and I'm sure that conjures up in their minds playing a guitar, something like that. I want to go on to the bat caves where my father used to get the excrement he used in his tomato fields, but there isn't enough time. It's over, and neither the forty-one-year-old man nor the ten-year-old within is going to be quite the same ever again.

FROM ARTHUR'S TOWN we set out for the northern tip of Eleuthera, a big island that's considered the most desirable part of the Bahamas by that part of the tourist population who prefer places less commercial than Nassau and Freeport. And after a few days there, our fabulous cruise is coming to an end, the whole group saddened by the thought that the real world is waiting to claim us the moment we step ashore at Nassau harbor. I must say about Sammy that this vacation is the most relaxed I've ever seen him. It's as if he's been wound down—he's moving differently, speaking differently, he's more fun to be with day by day, and in the end he's obviously pleased at having been able to turn "Sammy Davis, Jr.," off and just be a person.

He's not the only one affected by the trip, although the changes in the rest of us have more of a delayed bombshell effect, making big differences in the lives of each and every one of us. Quincy and Ula were soon to separate and eventually divorce. But Terry McNeeley, the bachelor of the century (in between his marriages), succumbed —Dolores caught him when his resistance was low, he said, but I think the boat trip solidified their relationship to a point where nearly all escape routes were sealed off and even Terry's legendary swiftness of foot failed him, allowing a patient, smiling Dolores to corner him, tag him, and remove him from circulation. Soon after Terry and Dolores got married, Quincy started dating the lovely young actress Sammy had originally brought along as his date—the girl who changed her mind and left before the trip got under way. Her name was Peggy Lipton. Quincy and Peggy developed a strong relationship, and soon *they* got married. Then Sammy began to realize how lucky he was to have a lovely woman like Altovise right there in his corner—someone who was really for him the person rather than him the superstar. He got wise, and he too got married.

There had been an understanding among Sammy, Terry, Quincy, and myself that there would be *no* marriages. Sammy had been married twice before, and that was going to be the end of marriages for Sammy Davis, Jr. Terry McNeeley had been married about three times before and he had absolutely no intentions *ever* of getting married again. Quincy Jones, with his two marriages, said to the rest of us at the time of his divorce from Ula, "If you hear of me getting married again, you come right over to where I am and beat the shit out of me because you'll know I've been hoodwinked or have lost my mind." I, too, was on record as having said, "Now listen here, let me tell you how I stand. I have been married once, and my history after that marriage is here for anybody to examine. The bottom line of which is: I ain't never, ever, going to get married no more. . . ."

Well, one day after my pals started falling—chickening out on me, leaving me with no comrades at the barricades —with my position weakened and my flank exposed, Joanna came home one day from a trip to the dentist with our two young daughters and told me of a dialogue she'd had with a new receptionist there. "May I help you?" "Yes, I have an appointment for Sydney and Anika Poitier." "Oh, yes—and who are you?" "Their mother." "And what is your name?" "Joanna Shimkus." At which point the receptionist looked up at her strangely.

By the time she had finished telling me this, I knew I was in trouble. That liberated woman with whom I had been living for eight happy, wonderful years stood before me now with sparks of fire flashing from her eyes. She said, "Now let me tell you something—you are going to have to do something about this, understand?" For the first time, my modern cosmopolitan woman was beginning to feel the pressure.

But I was ready also. I was ready. On January 23, 1976, we—the remaining survivors from a boat trip that held everybody's future in it—got married. And whether or not there was an unseen captain at the helm of our two ships is up to you to decide for yourself. As for me, whenever I confront the question, I simply count my blessings and give thanks to my ex-wife Juanita Marie Hardy Poitier (who now lives quietly and happily on her farm in upstate New York) for the many times she has reminded me that some things are best left resting on faith, in the hands of friendly heavenly forces.

27 The Young

I RECENTLY RECEIVED a call from a young woman named Nancy with whom I have an unusual family connection. Her mother Eva, now dead, was the wife of my brother Cedric, also now dead. Cedric and Eva were already the parents of four children when Eva left the Bahamas to work as a maid in the United States. In the years she was abroad she became pregnant again, by someone else, and after the birth of the baby, she returned to Nassau. There my brother Cedric, though conflicted in the extreme, took her and the child back into his home. He made a mighty try at standing tall, but with his long-established tendency toward self-doubt, he was not up to the battering his ego had to endure after her "unfortunate mistake" (for which he was willing to share part of the blame). So he fell deeper into a dependency on alcohol and then he died. His wife who survived him (but not for very long) was herself a study in contradictions. Having been born at a tough time in a world of struggle, to parents who weren't able to make much contribution to her growth and development, she arrived at her womanhood with very little education, completely unprepared for any true selfhood. Having crossed cultures as she did by leaving the Bahamas and going to work in Connecticut, she had no tools with which to work her way through the mass of conflicting values that naturally resulted from such a sudden transplanting. The new culture greeted her with impatience. No one in it seemed to have the time, or the willingness, to lend a guiding hand. Whatever she learned was by accident, by trial and error. How she survived and stayed in one piece as long as she did is a testament to the resilience of the human animal.

She was a domestic in Connecticut. I don't know that she was a particularly good domestic. I do know that she was neat, but neatness in an American upper-middle-class home is not enough. You have to be familiar with that kind of home. You have to know what it's like to deal with that kind of bedroom and how a dining room is kept and how a kitchen or bathroom is ordered. If you've never been exposed to that kind of kitchen, bathroom, or bedroom until you're thrust into the service of such a place, neatness is not enough.

And above and beyond all that, Eva was unaware (and probably remained so until she died) of the importance of appearances in American culture. She never knew that here in America people may have a self—a real self—and then also have an invented self that they put on when needed. My brother's wife didn't know that someone who cared not one whit about her might give her an enormous smile, a wonderful "Hello," and make what seemed to be genuine inquiries as to her health or her feelings. She never understood that often she was dealing with behavior that had no real relation to what the other person actually felt. It never dawned on her that in many cases the person who was smiling at her just wasn't interested in her, that what probably did matter to that person was that she ask for nothing beyond what she was receiving, and that she give her sixty dollars' worth of labor each week.

Eva Poitier was reeling from her employers' behavior: there was no one to explain to her that changing faces was a way of life in sophisticated societies. She came from a culture where it wasn't necessary, where you could be what you really were, where the essential human responses were still sufficient for the day-to-day dealings of human beings. Well, my poor sister-in-law, Nancy's dear mother Eva, wasn't sharp enough. She was victimized by the society and culture she was thrown into—fiercely victimized in many ways. In time, she lost her job. In that critical period when she needed to assess the signals around her, the smiles that didn't convey what she thought they conveyed, the relationships she thought she may have cultivated that in fact were not there at all, she found herself alone with her panic and confusion. Unable to deal with where she was, who she was, and how she was, she had to go back to where there was some security, so she returned to Nassau with the baby. If was difficult for her with my mother and sisters when she came back, but it was easier to brave the family's disapproval, which she understood, than to try to fashion some kind of coherence out of a relationship with a new, complex culture she didn't understand. She only knew for certain that she was no match for Darien, Connecticut.

Anyway, the baby named Nancy came to take her place among the many grandchildren of Evelyn and Reginald Poitier. After my brother's death, things became even more difficult for Eva: then quite dependent on alcohol, she was unable to keep any of several jobs. In time her deterioration was complete. But before she died, my favorite American niece had heard of Nancy. My niece was a hard-working, practical young woman who took advantage of her education to the tune of several degrees. She went into teaching and married a guy who was a teacher. They tried for many years to have children, but couldn't. She and her husband came to Nassau to see the two-year-old Nancy, fell in love with her, and asked Eva's permission to take her back with them to Florida for a little while. A "little while" turned into a few years, and my niece and her husband pleaded with Eva to consent to an adoption. In time, realizing it would be hopeless if the child had to depend on her for anything, Eva agreed, and Nancy found a permanent home with loving and able blood relations in Miami. Soon after that Eva died, leaving another girl and four boys.

Nancy had a far better shot at life than the others (although all but one of them are doing quite well today). Her happy adoptive parents gave her a decisive edge, not to mention a social and educational environment rich in opportunities. Therefore it was no surprise when sixteen years later she turned out to be a most attractive, intelligent, self-assured young woman who, God only knows why, wants to be an actress. (They are going to smother me in actors and actresses, my family. Whatever happened to aspirations toward doctoring and lawyering, I wonder?) Nancy called me recently and said, "Uncle Sidney, I'm having a problem. I can't decide what school I want to transfer to because here at Spellman College in Atlanta they don't have the kind of drama classes I need in order to develop as an actress."

I had heard the same pronouncements from two of my

own children—Pam and Sherri. And however much I dislike sounding like a high school adviser, I had to jump into my spiel. I said, "Nancy, what are you actually able to do at the age of nineteen? What can you do today if your parents don't send you any money to buy food, to pay your tuition—what can you do to ensure your survival?" "I don't know," she replied. "Can you do anything?" I asked. "Of course I can," she shot back. "So tell me— what?" There was silence. I began to prompt her, make suggestions. "Can you work in a Burger King? Can you work at McDonald's?" "Yes." "Can you work in a department store as a packer at Christmas time?" "Yes, I can." "Okay. Now do you know that those are the exact jobs that everybody who can't do anything else is looking for? Those are the jobs that attract nine hundred people for every possible opening, and those nine hundred people have one thing in common—they lack skills. So your competition is going to be extremely keen in those areas. Now, if you can't find that kind of job, what are you going to do? My point is, you are not self-sufficient, and you are not about to become self-sufficient by studying drama. Drama classes will not make you self-sufficient. How are you going to earn the money for the rent you pay for the roof over your head, the food you put in your refrigerator, the clothes you put on your back? When you're able to look the world in the eye and actually go out and do all that then, darling, you're self-sufficient. And until you're that self-sufficient, I don't want to hear talk about your being an actress. Two of my daughters are actresses and they're pounding the pavements in California and New York. I can only give them an occasional job because I don't make that many pictures anymore, and an occasional job doesn't suffice to characterize them as actresses. Neither one of those two young ladies is yet self-sufficient. With high hopes and crossed fingers, I pray they beat the odds. But if they don't, I expect them to be strong enough to carve some other niche for themselves in this tough world. Nancy, take it from one who has been out in the streets for a long, long time—there is no way you're going to deal with life out there if you're not able to take care of yourself, and I'm sure you'll agree that it would be unfair of you to expect two hard-working schoolteachers back in Florida to be paying your rent, buying your food, putting clothes on your back, while you waste precious years playing a long shot. So don't come telling me about drama classes. Take drama after you've got a degree in nursing or completed a secretarial course or graduated as a computer operator or a dental technician, or mastered any other of the highly saleable skills. It will take maybe three years of your young life. By the time you're twenty-two, you'll have locked into your head a skill, a craft, a profession. Then you can go almost anywhere in America and get a job that pays considerably above the minimum wage. Then you can take all the drama classes you want. Then you can be an actress in the evenings while you work days, or be an actress in the daytime while you work nights. Then you'll not only have been a source of pride and joy to your parents, but a relief to them, because you're not leaning on their already overstrained pocketbooks."

There was another silence, so long that I thought the girl had hung up on me. But finally she said, "I thank you, Uncle Sidney. I needed some guidance. I've heard the same things from my father and mother, but I just never thought about it very strongly, or maybe they didn't articulate it the way you did. But I do see your point, and their point, and I'm going to give it some serious thought."

I wish I could have left her with more, more in terms of making her feel good. But listen, feeling bad is sometimes necessary for us to clear our heads and get tuned into the way things are. It distresses me that so many young people want to be actors and actresses. I used to take great pride in the enormous upsurge of young blacks in this business fifteen years ago, but I don't anymore: so many of them are coming in for the wrong reasons. Fame and fortune represent the carrot, not the work itself. (I myself, as you now know, came into acting with no motive at all—it was pure accident, or if there was a plan, it wasn't mine. I certainly didn't foresee fame *or* fortune!)

So much of what we as black people are has to do directly with the fact that our forefathers were not able to pass on the good life to us. We knew that there was a good life to be had, and we knew what the passport would be—hard work. Of course, it wasn't always a guaranteed passport, but it was essential if you were to have any chance at all. With that philosophy, many black kids whose parents didn't have the means to send them to college worked their way through by busing dishes in the cafeteria, mowing lawns in town, working as maids, pumping gas, scrubbing floors, or whatever else was necessary to pay for their own educations. Black youngsters were not the only ones using the hard-work philosophy to move upward and onward—loads of white kids were doing the same thing—but to a greater extent the black youngsters' parents had to say to them: "If you want a better life—and I want a better life for you—I will help you as much as I can, but I cannot hand it to you. You are going to have to get it for yourself, for the most part, and getting it for yourself requires that, first, you have an education and, second, that you go out there and work for it." An impressive number of them did just that. The glittering list of America's most successful blacks is generously sprinkled with the names of those who pumped gas, scrubbed floors, bused dishes, and even shined shoes.

Thirty years ago when they came back from World War II, where they were used mostly as supply technicians in a segregated army, the majority of America's black ex-servicemen went immediately to work or back to school. They had children and they worked at helping their kids to be prepared for the better life that was sure to come.

Now—dissolve from them and come up on their kids who are the parents of today. Some fundamental values have shifted. For everyone—whites, blacks, Jews, Gentiles, northerners, southerners, everyone. There is a whole different approach to "making it" in the country. Pride of workmanship has lost its gloss. Getting the good life by a shortcut is the best way to get it.

The reconversion period after the war—a comparatively easy transition, all things considered—set the groundwork for a long stretch of prosperity, out of which portions of the good life came, in varying degrees, within reach of millions of American workers. In the wake of the switch from the bullets, tanks, and guns to consumer goods, services, and products that could be sold all over the world, the country prospered. Life in postwar America became an upward-mobility adventure that swept millions of Americans along on a material "high," to a point from which they could catch glimpses of the super-life glittering on the horizon of the future. In those years when American industrial energy was the healthiest in the world, most American parents were comforted by the thought that if they didn't make it to the good life or the supergood life, at the least everything would be better for their children.

Alas, throughout history "a better life for our children" has been an expectation, an incentive—or an excuse. Postwar American parents fell into a no-win situation in their relations with their children. It was in that generation that the age-old idea of going out and making it for oneself began to tarnish. The guy who once didn't have a pot found himself with a nice little house in the suburbs, with a maid who came in twice a week. With the upward thrust came status, and with status came subtle shifts in values. A child in the post–World War II home was the tender instrument on which those subtle shifts registered most strongly. More and more American youngsters, to a greater and greater extent, came to expect things to be done for them. Today, in a startling number of American homes—and I don't mean rich homes, upper-middle-class homes—young people just expect to find the refrigerator filled with food and never wonder at *how* the refrigerator got to be full. By the time they learn how the mortgage or the rent gets paid, they will already have become accustomed to its simply happening, so that learning the ritual doesn't arm them with any strength. "Hey, wow—oh, that's how Daddy did it." It doesn't tell them that doing it is an imperative for their dad, and that if he didn't do it their asses would be out in the cold—and Daddy's ass would be out in the cold —and Mommie's ass would be out in the cold. The new value system makes it easy for the modern youngster to ignore the survival energies spent by his father on his behalf and to fail to understand a damn thing about how the good life got into his house. Lay the question before him and he'll probably reply, "The good life got here because Daddy pays the bills. I go to a nice school because we live in a nice neighborhood where there are nice people. And nice people that live in a nice neighborhood are entitled to a nice school—that's why I have a nice school." And the post–World War II father is often reluctant to say, "Hold on there—wait a minute—that ain't the way it is. You're just blowing smoke up your own tail. In eight or ten years you'll be out in the street and you won't be able to do beans because you've been brought up on a lot of hogshit." The fathers of the fifties, sixties, and seventies didn't say that. Instead, they preened their feathers because they were now middle class, and a sign of their middle-class status was that their kids didn't have to spend any time worrying about surviving. It was no earth-shaking problem if the kids didn't pick up their clothes after themselves; it would be nice if they would, but if they don't, Mommie will pick them up. If there's no Jiffy peanut butter in the refrigerator, that's no crisis—all they have to do is put a note on the bulletin board and Mommie will go out and buy some tomorrow.

Now there's a lot that the new value system hasn't taught children: many of them have been seriously harmed by omissions that can be laid right at the doorsteps of the modern parent. In the years following the end of the war, things were good and everybody was scrambling to get ahead—buy a little house in the country, a car, a washing machine, a college education fund for the youngsters, a winter vacation in the sun—whatever was the newest symbol that American industry and ingenuity had created to certify one's arrival into the middle class. In every corner of America it was a time for looking up and moving on, and nobody wanted to be reminded of crunch times. So omissions were made, and lots of hard-nosed necessities were not passed on to our kids; omissions were a part of our peculiar way of "making it better for them."

With my prosperity reaching new heights in the late 1960s, I was proud that I represented a success symbol to young black people at a time when the heady wine of success was at the lips of the nation. It pleased me greatly to be thought of by those young people as someone who had done very well as an actor, for whom hard work had paid off in fame and money—someone about whom they could say, "I can do better than *that*, given half a chance." Then, because I, too, liked the taste of that heady wine, and because I enjoyed the status brought to me by my unique position, I fell prey to the sins of omission in my own prosperous home, in relation to my own American kids.

Had I examined the new values deeper instead of just enjoying what came in their wake, I would not have expected all our American youngsters to automatically follow their fathers. I wouldn't have expected them to be twice as productive as their dads. I would have known that there wasn't the same hunger in most of them. I would have known that in their heads was a new philosophy: That cat's got him some bread. He's got him some fame and some fortune and life is cool. That's what I want. Now how do I get it? I just get on a bus and go out there and tell them people I'm here! Many kids arrive in Hollywood and New York just that way, with the intention of becoming stars within a matter of weeks. I have seen them arrive year after year with a bankroll of five hundred dollars. They enroll in a class for a fast twelve weeks of drama study. They share a one-room efficiency apartment, sometimes three or four of them need to pool their resources in order to secure adequate housing. Generally, in less than three months their funds are gone—and so are they.

If one asks who in the black community is responsible for these youngsters' lack of clarity, I have to say the generation that went before them is responsible. And the white generation that went before the white kids who come and do the same thing is responsible. Because too many of us didn't face the facts in relation to our kids. Not enough of us were willing to say to our child, "You know, making it in this life, putting food in your mouth and putting clothes on your back, is beating the shit out of me." Too few of us wanted to acknowledge it at all, and fewer still wanted to pass it on to our kids. A multitude of us now wish we had spoken up at one time or another and said, "Sit down and let me tell you something. I'm having some of the hardest years I've ever experienced in my life. Do you know how much I don't like getting up in the morning? I've never liked getting up in the morning, but I have to get up and go out there and make it—the man I work for don't want to hear nothing about my problems. In fact he don't like me nohow and will probably fire me if I give him half a chance. It's very hard for me, and I want you to remember that when you pull open that refrigerator door tomorrow. Do you understand what I am saying? I just want you to understand where it's at for real."

We missed performing what could have been a true service to our children. And in no way would we have been putting more pressure on a kid than he could stand. Rather, in all probability, he would rear back one night before going to sleep and say to himself in the privacy of his thoughts: It's a damn relief to find that my father ain't no fucking Superman—that he has problems—that

368

he has moments when he's scared—that life is whipping on his tail and sometimes he don't know whether he's going to make it through the day. Hey, that's refreshing news, because I have times like that myself.

NANCY ISN'T UNIQUE. Nancy wants to be an actress. Nancy sees what my children see, those who want to be actresses—and my children see what thousands of other young black aspirants see: that it is possible for someone of their race to reach the heights. They see that it's possible to get rich and famous, that dynamite combination from which they spin their dreams. It's possible—there are living proofs of it. So they fantasize, and before you know it, they develop a want and a need to do something like that in their own lives. For them to say, "I'll do it like Poitier and James Earl Jones, Bill Cosby, Richard Pryor, Jim Brown, and Calvin Lockhart, those people—and when I've done it, I will have left my mark on the world. I will have made myself known and my presence felt"—that's an enormous statement; very seductive stuff. And to want to achieve it is very understandable. But lying one step beyond that want is the big question: How do I go about it? What is entailed? What is the price? Only a few of them seem to have considered these things when they arrive out here.

We have hidden too much from our modern children. When we're scared, we tend not to let them know: they see the bravest, toughest, and most impenetrable visage we can muster precisely at those times when we are most afraid. How many mothers have lied to their girls most profoundly when they, the mothers, were battling feelings of insecurity in their femininity or their womanhood? Like Nancy's mother, Eva, who ran into faces that were masks designed to mislead. How many parents who love each other have days when they don't like each other and never even admit to themselves or their children that such feelings are possible—that, in fact, it's all right to have such feelings sometimes? I guess I have to join the other mothers and fathers of my generation as perpetrator of the ritual of omission. We called it "making it better for our children." Protecting them. *From what?* The *truth* is what we were protecting those little people from.

As one post–World War II father, Louis Robinson, put it: "The kid is secure while I worry about the mortgage next month. I walk into the house, smiling as if everything is cool. I wanted the kid to just be lying on the floor by the open fireplace reading his book, so warm and snuggly and secure in the knowledge that there is nothing to worry about. Bullshit—there is a lot to worry about, and I'd better start telling the little bastard—start worrying!"

THE BEST IN BIOGRAPHY

The lives and legends of the famous and infamous alike, in prize-winning and bestselling biographies.

Learn to live with somebody... *yourself.*

16   NE-5